The
**Territories of the
Russian Federation**
2004

The
Territories of the Russian Federation
2004

5th Edition

Routledge
Taylor & Francis Group

LONDON AND NEW YORK

First published 1999 by Europa Publications
Fifth Edition 2004

Published 2014
by Routledge
2 Park Square, Milton Park, Abingdon, Oxon OX14 4RN

and by Routledge
711 Third Avenue, New York, NY, 10017, USA

Routledge is an imprint of the Taylor & Francis Group, an informa business

ISBN 13: 978-1-85743-248-0 (hbk)

ISSN 1465-461X

Editor: Imogen Gladman.

Typeset Unwin Brothers Limited
The Gresham Press, Old Woking, Surrey

Foreword

This, the fifth edition of *The Territories of the Russian Federation*, aims to furnish a clear and comprehensive introduction to Russia's regions. Even in the 2000s, Russia is emerging as a federal state, and the balance of power between the centre and the federal subjects is not yet settled; the long-term consequences of the efforts of President Vladimir Putin to re-evaluate the powers of regional governors and assert central dominance still remained to be seen, as the federal presidential elections approached in 2004.

Meanwhile, the diverging economic fortunes of the different territories continue to present a further challenge to the structures of the state. All the themes apparent in the Russian Federation as a whole are reflected in its 89 constituent parts, and issues such as the progress of economic and political reforms or the balance of power between the executive and legislative branches of government are present in the territories as much as in the national capital, Moscow.

This book is divided into four parts. Part One is an Introduction, with an authoritative article, revised and updated for this edition, providing a context for regional politics and a description of the place of the territories in the national economy. There is also a Chronology of Russian history and politics, some fully updated statistics, and information on the federal administration. The economic data clearly demonstrates the general trends of the economic situation, and that time has only consolidated the differences between the regions is often made clear in the text of the Territorial Surveys. This, Part Two, is the heart of the book, with individual chapters on each of the 89 federal units. The geographical and historical background, the current political situation and an economic outline are reinforced by the names and contact details of the main officials in every territory. Each chapter includes a map of the federal unit, and there are, in addition, five maps covering wider geographical areas. A Select Bibliography of books appears in Part Three. Finally, the Indexes of Part Four provide an alphabetic listing (including alternative or historical names) of the territories, as well as grouping them according to their geographical location within the Federal Okrugs and Economic Areas into which Russia is divided.

January 2004

Acknowledgements

The editors gratefully acknowledge the co-operation, interest and advice of all who have contributed to this volume. We are also indebted to many organizations within the Russian Federation, such as the territorial administrations that responded to our enquiries and, particularly, to the State Committee of Statistics.

Thanks are due to the authors of the introductory article, Professor Philip Hanson of the University of Birmingham and Professor Michael J. Bradshaw of the University of Leicester. We are also very grateful to Eugene Fleury, who originally prepared the maps included in this book.

Contents

PART THREE

Select Bibliography

List of Maps

Abbreviations

Acad.	Academician; Academy	Feb.	February
AD	anno domini	Fr	Father
Adm.	Admiral	Fri.	Friday
a/o	avtonomnyi okrug (autonomous okrug)	FSB	Federalnaya sluzhba bezopasnosti (Federal Security Service)
AOb	Autonomous Oblast	ft	foot (feet)
AOk	Autonomous Okrug		
ASSR	Autonomous Soviet Socialist Republic	g	gram(s)
		GDP	gross domestic product
Aug.	August	Gen.	General
		GNP	gross national product
BC	before Christ	Gov.	Governor
b/d	barrels per day	Govt	Government
Brig.	Brigadier	GRP	gross regional product
C	Centigrade	ha	hectares
c.	circa	hl	hectolitre(s)
Capt.	Captain		
CIS	Commonwealth of Independent States	IBRD	International Bank for Reconstruction and Development (World Bank)
cm	centimetre(s)		
CMEA	Council for Mutual Economic Assistance	IMF	International Monetary Fund
		in (ins)	inch (inches)
Co	Company; County	Inc, Incorp., Incd	Incorporated
Col	Colonel		
Commdr	Commander		
Commr	Commissioner	incl.	including
Corpn	Corporation	Is	Islands
CP	Communist Party		
CPSU	Communist Party of the Soviet Union	Jan.	January
cu	cubic	Jr	Junior
		kg	kilogram(s)
Dec.	December	KGB	Komitet Gosudarstvennoi Bezopasnosti (Committee for State Security)
Dep.	Deputy		
Dr	Doctor		
		km	kilometre(s)
EBRD	European Bank for Reconstruction and Development	kW	kilowatt(s)
		kWh	kilowatt hours
EC	European Community		
EEC	European Economic Community	lb	pound(s)
e.g.	exempli gratia (for example)	Lt, Lieut	Lieutenant
e-mail	electronic mail	Ltd	Limited
et al.	et alii (and others)		
etc.	et cetera	m	metre(s)
EU	European Union	m.	million
excl.	excluding	Maj.	Major
		mm	millimetre(s)
F	Fahrenheit	MWh	megawatt hour(s)
fax	facsimile		

x

n.a.	not available	RSFSR	Russian Soviet Federative Socialist Republic
nab.	naberezhnaya (embankment, quai)		
NATO	North Atlantic Treaty Organization	sel.	seleniyi (settlement)
NMP	net material product	Sept.	September
no.	number	sq	square (in measurements)
Nov.	November	SS	Saints
		SSR	Soviet Socialist Republic
obl.	oblast (region)	St	Saint
Oct.	October	Supt	Superintendent
OECD	Organisation for Economic Co-operation and Development	tel.	telephone
Ok	Okrug (district)	UK	United Kingdom
		ul.	ulitsa (street)
p.	page	UN	United Nations
p.a.	per annum (yearly)	UNDP	United Nations Development Programme
per.	pereulok (lane, alley)		
pl.	ploshchad (square)	UNEP	United Nations Environment Programme
PLC	Public Limited Company		
POB	Post Office Box	USSR	Union of Soviet Socialist Republics
pr.	prospekt (avenue)		
Prof.	Professor	VAT	value-added tax
		Ven.	Venerable
q.v.	quod vide (to which refer)	viz.	videlicet (namely)
		vol.(s)	volume(s)
retd	retired		
Rev.	Reverend	yr	year

PART ONE
Introduction

The Territories and the Federation: An Economic Perspective

Prof. PHILIP HANSON and Prof. MICHAEL J. BRADSHAW

It is customary in Russia to describe the Russian Federation as consisting of 89 'federal subjects'. To convey something of the reality of Russia's administrative regions, however, one must begin by emphasizing that these are not 89 units of equal status, nor is there comparable information on all of them. The status of one, the Chechen (Nokchi) Republic—Chechnya, is in dispute, and socio-economic data for the Republic are not reported by the State Committee of Statistics of the Russian Federation (Goskomstat). Of the remaining 88, the 10 autonomous okrugs (AOks—districts) and the one autonomous oblast (AOb—region) are, for most purposes, of lesser status than the 20 autonomous republics, six krais (provinces), 49 oblasts and two federal cities (Moscow and St Petersburg).

Nine of the autonomous okrugs officially form part of an oblast or krai. The Chukot AOk (Chukotka), in the far north-east of Russia, facing the US state of Alaska, is one of the two anomalies: it was taken out of Magadan Oblast in July 1992 and left as a free-standing okrug (free-standing, that is, in a purely administrative sense—in every other sense it was collapsing, and the population declined by approximately one-half between 1985 and 1999; its fortunes improved, however, with the election of oligarch Roman Abramovich as Governor in late 2000, although he subsequently made it clear that he would not seek re-election). The inappropriately named Jewish (Yevreiskaya) AOb—Birobidzhan, of which only 4.2% of the population was Jewish (according to the 1989 census), had, likewise, been separated from Khabarovsk Krai in 1991. This means that nine of the 11 'lesser autonomies', as they might be called, are parts of other regions (oblasts and krais). Many of the regional statistics available do not cover them separately.

In this chapter, we shall, therefore, refer mainly to the 79 territories (when Chechnya is excluded) that together cover the whole of Russia, whether they are autonomous republics, krais, oblasts, federal cities, an AOk (Chukotka) or an AOb (Birobidzhan). These 79 can, generically, be labelled as 'regions'. We shall not consider separately the nine AOks that form part of other regions. It should, however, be noted that of the nine sub-units, two, the Khanty-Mansii AOk—Yugra and the Yamal-Nenets AOk, are of considerable economic importance. Both form part of Tyumen Oblast and are isolated, undeveloped and sparsely inhabited districts in western Siberia, although they form part of the Urals, rather than the Siberian, Federal Okrug (Russia was divided into seven such districts in May 2000—see below). They also happen to be floating on oceans of petroleum and natural gas. As might be expected, their local politicians are considerably more assertive than their counterparts in the other lesser autonomies, and they are very closely linked to Russia's petroleum and gas companies. As a result, the nature of their administrative, electoral and fiscal relations with Tyumen Oblast is a matter of ongoing dispute and negotiation.

Following the election, in March 2000, of federal President Vladimir Putin, it was thought that he might simplify the federal structure by abolishing the autonomous okrugs and merging them with the regions to which they were subordinate—this might be welcomed by poorer autonomous okrugs, which would benefit from greater budgetary support in a larger federal subject; however, rich regions, such as the Khanty-Mansii—Yugra and the Yamal-Nenets AOks, were bound to resist the loss of autonomy. In practice, Putin proceeded cautiously. In late August 2002 he raised the possibility of absorbing the Taimyr (Dolgan-Nenets) and Evenk AOks into Krasnoyarsk Krai, thereby transforming three federal subjects into just one; however, he went on to state that any such change would be subject to a referendum.

In May 2000 the territorial-administrative structure was modified. Putin issued an edict (*ukaz*) establishing an additional level of administration: seven Federal Okrugs covering the whole country and headed by centrally appointed presidential representatives. The creation of these seven okrugs (Central—based in the capital, Moscow; North-Western—based in St Petersburg; Volga—based in Nizhnii Novgorod; Southern—based in Rostov-on-Don; Urals—based in Yekaterinburg; Siberian—based in Novosibirsk; and Far Eastern—based in Khabarovsk) was part of a series of measures designed to curtail the autonomy of regional leaders. In September a new State Council was created to provide a means by which governors (who, together with the heads of regional parliaments, were gradually being removed from the upper house of the national legislature, the Federation Council) could advise the President on regional issues. The presidium of the State Council, which consists of the President and one governor from each of the seven Federal Okrugs, rotates every six months; the implications of this are considered below. In January 2002 a new session of the Federation Council opened, with a reformed composition, comprising the full-time appointees of both regional leaders and chairmen of regional legislative assemblies. Governors were no longer to be members *ex officio* and, in practice, regional representatives were not necessarily close allies of their territory's governor.

In the remainder of this essay we shall: first describe the evolving status of the Russian federal territories and their relations with the central Government; then review the differences in the levels of economic development and the production structures they inherited from the Soviet past; next discuss the different economic trajectories that various regions have followed since 1991; then examine the differences in economic conditions between them and their greatly differing investment potential; and, finally, offer some thoughts about the likely longer-term evolution of these enormously different territorial economies.

THE FEDERALIZATION OF RUSSIA

In Soviet times Russia was a nominal federation within a nominal federation that was, in fact, a unitary state. The diverse patchwork of 15 Union Republics (Soviet Socialist Republics—SSRs), some of them sub-divided into autonomous republics and other administrative territories, was managed by the apparatus of the Communist Party of the Soviet Union (CPSU). The party's officials formed a clear hierarchy, with appointment from above; the territorial divisions were merely decorative. Part of that decoration consisted in assigning the names of particular national groups to areas historically associated with them. In general, this Soviet legacy has been preserved in the existing administrative divisions within the Russian Federation. The labels can, however, be grossly misleading. The Jewish AOb, as has already been noted, is one such oddity. Located on the Chinese border and containing very few people recorded as Jewish, it was more a message to Soviet Jewry than any sort of homeland. Many other 'ethnic' territories are more in the nature of heritage sites.

Thus, Evenks constituted 14.0% of the population of the Evenk AOk, while Khants comprised 0.9% and Mansi 0.5% of the inhabitants of the Khanty-Mansii AOk—Yugra. Even at the higher level of republics, ethnic Russians are often in the majority in what are nominally ethnic-minority territories: for example, they account for 73.6% of the population in Kareliya (Karelia), 57.7% in Komi, 60.8% in Mordoviya and 58.9% in the Udmurt Republic, according to 1989 census figures.

The results of the census that took place in October 2002 were thought likely to demonstrate a change in the relative importance of the so-called titular nationalities in such regions. In many instances, the actions of republican governments had served to favour the titular group at the expense of others (both Russian and non-Russian), resulting in out-migration by non-titular groups. In addition, the Muslim population of many republics in the Volga and Urals districts had continued to register relatively high birth rates, compared with the ethnic Russians in the region. However, there were concerns about the validity of the census results, and the census did not request information on religious affiliation, owing to historical reasons, as much as a desire to avoid causing offence.

When the USSR disintegrated into 15 states there was some discussion of reshaping Russia's internal administrative boundaries into units of comparable population size, without ethnic labels, but it came to naught. One consequence of this inheritance is that the 79 main territories or regions vary enormously in population size—from an estimated 74,000 in Chukot to 8.5m. (officially) in Moscow City at January 2002. (The 2002 census subsequently found Moscow to have a population of more than 10m., making the disparity even greater.) The territories also vary enormously in levels of economic development, a matter that is dealt with in the next section.

Boundaries within independent Russia may have changed very little since the Soviet era, but the formal status of several territories has been amended since 1991. While Russia was still part of the USSR, Boris Yeltsin (Russian leader from 1990 and President in 1991–99), notoriously advised the local leaderships throughout the USSR to 'grab as much sovereignty as you can'. He was engaged in doing just that for the Russian Federation, and the remark no doubt seemed appropriate at the time. The 1990–91 'parade of sovereignties', however, did not stop at the level of Russia and the other 14 SSRs. Autonomous republics (then known as Autonomous Soviet Socialist Republics—ASSRs) sought to become Union Republics and autonomous okrugs sought to become autonomous republics. At a later stage, in 1992–95, a number of the territorial regions (oblasts and krais) considered declaring themselves to be republics (within Russia), because the powers of republics were, in some ways, greater.

More precisely, it was members of the regions' political élite who initiated such claims. The extent of popular support for autonomist assertiveness varies greatly. In some republics, such as Tatarstan, it is strong, at least among ethnic Tatars. In others, a common attitude is that living in an autonomous republic merely means paying more to support a more elaborate and costly government—which is routinely assumed to be corrupt. On the whole, the most assertive republics have been those that are comparatively strong economically, such as Bashkortostan, Tatarstan and Sakha—Yakutiya.

Chechnya has been the main exception. Although a poor, mountainous region, its inhabitants fought Russian invaders throughout much of the 19th century, and in the last decade of the 20th century they saw an opportunity to express their dissatisfaction once more. The first Chechen war (1994–96) ended, effectively, with a retreat by the federal authorities. The second, which commenced in late 1999, led to the central Government securing troubled and uncertain control over Chechen territory north of the guerrillas' mountain strongholds. Official peace negotiations took place in November 2001, but international pressure on the Russian Government to halt what it presented as its 'anti-terrorism' activity in Chechnya declined substantially after the large-scale suicide attacks on the US cities of New York and Washington, DC, on 11 September of that year, attributed to the al-Qa'ida (Base) organization, led by the Islamist fundamentalist, Osama bin Laden. Putin made much of the fact that both Russia and the USA had suffered at the hands of terrorists, in a reference to bombings in Moscow and elsewhere, which had been attributed to Chechen rebels. In late October 2002 a Chechen-led hostage crisis at a Moscow theatre only added to Putin's determination to confront what he regarded as a terrorist threat, rather than a civil conflict, despite the Government's questionable handling of the incident (as a result of which, together with the kidnappers, over 100 hostages were killed by an incapacitating gas). In 2003 the federal Government attempted to convince its own citizens and the wider world that 'normalization' was under way. On 5 October the federal Government's ally, Akhmed Kadyrov, officially received 87.7% of the votes cast, with a rate of participation by the electorate of 82.6%, in a republican presidential election from which his most credible challengers had withdrawn or been excluded. Major international organizations, such as the Council of Europe, declined to recognize the election as free and fair, and did not send monitors, while there were media reports of widespread irregularities. By the end of 2003 fighting in Chechnya was continuing, at huge financial cost, and resulting in substantial human suffering.

Such jostling for autonomy, or even independence, became possible with the collapse of the communist monopoly on power. The regional élite was often little changed in terms of personnel (one study in the mid-1990s found that about two-thirds of the regional political élite were former members of the communist-era regional nomenklatura). The chain of command from Moscow, however, had been broken as early as 1988, when Mikhail Gorbachev (the last Soviet leader, 1986–91) introduced the local election of regional leaders, in place of their appointment from above. This opened the way for the local party chiefs of the old order (or, often, their deputies) to transform their party positions into post-communist power.

From the beginning of the post-communist Russian state, therefore, there was a shifting struggle, both between the regions and the centre, and between the regions themselves, over who was to have power, and at how high a level. It was further complicated by a struggle between different areas of government, notably the executive and legislative branches. Friction over budgets and other matters is a part of everyday political life in any federation and, indeed, in any state with different levels of government. What was exceptional in 1990s Russia was that a new state was being constructed. The rules of the political game were still to be established in 1992, a situation that persisted, to some extent, even in 2003. Insofar as the federal territories and the centre are concerned, the bargaining was described by some as a process of 'federalization', the making of a real federation from the smallest of bases. There are other Russians of influence, however, who do not even concede that Russia should be a federation, and who argue for the construction of a unitary state. This view was being reasserted under the Putin presidency (which effectively began at the beginning of 2000).

In March 1992, three months after Russia's emergence as an independent state, three federal treaties (sometimes known collectively as the Federation Treaty) were signed between the federal leadership, on the one hand, and, on the other, separately, the republics, krais, oblasts and autonomous okrugs. Two republics refused to sign: Tatarstan, on the middle Volga; and what was then the Checheno-Ingush ASSR, in the North Caucasus. (Later Ingushetiya was hived off as a separate republic and the cities of Moscow and St Petersburg were granted the status of federal units.) These treaties set out three areas of competence: those that were exclusively federal; those that were shared; and those that were exclusively sub-federal.

The powers of the federal centre were predictable. They included: defence; weapons production; foreign policy; the adoption, amendment and enforcement of federal laws; the establishment of federal legislative, executive and judicial bodies; the determination of internal boundaries; citizenship issues; the operation of the federal budget, the central bank and the money supply; and energy, transport and communications policies. The list of shared powers was long, and the treaties contained little guidance about just how these powers would be distributed. Exclusively sub-national powers were merely whatever was left over. Relations between regional and sub-regional (local) government were left for later legislation and, in many ways, remain legally unclear. For instance, there are no clear rules governing budgetary relations between regions and municipalities or rural districts.

Insofar as federal-territorial relations were concerned, the federal treaties of March 1992 left three important unresolved problems: the non-participation of two republics; the large and ill-defined area of shared powers; and language that appeared (although contradicted elsewhere in the text) to give republics more control than other regions over natural resources on their territories. These problems were compounded by two other circumstances. There was very little to guarantee that devolved responsibilities would be supported by devolved tax-raising powers—that is, the powers to set tax rates and tax bases. Moreover, the judicial system, in practice, was unsuited to act as an arbiter between the centre and the regions when disagreement over the interpretation of these agreements occurred.

The new Russian Constitution approved in late 1993 superseded the federal treaties. This specified that where the federal treaties disagreed with the Constitution, the latter had priority. Moreover, the federal Constitution had precedence, in any conflicts, over sub-national constitutions or their equivalent. The new federal Constitution gave the President of the Russian Federation exceptionally strong powers. These were used to ensure that, for the next three years (approximately), regional governors were appointed and subject to dismissal by the President. That, however, did not apply to the republics, where presidents were, and are, locally elected. It was only in 1996–97 that the executive heads of all the territories became formally answerable to their electorates rather than to the federal President.

Meanwhile, the Federation negotiated a series of so-called power-sharing treaties with individual territories. This began in February 1994 with Tatarstan, and had extended to more than one-half of the regions by late 1998. At that time the First Deputy Head of the Presidential Administration, Oleg Sysoev, spoke publicly of plans to discontinue the practice and, eventually, to reorder uniformly federal-territorial relations. The power-sharing treaties were anomalous, often allowing conflicting provisions in the federal and regional constitutions simply to co-exist. A number of the treaties also included special arrangements on the retention of larger-than-normal shares of taxes collected within the borders of the territory concerned.

This applied to Bashkortostan, Kareliya, Sakha and Tatarstan—all republics and all comparatively strong economically (Sakha, for instance, accounts for almost all Russia's diamond-mining). Finally, these budget deals were, typically, not published.

'Asymmetric federalism' would be a generous description of the network of centre-territory relations that emerged. None the less, many observers concluded that, however shocking the arrangements may seem to constitutional lawyers, they probably helped as interim measures to hold Russia together. For much of the 1990s the centre was weak and divided, with the President and parliament often in conflict, and successive governments unable to implement key parts of their agendas (notably in tax collection). Consequently, all the territories, not just the favoured, strong republics, had considerable leeway. In practice, even in 1993–97, regional governors often defied the centre and acted as though they were more beholden to the local élite than to a President who could, in theory, dismiss them. Thus, for example, Yevgenii Nazdratenko, in the Maritime (Primorskii) Krai on the Pacific coast, replaced a Yeltsin-nominated reformer. He subsequently ran a corrupt regime, while defying the centre's efforts to remove him, and was re-elected in December 1999 with a sizeable majority, largely owing to his ability to discredit the opposition and his control over the local media. Nazdratenko was eventually removed from the governorship in 2001, but the strength of such local power-bases was demonstrated by the fact that he was subsequently offered a federal post with ministerial status.

Until the 1998 financial crisis four developments had tended to stabilize centre-territorial political relations. First, the invasion of Chechnya in December 1994, although ill-managed, costly in human life and unsuccessful in its immediate aim, acted as a deterrent to less determined and less advantageously located secessionists elsewhere. Second, the development of the Federation Council as a body representing the territories facilitated accommodation between the centre and the periphery. Third, the eight associations of territories (based on the 11 Economic Areas) had, throughout 1997, begun to emerge as regular channels for informal policy consultation between the central Government and representatives of the regions, and had begun to supplement the Federation Council as an institutionalized communications channel. Finally, the Constitutional Court was beginning to act somewhat more independently and usefully in rulings over conflicts regarding the distribution of powers. The financial crisis undermined some of this progress. It brought to the fore an underlying problem: the centre's dwindling ability to provide economic help to weaker territories and to use economic levers to achieve some consistency in the implementation of economic policy across Russia. The crisis also revealed that many of Russia's poorest regions were simply being excluded from the country's new market economy, a fact that isolated them from the immediate impact of the crisis, but threatened the cohesion of Russia.

The measures introduced by Putin in May 2000 were designed to reclaim power from the regional governors, by strengthening the central Government's control over its federal agencies in the regions and by ensuring regional compliance with federal legislation. By enforcing greater central control, Putin hoped to create a single economic space across Russia. Unlike his predecessor, Putin was prepared to move openly and boldly against concentrations of power that limited his own authority. With the advantage of a more compliant parliament and a background in the security service, he was prepared to attack determinedly both regional governors and business tycoons who attempted to influence politics at the federal level. Whereas

Yeltsin had relied on negotiations that played region against region, Putin sought directly to limit regional political authority. He was assisted in this by the recovery of the Russian economy: the central Government was better resourced and, therefore, better able to fulfil its responsibilities. In the past, the poverty of the federal agencies often meant that they had to turn to regional presidents and governors for financial support, which made them pliable and more sympathetic to regional interests.

Putin's representatives in the seven Federal Okrugs come, for the most part, from a security or military background—in four cases directly from military or security posts. Their role is to oversee federal administrative work in the regions, monitoring the implementation of federal policies. They also monitor the legality of the actions of individual governors, and have appointed their own staff to help in this. Although they were not given direct authority over governors of regions or presidents of republics, it was intended that they would be able to assist the federal Government in removing difficult characters from office. In theory, a governor who enacts local legislation that contradicts federal law can be dismissed.

Thus far, the presidential representatives have proved largely ineffective. They lack a clear mandate and the President appears unwilling to give them the necessary political power and financial resources to carry out the tasks that they have set themselves. Each representative has to deal with a distinct set of problems and has approached the job somewhat differently. Some have received a hostile reception. The presidential representative in the Urals, Col-Gen. Petr Latyshev, for example, encountered difficulties with the Governor of Sverdlovsk Oblast, Eduard Rossel. The circumstances surrounding the resignation of Maritime Governor Nazdratenko, following an extended energy crisis in the region, and the subsequent gubernatorial election, also proved a major embarrassment for the presidential representative in the Far East, Lt-Gen. Konstantin Pulikovskii (based, significantly, in Khabarovsk city, rather than Vladivostok, the capital of Maritime Krai), who was unable to control Nazdratenko. He was eventually eased out of the governorship, but only by means of what was, apparently, a negotiated deal with the centre (see above). Sergei Darkin (who was alleged to have connections with Nazdratenko) won the election to succeed him as governor, standing against a candidate supported by Pulikovskii. In general, the efforts by the presidential representatives to increase their powers and gain access to additional resources have been thwarted, not only by the resistance of the regional leaders, many of whom refused to take them seriously, but also by the power of federal ministries. Agencies of the federal Government report to the Prime Minister and not, in any direct sense, to the President. These agencies have resisted efforts by the presidential administration's territorial representatives to exercise control over regional branches of federal ministries. Moreover, the economic ministries have not established branches at the federal okrug level; the only agencies to have done so are concerned with law and order: the Ministry of Justice; the Ministry of Internal Affairs; the Procuracy; and the Tax Police.

Russia is experiencing a recentralization of power, but it is not necessarily the result of the creation of the Federal Okrugs and the appointment of presidential representatives. Changes in the tax law and a shift in the distribution of revenue between the centre and the regions, in favour of the federal authorities, mean that the central Government has increasing control over state expenditure (see below). The removal of governors from the Federation Council has reduced their influence in national politics and stripped them of their immunity from prosecution. The centre has reasserted its power to appoint regional heads of police and the Procuracy.

Meanwhile, electricity-supply reform threatens the ability of governors to control electricity tariffs, and the re-investment of natural-resource-sector profits by Moscow-based, large-scale companies, for the acquisition of a wide range of other businesses, has, in several cases, disrupted what had been comfortable relationships between regional political leaders and regional entrepreneurs. By 2004 governors and presidents of republics were less frequently judged to be among the most influential people in Russia.

ECONOMIC DIFFERENTIATION

Russian regional inequality in Soviet times is impossible to assess, chiefly because such data as there were on rouble incomes and outputs concealed differences in availability that, in a geographically huge, shortage economy, were very large indeed. It was well known that the biggest cities had priority in the allocation of consumer goods. Many everyday items that were widely available in Moscow were completely unobtainable in many lesser cities and small towns. Then, as now, barter and subsistence food production were predominant in rural areas, and were poorly accounted for in statistical reporting.

It is, nevertheless, clear that in 1992 the new Russian state had inherited an exceptionally uneven array of regional development levels. Underdeveloped, rural territories had little in common with the very big cities such as Moscow, St Petersburg, Yekaterinburg, Nizhnii Novgorod and Samara. In 1991 both Dagestan and Tyva, for example, had rural populations of more than 50% of the total, while, at the other end of the scale (omitting the far northern districts and cities with regional status), Kemerovo's rural population consisted of only 13% of the total and Samara's 19%. (The Russian average was 26%.) In a country where poverty was concentrated in rural areas, as it was in the USSR, these differences dictated large inequalities in average real incomes across the regions.

Later in the 1990s, as local food-price controls waned and the measurement of regional inequalities became a little less problematic, it was clear that differences in territorial, per-head, real output and personal incomes were very large indeed. They were also becoming larger over time. In 1998 per-head gross regional product (GRP—which approximates to regional gross domestic product—GDP) was 19 times higher in petroleum-rich Tyumen than in Ingushetiya. In mid-2002 the average money income in Moscow City, divided by the cost of the 'subsistence minimum' basket of goods at local prices, was more than eight times the equivalent measure for Tyva. This was substantially greater than the range from poorest to richest region in the European Union (EU), using the EU's second-tier definition of 'region' (in which the average population size happens to be very close to that for Russian regions— 1.9m.). The Moscow–Tyva difference is probably overstated by this measure, because uncounted subsistence food production will play a larger role in Tyva. Nevertheless, even if one guesses at a 'true' ratio of 6:1, the range is still enormous.

A more comprehensive measure of dispersion among regional average real incomes, the co-efficient of variation, shows a clear, rapid increase throughout 1998. In 1992 it was 0.31. In 1998 it was 0.56, although the economic recovery that followed the rouble devaluation of that year seemed to lessen substantially this dispersion, bringing the indicator down to 0.40 by mid-1999, before edging up slightly, to 0.42, by mid-2002. It is clear that the regions' economic fortunes diverged rapidly from the end of communist rule. This suggests that there is a large capacity for inter-regional discord under the new economic order, and one that may, despite some fluctuation, increase in the long term. The growing concentration of state resources within the federal Government in Moscow makes it all the more important for the Government to create a mechanism to redistribute wealth from richer to poorer regions. The sum of federal transfers to sub-national budgets has indeed increased, but, at 2.9% of GDP in 2002, transfers remain modest, relative to national income. (In 1998 the equivalent figure for the USA, with 50, less unevenly developed states was also 2.9%. In the late 1990s the figure in Argentina, with 24 provinces demonstrating extremely uneven development, was about 6%.)

THE PROCESSES OF CHANGE AND THE ROLE OF THE CENTRE

Insofar as a territory's economic fortunes are concerned, the fundamental measure must be the standard of living of its inhabitants. The real-income measures that can be made for contemporary Russia are full of problems: neither the data on money incomes nor the data on regional price levels are of good quality, and one cannot assume that these defects produce a bias that is uniform across regions. Regions with particularly large informal economies, such as Kaliningrad, are doing better than the official figures suggest; casual observation certainly supports this where the Baltic oblast is concerned. Nevertheless, the regions that are doing particularly well or particularly badly are probably reasonably well identified by the official statistics. To put these differences in perspective, it should be said that post-communist economic adaptation in Russia as a whole has taken the form of collapse. In 2002 measured national income (GDP) was about 68% of the 1989 level. Only one region, Moscow City, has shown all the outward signs of economic success; and even in Moscow a large proportion of the population has been left behind. However, a small number of other regions have adapted comparatively well; typically, these are territories that began to show real growth in output in 1997, well above the marginal improvement of 1.4% recorded for Russian GDP as a whole.

Analyses of inter-regional differences in average real incomes suggest that two kinds of territory fared better than the Russian average: those with particularly strong reserves of exploitable petroleum, gas, metals and hydroelectric power (such as Tyumen Oblast, and Irkutsk Oblast in Eastern Siberia); and a small number of regions that contain emerging commercial and financial 'hubs' (Moscow, Nizhnii Novgorod, St Petersburg, Samara and Sverdlovsk). St Petersburg apart, maritime 'gateway' territories, such as Kaliningrad (on the Baltic), Krasnodar (Black Sea) and the Maritime Krai (Pacific), have fared far less well than might have been expected. The reasons for this are not clear, but each has had, for most of the post-communist period, a traditionalist, even xenophobic, leadership. In addition, the Maritime Krai has suffered for reasons common to the Russian Far East as a whole (on which, more below). A study by the Russian economy ministry confirmed this analysis. It suggested that the number of regions enjoying an 'above average' level of economic development increased from 20 in 1998 to 25 in 2000. Of these 25 regions, 17 were characterized as resource-processing, two (Moscow and St Petersburg) as financial-economic centres, and the remainder (including Samara, Moscow Oblast, Belgorod and Tatarstan) as industrial centres. This list reflects the regional consequences, post-1998, of high resource prices, which are of benefit to resource-exporting regions, and of a devalued rouble, which increased the costs of imports and provided import-substitution benefits for the major industrial regions.

Those regions where economic adaptation has been more uniformly gloomy are, not to put too fine a point upon it, all the rest. They fall into two main categories:

the strongly rural and agricultural regions; and what might be called 'typical Russian regions', mainly industrial, but without the particular attributes that have favoured the emerging hub and natural-resource regions or the industries that have been able to respond to domestic market opportunities post-1998. The former have suffered from a lack of farm restructuring and a massive deterioration in agricultural prices relative to all other prices; the latter have been victims of the lack of competitiveness of Russian industry and have failed to develop new activities on any scale. The natural-resource and the hub regions have in common an engagement with the outside world, either as generators of exports to the West or as magnets for foreign business and for trading in imports, or both. During 1994 the per-head inflow of foreign currency into a region was a statistically significant, positive influence on per-head real incomes. This influence showed up less clearly thereafter, as currency markets within Russia became more integrated, but it probably provides a clue to early adaptation. If so, this is not surprising. The domestic economy was collapsing, but Western demand for Russian energy and materials was growing; also, Russians' appetite for imports was massive, and incomes from the domestic distribution of imports increased rapidly.

The reasons why these particular hub regions have emerged are harder to determine. Econometric studies suggest that small business, the development of which has been generally very weak, has grown rather better in regions with large urban populations and, therefore, large and concentrated domestic markets, other things being equal. It also seems the case that those regions that have a positive attitude towards economic reform, in addition to a well-educated population, have the highest level of new-enterprise formation. It appears highly plausible that the development of financial and other services, stunted during the Soviet era, and of new lines of economic activity generally, would be easier in very large cities. In these very large communities a wide range of skills and lines of production are available. This must facilitate the recombining of capital and labour resources into new activities, as well as providing a large market for those activities, and explains why those same hub regions seem to be leading the way in the development of 'new economy' activities, relating, for example, to the mobile telephone network and the internet.

It may be the case that the advantage of being a hub region is more durable than that of being a natural-resource region. Energy and raw materials reserves become depleted and their prices fluctuate. The slide in petroleum and natural gas prices in 1996–99 and again, briefly, between late 2001 and early 2002, made a difference to the regional rankings. In addition, it is in petroleum, gas, gold, aluminium and diamonds that the Russian élite is most determined to maintain control of what it views as the serious earners. In many cases it is concerned simply to make private fortunes out of these assets, regardless of the long-term development of the business. Seeking Western partners, with a view to long-term development, has been the exception rather than the rule. In June 2003 the finalization of a joint venture between British Petroleum (BP) and the Tyumen Oil Company (TNK), creating TNK-BP, suggested that this pattern might be changing, but the attitude to such developments of both Russian business and the Russian authorities remains ambivalent, at best. Meanwhile, the months-long government campaign, targeting Russia's largest oil company, Yukos, which culminated, in October, in the arrest of its Chairman, Mikhail Khodorovskii, on charges of fraud and tax evasion, undermined the faith of domestic and foreign investors alike. As a result, many foreign companies, together with international credit rating agencies, were reconsidering their opinion of Russia, and capital 'flight' (the export of funds for legitimate investment reasons, as well as tax avoidance) was increasing once again.

It is clear that Russia's current economic recovery (with GDP growth averaging around 6% per year in 1999–2003) has been associated with some amelioration of inter-regional inequality, probably because the massive devaluation of the rouble enabled moribund industries like engineering, textiles and food-processing, which dominate many ordinary Russian regions, to revive as producers of import substitutes. However, the continuing real appreciation of the rouble may well undermine those gains and again lead to greater regional differentiation, as a relatively small number of regions enjoy sustained economic recovery, while the vast majority of the remainder remain depressed. Russia's politicians are increasingly concerned about the development gap between Moscow and the rest of Russia, but outside Moscow there is also a huge gap between the winners in Russia's new economy and the losers from the old.

One other factor has been of great importance for the territories of Russia's Far North and Far East. This is the erosion of the enormous subsidies to transport, energy and food supplies that had supported their development in the Soviet era. Most of that development would not have occurred in a market economy; now that a market economy is being established, these regions have experienced an exceptionally severe decline. One reaction was substantial out-migration from those areas during the 1990s, and the Russian Government received financial assistance from the World Bank to support further out-migration from the Far North and the Far East. However, it is not the case that everyone wants to leave, since these regions are the homelands of indigenous ethnic groups, and there are also many ethnic Russians, mainly among the elderly, who consider these regions home. The net result is that the economically active are leaving behind a welfare-dependent population in regions that the federal Government is no longer inclined to support, a stark reminder of the human consequences of the collapse of Soviet socialism.

These, then, are (in very crude summary) the factors that lie behind the sharp divergence of regional fortunes. It is doubtful whether differences in policies among regional leaders have made much difference to the outcome. The economic structure inherited from the past, including population size and the presence or absence of major conurbations and natural-resource industries, seem to have been far more important, as have basic geographical characteristics, such as accessibility and remoteness. A few regional leaders, such as Boris Nemtsov in Nizhnii Novgorod (1991–97) and Mikhail Prusak in Novgorod (1995–), gained reputations as serious reformers, but such cases are rare, and even they worked with the grain of their region's inheritance. Governors who were overtly hostile to foreign business activity and economic restructuring, as in Krasnodar and Maritime Krais, were probably capable of making matters worse, although they were usually at odds with the mayors of their major cities. The latter, like most governors, tended to be pragmatists who saw little personal benefit in making special efforts to block change.

By the end of the Yeltsin era an impasse had been reached. Regional politicians still looked to the centre and lobbied institutions in Moscow, but there was an element of inertia in this. In interviews, regional officials were apt to complain that the centre had become merely a source of trouble. Some regional policy-makers and administrators openly questioned the system of remittances of tax revenue to the centre and transfers back to the federal territories. There may have been little appetite for secession, but there was also little expectation that the central Government would do much to help a region deal with its most pressing problems. Meanwhile, the centre and regions competed to obtain revenue from the same sources (under tax-sharing arrangements), which led both to damagingly high nominal rates of tax and to collusion between regional governments and local businesses to conceal resources from the central budget—a process aided by the use of barter and money surrogates. At the same time, the centre had devolved some major responsibilities for public provision, notably welfare and housing, to sub-national levels, without making available the means to pay for them. It was estimated that in 1998 such 'unfunded mandates' amounted to at least 5% of GDP—an amount that should, in international accounting practice, have been added to the officially reported government deficit.

Putin changed things radically. He may not have succeeded in resolving the complex issue of centre-regional financial relations, but he was certainly prepared to tackle it directly. In 2000 sub-national government revenue before transfers from the federal budget was 13.0% of GDP, and transfers added 1.4% of GDP to this figure. In 2002 the corresponding figures were 12.1% and 2.9%. Thus, the regions (and the local governments below them) were receiving a somewhat larger proportion of a larger national total, but were receiving less of it directly, and more at the discretion of the central Government. If the economy slowed and profits declined, then the regions would begin to come under financial pressure. By removing the influence of the governors from the federal policy-making process, and by increasing their reliance on funds channelled through the federal Government, Putin was strengthening central control by stealth. If the Yeltsin era witnessed a shift in centre-regional relations that favoured the regions, the Putin presidency appeared to be heralding a reassertion of central influence. By 2003, at least, this had been achieved without open conflict, and most governors remained supportive of the President.

However, other developments had an ambiguous effect on presidential power. From 1999 the expansion of large, Moscow-based firms into the regions both disrupted 'crony' relations between regional politicians and regional-level business magnates, and offered the possibility of new alliances. Many governors sought to build alliances with large-scale Russian enterprises, and in 2002 a World Bank study confirmed that the concentration of market power in a small number of firms was much greater at the regional than the national level. However, the relationship between a particular region and the dominant company varies. In the 2000–01 cycle of gubernatorial elections, large-scale businesses sought to ensure the election of governors who would promote their interests, as did the federal Government. In the gubernatorial election held in Krasnoyarsk Krai in September 2002 both leading candidates were supported by rival large firms. The most prominent cases of business executives becoming governors were those of the Chukot, Evenk and Taimyr AOks. In other regions there were close relationships between governors and corporations, for example, between the state-controlled gas monopoly, Gazprom, and Yurii Neyelov in the Yamal-Nenets AOk. However, in a number of other regions businesses supported losing candidates. For example, in the Nenets AOk the petroleum company LUKoil tried, and failed, to oust the incumbent, Vladimir Butov.

Although governors are happy to receive the tax revenue that may be associated with having a high-placed corporate citizen located in their region, companies can benefit at the same time, by securing their own regional bases outside Moscow. Meanwhile, if governors are perceived to be interfering in the interests of businesses, the penalties can be severe, as was indicated by the murder of the Governor of Magadan Oblast in Moscow in October 2002.

INVESTMENT POTENTIAL

Throughout 1998 investment in Russia declined even more rapidly than output. The country's capital stock shrank, although the decline could not be measured with any confidence. Not surprisingly, while domestic investment was collapsing, foreign investment was small. A surge of foreign investment in 1996–97 was dominated by portfolio debt investment, mainly in government treasury bills (GKOs). Foreign portfolio investment in Russia merely rearranged the liabilities. Domestic investment recovered, increasing strongly in 1999–2003, and profits from natural-resource exports at last began to be channelled in significant quantities into internal investment, rather than placed off shore. Although this investment was heavily concentrated in the natural-resource sectors, there was some expansion into other sectors. Domestic investment growth was about 12% year-on-year in the first nine months of 2003.

Foreign direct investment (FDI) should also have helped to support production capacity, but it continued to languish. Accurate statistics on FDI are difficult to come by; estimates for the 1990s range from around US $17,000m., to almost $20,000m. by the end of 1999. In its *World Investment Report*, the UN Conference on Trade and Development estimated the value of FDI inward stock in Russia at the end of 2001 to be $18,579m., and the flow into Russia in 2001 to represent 0.35% of global FDI—compared with Russia's 2.6% share of global GDP. Subsequently, the rate of inward FDI rose somewhat. In January–September 2003 it totalled $3,900m., compared with $2,100m. in the first nine months of 2002; however, in terms of international perspective, that figure was still rather small for an economy of Russia's size. Despite its modest total, this FDI, establishing or expanding joint ventures and wholly foreign-owned firms, has a special role in channelling the flow of investment to different Russian regions. The regional distribution of FDI reflects the perceived economic potential of activities in each region, allowing for the barriers to foreigners gaining significant control in those activities. In turn, FDI influences regional outcomes: it must usually have beneficial effects on a region's output.

In practice, FDI has been heavily concentrated in Moscow City, although that dominance is dwindling quite significantly. During 2002 Moscow City accounted for 37.7% of total FDI in Russia, compared with some 29% in 2001, well below its peak level of 76.9% in 1997. The surrounding Moscow Oblast accounted for a further 14.7% of FDI in 2002, bringing the share of the capital region to 52.4%. Such a concentration on the capital city is not unusual for FDI in former communist countries. Some of it was recorded in Moscow only because head offices of large companies are often based there; insofar as the resource inflow goes through that head office to provincial production, the real concentration of FDI resources on the metropolis will be somewhat less. Despite the declining dominance of Moscow, there are still many Russian regions that have received little or no foreign investment. According to the official figures, the 10 leading regions for foreign investment in 1995–2002 received, on average, over 80% of all inward FDI; of this, around one-half went to Moscow City and the rest was distributed in small amounts around an array of regions, which changed from year to year. Moscow Oblast, St Petersburg, Tyumen and Samara feature with some regularity and prominence. It is clear, however, that, in a number of second-tier regions, a particular investment project in a particular year can push that region, a little fortuitously, into a leading ranking.

Sakhalin Oblast is the most notable case, home to two very large offshore petroleum and gas projects involving the Anglo-Dutch company, Shell, and a US company, ExxonMobil, which are being developed under production-sharing agreements. In the period following the financial crisis of 1998 the regional pattern of foreign investment, measured both in terms of capital stock and number of enterprises with foreign involvement, moved away from the resource regions and favoured regions involved in import-substitution manufacturing. It is also noteworthy that, despite their political complexion, the major port regions—St Petersburg/Leningrad, Krasnodar/Rostov and Maritime, consistently appear in the top 10. This pattern reflects the impact of rouble devaluation on the cost of imported consumer goods and the failure of the resource sector to capture substantial amounts of investment; the latter is partly the result of problems in reforming Russia's production-sharing legislation, and partly owing to the reluctance, thus far, of large-scale businesses to loosen their control over major hard-currency-earning assets. The profile of Krasnodar Krai was also raised as a result of the construction of a petroleum-export pipeline from Tengiz, Kazakhstan, to the port of Novorossiisk, which opened in late 2001.

Whether the pattern of foreign investment corresponds to the potential of different Russian territories is not clear. Western investors can be assumed to know what they are doing, but one of the things they are forced to do is to take into account the obstacles placed in their way, often by regional administrations. There are, for instance, a number of natural-resource developments from which, as noted earlier, foreign business has been more or less excluded. There are also some regions, such as Archangel (Arkhangelsk) Oblast, where Russian interests, assisted by the local political élite, have served to exclude investors. Apart from direct investment, a number of research organizations have been evaluating the economies of Russia's territories. These organizations are mainly found in Russia itself. Typically, regions are evaluated in term of investment potential and/or risk, on the basis of a collection of diverse indicators. Some of the major producers of regional ratings are *Ekspert* magazine, the (unrelated) Expert Institute of the Russian Union of Industrialists and Entrepreneurs, the Federal Fund for the Support of Small Business, Troika Dialog and BankAustria (commissioning studies from the Institute for Advanced Studies in Vienna, Austria).

The purposes of these rankings are broadly similar: to assess the business climate, attractiveness for investment and risk levels associated with the various federal subjects. Their methods vary, but all perforce operate with official Russian statistics. The indicators used include a core of measures that are used by almost all of the ratings analysts: GRP, population size, per-head incomes (sometimes with adjustment for the still large differences in regional prices, some without), strength of the regional budget (deficit as a percentage of expenditure, for example) and volume of industrial output. Several try to incorporate measures of human capital, such as average years of education of the work-force, or infrastructural indicators, such as the number of telephones per 1,000 inhabitants. The weighting given to different indicators varies and is sometimes far from clear. We have taken three ratings that are very similar in purpose and devised a kind of 'poll of polls'. The three are the ratings of Troika Dialog (August 1997), BankAustria (1998) and *Ekspert* (1998–2002). They differ little in their selection of the most promising 10 territories; they differ rather more in their rankings within the 10, except that Moscow City comes out first in each of them. Combining the three (and assigning a ranking of 11th in the list in question to any region that is omitted from that particular list but does appear in the others), we get the following ranking of 10 (in descending order): Moscow City; St Petersburg; Tyumen Oblast; Sverdlovsk Oblast; Samara Oblast; Nizhnii Novgorod Oblast; Moscow Oblast; Krasnoyarsk Krai; Tatarstan; and Irkutsk Oblast.

This selection displays the mixture of emerging commercial hubs and natural-resource regions described earlier. They form the minority of Russian territories that have adapted less badly than most to the market, and they correspond fairly well to the rankings by inward FDI. However, the changing pattern of investment, away from the dominance of Moscow and the resource regions, and towards the port regions and market-orientated centres, suggests that post-1998 foreign investment is playing a much more constructive role in Russia's economic recovery.

PROSPECTS

Output in Russia declined between 1989 and 1998, with a brief halt in 1997. Thereafter, GDP recovered, rising by a total of about 36% in the five subsequent years. Putin hoped to double GDP within a decade (through average annual growth of 7.2%), although few economists consider this to be possible in the medium term. Many analysts regard the massive devaluation of the rouble in 1998 and the unrelated subsequent strengthening of world petroleum prices as generating an upturn that can be sustained only if basic structural reforms are undertaken—not merely legislated, as was the case in 2001–02, but also implemented in everyday practice. Some continued growth, but at a slower rate (of, say, 3%–5% per year) seems more likely, while pervasive government intervention continues to hinder the competitive process. A World Bank study suggested that about 3%, out of the overall growth rate of 7%, was the result of the direct and indirect benefits of high petroleum prices. Thus, if petroleum prices declined, the real effectiveness of Russia's economic reforms would rapidly be revealed. One factor in favour of effective reform was Russia's attempt to join the World Trade Organization (WTO). Members of the WTO were insisting on strong, further liberalization that would open the Russian financial services, telecommunications and energy sectors to Western business, introducing more competition to the system. Putin and a section of the Russian business élite had apparently chosen to pursue WTO membership on such terms.

Whatever the outcome for Russia in the medium term, the fortunes of individual regions will continue to differ enormously. Sustained convergence of regional living standards requires a strengthening of market institutions, to facilitate the establishment of new business in low-wage areas and the freer movement of people to high-wage areas. Even that, however, although desirable in itself, may not be sufficient to prevent inter-regional inequalities from increasing. Russia's regions differ so markedly in natural-resource endowments, infrastructure, location and human capital, that agglomeration in a number of comparatively successful places may well be stronger than the forces making for convergence.

Putin's evident desire to impose greater central control could help economic change. Regional governments have played a key role in blocking structural change by supporting favoured large enterprises and helping to generate barter and money-surrogate transactions. All other things being equal, the weakening of regional governments should aid economic adjustment. There are, however, two reasons for being cautious about this scenario. First, the power of regional networks of politicians and businessmen may be such that the new federal okrugs and other measures, designed to give the centre more leverage, may turn out, in practice, to make very little difference. Second, even if regional power actually is reduced, there is no guarantee that a strengthened national centre will put an end to corrupt and ineffective government. Russia's problem may be not so much that regional government works poorly, but that all levels of government work poorly.

Chronology of Russia

c. 878: Kievan Rus, the first unified state of the Eastern Slavs, was founded, with Kiev (Kyiv) as its capital.

c. 988: Vladimir (Volodymyr) I—'the Great', ruler of Kievan Rus, converted to Orthodox Christianity.

1237–40: The Rus principalities were invaded and conquered by the Mongol Tatars.

1462–1505: Reign of Ivan III of Muscovy (Moscow), who consolidated the independent Rus domains into a centralized state.

1480: Renunciation of Tatar suzerainty.

1533–84: Reign of Ivan IV—'the Terrible', who began the eastern expansion of Russian territory.

1547: Ivan IV was crowned 'Tsar of Muscovy and all Russia'.

1552: Subjugation of the Khanate of Kazan.

1556: Subjugation of the Khanate of Astrakhan.

1581: A Russian adventurer, Yermak Timofeyev, led an expedition to Siberia, pioneering Russian expansion beyond the Ural Mountains.

1645: A Russian settlement was established on the Sea of Okhotsk, on the coast of eastern Asia.

1654: Eastern and central Ukraine came under Muscovite rule as a result of the Treaty of Pereyaslavl.

1679: Russian pioneers reached the Kamchatka Peninsula and the Pacific Ocean.

1682–1725: Reign of Peter (Petr) I—'the Great', who established Russia as a European Power, expanded its Empire, and modernized the civil and military institutions of the state.

1703: St Petersburg was founded at the mouth of the River Neva, in north-west Russia.

1721: Peter I, who was declared the 'Tsar of all the Russias', proclaimed the Russian Empire.

1728: The Treaty of Kyakhta with China secured the Russian annexation of Transbaikal.

1762–96: Reign of Catherine (Yekaterina) II—'the Great'.

1774: As a result of the Treaty of Kuçuk Kainavci with the Turks, the Black Sea port of Azov was annexed.

1783: Annexation of the Khanate of Crimea (now in Ukraine).

1801–25: Reign of Alexander (Aleksandr) I.

1809: Finland became a possession of the Russian Crown.

1812: The French, under Napoleon I, invaded Russia.

1825: On the death of Alexander I, a group of young officers, the 'Decembrists', attempted to seize power; the attempted *coup d'état* was suppressed by troops loyal to the new Tsar, Nicholas (Nikolai) I, who reigned until 1855.

1853–56: The Crimean War was fought, in which the United Kingdom and France aided Turkey against Russia.

1855–81: Reign of Alexander II, who introduced economic and legal reforms.

1859: The conquest of the Caucasus was completed, following the surrender of rebel forces.

1860: Acquisition of provinces on the Sea of Japan from China and the establishment of Vladivostok.

1861: Emancipation of the serfs.

1864: Final defeat of the Circassian peoples and the confirmation of Russian hegemony in the Caucasus.

1867: The North American territory of Alaska was sold to the USA for US $7m.

1875: Acquisition of Sakhalin from Japan in exchange for the Kurile Islands.

1876: Subjugation of the last of the Central Asian khanates.

1881–94: Reign of Alexander III, who acceded following the assassination of his father and re-established autocratic principles of government.

1891: Construction of the Trans-Siberian Railway was begun.

1894–1917: Reign of Nicholas II, the last Tsar.

1898: The All-Russian Social Democratic Labour Party (RSDLP), a Marxist party, was founded, five years later dividing into 'Bolsheviks' (led by Lenin—Vladimir Ilych Ulyanov) and 'Mensheviks'.

1905: Russia's defeat in the Russo–Japanese War contributed to unrest, which eventually forced the Tsar to introduce limited political reforms, including the holding of elections to a Duma (parliament).

January 1912: The Bolsheviks formally established a separate party, the RSDLP (Bolsheviks).

1 August 1914: Russia entered the First World War against Austria-Hungary, Germany and the Ottoman Empire (the Central Powers).

2 March (New Style: 15 March) 1917: Abdication of Tsar Nicholas II after demonstrations and strikes in Petrograd (as St Petersburg was renamed in 1914); a Provisional Government took power.

25 October (7 November) 1917: The Bolsheviks overthrew the Provisional Government; the Russian Soviet Federative Socialist Republic (RSFSR or Russian Federation) was proclaimed.

6 January (19 January) 1918: The Constituent Assembly, which had been elected in November 1917, was dissolved by the Bolsheviks, which were by this time engaged in a civil war against various anti-communist leaders (the 'Whites').

14 February (Old Style: 1 February) 1918: Adoption of the Gregorian Calendar by the Russian civil authorities.

3 March 1918: Treaty of Brest-Litovsk: the Bolsheviks ceded large areas of western territory to Germany and recognized the independence of Finland and Ukraine.

6–8 March 1918: The RSDLP (Bolsheviks) was renamed the Russian Communist Party (Bolsheviks)—RCP (B).

9 March 1918: The capital of Russia was moved from Petrograd (renamed Leningrad in 1924) to Moscow.

10 July 1918: The first Constitution of the RSFSR was adopted by the Fifth All-Russian Congress of Soviets.

18 July 1918: Tsar Nicholas II and his family were murdered in Yekaterinburg (Sverdlovsk, 1924–91) by Bolshevik troops.

11 November 1918: The Allied Armistice with Germany (which was denied its gains at Brest-Litovsk) ended the First World War.

March 1921: As the civil war ended, the harsh policy of 'War Communism' was replaced by the New Economic Policy (NEP), which allowed peasants and traders some economic freedom.

3 April 1922: Stalin (Iosif V. Dzhugashvili) was elected General Secretary of the RCP (B).

30 December 1922: The Union of Soviet Socialist Republics (USSR) was formed at the 10th All-Russian (first All-Union) Congress of Soviets by the RSFSR, the Transcaucasian Soviet Federative Socialist Republic (TSFSR), the Ukrainian SSR (Soviet Socialist Republic), the Belarusian SSR, and the Central Asian states of the Khorezm People's Socialist Republic and the People's Soviet Republic of Bukhara.

6 July 1923: Promulgation of the first Constitution of the USSR (the Constitution was ratified by the Second All-Union Congress of Soviets in January 1924).

21 January 1924: Death of Lenin.

1928: The NEP was abandoned; the forced collectivization of agriculture resulted in widespread famine.

5 December 1936: The second Constitution of the USSR (the 'Stalin' Constitution) was adopted; two new Union Republics (the Kyrgyz and Kazakh SSRs) were created, and the TSFSR was dissolved into the Georgian, Armenian and Azerbaijani SSRs. The decade was also dominated by a number of ruthless political purges.

1939: Following the signature of the Treaty of Non-Aggression with Germany (the Nazi-Soviet Pact) on 23 August, Soviet forces invaded eastern Poland and then Finland (the Baltic states and Bessarabia were annexed the following year).

22 June 1941: Germany invaded the USSR.

2 February 1943: German forces surrendered at Stalingrad (now Volgograd), marking the first reverse for the German Army. Soviet forces began to regain territory.

1944: In a consolidation of domestic authority, Stalin ordered a number of mass deportations of populations from the North Caucasus and Crimea. Tannu-Tuva (Tyva), a Russian protectorate from 1914, was formally incorporated into the USSR (as part of the RSFSR).

8 May 1945: German forces surrendered to the USSR in Berlin, and Germany subsequently capitulated; most of Eastern and Central Europe had come under Soviet control.

8 August 1945: The USSR declared war on Japan and occupied Sakhalin and the Kurile Islands.

25 January 1949: The Council for Mutual Economic Assistance (CMEA or Comecon) was established, as an economic alliance between the USSR and its Eastern European allies.

14 July 1949: The USSR exploded its first atomic bomb.

5 March 1953: Death of Stalin; he was replaced by a collective leadership.

September 1953: Nikita Khrushchev was elected First Secretary of the Central Committee of the Communist Party of the Soviet Union (CPSU).

14 May 1955: The Warsaw Treaty of Friendship, Co-operation and Mutual Assistance was signed by the USSR and its Eastern European satellites, establishing a military alliance known as the Warsaw Treaty Organization (or the Warsaw Pact).

4 November 1956: Soviet forces invaded Hungary to overthrow Imre Nagy's reformist Government.

4 October 1957: The USSR placed the first man-made satellite (Sputnik I) in orbit around the earth.

18–28 October 1962: The discovery of Soviet nuclear missiles in Cuba by the USA led to the 'Cuban Missile Crisis'; tension eased when Khrushchev announced the withdrawal of the missiles, following a US blockade of the island.

13–14 October 1964: Khrushchev was deposed and replaced as First Secretary of the CPSU by Leonid Brezhnev.

20–21 August 1968: Soviet and other Warsaw Pact forces invaded Czechoslovakia to overthrow the reformist Government of Alexander Dubček.

May 1972: The US President, Richard Nixon, visited Moscow, thus marking a relaxation in US-Soviet relations, a process which came to be known as *détente*.

16 June 1977: Brezhnev became Chairman of the Presidium of the Supreme Soviet (titular head of state).

7 October 1977: The third Constitution of the USSR was adopted.

24 December 1979: Soviet forces invaded Afghanistan (troops were withdrawn between July 1986 and February 1989).

10 November 1982: Death of Brezhnev; Yurii Andropov succeeded him as party leader.

9 February 1984: Death of Andropov; Konstantin Chernenko succeeded him as General Secretary.

10 March 1985: Death of Chernenko; he was succeeded as General Secretary by Mikhail Gorbachev.

24 February–6 March 1986: At the 27th Congress of the CPSU, Gorbachev proposed radical economic and political reforms and 'new thinking' in foreign policy; emergence of the policy of *glasnost* (openness).

26 April 1986: An explosion occurred at a nuclear reactor in Chernobyl (Chornobyl), Ukraine, which resulted in discharges of radioactive material.

January 1987: At a meeting of the CPSU Central Committee, Gorbachev proposed plans for the restructuring of the economy and some democratization of local government and the CPSU (*perestroika*).

21 October 1987: Boris Yeltsin, who had been appointed First Secretary of the Moscow City Party Committee in 1985, resigned from the Politburo of the CPSU.

8 December 1987: In Washington, DC, USA, Gorbachev and US President Ronald Reagan signed a treaty to eliminate all intermediate-range nuclear forces in Europe.

6 December 1988: With the pace of domestic reform quickening, in a speech at the UN Gorbachev outlined his 'new thinking' on foreign policy.

25 March 1989: Multi-party elections to the newly established legislature, the Congress of People's Deputies, took place.

4 March 1990: Elections took place to the local and republican legislatures of the Russian Federation; reformists made substantial gains in the larger cities, notably Moscow and Leningrad (elections elsewhere in the USSR produced overtly nationalist majorities in the Baltic republics and Moldova).

15 March 1990: The all-Union legislature approved the establishment of the post of President of the USSR and elected Mikhail Gorbachev to that office.

29 May 1990: Boris Yeltsin was elected as Chairman of the Supreme Soviet of the Russian Federation. On 12 June, against a background of increasing restiveness in a number of other Union Republics, Congress adopted a declaration of Russian sovereignty within the USSR.

5 June 1990: More than 500 people were killed in inter-ethnic violence in Kyrgyzstan, as protests increased throughout the USSR.

17 March 1991: In an all-Union referendum on the issue of the future state of the USSR, some 75% of participants approved Gorbachev's concept of a 'renewed federation' (several republics did not participate).

12 June 1991: Yeltsin was elected President of the Russian Federation in direct elections, with Aleksandr Rutskoi as Vice-President; residents of Leningrad voted to change the city's name back to St Petersburg.

1 July 1991: The USSR and the other member countries of the Warsaw Pact signed a protocol, formalizing the dissolution of the alliance.

18–21 August 1991: An attempted *coup d'état* was frustrated by popular and institutional opposition, with Yeltsin prominent in the successful campaign to reinstate Gorbachev.

6 September 1991: The newly formed State Council, which comprised the supreme officials of the Union Republics, recognized the independence of Estonia, Latvia and Lithuania.

8 December 1991: The leaders of the Russian Federation, Belarus and Ukraine, meeting at Belovezhskaya Pushcha, Belarus, agreed to form a Commonwealth of Independent States (CIS) to replace the USSR, as stated in the so-called Minsk Agreement.

21 December 1991: At a meeting in Almaty, Kazakhstan, the leaders of 11 former Union Republics of the USSR signed a protocol on the formation of the new CIS.

25 December 1991: Mikhail Gorbachev formally resigned as President of the USSR, thereby confirming the effective dissolution of the Union.

2 January 1992: A radical economic reform programme was introduced in Russia.

31 March 1992: President Yeltsin and the leaders of the country's administrative units signed three documents together known as the Federation Treaty; representatives from the Chechen-Ingush ASSR and Tatarstan did not participate.

June 1992: Ingushetiya was recognized as a federal republic separate from Chechnya.

9 December 1992: The Congress rejected Yeltsin's nomination of a supporter of radical economic reform, Yegor Gaidar, as Prime Minister (Gaidar had been serving as premier, in an acting capacity, since mid-June); Yeltsin subsequently appointed Viktor Chernomyrdin to the post.

25 April 1993: In a referendum organized by President Yeltsin, in order to resolve the increasing conflict between the executive and the legislature, 57.4% of the electorate endorsed the President and 70.6% voted in favour of early parliamentary elections.

31 August 1993: A majority of territorial leaders approved Yeltsin's proposal for the establishment of a Federation Council, which convened in mid-September.

21 September 1993: Yeltsin issued a decree 'On Gradual Constitutional Reform' (Decree 1,400), which suspended the powers of the legislature with immediate effect. The defiance of the legislators, and Vice-President Rutskoi, eventually prompted a state of emergency to be declared in Moscow on 3 October.

4 October 1993: The White House, the seat of the legislature, was shelled by government forces and severely damaged by fire, and over 140 people were killed; the leaders of the parliamentary revolt surrendered.

12 December 1993: A proposed new Constitution was approved by 58.4% of participating voters in a referendum. On the same day elections to the new Federal Assembly (comprising the Federation Council and the State Duma) were held.

11 October 1994: The rouble collapsed, losing almost one-quarter of its value against the US dollar.

11 December 1994: Following the collapse of peace negotiations earlier in the month, Yeltsin ordered the invasion of Chechnya (which had ambitions to secede) by some 40,000 federal ground troops, who met with bitter resistance.

30 July 1995: Opposition to the continuing war in Chechnya prompted a military accord on the gradual disarmament of the Chechen rebels, in return for the partial withdrawal of federal troops from Chechnya; it remained in effect until October.

17 December 1995: In a general election the Communist Party of the Russian Federation (CPRF) achieved the greatest success, winning 22.7% of the votes cast; the radical nationalist Liberal Democratic Party of Russia (LDPR) won 11.2%, Our Home is Russia (a centre-right electoral bloc headed by Chernomyrdin) 10.1% and the liberal Yabloko 6.9%.

16 June 1996: Eleven candidates contested the presidential election; Yeltsin secured the greatest number of votes (35%), followed by the leader of the CPRF, Gennadii Zyuganov (32%); Lt-Gen. (retd) Aleksandr Lebed won an unexpectedly high level of support, with 15% of the votes cast, and was later appointed to the Government.

3 July 1996: Amid increasing speculation about his health, Boris Yeltsin won the second round of voting in the presidential election, with 53.8% of the votes cast. Yeltsin was inaugurated as President on 9 August.

31 August 1996: Lebed, who only survived in government until October, negotiated a cease-fire with the Chechen rebels; the so-called Khasavyurt Accords included postponing resolution of the issue of sovereignty until 2001.

27 March 1998: Following the dismissal, four days earlier, of Chernomyrdin and his Government, Sergei Kiriyenko, a reformist, but hitherto not a prominent minister, was nominated as premier. Kiriyenko was confirmed as Prime Minister by the State Duma on 24 April, having been rejected twice earlier in the month.

17 August 1998: In response to an escalating financial crisis, and in a complete reversal of its monetary policies, the Government announced a series of emergency measures, which included the effective devaluation of the rouble.

23 August 1998: President Yeltsin dismissed Kiriyenko's administration and reappointed Chernomyrdin premier.

11 September 1998: Following the State Duma's second conclusive rejection of Chernomyrdin's nomination as Prime Minister, the Minister of Foreign Affairs, Yevgenii Primakov, was confirmed as premier.

5 November 1998: The Constitutional Court ruled that Boris Yeltsin was ineligible to seek a third presidential term.

24 March 1999: Russia condemned airstrikes by the North Atlantic Treaty Organization (NATO) against Yugoslav targets, initiated in response to the repression of ethnic Albanians in the Serbian province of Kosovo and Metohija (Kosovo), and suspended relations with the Alliance.

12 May 1999: The dismissal of Primakov and his Government was effected by Yeltsin, who appointed Sergei Stepashin, hitherto First Deputy Prime Minister and Minister of the Interior, as acting premier; he was approved by the State Duma one week later.

7 August 1999: Armed Chechen guerrillas invaded neighbouring Dagestan and seized control of two villages. Federal troops retaliated and claimed, by the end of the month, to have quelled the rebel action.

9 August 1999: Stepashin was dismissed by Yeltsin, and replaced as premier by Vladimir Putin, hitherto the Secretary of the Security Council and head of the Federal Security Service (FSB).

9 and 13 September 1999: Two bomb attacks, which targeted apartment blocks in Moscow, killing almost 200 people, were attributed by the federal authorities to Chechen rebels. In August a bomb explosion at a Moscow shopping centre had injured more than 30 people, and further bombings in southern Russian, against both civilian and military targets, took place in mid-September.

23 September 1999: Russia initiated airstrikes against Chechnya, officially in retaliation for the bombings, and as part of a declared 'anti-terrorism' campaign. A full-scale invasion of Chechnya was initiated at the beginning of November, and in December a ground offensive commenced against the republic's capital, Groznyi.

19 December 1999: In elections to the State Duma, the CPRF secured the most seats, with 113. Unity, formed by 31 leaders of Russia's regions, obtained 72 seats, and the Fatherland—All Russia bloc obtained 67. The pro-market Union of Rightist Forces, led by Sergei Kiriyenko, obtained 29 seats, Yabloko took 21, and the Zhirinovskii bloc (contesting the election in place of the LDPR) won 17. The participation rate was 62%; the Chechen constituency remained vacant, owing to the continuing conflict.

31 December 1999: Yeltsin unexpectedly resigned as President; Putin assumed the role in an acting capacity.

26 March 2000: Putin achieved a clear victory in the first round of the presidential election, with 52.9% of the votes cast. He was inaugurated on 7 May, and subsequently formed a new Government, headed by the former First Deputy Prime Minister, Mikhail Kasyanov.

5 May 2000: Putin decreed that, henceforth, Chechnya was to come under direct federal, rather than direct presidential, rule.

13 May 2000: The President issued a decree dividing Russia's 89 constituent regions and republics between seven federal districts (okrugs). Each district was to come under the control of a presidential envoy, who was to oversee local regions' compliance with federal legislation. Of the new presidential envoys, five were senior officers of the security services or the military.

31 May 2000: Three pieces of legislation, proposed by Putin to extend the powers of the President and curtail those of the regional governors, were passed by the State Duma. The first proposed that regional governors should lose their seats in the Federation Council, and be replaced by representatives elected from regional legislatures; following its ratification by the Federation Council in July, all existing Council members were to be replaced by the beginning of 2002. The second bill accorded the President the right to dismiss regional governors, and the third allowed governors to remove from office elected officials who were subordinate to them.

23 November 2000: The State Council, a body comprising the President and the territorial governors and formed as part of the ongoing reform of the Federation Council, convened for the first time.

22 January 2001: Putin signed a decree transferring control of operations in Chechnya from the Ministry of Defence to the FSB.

12 July 2001: New conditions for the registration of political parties were introduced, which were intended to facilitate the consolidation of national parties.

1 September 2001: Following condemnation by the Minister of Defence of the reported appointment of the Islamist extremist, Osama bin Laden, as Commander-in-Chief of the defence force of the Taliban leadership in Afghanistan, the military districts of Russia were reformed; the former Volga and Urals regions were combined in a new, strengthened Trans-Volga region, in response to the perceived heightened security threat from the Central Asian region.

16 January 2002: A new session of the Federation Council opened; for the first time, the Council comprised the full-time appointees of both regional governors and the chairmen of regional legislative assemblies. Sergei Mironov, an ally of Putin, had replaced Yegor Stroyev as Chairman of the Council in the previous month.

25 April 2002: Federal sources reported that the rebel Islamist leader, al-Khattab, who had led a faction in the war in Chechnya, had been killed, a report that was subsequently confirmed by rebel sources.

9 May 2002: During Victory Day processions in Kaspiisk, Dagestan, 45 people were killed, and more than 130 others injured as the result of a bomb attack attributed to Chechen militants.

24 May 2002: Putin and the US President, George W. Bush, signed an agreement, in accordance with which Russia and the USA were each to reduce their stocks of strategic nuclear warheads by more than one-half over a period of 10 years. This development followed an announcement by the USA in late 2001 that it was to withdraw from the Anti-Ballistic Missiles (ABM) Treaty, signed between the USA and the USSR in 1972, with effect from June 2002. On 13 June Russia withdrew from the second Strategic Arms Reduction Treaty (START 2), which had been superseded by the new nuclear arms reduction agreement.

28 May 2002: The new NATO-Russia Council, which made Russia a full partner of NATO in discussions on a number of issues, including counter-terrorism, non-proliferation and emergency planning, was inaugurated at a NATO conference in Rome, Italy.

19 August 2002: In the single largest loss of life since the recommencement of military operations in Chechnya in 1999, some 118 federal troops were killed when rebels shot down a military helicopter.

23 October 2002: Some 50 heavily armed Chechen rebels took more than 700 people hostage in a Moscow theatre, demanding the immediate withdrawal of federal troops from Chechnya. On 26 October élite Russian troops stormed the theatre, killing the rebels in an operation that also resulted in the deaths of some 129 hostages. It rapidly emerged that the vast majority of these deaths had resulted from the use of an incapacitating gas by the federal troops.

7 November 2002: In a move that was generally regarded as a promotion, Stanislav Ilyasov, hitherto Chairman of the Government of Chechnya, was appointed to the federal Government as Minister without Portfolio, responsible for the Social and Economic Development of Chechnya. Capt (retd) Mikhail Babich was appointed as the new premier of Chechnya; Babich resigned in January 2003 and was replaced in the following month by Anatolii Popov, hitherto the Deputy Chairman of the State Commission for the Reconstruction of Chechnya.

27 December 2002: At least 83 people died, and more than 150 others were injured, when suicide bombers detonated bombs in two vehicles stationed outside the headquarters of the Chechen republican Government in Groznyi.

11 March 2003: Putin removed Valentina Matviyenko from her post as Deputy Chairman of the Government, responsible for Social Affairs, appointing her as Presidential Representative in the North-Western Federal District, based in St Petersburg.

23 March 2003: A referendum was held in Chechnya on a draft republican constitution, which described the region as an integral part of the Russian Federation. According to the official results, some 88.4% of the electorate participated in the plebiscite, of whom 96.0% voted in favour. Two further questions, on the method of electing the president and the parliament of the republic, were also approved, receiving the support of 95.4% and 96.1% of the votes cast, respectively.

12 May 2003: At least 59 people were killed when suicide bombers attacked offices of the Chechen Government in Znamenskoye, in the north of the republic. Two days later another suicide bombing in Chechnya, at a religious festival attended by Kadyrov, resulted in at least 14 deaths.

16 June 2003: Vladimir Yakovlev, hitherto Governor of St Petersburg, was appointed to the federal Government as a Deputy Chairman, with particular responsibility for housing and utilities.

21 June 2003: An interim legislative body in Chechnya, the State Council, was inaugurated.

6 July 2003: Fifteen people were killed as the result of a suicide bombing, attributed to Chechen militants, at a music festival outside Moscow.

1 September 2003: The overall command for military operations in Chechnya was transferred from the FSB to the Ministry of Internal Affairs. Moreover, the Minister of Internal Affairs, Boris Gryzlov, stated that such operations were no longer regarded as having an 'anti-terrorist' character, but were rather, henceforth, to form part of an 'operation to protect law and constitutional order'.

5 October 2003: At a second round of voting, Matviyenko was elected as Governor of St Petersburg, having received the support of Putin. On the same day Kadyrov was elected as President of Chechnya, with 88% of the votes cast, according to official figures. However, many observers were critical of the conduct of voting in Chechnya, citing a heightened military presence at polling stations, and noting that several of Kadyrov's principal rivals had withdrawn, or been obliged to withdraw, their candidacies.

7 December 2003: Elections to the State Duma took place. Observers from the Organization for Security and Co-operation in Europe declared the elections to have been free but not fair, noting, in particular, widespread media bias in favour of Unity and Fatherland-United Russia, supportive of Putin, which secured 226 seats in the 450-seat State Duma. The CPRF was the second-placed party, obtaining 53 seats, while nationalist parties, including the LDPR (with 38 seats), attracted increased support. Liberal parties, such as Yabloko and the Union of Rightist Forces, lost their representation in the Duma, at least partly owing to their unpopular association with the so-called 'oligarchy'. The rate of participation by the electorate was low, at around 50%, and some 5% of votes were cast 'against all candidates'.

9 December 2003: Six people were killed when a bomb exploded in Moscow, outside a hotel located close to the Kremlin; the intended target was thought to have been the State Duma building and the attack was widely attributed to female Chechen suicide bombers (often referred to as 'black widows'). Four days earlier a bomb attack had targeted a passenger train in Stavropol Krai, killing some 45 people and injuring about 170.

29 December 2003: Boris Gryzslov, who had resigned his ministerial portfolio, was elected Chairman of the State Duma.

Statistics

MAJOR DEMOGRAPHIC AND ECONOMIC INDICATORS

	Area ('000 sq km)	Population at 2002 census ('000, preliminary data)	Population density, 2002 census (per sq km, preliminary data)	Average annual change in population, 1991–2002 (%)*	Life expectancy at birth, 2001
Central Federal Okrug	650.7	37,991	58.4	−0.4	65.26
Belgorod Oblast . . .	27.1	1,512	55.8	0.6	67.38
Bryansk Oblast . . .	34.9	1,379	39.5	−0.3	65.05
Ivanovo Oblast . . .	21.8	1,149	52.7	−0.7	63.18
Kaluga Oblast . . ,. .	29.9	1,041	34.8	−0.2	64.27
Kostroma Oblast	60.1	738	12.3	−0.5	63.65
Kursk Oblast	29.8	1,236	41.5	−0.3	65.87
Lipetsk Oblast	24.1	1,213	50.3	0.0	66.53
Moscow City	1.0	10,400	10,462.8	−0.4	67.40
Moscow Oblast[1] . . .	46.0	6,627	144.1	−0.4	64.77
Orel Oblast	24.7	861	34.8	−0.2	65.37
Ryazan Oblast	39.6	1,228	31.0	−0.7	64.71
Smolensk Oblast . . .	49.8	1,051	21.1	−0.5	62.70
Tambov Oblast . . .	34.3	1,180	34.4	−0.5	65.93
Tula Oblast	25.7	1,676	65.2	−0.8	63.00
Tver Oblast	84.1	1,473	17.5	−0.7	61.94
Vladimir Oblast . . .	29.0	1,525	52.6	−0.5	63.56
Voronezh Oblast . . .	52.4	2,379	45.4	−0.2	66.17
Yaroslavl Oblast . . .	36.4	1,368	37.6	−0.6	64.22
North-Western Federal Okrug	1,677.9	13,986	8.3	−0.6	64.42
Archangel Oblast[2]	587.4	1,336	2.3	−0.9	63.87
Nenets AOk . . .	176.7	42	0.2	−1.6	61.87
Kaliningrad Oblast . .	15.1	955	63.3	0.6	63.00
Kareliya (Republic) . .	172.4	717	4.2	−0.5	62.96
Komi (Republic) . .	415.9	1,019	2.5	−1.0	64.79
Leningrad Oblast[3]. . .	85.3	1,671	19.4	−0.1	61.99
Murmansk Oblast . . .	144.9	893	6.2	−1.7	65.87
Novgorod Oblast . . .	55.3	695	12.6	−0.5	62.32
Pskov Oblast	55.3	761	13.8	−0.7	61.58
St Petersburg Federal City	0.6	4,669	8,191.9	−0.8	66.19
Vologda Oblast	145.7	1,270	8.7	−0.4	64.37

* According to official estimates at 1 Jan.
[1] Excluding Moscow city.
[2] Including Nenets AOk.
[3] Excluding St Petersburg.

Gross regional product (GRP), 2000 (m. roubles)	GRP per head, 2000 (roubles)	Rate of un-employment, 2001 (%)	Inflation rate, 2001 (%)†	Foreign investment, 2001 (US $m.)	
2,079,743	56,158	6.3	19.2	6,469.9	**Central Federal Okrug**
44,346	29,574	6.5	19.2	40.0	Belgorod Oblast
26,154	18,213	10.0	17.3	9.1	Bryansk Oblast
18,093	14,885	5.6	17.1	0.4	Ivanovo Oblast
26,107	24,257	6.0	19.9	103.0	Kaluga Oblast
18,174	23,204	6.0	19.6	0.9	Kostroma Oblast
31,949	24,403	10.4	19.8	24.2	Kursk Oblast
48,236	38,980	6.6	17.1	81.3	Lipetsk Oblast
1,342,997	155,543	2.1	20.4	5,654.0	Moscow City
193,614	29,800	5.5	21.8	372.7	Moscow Oblast[1]
25,456	28,423	7.9	16.7	18.5	Orel Oblast
31,966	25,044	11.2	19.2	1.6	Ryazan Oblast
29,906	26,565	9.9	16.6	9.9	Smolensk Oblast
25,871	20,498	12.4	15.5	20.1	Tambov Oblast
43,722	25,215	5.2	17.2	43.7	Tula Oblast
38,749	24,338	7.8	19.0	24.3	Tver Oblast
35,450	22,135	9.9	20.5	22.7	Vladimir Oblast
52,100	21,268	9.6	17.1	29.2	Voronezh Oblast
46,853	33,278	7.1	20.8	14.1	Yaroslavl Oblast
615,064	42,541	7.7	18.3	1,789.1	**North-Western Federal Okrug**
58,465	40,277	8.8	19.6	50.5	Archangel Oblast[2]
n.a.	n.a.	7.2	20.0	20.1	Nenets AOk
26,151	27,592	9.6	21.0	24.6	Kaliningrad Oblast
28,509	37,310	8.7	18.3	41.7	Kareliya (Republic)
72,346	64,068	14.0	20.5	76.8	Komi (Republic)
59,342	35,528	6.9	19.6	327.0	Leningrad Oblast[3]
58,370	59,747	12.9	22.6	12.4	Murmansk Oblast
20,920	28,863	6.4	16.8	50.1	Novgorod Oblast
17,110	21,493	10.3	18.4	5.2	Pskov Oblast
205,399	43,914	3.9	18.1	1,171.3	St Petersburg Federal City
68,453	51,857	8.9	15.4	29.6	Vologda Oblast

† Percentage change in the Consumer Price Index, Dec.–Dec.

MAJOR DEMOGRAPHIC AND ECONOMIC INDICATORS (continued)

	Area ('000 sq km)	Population at 2002 census ('000, preliminary data)	Population density, 2002 census (per sq km, preliminary data)	Average annual change in population, 1991–2002 (%)	Life expectancy at birth, 2001
Southern Federal Okrug	589.2	22,914	38.9	0.3	67.24
Adygeya (Republic) . .	7.6	447	58.8	0.2	68.77
Astrakhan Oblast . . .	44.1	1,007	22.8	0.1	65.18
Chechnya (Republic) . .	n.a.	1,100	n.a.	−4.9‡	n.a.
Dagestan (Republic) . .	50.3	2,584	51.3	1.5	71.56
Ingushetiya (Republic) .	n.a.	469	n.a.	7.7‡	74.60
Kabardino-Balkariya (Republic)	12.5	901	72.0	−1.9	67.96
Kalmykiya (Republic) .	75.9	292	3.9	8.2	66.32
Karacheyevo-Cherkessiya	14.1	440	31.2	−3.0	69.38
Krasnodar Krai . . .	76.0	5,124	67.4	0.6	67.00
North Osetiya—Alaniya (Republic)	8.0	710	88.7	−3.6	69.43
Rostov Oblast	100.8	4,407	43.7	−0.1	66.23
Stavropol Krai. . . .	66.5	2,731	41.1	0.6	67.75
Volgograd Oblast . . .	113.9	2,703	23.7	0.0	65.88
Volga Federal Okrug .	1,038.0	31,158	30.0	−0.1	65.75
Bashkortostan (Republic)	143.6	4,103	28.6	0.3	66.68
Chuvash Republic. . .	18.3	1,314	71.8	0.0	66.36
Kirov Oblast	120.8	1,504	12.4	−0.6	65.88
Marii-El (Republic) . .	23.2	728	31.4	−0.1	64.58
Mordoviya (Republic) .	26.2	889	33.9	−0.5	67.38
Nizhnii Novgorod Oblast	76.9	3,524	45.8	−0.4	64.92
Orenburg Oblast . . .	124.0	2,178	17.6	0.2	65.21
Penza Oblast	43.2	1,453	33.6	−0.3	66.54
Perm Oblast[4]	160.6	2,824	17.6	−0.4	63.85
Komi-Permyak AOk .	32.9	136	4.1	−0.6	61.15
Samara Oblast	53.6	3,240	60.4	0.0	64.73
Saratov Oblast. . . .	100.2	2,669	26.6	−0.1	65.42
Tatarstan (Republic) . .	67.8	3,780	55.7	0.2	67.63
Udmurt Republic . . .	42.1	1,571	37.3	−0.1	65.26
Ulyanovsk Oblast . . .	37.3	1,382	37.1	0.1	65.99
Urals Federal Okrug .	1,788.9	12,382	6.9	−0.2	65.28
Chelyabinsk Oblast . .	87.9	3,606	41.0	−0.2	65.08
Kurgan Oblast . . .	71.0	1,020	14.4	−0.3	64.95
Sverdlovsk Oblast. . .	194.8	4,490	23.0	−0.4	64.72
Tyumen Oblast[5] . . .	1,435.2	3,266	2.3	0.3	66.73
Khanti-Mansii AOk— Yugra	523.1	1,433	2.7	0.6	68.15
Yamal-Nenets AOk .	750.3	507	0.7	0.1	69.74

* According to official estimates at 1 Jan.
‡ 1996–2002 figure.
[4] Including Komi-Permyak AOk.
[5] Including Khanty-Mansii—Yugra and Yamal-Nenets AOks.

Gross regional product (GRP), 2000 (m. roubles)	GRP per head, 2000 (roubles)	Rate of unemployment, 2001 (%)	Inflation rate, 2001 (%)†	Foreign investment, 2001 (US $m.)	
488,075	23,151	13.6	20.2	985.6	**Southern Federal Okrug**
5,811	12,980	14.1	21.5	1.7	Adygeya (Republic)
32,274	31,587	10.5	21.6	1.8	Astrakhan Oblast
n.a.	n.a.	n.a.	n.a.	n.a.	Chechnya (Republic)
21,328	9,885	28.8	17.4	0.1§	Dagestan (Republic)
6,021	12,690	34.9	38.7	n.a.	Ingushetiya (Republic)
16,219	20,509	16.8	22.5	0.2‖	Kabardino-Balkariya (Republic)
8,845	28,080	19.1	19.8	1.6¶	Kalmykiya (Republic)
5,795	13,353	18.6	19.2	0.0	Karacheyevo-Cherkessiya
151,405	29,095	10.7	22.3	793.4	Krasnodar Krai
11,691	17,290	16.7	17.5	n.a.	North Osetiya—Alaniya (Republic)
96,000	22,090	12.9	22.3	84.0	Rostov Oblast
58,807	21,884	9.8	19.8	20.9	Stavropol Krai
73,878	27,680	9.8	20.5	82.8	Volgograd Oblast
1,120,575	35,085	8.5	18.2	1,220.0	**Volga Federal Okrug**
160,751	39,083	10.7	17.4	29.6	Bashkortostan (Republic)
25,189	18,603	9.6	19.1	34.7	Chuvash Republic
38,065	24,058	7.7	17.3	3.8	Kirov Oblast
11,863	15,669	9.4	18.2	0.1	Marii-El (Republic)
24,005	25,952	10.5	19.7	1.6	Mordoviya (Republic)
104,296	28,634	8.3	19.7	20.9	Nizhnii Novgorod Oblast
82,646	37,223	8.5	15.8	88.8	Orenburg Oblast
27,371	17,961	13.9	18.5	1.7	Penza Oblast
131,388	44,424	6.9	22.5	97.6	Perm Oblast[4]
2,017	n.a.	12.2	18.0	n.a.	Komi-Permyak AOk
155,732	47,339	6.0	16.7	260.4	Samara Oblast
67,908	25,103	10.0	19.0	8.9	Saratov Oblast
202,734	53,695	6.3	17.4	651.0	Tatarstan (Republic)
55,766	34,216	7.5	20.4	6.8	Udmurt Republic
32,860	22,462	9.0	28.1	2.2	Ulyanovsk Oblast
939,797	74,685	9.2	20.5	1,800.1	**Urals Federal Okrug**
136,063	37,131	8.7	24.8	767.1	Chelyabinsk Oblast
19,941	18,246	13.3	27.8	0.9	Kurgan Oblast
165,761	36,056	7.7	20.1	747.8	Sverdlovsk Oblast
618,032	191,412	10.4	19.9	284.4	Tyumen Oblast[5]
n.a.	n.a.	11.0	19.2	201.0	Khanti-Mansii AOk—Yugra
n.a.	n.a.	7.1	22.9	73.2	Yamal-Nenets AOk

† Percentage change in the Consumer Price Index, Dec.–Dec.
§ 1998 figure.
‖ 2000 figure.
¶ 1995 figure.

MAJOR DEMOGRAPHIC AND ECONOMIC INDICATORS (continued)

	Area ('000 sq km)	Population at 2002 census ('000, preliminary data)	Population density, 2002 census (per sq km, preliminary data)	Average annual change in population, 1991–2002 (%)*	Life expectancy at birth, 2001
Siberian Federal Okrug	5,114.8	20,064	3.9	−0.3	64.00
Altai Krai	169.1	2,607	15.4	−0.1	66.30
Altai (Republic) . . .	92.6	203	2.2	0.4	62.37
Buryatiya (Republic) . .	351.3	981	2.8	−0.3	62.47
Chita Oblast	412.5[6]	1,084[6]	2.6[6]	−0.6	61.48
Aga-Buryat AOk . .	19.0	72	3.8	0.2	63.91
Irkutsk Oblast	745.5[7]	2,446[7]	3.3[7]	−0.3	61.82
Ust-Orda Buryat AOk .	22.4	136	6.0	0.3	61.93
Kemerovo Oblast . . .	95.5	2,900	30.4	−0.5	62.77
Khakasiya (Republic). .	61.9	546	8.8	0.0	63.57
Krasnoyarsk Krai[8]. . .	2,339.0	2,966	1.3	−0.5	63.34
Evenk AOk	767.6	18	0.0	−2.9	59.26
Taimyr (Dolgano-Nenets) AOk . .	862.1	40	0.1	−1.8	63.51
Novosibirsk Oblast . .	178.2	2,692	15.1	−0.1	66.26
Omsk Oblast	139.7	2,079	14.9	−0.2	66.65
Tomsk Oblast	316.9	1,046	3.3	−0.2	65.49
Tyva (Republic) . . .	170.5	306	1.8	0.1	56.48
Far Eastern Federal Okrug	6,215.9	6,687	1.1	−1.2	63.49
Amur Oblast	363.7	903	2.5	−0.7	62.43
Chukot AOk	737.7	54	0.1	−6.8	62.54
Jewish (Birobidzhan) AOb	36.0	191	5.3	−1.0	62.27
Kamchatka Oblast. . .	170.8[9]	334[9]	2.0[9]	−2.1	63.79
Koryak AOk . . .	301.5	25	0.1	−3.2	59.32
Khabarovsk Krai . . .	788.6	1,435	1.8	−0.8	63.02
Magadan Oblast . . .	461.4	183	0.4	−4.6	59.73
Maritime (Primorskii) Krai	165.9	2,068	12.5	−0.7	64.37
Sakha—Yakutiya (Republic)	3,103.2	948	0.3	−1.2	64.37
Sakhalin Oblast . . .	87.1	546.5	6.3	−1.9	62.73
Russian Federation . .	17,075.4	145,182	8.5	−0.3	65.29

* According to official estimates at 1 Jan.
[6] Excluding Aga-Buryat AOk.
[7] Excluding Ust-Orda Buryat AOk.
[8] Figures for Krasnoyarsk Krai include Evenk and Taimyr (Dolgano-Nenets) AOks.
[9] Excluding Koryak AOk.

Source: Goskomstat, Moscow.

Gross regional product (GRP), 2000 (m. roubles)	GRP per head, 2000 (roubles)	Rate of un-employment, 2001 (%)	Inflation rate, 2001 (%)†	Foreign investment, 2001 (US $m.)	
715,199	34,487	11.3	18.0	1,226.3	**Siberian Federal Okrug**
48,691	18,391	9.9	19.4	1.5	Altai Krai
4,027	19,625	9.7	13.7	0.1‡	Altai (Republic)
22,479	21,782	18.5	20.9	0.2	Buryatiya (Republic)
31,549	25,154	17.0	19.3	6.0	Chita Oblast
n.a.	n.a.	23.0	13.7	n.a.	Aga-Buryat AOk
106,909	38,999	10.9	16.9	101.1	Irkutsk Oblast
n.a.	n.a.	14.2	10.9	n.a.	Ust-Orda Buryat AOk
93,636	31,448	10.0	18.0	33.9	Kemerovo Oblast
17,441	30,036	8.8	17.8	0.1	Khakasiya (Republic)
217,292	71,730	9.7	24.3	30.1	Krasnoyarsk Krai[8]
n.a.	n.a.	2.9	34.2	n.a.	Evenk AOk
n.a.	n.a.	7.3	23.9	n.a.	Taimyr (Dolgano-Nenets) AOk
76,948	28,093	12.4	14.2	103.9	Novosibirsk Oblast
48,704	22,608	10.0	15.4	925.2	Omsk Oblast
43,765	41,055	9.8	23.5	24.6	Tomsk Oblast
3,761	12,081	23.9	15.0	0.4	Tyva Oblast
319,335	44,795	10.2	17.8	766.8	**Far Eastern Federal Okrug**
26,954	26,908	12.2	19.7	0.2	Amur Oblast
4,129	58,520	7.4	10.5	n.a.	Chukot AOk
3,824	19,282	9.5	19.0	0.0	Jewish (Birobidzhan) AOb
18,348	48,190	14.5	15.4	78.4	Kamchatka Oblast
n.a.	n.a.	15.2	21.6	4.3	Koryak AOk
68,684	45,424	10.3	23.5	19.9	Khabarovsk Krai
12,760	55,480	11.7	17.5	26.4	Magadan Oblast
66,342	30,628	8.6	19.1	108.6	Maritime (Primorskii) Krai
81,919	84,011	8.2	13.1	144.5	Sakha—Yakutiya (Republic)
36,376	61,208	12.0	19.4	388.9	Sakhalin Oblast
6,277,787	43,306	9.1	18.6	14,257.8	**Russian Federation**

† Percentage change in the Consumer Price Index, Dec.–Dec.
‡ 2000 figure.

RUSSIAN CURRENCY AND EXCHANGE RATES

Monetary Units
   100 kopeks = 1 Russian rouble (rubl or ruble).

Sterling, Dollar and Euro Equivalents (31 October 2003)
   £1 sterling = 50.51 roubles;
   US $1 = 29.86 roubles;
   €1 = 34.70 roubles;
   1,000 roubles = £19.80 = $33.49 = €28.82.

Average Exchange Rate (roubles per US dollar)
   2000   28.1292
   2001   29.1685
   2002   31.3485

Note: On 1 January 1998 a new rouble, equivalent to 1,000 of the former units, was introduced. Figures in this Survey are expressed in terms of new roubles, unless otherwise indicated.

RUSSIAN INFLATION
The annual increase in consumer prices in the Russian Federation as a whole, according to official figures, for the year to December was:
   2000   20.2%
   2001   18.6%
   2002   15.1%
   2003   12.0%

The Government of the Russian Federation

(January 2004)

According to the Constitution of December 1993, the Russian Federation is a democratic, federative, multi-ethnic republic, in which state power is divided between the executive, the legislature and the judiciary, which are independent of one another. The President of the Russian Federation is Head of State and Commander-in-Chief of the Armed Forces. The President, who wields considerable executive authority, is elected for a term of four years by universal direct suffrage. The President appoints the Chairman (Prime Minister) of the Government, but the cabinet must be approved by the legislature. Supreme legislative power is vested in a bicameral Federal Assembly.

There are 89 members (federal territorial units) of the Russian Federation. The recognized territories consist of 21 autonomous republics, six krais (provinces), 49 oblasts (regions), two cities of federal status, one autonomous oblast and 10 autonomous okrugs (districts). Largely based on the old Soviet divisions, their status as constituent members of the Federation began to be regularized by the so-called Federation Treaty of 31 March 1992. These three documents provided for a union of 20 republics (16 of which had been Autonomous Soviet Socialist Republics— ASSRs under the old regime, and four of which were autonomous oblasts), six krais and one autonomous oblast. The 10 autonomous okrugs remained under the jurisdiction of the krai or oblast within which they were located (a situation which largely continued thereafter) but, as federal units, were raised to the same status as oblasts and krais. The former republic of Chechno-Ingushetiya was divided into two republics in June 1992, by the formal recognition of a republic of Ingushetiya. Moscow and St Petersburg subsequently assumed the status of federal cities.

Under the terms of the 1992 treaties, republics were granted far wider-reaching powers than the other federal units, specifically over the use of natural resources and land. They consequently represent autonomous states within the Russian Federation, as opposed to being merely administrative units of a unitary state. From 1995 agreement of bilateral treaties to delineate powers between the federal Government and the regional authorities became increasingly commonplace. This resulted in the establishment, in March 1996, of the precise terms of the delimitation of jurisdiction and powers between federal and regional authorities; no treaty could change the status of a federal unit, threaten the territorial integrity of the Russian Federation or violate the terms of the federal Constitution. Fears that the country was being transformed from a constitution-based to a treaty-based federation became more widespread as these power-sharing agreements were signed by a majority of federal subjects.

Attempts to regulate the subsequent peripheral–central tensions in the governance of Russia took a variety of forms, particularly after the election of Vladimir Putin to the presidency in March 2000. In particular, the establishment of the Federal Okrugs (see below), each of which was headed by a presidential appointee, was considered by many to be a device to ensure closer central supervision of regional activity. The federal President also assumed the right to dismiss governors at will, extending such a right over local officials to regional governors themselves, hence encouraging a more efficient form of government, with a clearer hierarchy, which Putin referred to as 'vertical power'. In the event, however, these powers were seldom used in the three years following their introduction. Instead, a series of presidential decrees in 2000–01 ruled that laws specific to certain regions were unconstitutional and must be amended. The federal republics, which had the greatest degree of autonomy to lose under the new arrangements, were most severely affected; by April 2002 28 of the 42 'power-sharing treaties' signed between the regional and federal authorities had been annulled, and many of those which remained had been amended, in order to bring regional legislation into conformity with the federal norm. A new body, the State Council of the Russian Federation, was created by presidential decree in September 2000, the members of which were the heads of the 89 constituent parts of the Russian Federation. Since the Russian Constitution remained unchanged, the State Council's functions were consultative, and participation in it was voluntary. According to its founding decree, the body was to advise the President mainly on issues concerning the relationship between the central administration and Russia's regions.

Autonomous republics, autonomous okrugs and the autonomous oblast are ethnically defined, while krais and oblasts are defined on territorial grounds. One of Putin's earliest actions after his election as federal President was to group the federal subjects into seven large Federal Okrugs. These seven districts, broadly similar to the organizational units of the Federation's armed forces in existence at that time, are the Central Federal Okrug (based in the capital, Moscow), the North-Western Federal Okrug (St Petersburg), the Southern Federal Okrug (Rostov-on-Don), the Volga Federal Okrug (Nizhnii Novgorod), the Urals Federal Okrug (Yekaterinburg), the Siberian Federal Okrug (Novosibirsk) and the Far Eastern Federal Okrug (Khabarovsk). Additionally, each of the federal units is grouped into one of 11 economic areas (see the indexes). These are the Central Economic Area, the Central Chernozem (Black Earth) Economic Area, the Eastern Siberian Economic Area, the Far Eastern (sometimes known as the Pacific) Economic Area, the North Caucasus Economic Area, the North-Western Economic Area, the Northern Economic Area, the Urals Economic Area, the Volga Economic Area, the Volga-Vyatka Economic Area and the Western Siberian Economic Area.

Of the 89 members of the Russian Federation, the 21 republics are each administered by a president and/or prime minister. The republics each have their own governments and ministries. The remaining federal units are governed by a local administration, the head (governor) of which is the highest official in the territory, and a representative assembly (usually known as a soviet or duma). Governors are able to veto regional legislation, although their vetoes may be overridden by a two-thirds' parliamentary majority. The federal legislature, which created the post of governor in August 1991, intended that the official be elected by popular vote. The federal President, Boris Yeltsin, however, secured an agreement that the governors be appointed. In many regions conflict subsequently arose between the executive and legislative bodies, as the presidential appointees encountered much resistance from the communist-dominated assemblies. In those cases where a vote of 'no confidence' was passed in the governor, elections were permitted. (This occurred in seven oblasts and one krai in December 1992.) Following Yeltsin's dissolution of the Russian legislature in September 1993, and parliament's violent resistance, it was announced that all heads of local administrations would, henceforth, be appointed and dismissed by presidential decree. In response to increasing pressure, however, this ruling was relaxed in December 1995, when gubernatorial elections were held in one krai and 11 oblasts. From the late 1990s elected governors became the norm in all federal subjects.

Presidential Representative in the Central Federal Okrug: Lt-Gen. GEORGII S. POLTAVCHENKO; 103132 Moscow, Nikolskii per. 6; tel. (095) 206-12-76; e-mail malakhov_dm@gov.ru; internet www.cfopolpred.ru.

Presidential Representative in the Far Eastern Federal Okrug: Lt-Gen. KONSTANTIN B. PULIKOVSKII; 680030 Khabarovsk, ul. Sheronova 22; tel. (4212) 31-39-78; fax (4212) 31-38-04; internet www.dfo.ru.

Presidential Representative in the North-Western Federal Okrug: ILYA I. KLEBANOV; 193015 St Petersburg, ul. Shpalernaya 47; tel. (812) 346-20-09; fax (812) 326-64-84.

Presidential Representative in the Siberian Federal Okrug: LEONID V. DRACHEVSKII; 630091 Novosibirsk, ul. Derzhavina 18/120; tel. (3832) 20-17-56; fax (3832) 20-13-90; e-mail sibokrug@online.sinor.ru; internet www.sfo.nsk.su.

Presidential Representative in the Southern Federal Okrug: Col-Gen. VIKTOR G. KAZANTSEV; 344006 Rostov-on-Don, ul. B. Sadovaya 73; tel. (8632) 44-16-16; fax (8632) 40-39-40; e-mail polpred@polpred-ug.donpac.ru.

Presidential Representative in the Urals Federal Okrug: Col-Gen. PETR M. LATYSHEV; 620031 Sverdlovsk obl., Yekaterinburg, pl. Oktyabrskaya 3; tel. (3432) 77-18-96; e-mail support@uralfo.ru; internet www.uralfo.ru.

Presidential Representative in the Volga Federal Okrug: SERGEI V. KIRIYENKO; 603082 Nizhnii Novgorod, Kreml, kor. 1; tel. (8312) 31-46-07; fax (8312) 31-47-51; internet www.pfo.ru.

HEAD OF STATE

President of the Russian Federation: VLADIMIR V. PUTIN (elected 26 March 2000; inaugurated 7 May 2000).

PRESIDENTIAL ADMINISTRATION

Office of the President: 103073 Moscow, Kremlin; tel. (095) 925-35-81; fax (095) 206-51-73; e-mail president@gov.ru; internet president.kremlin.ru.

THE GOVERNMENT
(January 2004)

Chairman (Prime Minister): MIKHAIL M. KASYANOV.

Deputy Chairman and Minister of Agriculture and Foodstuffs: ALEKSEI V. GORDEYEV.

Deputy Chairman and Minister of Finance: ALEKSEI L. KUDRIN.

Deputy Chairman, responsible for Industrial Policy: BORIS S. ALESHIN.

Deputy Chairman, responsible for Social Affairs: GALINA N. KARELOVA.

Deputy Chairmen: VIKTOR B. KHRISTENKO, VLADIMIR A. YAKOVLEV.

Minister for Antimonopoly Policy and Support for Entrepreneurship: ILYA A. YUZHANOV.

Minister of Atomic Energy: ALEKSANDR YU. RUMYANTSEV.

Minister of Civil Defence, Emergencies and Clean-up Operations: Lt-Gen. SERGEI K. SHOIGU.

Minister of Communications and Information Technology: LEONID D. REIMAN.

Minister of Culture: MIKHAIL YE. SHVYDKOI.

Minister of Defence: SERGEI B. IVANOV.

Minister of Economic Development and Trade: GERMAN O. GREF.

Minister of Education: VLADIMIR M. FILIPPOV.

Minister of Energy: IGOR KH. YUSUFOV.

Minister of Foreign Affairs: IGOR S. IVANOV.

Minister of Health: YURII L. SHEVCHENKO.

Minister of Industry, Science and Technology: ANDREI A. FURSENKO (acting).

Minister of Internal Affairs: Col-Gen. RASHID NURGALIYEV (acting).

Minister of Justice: YURII YA. CHAIKA.

Minister of Labour and Social Development: ALEKSANDR P. POCHINOK.

Minister of Natural Resources: VITALII G. ARTYUKHOV.

Minister of the Press, Broadcasting and Mass Media: MIKHAIL YU. LESIN.

Minister of Railways: VADIM N. MOROZOV.

Minister of State Property: FARIT R. GAZIZULLIN.

Minister of Taxes and Levies: GENNADII I. BUKAYEV.

Minister of Transport: SERGEI O. FRANK.

Head of the Presidential Administration and Minister without Portfolio: KONSTANTIN E. MERZLIKIN.

Minister without Portfolio, responsible for the Social and Economic Development of Chechnya: STANISLAV V. ILYASOV.

Minister without Portfolio, responsible for Nationalities Policy: VLADIMIR YU. ZORIN.

Minister without Portfolio: VLADIMIR V. YELAGIN.

MINISTRIES

Office of the Government: 103274 Moscow, Krasnopresnenskaya nab. 2; tel. (095) 205-57-35; fax (095) 205-42-19; internet www.government.ru.

Ministry of Agriculture and Foodstuffs: 107139 Moscow, Orlikov per. 1/11; tel. (095) 207-83-86; fax (095) 207-95-80; e-mail info@aris.ru; internet www.aris.ru.

Ministry for Antimonopoly Policy and Support for Entrepreneurship: 123231 Moscow, ul. Sadovaya-Kudrinskaya 11; tel. (095) 254-74-45; fax (095) 254-75-21; e-mail gak1@infpres.ru; internet www.maprf.ru.

Ministry of Atomic Energy: 109017 Moscow, ul. B. Ordynka 24/26; tel. (095) 239-45-45; fax (095) 230-24-20; e-mail info@minatom.ru; internet www.minatom.ru.

Ministry of Civil Defence, Emergencies and Clean-up Operations: 103012 Moscow, Teatralnyi proyezd 3; tel. (095) 926-39-01; fax (095) 924-19-46; e-mail pressa@emercom.gov.ru; internet www.emercom.gov.ru.

Ministry of Communications and Information Technology: 103375 Moscow, ul. Tverskaya 7; tel. (095) 292-71-44; fax (095) 292-74-55; internet www.minsvyaz.ru.

Ministry of Culture: 103074 Moscow, Kitaigorodskii proyezd 7; tel. (095) 925-11-95; fax (095) 928-17-91; e-mail root@mincult.isf.ru; internet www.mincultrf.ru.

Ministry of Defence: 105175 Moscow, ul. Myasnitskaya 37; tel. (095) 293-38-54; fax (095) 296-84-36; internet www.mil.ru.

Ministry of Economic Development and Trade: 125993 Moscow, ul. Tverskaya-Yamskaya 1/3; tel. (095) 200-03-53; e-mail presscenter@economy.gov.ru; internet www.economy.gov.ru.

Ministry of Education: 113833 Moscow, ul. Lyusinovskaya 51; tel. (095) 237-61-55; fax (095) 237-83-81; e-mail mail@ministry.ru; internet www.ed.gov.ru.

Ministry of Energy: 103074 Moscow, Kitaigorodskii proyezd 7/191; tel. (095) 220-51-33; fax (095) 220-56-56; e-mail abs@cdu.oilnet.ru; internet www.mte.gov.ru.

Ministry of Finance: 103097 Moscow, ul. Ilinka 9; tel. (095) 298-91-01; fax (095) 925-08-89; internet www.minfin.ru.

Ministry of Foreign Affairs: 119200 Moscow, Smolenskaya–Sennaya pl. 32/34; tel. (095) 244-16-06; fax (095) 230-21-30; e-mail ministry@mid.ru; internet www.mid.ru.

Ministry of Health: 101431 Moscow, ul. Neglinnaya 25; tel. (095) 927-28-48; fax (095) 928-58-15; e-mail press-center@minzdrav-rf.ru; internet www.minzdrav-rf.ru.

Ministry of Industry, Science and Technology: 125889 Moscow, pl. Miusskaya 3; tel. (095) 972-70-51; fax (095) 229-55-49; e-mail info@mpnt.gov.ru; internet www.mptn.gov.ru.

Ministry of Internal Affairs: 117049 Moscow, ul. Zhitnaya 16; tel. (095) 237-75-85; fax (095) 293-59-98; e-mail uimvd@mvdinform.ru; internet www.mvdinform.ru.

Ministry of Justice: 109830 Moscow, ul. Vorontsovo Pole 4A; tel. (095) 206-05-54; fax (095) 916-29-03; internet www.minjust.ru.

Ministry of Labour and Social Development: 101999 Moscow, Birzhevaya pl. 1; tel. (095) 298-88-88; fax (095) 230-24-07; e-mail press_mt@zanas.ru; internet www.mintrud.ru.

Ministry of Natural Resources: 123812 Moscow, ul. B. Gruzinskaya 4/6; tel. (095) 254-48-00; fax (095) 254-43-10; e-mail admin@mnr.gov.ru; internet www.mnr.gov.ru.

Ministry of the Press, Broadcasting and Mass Media: 127994 Moscow, Strastnoi bulv. 5; tel. (095) 229-66-93; fax (095) 200-22-81; internet www.mptr.ru.

Ministry of Railways: 107174 Moscow, ul. Novobasmannaya 2; tel. (095) 262-10-02; e-mail info@mps.ru; internet www.mps.ru.

Ministry of State Property: 103685 Moscow, Nikolskii per. 9; tel. (095) 298-75-62; fax (095) 206-11-19; e-mail mgi1@ftcenter.ru; internet www.mgi.ru.

Ministry of Taxes and Levies: 103381 Moscow, ul. Neglinnaya 23; tel. (095) 200-38-48; fax (095) 200-11-78; e-mail mns@nalog.ru; internet www.nalog.ru.

Ministry of Transport: 109012 Moscow, ul. Rozhdestvenka 1/1; tel. (095) 926-10-00; fax (095) 200-33-56; e-mail mcc@morflot.ru; internet www.mintrans.ru.

FEDERAL ASSEMBLY

The Federal Assembly of the Russian Federation is the bicameral national parliament. Its upper chamber, the Federation Council, comprises 178 deputies, two appointed from each of the federal units, representing the executive and legislative branches of power in each territory. The lower chamber is the State Duma, with 450 deputies elected for a four-year term (the last general election was held on 7 December 2003).

Chairman of the Federation Council: SERGEI M. MIRONOV, 103426 Moscow, ul. B. Dmitrovka 26; tel. (095) 203-90-74; fax (095) 203-46-17; e-mail post_sf@gov.ru; internet www.council.gov.ru.

Chairman of the State Duma: BORIS V. GRYZLOV, 103265 Moscow, Okhotnyi ryad 1; tel. (095) 292-83-10; fax (095) 292-94-64; e-mail www@duma.ru; internet www.duma.ru.

THE STATE COUNCIL

The State Council is a consultative body, established in September 2000, and intended to improve co-ordination between federal and regional government, and to strengthen federal control in the regions. The membership of the Council comprises the leaders of the 89 federal subjects and the President of the Russian Federation, who chairs the Council. The President appoints a presidium, comprising seven-members of the Council, who serve for a period of six months.

PART TWO
Territorial Surveys

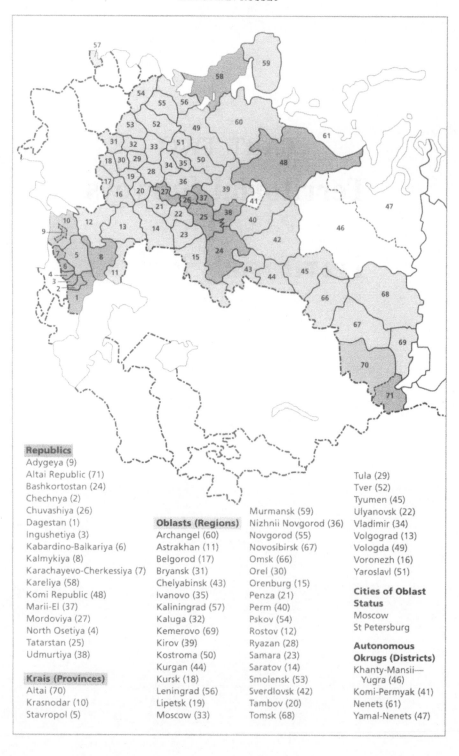

Republics

Adygeya (9)
Altai Republic (71)
Bashkortostan (24)
Chechnya (2)
Chuvashiya (26)
Dagestan (1)
Ingushetiya (3)
Kabardino-Balkariya (6)
Kalmykiya (8)
Karachayevo-Cherkessiya (7)
Kareliya (58)
Komi Republic (48)
Marii-El (37)
Mordoviya (27)
North Osetiya (4)
Tatarstan (25)
Udmurtiya (38)

Krais (Provinces)

Altai (70)
Krasnodar (10)
Stavropol (5)

Oblasts (Regions)

Archangel (60)
Astrakhan (11)
Belgorod (17)
Bryansk (31)
Chelyabinsk (43)
Ivanovo (35)
Kaliningrad (57)
Kaluga (32)
Kemerovo (69)
Kirov (39)
Kostroma (50)
Kurgan (44)
Kursk (18)
Leningrad (56)
Lipetsk (19)
Moscow (33)

Murmansk (59)
Nizhnii Novgorod (36)
Novgorod (55)
Novosibirsk (67)
Omsk (66)
Orel (30)
Orenburg (15)
Penza (21)
Perm (40)
Pskov (54)
Rostov (12)
Ryazan (28)
Samara (23)
Saratov (14)
Smolensk (53)
Sverdlovsk (42)
Tambov (20)
Tomsk (68)

Tula (29)
Tver (52)
Tyumen (45)
Ulyanovsk (22)
Vladimir (34)
Volgograd (13)
Vologda (49)
Voronezh (16)
Yaroslavl (51)

Cities of Oblast Status

Moscow
St Petersburg

Autonomous Okrugs (Districts)

Khanty-Mansii—
   Yugra (46)
Komi-Permyak (41)
Nenets (61)
Yamal-Nenets (47)

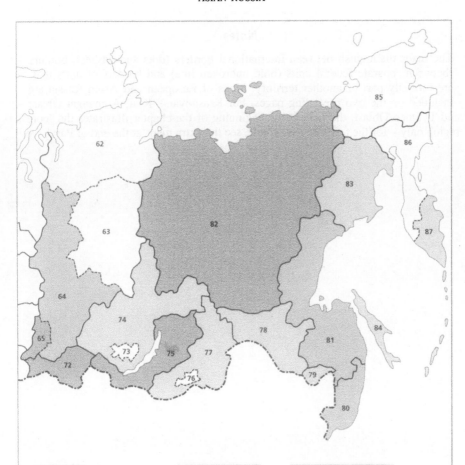

Republics
Buryatiya (75)
Khakasiya (65)
Tyva (72)
Republic of Sakha (82)
(Yakutiya)

Krais (Provinces)
Khabarovsk (81)
Krasnoyarsk (64)
Maritime (Primorskii) (80)

Oblasts (Regions)
Amur (78)
Chita (77)
Irkutsk (74)
Kamchatka (87)
Magadan (83)
Sakhalin (84)

Autonomous Oblast
Jewish Autonomous Oblast (79)

**Autonomous
Okrugs (Districts)**
Aga-Buryat (76)
Chukot (85)
Evenk (63)
Koryak (86)
Taimyr (Dolgan-Nenets) (62)
Ust-Orda Buryat (73)

Notes

The maps distinguish between international borders (dots and dashes), borders between separate federal units (bold unbroken line) and borders of units that are formally part of another territory. Maps of European and Asian Russia are included on the two preceding pages. For Krasnoyarsk Krai, Archangel Oblast and Tyumen Oblast, the map at the beginning of the chapter illustrates the 'core' region only—for the territory as a whole, see the extra maps at the end of Part Two.

CENTRAL FEDERAL OKRUG

Belgorod Oblast

Belgorod Oblast is situated in the south-west of the Central Russian Highlands. It forms part of the Central Federal Okrug and the Central Chernozem Economic Area. The Oblast lies on the international border with Ukraine, with the Oblasts of Kursk to the north and Voronezh to the east. Its main rivers are the Severnii Donets, the Vorskla and the Oskol. The territory occupies 27,100 sq km (10,460 sq miles) and measures around 260 km (160 miles) from west to east. It is divided into 21 administrative districts and 10 cities. According to the preliminary results of the census of 9–16 October 2002, Belgorod Oblast had a total population of 1,512,400, giving a population density of 55.8 per sq km. Some 65.2% of the population inhabited urban areas at that time. According to the 1989 census, 92.9% of the Oblast's inhabitants were ethnic Russians. The Oblast's administrative centre is at Belgorod, which had 337,600 inhabitants in October 2002, according to provisional census results. A further major city is Staryi Oskol (216,000).

History

Belgorod was established as a bishopric during the early days of Orthodox Christianity. The region was part of Lithuania until 1503, when it was annexed by the Muscovite state. The new city of Belgorod was founded in 1593 and a local regiment was based there for much of the tsarist period. On 12 July 1943, at Prokhorovka, north-east of the city of Belgorod, the Red Army defeated the Germans in the largest single tank battle in history (some 1,200 tanks are supposed to have taken part), the most vital action in the wider, so-called Kursk offensive. Belgorod Oblast was formally established on 6 January 1954.

In late 1993 President Boris Yeltsin dismissed the region's Governor and arranged for elections to a new Regional Duma to be held in 1994. The communists enjoyed a majority in this body, too, and there was constant conflict with the administration, the head of which, however, also enjoyed popular support. For this reason, the Oblast was one of only 12 areas in the Federation to be permitted gubernatorial elections in December 1995. The incumbent, Yevgenii Savchenko, was duly elected. Savchenko was re-elected in May 1999, with the leader of the Liberal Democratic Party of Russia, Vladimir Zhirinovskii, coming third in the poll, as part of his unsuccessful campaign to become a regional governor. Savchenko was elected to a further term of office, as an independent candidate, on 25 May 2003, receiving 61.2% of the votes cast in a poll contested by three candidates.

Economy

In 2000 Belgorod Oblast's gross regional product amounted to 44,346m. roubles, or 29,574 roubles per head. The main industrial centres in the territory are situated at Belgorod, Shebekino and Alekseyevka. At the end of 2001 there were 694 km of railway lines and 6,471 km of paved roads on the Oblast's territory.

Belgorod Oblast's principal crops are grain, sugar beet, sunflower seeds and essential-oil plants. Horticulture, animal husbandry and bee-keeping are also important. In 2001 24.3% of the region's working population were engaged in the agricultural sector, which generated a total of 19,936m. roubles, with crop sales accounting for 50.2% of total production and animal husbandry for 49.8%. The Oblast has substantial reserves of bauxite, iron ore and apatites. Its main industries are ore-mining (iron ores), the production of electricity, mechanical engineering, metal-working, chemicals, the manufacture of building materials and food-processing. Industry employed 21.5% of the work-force in 2001, and total industrial production was worth 50,941m. roubles.

The economically active population in Belgorod Oblast numbered 738,000 in 2001, when 6.5% of the region's labour force were unemployed. In mid-2002 the average monthly salary was 4,599.6 roubles. There was a budgetary deficit of 327m. roubles in 2001. In that year export trade totalled US $719.3m., while import trade amounted to $789.2m. In 2001 a treaty was signed between the Russian and Ukrainian authorities, initially on an experimental basis, which provided for a simplification of the customs and border formalities for residents of the Oblasts of Belgorod (in Russia) and Kharkhiv (Kharkov—in Ukraine), with a view to facilitating increased cross-border trade. This measure was widely regarded as a success, and by early 2003 annual trade between the two regions was estimated at $800m. Foreign investment in the Oblast totalled $40.0m. in 2001, compared with $156.1m. in 1998. At the end of 2001 there were 4,589 small businesses in the Oblast.

Directory

Head of the Regional Administration (Governor): YEVGENII S. SAVCHENKO; 308005 Belgorod, pl. Revolyutsii 4; tel. (0722) 22-42-47; fax (0722) 22-33-43; e-mail admin@regadm.bel.ru; internet beladm.bel.ru.

Chairman of the Regional Duma: ANATOLII YA. ZELIKOV; 308005 Belgorod, pl. Revolyutsii 4; tel. (0722) 32-24-37; fax (0722) 27-65-88; e-mail duma@bel.ru; internet duma.bel.ru.

Chief Representative of Belgorod Oblast in the Russian Federation: ALEKSANDR G. MATSEPURO; 113052 Moscow, Zagorodnoye shosse 5/21; tel. (095) 952-02-03; fax (095) 952-28-36; e-mail moscow@ bel.ru.

Head of Belgorod City Administration: VASILII N. POTRYASAYEV; 308800 Belgorod, ul. Lenina 38; tel. (0722) 27-72-06.

Bryansk Oblast

Bryansk Oblast is situated in the central part of the Central Russian Highlands and is in the Central Federal Okrug and the Central Economic Area. It has international borders to the west (Belarus) and south (Ukraine), and domestic borders with Kursk and Orel Oblasts to the east, Kaluga to the north-east and Smolensk to the north-west. Bryansk's main river is the Desna, a tributary of the Dnepr (Dnieper), and just under one-third of its area is forested. The Oblast occupies 34,900 sq km (13,480 sq miles) of territory and measures 245 km (152 miles) from south to north and 270 km from west to east. It is divided into 27 administrative districts and 16 cities. According to the preliminary results of the census of 9–16 October 2002, the region had a total population of 1,378,900, giving a population density of 39.5 per sq km. Some 68.4% of the population inhabited urban areas. Bryansk, with a population of 431,600, according to provisional census results, is the Oblast's administrative centre.

History

The ancient Russian city of Bryansk (first mentioned in 1146) was part of the independent principality of Novgorod-Serversk until 1356. It was an early Orthodox Christian bishopric. The Muscovite state acquired the city from Lithuania in the 16th century. In the early 17th century the city figured in the insurrections associated with the pretenders to the tsarist throne known as the 'false Dmitriis'. Generally, it was a loyal garrison town. Bryansk Oblast was founded on 5 July 1944.

In the 1990s and early 2000s the region was considered part of the communist-dominated 'red belt'. Bryansk was one of eight federal territories permitted gubernatorial elections in December 1992. The incumbent, a supporter of the federal President, Boris Yeltsin, was defeated by the communist-backed candidate, Yurii Lodkin. After the constitutional crisis of September–October 1993 Lodkin was dismissed and the Soviet disbanded, and a Regional Duma formed. The Communist

Party of the Russian Federation (CPRF) secured about 35% of the votes cast in the region for the elections to the State Duma in December 1995. After a series of scandals involving successive, short-lived (and non-communist) governors, Lodkin returned to the post of governor, following elections in December 1996. Relations with the federal centre improved after the signature of a power-sharing agreement in July 1997, although the CPRF dominated the local elections held in the previous month and maintained its influence in the federal presidential election of March 2000. Lodkin was re-elected as Governor in December, although he obtained only 29% of the votes cast. In the early 2000s concerns were expressed regarding the regulation of the media by the oblast authorities; notably, in September 2003 the oblast electoral commission formally warned three newspapers that had violated recently introduced amendments to the federal electoral law on the coverage of election campaigns, representing the first application of the new legislation. In early October the federal Minister of the Press, Broadcasting and Mass Media, Mikhail Lesin, stated that actions such as those taken by the Bryansk electoral commission could have the effect of reducing informed political coverage in the press, and in late October the federal Constitutional Court ruled the legislation to be in breach of the Constitution.

Economy

Bryansk Oblast is one of the Russian Federation's major industrial regions. The territory's gross regional product was 26,154m. roubles in 2000, equivalent to 18,213 roubles per head. Its main industrial centres are at Bryansk and Klintsy. At the end of 2001 there were 1,009 km of railway track on its territory, and 6,318 km of paved roads.

The Oblast's agriculture, which employed 17.9% of its work-force in 2001, consists mainly of grain, sugar beet and potato production, and animal husbandry. Around one-half of the territory's area is used for agricultural purposes. In 2001 total production in the sector was worth 11,310m. roubles, of which crop sales contributed 49.3% and animal husbandry 50.7%. The Oblast's main industries are mechanical engineering, food-processing, electrical energy, the manufacture of building ma-terials and timber-working. Industry employed 21.1% of the work-force in 2001 and generated 18,660m. roubles.

In 2001 the economically active population of Bryansk Oblast numbered 653,000, and some 10.0% of the region's labour force were unemployed. In mid-2002 the average monthly wage was 2,641.7 roubles. There was a regional government budgetary surplus of 133m. roubles in 2001. In that year international trade comprised US $116.9m. of exports and $181.9m. of imports. Foreign investment amounted to $9.1m. At 31 December 2001 there were 3,195 small businesses registered in the region.

Directory

Head of the Regional Administration (Governor): Yurii Ye. Lodkin; 241002 Bryansk, pr. Lenina 33; tel. (0832) 46-26-11; fax (0832) 41-38-95; e-mail press@admin.debryansk.ru; internet www.bryanskobl.ru.

Chairman of the Regional Duma: Stepan N. Ponasov; 241000 Bryansk, pl. K. Marksa 2; tel. (0832) 43-36-91; fax (0832) 74-31-95.

Chief Representative of Bryansk Oblast in the Russian Federation: Nikolai I. Moskin; 103025 Moscow, ul. Novyi Arbat 19; tel. and fax (095) 203-50-52.

Head of Bryansk City Administration (Mayor): Valerii Polyakov; 241002 Bryansk, pr. Lenina 35; tel. (0832) 74-30-13; fax (0832) 74-47-30; e-mail postmaster@comimm.bryansk.su.

Ivanovo Oblast

Ivanovo Oblast is situated in the central part of the Eastern European Plain. It forms part of the Central Federal Okrug and the Central Economic Area. It is surrounded by the Oblasts of Kostroma (to the north), Nizhnii Novgorod (east), Vladimir (south) and Yaroslavl (north-west). Its main river is the Volga and one-half of its territory is forested. The Oblast covers a total area of 21,800 sq km (9,230 sq miles), and includes 21 administrative districts and 17 cities. According to the preliminary results of the census of 9–16 October 2002, the Oblast's population numbered 1,148,900, giving a population density of 52.7 per sq km. Some 82.7% of the population inhabited urban areas. The Oblast's administrative centre, Ivanovo, had a population of 432,200 at that time, according to provisional census results.

History

A village of Ivanovo was first mentioned in 1561. From the 18th century it became famous for its textiles trade. Palekh, in the east, was an important centre for the painting of icons. The city of Ivanovo was founded in 1871 and was known as Ivanovo-Voznesensk until 1932. It was an important centre of anti-government activity during the strikes of 1883 and 1885 and in the 1905 Revolution. Ivanovo Oblast was founded on 20 July 1918.

In the post-Soviet era the region displayed support for political diversity. Although the Communist Party of the Russian Federation (CPRF) and Vladimir Zhirinovskii's nationalist Liberal Democratic Party of Russia both performed well in elections in 1994–95, moderates were successful in the gubernatorial and regional legislative elections held in 1996, and in the elections to the State Duma in 1999. However, in the gubernatorial elections held in two rounds in December 2000, the CPRF candidate, Vladimir Tikhonov, defeated the regional premier, Vladimir Golovkov. Legislative elections took place in the same month.

Economy

In 2000 Ivanovo Oblast's gross regional product totalled 18,093m. roubles, equivalent to 14,885 roubles per head. The region's main industrial centres are at Ivanovo (a major producer of textiles), Kineshma, Shuya, Vichuga, Furmanov, Teikovo and Rodniki. There are well-developed rail, road and river transport networks in the region and the largest international airport in central Russia. At the end of 2001 there were 341 km (212 miles) of railways and 3,510 km of paved roads on the Oblast's territory.

Ivanovo Oblast was the historic centre of Russia's cotton-milling industry and was known as the 'Russian Manchester' at the beginning of the 20th century. Flax production was still an important agricultural activity in the region in the 2000s, as were grain and vegetable production and animal husbandry. However, agriculture employed just 10.7% of the work-force in 2001, and total agricultural production in that year amounted to a value of 4,910m. roubles, 43.7% of which was represented by crop production and 56.3% by animal husbandry. The region's main industries are light manufacturing (especially textiles), electrical energy, mechanical engineering and metal-working, food-processing and handicrafts (especially lacquerware). Some 33.6% of the working population were engaged in the sector, which generated 18,727m. roubles in 2001.

The territory's economically active population amounted to 588,000 in 2001, when just 5.6% of the labour force were unemployed, compared with 18.6% in 1998. The average wage was 2,631.5 roubles per month in mid-2002. In 2001 the budget recorded a surplus of 28m. roubles. External trade was relatively low in that year, amounting to a value of US $73.6m. in exports and $180.5m. in imports. Foreign investment amounted to just $368,000 in 2001, and in 2000 there were only nine enterprises with foreign capital in the Oblast, fewer than in any other region of the Central Federal Okrug. At 31 December 2001 there were 5,165 small businesses registered in the region.

Directory

Head of the Regional Administration (Governor): VLADIMIR I. TIKHONOV; 153000 Ivanovo, ul. Baturina 5; tel. (0932) 41-77-05; fax (0932) 41-92-31; e-mail 001@ adminet.ivanovo.ru; internet ivadm.ivanovo.ru.

Chairman of the Legislative Assembly: VLADIMIR S. GRISHIN; 153461 Ivanovo, ul. Pushkina 9; tel. and fax (0932) 41-60-68; e-mail zsio@gov.ivanovo.ru.

Representation of Ivanovo Oblast in the Russian Federation: 127025 Moscow, ul. Novyi Arbat 16/1714; tel. (095) 203-41-34; fax (095) 203-93-45.

Head of Ivanovo City Administration: ALEKSANDR V. GROSHEV; 153001 Ivanovo, pl. Revolyutsii 6; tel. (0932) 32-70-20; fax (0932) 41-25-12; e-mail info@goradm .ivanovo.ru; internet ivgoradm.ivanovo.ru.

Kaluga Oblast

Kaluga Oblast is situated in the central part of the Eastern European Plain, its administrative centre, Kaluga, being 188 km (177 miles) south-west of Moscow. It forms part of the Central Federal Okrug and the Central Economic Area. Tula and Orel Oblasts lie to the south-east, Bryansk Oblast to the south-west, Moscow Oblast to the north-east and Smolensk Oblast to the north-west. Kaluga's main river is the Oka and some two-fifths of its territory is forested. It occupies 29,900 sq km (11,540 sq miles) and is divided into 24 administrative districts and 19 cities. According to the preliminary results of the census of 9–16 October 2002, the Oblast's population totalled 1,040,900, giving a population density, therefore, of 34.8 per sq km. Some 74.9% of the population inhabited urban areas. The administrative centre is at Kaluga, a river-port on the Oka river, which had a population of 335,100, according to provisional census results. Other major cities in the Oblast include Obninsk (105,800), the site of the world's first nuclear power station.

History

The city of Kaluga, first mentioned in the letters of a Lithuanian prince, Olgerd, in 1371, was founded as a Muscovite outpost. The region was the scene of an army mutiny in 1905 and was seized by Bolshevik troops at the end of 1917. Kaluga Oblast was founded on 5 July 1944.

Communist-affiliated managers of industrial and agricultural bodies dominated the new representative body, the Legislative Assembly, elected in March 1994. The Communist Party of the Russian Federation (CPRF) won over one-quarter of the region's votes in the 1995 elections to the State Duma. However, in elections to the Legislative Assembly in 1996 the CPRF failed to win any seats. Valerii Sudarenkov, the Governor from 1996, had previously been the Deputy Prime Minister of the Uzbek Soviet Socialist Republic (Uzbekistan). Sudarenkov did not stand for re-election in November 2000; his former deputy, Anatolii Artamonov, was elected to succeed him, with 56.7% of the votes cast.

Economy

In 2000 gross regional product in Kaluga Oblast totalled 26,107m. roubles, equivalent to 24,257 roubles per head. Apart from Kaluga, the region's main industrial centres are at Lyudinovo, Kirov, Maloyaroslavets and Sukhinichi. At the end of 2001 there were 872 km of railway track in the Oblast, and 5,028 km of paved roads.

Certain areas of the Oblast contain fertile black earth (*chernozem*). Agriculture employed 11.8% of the work-force in 2001, comprising mainly animal husbandry and vegetable production. Agricultural output amounted to a value of 7,644m. roubles, of which 49.2% was generated by crop sales and 50.8% by animal husbandry. The Oblast's main industries are mechanical engineering, food-processing, timber and timber-processing, and wood-working. The industrial sector employed 26.1% of the working population in 2001 and generated 29,955m. roubles.

The territory's economically active population totalled 550,000 in 2001, when 6.0% of the labour force were unemployed. The average monthly wage in Kaluga Oblast was 3,503.4 roubles in mid-2002. In 2001 there was a budgetary deficit of 43m. roubles. In that year export trade amounted to a value of US $69.2m.; imports amounted to $135.8m. Total foreign investment amounted to $103.0m. in 2001. At the end of that year there were 5,866 small businesses registered in the region.

Directory

Head of the Regional Administration (Governor): ANATOLII D. ARTAMONOV; 248661 Kaluga, pl. Staryi Torg 2; tel. (0842) 56-23-57; fax (0842) 53-13-09; e-mail postmaster@admobl.kaluga.su; internet www.admobl.kaluga.ru.

Chairman of the Legislative Assembly: VALERII I. KRESTYANINOV; 248600 Kaluga, pl. Staryi Torg 2; tel. (0842) 57-45-00; fax (0842) 59-15-63.

Chief Representative of Kaluga Oblast in the Russian Federation: VLADIMIR V. POTEMKIN; 121002 Moscow, per. Glazovskii 8; tel. (095) 203-17-12; fax (095) 229-98-05; e-mail kaluga@orc.ru.

Head of Kaluga City Administration: VALERII V. IVANOV; 248600 Kaluga, ul. Lenina 93; tel. (0842) 56-26-46; fax (0842) 24-41-78; e-mail uprava@kaluga.ru; internet users.kaluga.ru/uprava.

Kostroma Oblast

Kostroma Oblast is situated in the central part of the Eastern European Plain. It forms part of the Central Federal Okrug and the Central Economic Area. It is bordered by Vologda Oblast to the north, Kirov Oblast to the east, Nizhnii Novgorod and Ivanovo Oblasts to the south and Yaroslavl Oblast to the west. Its main rivers are the Volga, the Kostroma, the Unzha, the Vokhma and the Vetluga. It has two major lakes—the Galichskoye and the Chukhlomskoye. The total area of Kostroma Oblast is 60,100 sq km (23,200 sq miles), almost three-quarters of which is forested. It is divided into 24 administrative districts and 12 cities. According to the preliminary results of the census of 9–16 October 2002, the region had a total population of 737,500, giving a population density of 12.3 per sq km. Some 67.4% of the population inhabited urban areas. The Oblast's administrative centre is at Kostroma, a river-port situated on both banks of the Volga (a popular tourist resort of the 'Golden Ring'), which had 279,400 inhabitants, according to provisional census results.

History

The city of Kostroma was founded in the 12th century and became the base of the Gudunov family, as well as, later, an important centre for the Romanovs. The city became an industrial centre from the mid-18th century. Kostroma Oblast was formed on 13 August 1944. The region remained loyal to the communist nomenklatura in the 1990s—its oblast Soviet supported the federal parliament in its 1993 defiance of the Russian President, Boris Yeltsin, and was replaced by a new representative body, the Duma, in 1994. The Communist Party of the Russian Federation (CPRF) was the predominant party in this body, and the CPRF candidate, Viktor Shershunov, was elected as Governor in December 1996 (although Yeltsin had been the Oblast's preferred candidate in the presidential election held earlier that year). Shershunov was re-elected to serve a further term of office in December 2000.

Economy

In 2000 gross regional product in Kostroma Oblast amounted to 18,174m. roubles, or 23,204 roubles per head. The Oblast's main industrial centres are at Kostroma, Sharya, Nerekhta, Galich, Bui, Manturovo and Krasnoye-on-Volga (Krasnoye-na-Volge). The region has major road and rail networks—at the end of 2001 there were 640 km (398 miles) of railways in use on its territory and 5,549 km of paved roads. There were 985 km of navigable waterways in 1998.

Agriculture in Kostroma Oblast, which employed 9.6% of the work-force in 2001, consists mainly of production of grain, flax (the region is one of Russia's major producers of linen) and vegetables, and animal husbandry. Total agricultural output in 2001 was worth 6,999m. roubles, of which 50.5% was generated by crop sales and 49.5% by animal husbandry. Adverse weather conditions in mid-2003 caused severe disruption to the regional harvest. The region has an energy surplus, exporting some four-fifths of electrical energy produced. Electricity generation comprised 32.0% of total industrial production in Kostroma Oblast in 2001. The other main industries in the region are light manufacturing, wood-working, mechanical engineering, food- and timber-processing and handicrafts (especially jewellery). The territory is also an important military centre, with numerous rocket silos, of which 23 had been converted to agricultural use by early 1996, with plans to recultivate a further 20. Some 25.5% of the Oblast's working population was engaged in industry in 2001, when industrial production amounted to a value of 16,618m. roubles.

The economically active population numbered 380,000 in 2001, when 6.0% of the labour force of the region were unemployed. The average wage in the Oblast was 3,164.1 roubles per month in mid-2002. There was a budgetary deficit of some 78m. roubles in 2001. In that year external trade comprised US $91.6m. of exports and $14.1m. of imports, one of the lowest levels in the Central Federal Okrug. Foreign investment totalled $927,000. At 31 December 2001 there were 3,247 small businesses registered in the Oblast.

Directory

Head of the Regional Administration (Governor): VIKTOR A. SHERSHUNOV; 156001 Kostroma, ul. Dzerzhinskogo 15; tel. (0942) 31-34-72; fax (0942) 31-33-95; e-mail shershunov@kos-obl.kmtn.ru; internet www.region.kostroma.net.

Chairman of the Regional Duma: VALERII P. IZHITSKII; 156000 Kostroma, Sovet-skaya pl. 2; tel. (0942) 31-62-52; fax (0942) 31-21-73; e-mail info@kosoblduma.ru; internet www.kosoblduma.ru.

Chief Representative of Kostroma Oblast in the Russian Federation: GALINA M. PSHENITSYNA; 127025 Moscow, ul. Novyi Arbat 19/1811; tel. (095) 203-42-44; fax (095) 203-41-69.

Head of Kostroma City Administration: IRINA PEREVERZEVA; 156000 Kostroma, pl. Sovetskaya 1; tel. (0942) 31-44-40; fax (0942) 31-39-32.

Kursk Oblast

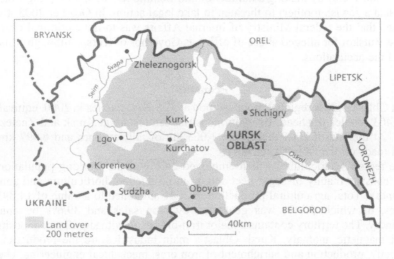

Kursk Oblast is situated within the Central Russian Highlands. It forms part of the Central Federal Okrug and the Central Chernozem Economic Area. An international boundary with Ukraine lies to the south-west, with neighbouring Russian federal territories consisting of Bryansk in the north-west, Orel and Lipetsk in the north, Voronezh in the east and Belgorod in the south. Its main river is the Seim. The Oblast measures 171 km (106 miles) from south to north and 305 km from west to east. It occupies 29,800 sq km (11,500 sq miles) and is divided into 28 administrative districts and 10 cities. According to the preliminary results of the census of 9–16 October 2002, the Oblast had a total population of 1,235,600, giving a population density of 41.5 per sq km. Some 61.2% of the population inhabited urban areas. The Oblast's administrative centre is at Kursk, with 412,600 inhabitants, according to provisional census results.

History

The city of Kursk, one of the most ancient in Russia, was founded in 1032, destroyed by the Tatars in 1240 and fortified as a Muscovite outpost in the 16th century. The city became famous for its nightingales and Antonovka apples. The region was the scene of an army mutiny in 1905 and, in 1943, of a decisive battle against German forces during the Second World War. Kursk Oblast was formed on 13 July 1934, and was regarded as part of the communist-supporting 'red belt' in the 1990s and early 2000s.

The Communist Party of the Russian Federation (CPRF) dominated the regional assembly, a Duma, elected in 1994, and in its successors, elected in 1996 and 2001. The former federal Vice-President, Aleksandr Rutskoi, a noted opponent of liberal reforms, was elected regional Governor on 20 October 1996. However, one day before the election of 22 October 2000 he was prevented from standing as a candidate owing to a legal technicality. In a second round of voting on 5 November the CPRF candidate, Aleksandr Mikhailov, defeated the pro-Government, former Federal Security Service general, Viktor Surzhikov (who was elected Mayor of

Kursk city in September 2003). Immediately after being elected, Mikhailov provoked controversy by making a number of anti-Semitic remarks, prompting Rutskoi (who had a Jewish mother) to threaten to take legal action. In October 2003 it was reported that the federal Ministry of Internal Affairs was to issue criminal charges against Rutskoi for alleged abuse of office as Governor of Kursk, although Rutskoi denied the accusations.

Economy

Kursk Oblast's gross regional product stood at 31,949m. roubles in 2000, equivalent to 24,403 roubles per head. Its main industrial centres are at Kursk and Zheleznogorsk. At the end of 2001 there were 1,063 km of railway lines and 6,097 km of paved roads on the Oblast's territory.

The region's agriculture, which employed 24.8% of the working population in 2001, consists mainly of sugar beet and grain production, horticulture and animal husbandry. Total agricultural production in 2001 amounted to a value of 14,891m. roubles, of which 61.4% was generated by crop sales and 39.6% by animal husbandry. The territory contains a major iron-ore basin, with significant deposits of Kursk magnetic anomaly. Kursk Oblast's main industries are the production of electricity, production and enrichment of iron ores, mechanical engineering, chemicals and petrochemicals, ferrous metallurgy and food-processing. Some 20.6% of the work-force were engaged in industry in 2001, when the sector's output was worth 30,779m. roubles.

The economically active population in Kursk Oblast numbered 623,000 in 2001, when 10.4% of the labour force were unemployed. The average monthly wage in the region was 2,719.0 roubles in mid-2002. In 2001 there was a budgetary deficit of 1m. roubles. From the mid-1990s the Oblast's main foreign trading partners were Poland and the Czech Republic, although it also had economic links with other European countries, North America, India and Turkey, and was undertaking measures that would, it was hoped, facilitate greater cross-border trade with Ukraine. Its principal exports comprised iron ore and concentrate, automobiles and machinery. In 2001 the total value of external trade was US $246.9m., of which imports accounted for $150.8m. Following the success of a scheme to promote cross-border trade established by Belgorod Oblast with Kharkiv (Kharkov) Oblast in Ukraine, in November 2001 the Kursk Oblast authorities signed a trade agreement with the neighbouring Sumy Oblast, in Ukraine; by the following year it was reported that cross-border merchandise trade had increased by 500%. Foreign investment in 2001 amounted to $24.2m. At 31 December 2001 2,795 small businesses were registered in the Oblast.

Directory

Head of the Regional Administration (Governor): ALEKSANDR N. MIKHAILOV; 305002 Kursk, Krasnaya pl., Dom Sovetov; tel. (07122) 2-62-62; fax (0712) 56-65-73; e-mail intercom@region.kursk.ru; internet www.region.kursk.ru.

Chairman of the Regional Duma: ALEKSANDR N. ANPILOV; 305001 Kursk, ul. S. Perovskoi 24; tel. (0712) 56-09-91; fax (0712) 56-20-06; e-mail oblduma@kursknet .ru; internet oblduma.kursknet.ru.

Representation of Kursk Oblast in the Russian Federation: Moscow; tel. (095) 917-08-69.

Head of Kursk City Administration: VIKTOR SURZHIKOV; 305000 Kursk, ul. Lenina 1; tel. (07122) 2-63-63; fax (07122) 2-43-16; e-mail kursk@pub.sovest.ru; internet www.kurskadmin.ru.

Lipetsk Oblast

Lipetsk Oblast is situated within the Central Russian Highlands, some 508 km (315 m) south-east of Moscow. It forms part of the Central Federal Okrug and the Central Chernozem Economic Area. It is bordered by Voronezh and Kursk Oblasts to the south, Orel Oblast to the west, Tula Oblast to the north-west, Ryazan Oblast to the north and Tambov Oblast to the east. Its main rivers are the Don and the Voronezh. The Oblast occupies 24,100 sq km (9,300 sq miles) and is divided into 18 administrative districts and eight cities. According to the preliminary results of the census of 9–16 October 2002, Lipetsk Oblast had a total population of 1,213,400, and its population density was, therefore, 50.3 per sq km. Some 64.3% of the Oblast's population inhabited urban areas. Its administrative centre is at Lipetsk, with a population of 506,000, according to provisional census results. The Oblast's second largest city is Yelets (116,700), one of the oldest in Russia.

History

Lipetsk city was founded in the 13th century and was later famed for containing one of Russia's oldest mud-bath resorts and spas. In the late tsarist and Soviet periods the region became increasingly industrialized. Lipetsk Oblast was formed on 6 January 1954. By the 1990s it was considered part of the 'red belt' of support for the Communist Party of the Russian Federation (CPRF) across central Russia. Thus, in December 1992, when Lipetsk was one of eight territorial units permitted to hold gubernatorial elections (in an attempt to resolve the dispute between the head of the administration and the regional assembly), the incumbent, a supporter of the federal Government, was defeated by the CPRF candidate. In September 1993 both the Regional Soviet and the Governor, therefore, denounced the Russian President's dissolution of the federal parliament. Subsequently, the territory was obliged to comply with the directives of the federal Government.

Legislative elections were held in the region on 6 March 1994, but were invalidated, owing to a low level of attendance. Further elections were held later that year. Political apathy also contributed to a relatively low level of support for the CPRF, in comparison to other 'red belt' regions, in the election to the State Duma held in December 1995 (29%). However, in the elections to the federal presidency of March 2000, Lipetsk Oblast awarded the CPRF candidate, Gennadii Zyuganov, a higher proportion of the votes (47.4%) than did any other federal subject. On 12 April 1998 the Chairman of the Regional Council of Deputies (legislature), Oleg Korolev, won an overwhelming victory (some 79% of the votes cast) in the gubernatorial election. He was supported primarily by the CPRF, but also by the local branch of Yabloko and other political movements. Korolev, who was regarded as the candidate supported by the federal Government, was re-elected on 14 April 2002, with 73% of the votes cast, after his principal rival withdrew his candidacy.

Economy

In 2000 Lipetsk Oblast's gross regional product totalled 48,236m. roubles, or 38,980 roubles per head—the highest level in the Central Federal Okrug, after Moscow City. Its main industrial centres are at Lipetsk, Yelets, Dankov and Gryazi. At the end of 2001 there were 746 km (464 miles) of railway lines and 5,174 km of paved roads on the Oblast's territory. Yelets and Gryazi contain the region's major railway junctions.

The region's agriculture consists mainly of animal husbandry and the production of grain, sugar beet and sunflower seeds. Some 17.8% of the work-force was engaged in agriculture in 2001. Agricultural output in that year amounted to a value of 12,741m. roubles, of which crop sales accounted for 60.2% and animal husbandry 39.8%. The Oblast's main industries are ferrous metallurgy (which comprised 67% of the region's total industrial output in 2001), mechanical engineering, metal-working and food-processing. Novolipetsk MetKom (New Lipetsk Metallurgical Group), based in the region, is one of the country's major industrial companies. In 2001 the industrial sector employed 24.3% of the region's working population and industry generated 67,501m. roubles.

The economically active population totalled 600,000 in 2001, when 6.6% of the labour force were unemployed. Those in employment earned, on average, 3,475.2 roubles per month in mid-2002. In 2001 the regional budget recorded a deficit of 331m. roubles. In that year exports amounted to US $923.6m. and imports were worth $223.2m. Foreign investment amounted to $81.3m. in 2001. At 31 December 2001 there were 4,271 small businesses registered in the territory.

Directory

Head of the Regional Administration (Governor): OLEG P. KOROLEV; 398014 Lipetsk, Sobornaya pl. 1; tel. (0742) 77-65-96; fax (0742) 72-24-26; e-mail office@ admlr.lipetsk.ru; internet www.admlr.lipetsk.ru.

Chairman of the Regional Council of Deputies: ANATOLII I. SAVENKOV; 398014 Lipetsk, Sobornaya pl. 1; tel. (0742) 74-35-08; fax (0742) 72-24-15.

Representation of Lipetsk Oblast in the Russian Federation: Moscow.

Head of Lipetsk City Administration (Mayor): MIKHAIL GULEVSKII; 398600 Lipetsk, ul. Sovetskaya 22; tel. (0742) 77-66-17; fax (0742) 77-44-30.

Moscow City

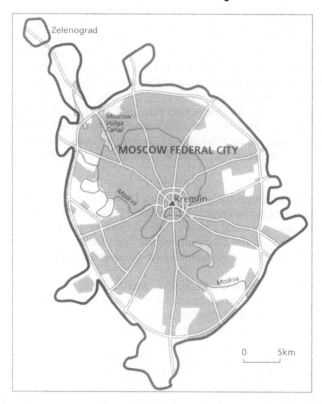

Moscow (Moskva) is located in the west of European Russia, on the River Moskva, which crosses the city from the north-west to the south-east. It is connected to the Volga river system by the Moscow–Volga Canal. Moscow is included in the Central Federal Okrug and the Central Economic Area. The city's total area is 994 sq km (384 sq miles). Moscow is the largest city in the Russian Federation and had a total population of 10.4m., according to the preliminary results of the census of 9–16 October 2002, and a population density, therefore, of 10,462.8 per sq km. In 1999 around 89.7% of the city's population were ethnic Russians, 2.9% were Ukrainians and 2.0% were Jews.

History
Moscow city was founded in about 1147. In 1325 it became the seat of the Eastern Orthodox Metropolitan of Rus (from 1589–1721 and after 1917 the Patriarch of Moscow and all Rus) and the steadily expanding Muscovite state became the foundation for the Russian Empire. The centre of tsarist government was moved to St Petersburg in 1712, but Moscow was restored as the Russian and Soviet capital in March 1918.

In the 1980s and 1990s reformists enjoyed considerable support in the city. On 12 June 1991 the democrat Gavriil Popov won the city's first mayoral elections.

However, Popov resigned in 1992, after the economic situation deteriorated to such an extent that food-rationing was introduced, and Yurii Luzhkov, head of the City Government, and also regarded as a reformist, was appointed by federal President Boris Yeltsin in his place. In October 1993 a presidential decree suspended the powers of the City Soviet; elections to a new 35-member Municipal Duma were held on 12 December. The Duma held its first session on 10 January 1994.

In a mayoral election held simultaneously with the federal presidential election on 16 June 1996 Luzhkov was re-elected with 89.7% of the votes cast. Thereafter, Luzhkov became an increasingly high-profile political figure nation-wide. In June 1998 he signed a power-sharing treaty with the federal authorities, following a protracted period of negotiation that resulted in the city receiving taxation and budget privileges. By late 1998 the Moscow City Government owned controlling stakes in a television station, a bank, and a range of other businesses; moreover, Luzhkov concluded a number of trade agreements with other regions, and in 1998 founded the nation-wide, centrist, generally anti-Government political movement, Fatherland. Meanwhile, in February the federal Constitutional Court had ruled Moscow City's strict controls over residence permits to be illegal, and the Supreme Court outlawed such permits (*propiski*, a legacy of the Soviet era) in July. However, Luzhkov opposed or ignored his critics, and even the ruling of the Constitutional Court. Indeed, following a number of bomb attacks in the city in late 1999, which killed over 200 people, and which were officially attributed to supporters of Chechen independence, the city's unconstitutional laws were implemented yet more firmly.

Although Luzhkov was re-elected as Mayor, with 69.9% of votes cast, on 19 December 1999, in the simultaneous nation-wide elections to the State Duma Fatherland—All Russia (FAR—as Fatherland had become, following its merger with the All Russia union of regional governors) came third, behind the Communist Party of the Russian Federation and the newly formed pro-Government bloc, Unity. Many of FAR's supporters in the regions backed the candidacy of Vladimir Putin in the presidential campaign and, after a period of neutrality (during which time Luzhkov was reportedly a candidate for the presidency), Luzhkov also announced his support for Putin. (Indeed, in 2001 FAR merged with Unity to form a new bloc, Unity and Fatherland-United Russia—UF-UR.) In elections to the Municipal Duma held in December 2001 Fatherland and Unity secured a total of 14 seats, followed by the pro-market Union of Rightist Forces with six seats, and the liberal Yabloko with four.

In the early 2000s Luzhkov remained a prominent advocate of more widespread use of identity checking, and of permit-based systems as a means of combating illicit activity, in particular as bombings and other attacks attributed to Chechen militants, notably an armed siege in a Moscow theatre in October 2002, as a result of which 129 hostages died, continued. In January 2003 the city court ruled that a provision of the city council permitting the direct election of the vice-mayor concurrently with that of the mayor (as had occured in 1999) contradicted federal law; at the end of March this ruling was upheld by the Supreme Court. In advance of mayoral elections, scheduled to be held on 7 December 2003, Luzhkov, who had become increasingly critical of the federal Government's policies (particularly with regard to a perceived recentralization of various social and economic powers), confirmed that he would seek a further term; it was also announced that Luzhkov had been appointed to the third position on the UF-UR federal list in the concurrent elections to the State Duma (in which UF-UR secured the majority of the votes cast). In the mayoral election, which took place as scheduled, Luzhkov was re-elected, with some 75.5% of the votes cast. The rate of participation by the electorate was some 56.7%.

Economy

In 2000 the city of Moscow's gross regional product amounted to 1,342,997m. roubles, equivalent to 155,543 roubles per head—by far the highest level in the Central Federal Okrug. There are nine railway termini in the city and 11 electrified radial lines. The metro system includes 11 lines and 164 stations and extends for 266 km (165 miles); a suburban light railway extension was scheduled to open in late 2003. The city's trolleybus and tram routes are 1,700 km long, its bus routes 5,700 km. The public-transport system carries around 6.5m. passengers per day. Moscow's waterways connect with the Baltic, White, Caspian and Black Seas and the Sea of Azov. There are also four airports on the city's territory.

Moscow's industry consists primarily of mechanical engineering, metal-working, electricity production, production of chemicals and petrochemicals, petroleum-refining and food-processing. Industry employed around 13.2% of the city's working population in 2001 (in contrast to the 0.2% engaged in agriculture) and generated 330,306m. roubles, a figure surpassed in the Russian Federation only by Tyumen Oblast, which has the majority of gas and petroleum deposits in the Federation. The Moskvich Inc. Automobile Plant, in which the City Government held a controlling stake from 1998, is one of Moscow's principal companies. There are also significant defence-sector industries in the city. In 2001 some 15.2% of the working population of Moscow City were engaged in the construction sector. The services sector is also significant in the city economy, with the city authorities having successfully consolidated its leading position within Russia during the 1990s: in 2000 some 18.9% of the working population of the city were employed in the services sector. (Although the financial crisis of August 1998 led to a restructuring of the banking and financial sector, the city had sufficient resources to recover.) As the Russian capital, the city is the site of a large number of government offices, as well as the centre for major business and financial companies. Tourism is another important service industry.

In 2001 the economically active population of the city stood at 4.38m., and the proportion of the labour force that was unemployed, at 2.1%, was the lowest in the Russian Federation. In mid-2002 those in employment earned, on average, 6,845.2 roubles per month, one of the highest rates in the Federation. The 2001 budget showed a surplus, of 4,652m. roubles, but the city finances are notoriously lacking in transparency. In 2001 international trade amounted to a value of US $24,417.7m. in exports and $14,480.6m. in imports, by far the highest level of any federal subject. Capital investment in the city represents around one-10th of that in Russia as a whole. In 2000 some 47% of Russian enterprises and organizations involving foreign capital were situated in Moscow City and the surrounding Moscow Oblast; in 2000 there were some 5,849 such enterprises and organizations in the region, of which 632 were joint ventures with partners from the USA, 587 had Cypriot partners, 535 Chinese and 512 German. Total foreign investment in the city amounted to $5,654m. in 2001. In September 1997 Moscow became the first city in Russia to enter the international capital market and place a Eurobonds issue. Local companies also flourished, in one of the few regions of Russia that could claim significant economic growth during the 1990s. At the end of 2001 there were 182,218 small companies registered in the city.

Directory

Mayor and Prime Minister of the Government of Moscow City: YURII M. LUZHKOV; 103032 Moscow, ul. Tverskaya 13; tel. (095) 229-58-03; fax (095) 232-18-74; internet www.mos.ru.

Chairman of the Municipal Duma: VLADIMIR M. PLATONOV; 103051 Moscow, ul. Petrovka 22; tel. (095) 923-50-80; fax (095) 921-92-02; e-mail d29@mcd.mos.ru; internet duma.mos.ru.

Representation of Moscow City in the Russian Federation: Moscow.

Moscow Oblast

Moscow Oblast is situated in the central part of the Eastern European Plain, at the Volga-Oka confluence. It forms part of the Central Federal Okrug and the Central Economic Area. Moscow is surrounded by seven other oblasts: Tver and Yaroslavl to the north, Vladimir and Ryazan to the east, Tula and Kaluga to the south-west and Smolensk to the west. Most of the region is forested and its main rivers are the Moskva and the Oka. The territory of the Oblast (including Moscow City) covers an area of 47,000 sq km (18,147 sq miles) and has 39 administrative districts and 75 cities. According to the preliminary results of the census of 9–16 October 2002, the Oblast's total population, excluding Moscow City, was 6,627,000. Inhabitants of urban areas comprised some 79.3% of the region's total population. The Oblast's administrative centre is in Moscow City. Within the Oblast proper, there are several cities with a population of over 100,000, including (in order of size) Podolsk (181,500), Mytishchi (159,200), Lyubertsy (156,900), Kolomna (150,100), Bala-shikha (148,200), Elektrostal (146,100), Korolev (143,100), Khimki (141,300), Odintsovo (134,700), Serpukhov (131,200), Orekhovo-Zuyevo (122,300), Noginsk (118,000), Sergiyev-Posad (formerly Zagorsk—113,800) and Shchelkovo (113,700). Sergiyev-Posad is an important centre of Russian Orthodoxy, containing Russia's foremost monastery and two medieval cathedrals.

History

The city of Moscow was established in the mid-12th century and became the centre of a burgeoning Muscovite state. The region soon became an important trade route between the Baltic Sea in the north and the Black and Caspian Seas in the south. It first became industrialized in the early 18th century, with the development of the textiles industry, in particular the production of wool and cotton. The region and the city of Moscow were captured by the troops of Emperor Napoleon I of France in

68

1812, but the invaders were forced to retreat later that year. German invaders reached the Moscow region (which had been formed as Moscow Oblast on 14 January 1929) in 1941, and the Soviet Government was removed from the city until 1943. Between late 1941 and early 1942 the German forces were driven from the Oblast's territory. Otherwise, the region and the city have benefited from Moscow being the Soviet, and the Russian, capital.

As the seat of government, in the 1990s the federal executive could rely on a reasonable level of support in the Moscow region. The gubernatorial elections of December 1999–January 2000 were closely fought, with Col-Gen. Boris Gromov, an ally of Moscow City Mayor Yurii Luzhkov, and a former member of the State Duma and Deputy Minister of Defence, emerging the victor. Relative prosperity kept discontent to a minimum and the region did not experience the problems of wage arrears to the same extent as elsewhere in the Federation. In the gubernatorial election held on 7 December, concurrently with elections to the federal State Duma, Gromov was re-elected, with 85.5% of the valid votes cast; the rate of participation by the electorate was 51.9%.

Economy

In 2000 Moscow Oblast's gross regional product amounted to 193,614m. roubles, or 29,800 roubles per head. The main industrial centres are at Podolsk, Lyubertsy, Kolomna, Mytishchi, Odintsovo, Noginsk, Serpukhov, Orekhovo-Zuyevo, Shchel-kovo and Sergiyev-Posad. At the end of 2001 there were 2,699 km (1,677 miles) of railways and 16,299 km of paved roads on the Oblast's territory. In mid-2003 proposals for the construction of the first toll motorway in Russia were announced by the Government of Moscow Oblast.

Moscow Oblast's agriculture, which employed 7.7% of the region's work-force in 2001, consists mainly of animal husbandry and the production of vegetables. Total agricultural production generated 26,458m. roubles in 2001. Of this total, 50.5% was contributed by crop sales and 49.5% by animal husbandry. The Oblast's industry, in which some 22.9% of the working population were engaged in 2001, mainly comprises heavy industry. The region's major industries are mechanical engineering, radio electronics, chemicals, light manufacturing, textiles, ferrous and non-ferrous metallurgy, metal-working, the manufacture of building materials, wood-working and handicrafts (ceramics, painted and lacquered wooden ornaments). The region's military-industrial complex is also important. Industrial output was worth 174,789m. roubles in 2001.

The economically active population of the Oblast was 3,443,000 in mid-2001, when 5.5% of the labour force were unemployed. The average monthly wage was 4,741.7 roubles in mid-2002. In 2001 there was a regional budgetary deficit of 574m. roubles. In 2001 the value of the Oblast's export trade amounted to US $1,592.4m., and imports were worth $2,524.3m. Total foreign investment in Moscow Oblast amounted to $372.7m. In 1997 there was a total of 110 joint enterprises operating in the Oblast, of which 78 had foreign partners, particularly from Germany, Italy and the USA. At the end of 2001 there were 45,991 small businesses registered in the Oblast.

Directory

Governor: Boris V. Gromov; 103070 Moscow, pl. Staraya 6; tel. (095) 206-60-93; fax (095) 206-61-23; e-mail amo@mosreg.ru; internet www.mosreg.ru.

Chairman of the Regional Duma: VIKTOR A. AKSKAKOV; 103070 Moscow, pl. Staraya 6; tel. (095) 206-61-32; fax (095) 925-17-46.

Representation of Moscow Oblast in the Russian Federation: Moscow.

Orel Oblast

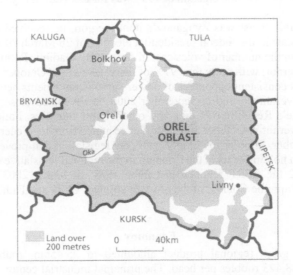

Orel Oblast is situated in the central part of the Eastern European Plain within the Central Russian Highlands. The Oblast forms part of the Central Federal Okrug and the Central Economic Area. It is surrounded by five other oblasts: Kursk (to the south), Bryansk (west), Kaluga (north-west), Tula (north-east) and Lipetsk (east). The Ukrainian border lies some 180 km (just over 100 miles) to the south-west. The Oblast's major river is the Oka, the source of which is found in the south-west. There are a total of around 2,000 rivers, with a combined length of 9,100 km, although none is navigable. Just over 7% of the Oblast's area is forested. The territory of Orel Oblast covers an area of 24,700 sq km (9,530 sq miles) and is divided, for administrative purposes, into 24 districts and seven cities. According to the preliminary results of the census of 9–16 October 2002, the total population of the Oblast was 860,600 and the population density was 34.8 per sq km. Some 63.5% of the inhabitants of the region lived in urban areas. The Oblast's administrative centre is at Orel, which had 333,600 inhabitants, according to provisional census results.

History

Orel was founded as a fortress in 1566. In the 1860s it served as a place of exile for Polish insurgents and was later a detention centre for prisoners on their way to exile in Siberia. Orel Oblast was formed on 27 September 1937. In post-Soviet Russia it formed part of the political 'red belt'. The Communist Party candidate defeated the pro-Government incumbent in elections for a head of the regional administration in December 1992. The victor was eventually dismissed and the regional legislature dissolved by presidential decree, following its criticism of the federal Government during the constitutional crisis of 1993. A 50-seat Regional Duma, elected in March 1994, was dominated by the Communist Party of the Russian Federation (CPRF), which received 45% of the votes cast in the Oblast during the 1995 elections to the State Duma. Despite the loyalty to President Yeltsin shown by the head of the regional administration, Yegor Stroyev (a former cabinet member and the speaker of the upper house of the federal parliament, the Federation Council), the greatest show of support in the presidential election of 1996 was for Gennadii Zyuganov, the CPRF candidate.

Although Orel Oblast was Zyuganov's home region, he received 44.6% of the regional votes cast in the federal presidential election of 26 March 2000, which was 1.2% fewer than the number of votes cast in support of Vladimir Putin. Stroyev was re-elected Governor, with more than 97% of the votes cast, in October 1997. He was one of the most consistent opponents of power-sharing agreements between regional and federal government, and in September 2000 he advocated closer co-operation with the People's Republic of China and other Asian countries. Following his re-election as Governor in October 2001, Stroyev resigned from the Federation Council in early December, in order to comply with new legislation that prevented regional governors from holding seats in the Council. In the regional legislative elections held in March 2002 the CPRF retained just three seats. In March 2003 Stroyev was elected to the Supreme Council of the pro-Government Unity and Fatherland-United Russia party.

Economy

Orel Oblast's gross regional product amounted to 25,456m. roubles in 2000, equivalent to 28,423 roubles per head. The principal industrial centres in the region are at Orel, Livny and Mtsensk. Orel city lies on the Moscow–Simferopol (Crimea, Ukraine) highway and is an important railway junction. At the end of 2001 there were 595 km of railway track in the Oblast and 4,085 km of paved roads.

Orel Oblast is an important agricultural trade centre. In 2001 around 21.4% of the economically active population were engaged in agriculture. Agricultural production, which amounted to a total value of 11,317m. roubles in 2001, consists mainly of the cultivation of grain and sugar beet, while animal husbandry accounted for 39.9% of production in that year. There are some 17.5m. cu m of timber reserves in the Oblast and a major source of iron ore, at Novoyaltinskoye. However, this and reserves of other minerals in the region have generally not been exploited to their full potential. The industrial sector employed around 22.0% of the economically active population in 2001 and generated some 16,327m. roubles. The Oblast's main industries are mechanical engineering, metal-working, the production of building materials and food-processing. It produces around one-third of its electrical-energy requirements, the remainder being supplied by neighbouring oblasts (Tula, Kursk and Lipetsk).

The region's economically active population numbered 434,000 in 2001, when 7.9% of the labour force were unemployed. In mid-2002 those in employment earned an average of 3,079.6 roubles per month. There was a budgetary deficit of 454m. roubles in 2001. In that year external trade amounted to a value of US $131.2m. in exports and $115.4m. in imports. Total foreign investment in Orel Oblast amounted to $18.5m. At 31 December 2001 there were some 2,636 small businesses in operation in the region.

Directory

Head of the Regional Administration (Governor): Yegor S. Stroyev; 302021 Orel, pl. Lenina 1; tel. (0862) 41-63-13; fax (0862) 41-25-30; e-mail post@adm.orel .ru; internet www.adm.orel.ru.

Chairman of the Regional Council of People's Deputies: Nikolai A. Volodin; 302021 Orel, pl. Lenina 1; tel. (0862) 41-58-53; fax (0862) 41-60-22.

Chief Representative of Orel Oblast in the Russian Federation: Marina G. Rogacheva; 109240 Moscow, ul. Goncharnaya 12/3; tel. (095) 915-85-51; fax (095) 915-86-14.

Head of Orel City Administration (Mayor): Vasilii I. Uvarov; 302000 Orel, Proletarskaya gora 1; tel. (0862) 43-33-12; fax (08622) 6-39-44.

Ryazan Oblast

Ryazan Oblast is situated in the central part of the Eastern European Plain and forms part of the Central Federal Okrug and the Central Economic Area. Ryazan city lies some 192 km (just under 120 miles) south-east of Moscow. The other neighbouring regions are Vladimir (to the north), Nizhnii Novgorod (north-east), the Republic of Mordoviya (east), Penza (south-east), Tambov and Lipetsk (south), and Tula (west). There are some 2,800 lakes in the region (the largest being the Velikoye and the Dubovoye) and its major rivers are the Oka and the Don and their tributaries. The Oka extends 489 km (304 miles) between the borders of Moscow and Vladimir Oblasts. Its catchment area amounts to over 95% of the region's territory, which occupies an area of 39,600 sq km (15,290 sq miles) and is divided into 25 administrative districts and 12 cities. According to the preliminary results of the census of 9–16 October 2002, the population of Ryazan Oblast totalled 1,228,000, giving a population density of 31.0 per sq km. Some 68.9% of the population inhabited urban areas. The Oblast's principal city is Ryazan, with a population of 521,700, according to provisional census results.

History

Ryazan city was an early Orthodox Christian bishopric. The Oblast was formed on 26 September 1937. In the 1990s it was described as part of the 'red belt' of communist support in Russia. With 31% of the Oblast's participating electorate voting for the Communist Party of the Russian Federation (CPRF) in the general election of December 1995, this party was also able to dominate the Regional Duma. In October 1998 the incumbent Governor was removed by the federal Government; the acting Governor, Igor Ivlev, lost the subsequent election to the CPRF candidate, Vyacheslav Lyubimov.

In April 1999, at the time of the aerial bombardment of Serbia and Montenegro, then known as the Federal Republic of Yugoslavia, by North Atlantic Treaty Organization (NATO) forces, Lyubimov was one of the leading supporters in the Federation Council of the expansion of the Russia-Belarus Union to include

Yugoslavia. From the late 1990s Ryazan obtained notoriety as a region in which far-right groups, notably Russian National Unity and its successor organization, Russian Rebirth, were able to operate. The most dramatic example was an attack on a Jewish Sunday school class by 15 youths in September 2000. Lyubimov was re-elected as Governor in December of that year.

Economy

In 2000 Ryazan Oblast's gross regional product amounted to 31,966m. roubles, or 25,044 roubles per head. The Oblast's industrial centres are at Ryazan, Skopin, Kasimov and Sasovo. At the end of 2001 there were 974 km of railways and 6,697 km of paved roads in the region.

The Oblast's warm, moist climate is conducive to agriculture, which consists mainly of production of grain, vegetables, fruit, potatoes and sugar beet, and animal husbandry, and employed 15.5% of the work-force in 2001. Total agricultural production amounted to a value of 11,077m. roubles in that year, of which crop sales accounted for 55.4% and animal husbandry for 44.6%. There are 162.8m. cu m of timber reserves in the region and substantial reserves of brown coal and peat, estimated at around 302m. metric tons and 222m. tons, respectively. Deposits of peat are concentrated in the north, the east and the south-west of the region. The Oblast's main industries are mechanical engineering, metal-working, the generation of electrical energy, petroleum-processing, the production of building materials, light manufacturing and food-processing. In 2001 some 23.8% of the working population were engaged in industry, which generated a total of 30,406m. roubles.

The economically active population numbered 595,000 in 2001, when 11.2% of the labour force were unemployed. In mid-2002 those in employment earned, on average, 3,425.3 roubles per month. The 2001 budget showed a surplus of 152m. roubles, and foreign investment in the region totalled US $1.6m. in that year. In 2001 external trade amounted to a value of $765.9m. in exports and $94.3m. in imports. At 31 December 2001 there were 6,437 small businesses registered in the Oblast.

Directory

Head of the Regional Administration (Governor): VYACHESLAV N. LYUBIMOV; 390000 Ryazan, ul. Lenina 30; tel. (0912) 27-21-25; fax (0912) 44-25-68; e-mail korn@adm1.ryazan.su; internet www.gov.ryazan.ru.

Chairman of the Regional Duma: VLADIMIR N. FEDOTKIN; 390000 Ryazan, ul. Pochtovaya 50/57; tel. (0912) 77-48-82; fax (0912) 21-64-22; e-mail duma@org.etr .ru.

Representation of Ryazan Oblast in the Russian Federation: 127025 Moscow, ul. Novyi Arbat 19/2213; tel. (095) 203-61-78; fax (095) 203-61-85.

Head of Ryazan City Administration (Mayor): PAVEL D. MAMATOV; 390000 Ryazan, ul. Radishcheva 28; tel. (0912) 77-34-02; fax (0912) 24-05-70; e-mail glava@cityadmin.ryazan.ru.

Smolensk Oblast

Smolensk Oblast is situated in the central part of the Eastern European Plain on the upper reaches of the Dnepr (Dnieper). It forms part of the Central Federal Okrug and the Central Economic Area. An international boundary with Belarus lies to the south-west, while Pskov and Tver Oblasts lie to the north, Moscow to the north-east and Kaluga and Bryansk to the south-east. The Oblast covers an area of 49,800 sq km (19,220 sq miles) and extends for some 280 km (175 miles) from south to north and 250 km from west to east. It is divided into 25 administrative districts and 15 cities. According to the preliminary results of the census of 9–16 October 2002, the total population numbered 1,050,500, giving a population density of 21.1 per sq km. Some 70.9% of the region's inhabitants lived in urban areas. The Oblast's administrative centre is at Smolensk, a river-port on the Dnepr, with 325,500 inhabitants, according to provisional census results.

History

Smolensk city was first documented in 863, as the chief settlement of the Krivichi, a Slavic tribe. It became an Orthodox Christian bishopric in 1128. It achieved prosperity during the 14th and 15th centuries as it was situated on one of the Hanseatic trade routes. Smolensk was the site of a major battle in 1812, between the Russian imperial army and the forces of Emperor Napoleon I of France, who subsequently went on to occupy the city of Moscow for a time. It was seized by the Bolsheviks in late 1917 and remained under their control for the duration of the civil war. Smolensk Oblast was formed on 27 September 1937.

The communist establishment remained in control of the region in the early years of Russia's restored independence. The Communist Party of the Russian Federation (CPRF) won the most seats in the Regional Duma elected in 1994 and secured the highest proportion of the votes of any party in elections to the State Duma in both 1995 and 1999. In the gubernatorial election of April–May 1998, after a second round of voting, the CPRF candidate and Mayor of Smolensk, Aleksandr Prokhorov, defeated the incumbent. However, support for the CPRF declined significantly in the regional legislative elections held in May 2002. In the same month Viktor Maslov, a general in the Federal Security Service, was elected as the new Governor of Smolensk Oblast, receiving 41.6% of the votes cast, compared with the 35.3% received by Prokhorov. Maslov's campaign had concentrated on issues of law and order, and concern about, in particular, organized crime, which was subsequently heightened, following the assassination of Vladimir Prokhorov, the First Deputy Governor and Maslov's campaign manager, in early August.

Economy

In 2000 Smolensk Oblast's gross regional product amounted to 29,906m. roubles, or 26,565 roubles per head. Its major industrial centres are at Smolensk, Roslavl, Safonovo, Vyazma, and Yartsevo. At the end of 2001 there were 1,258 km of railway lines and 8,879 km of paved roads in the Oblast.

Agriculture in Smolensk Oblast, which employed 15.8% of the work-force in 2001, mainly consists of animal husbandry (accounting for 56.3% of production in 2001), bee-keeping, and the production of flax, potatoes, fruit and vegetables, grain, sugar beet and sunflower seeds. Total agricultural output was worth 7,605m. roubles in 2001. The Oblast's main industries are mechanical engineering (in particular the production of automobiles), metal-working, chemicals and petrochemicals, food-processing and electrical-energy production. In 2001 23.1% of the work-force were engaged in industry. Total industrial production in that year amounted to a value of 32,639m. roubles.

The region's economically active population numbered 556,000 in 2001, when 9.9% of the labour force were unemployed. The average wage in the Oblast stood at 3,305.6 roubles per month in mid-2002. The 2001 budget showed a deficit of 188m. roubles. The value of external trade in that year amounted to US $419.8m. in exports and $133.4m. in imports. Total foreign investment in the region amounted to $9.9m. At 31 December 2001 there were 2,355 small businesses in operation.

Directory

Head of the Regional Administration (Governor): Viktor N. Maslov; 214008 Smolensk, pl. Lenina 1; tel. (08122) 3-65-71; fax (08122) 3-68-51; e-mail maslov@ admin.smolensk.ru; internet admin.smolensk.ru.

Chairman of the Regional Duma: Vladimir I. Anisimov; 214008 Smolensk, pl. Lenina 1; tel. (08122) 3-67-00; fax (08122) 3-71-85; e-mail duma@admin.smolensk .ru; internet admin.smolensk.ru/~duma.

Representation of Smolensk Oblast in the Russian Federation: Moscow.

Head of Smolensk City Administration: Vladislav N. Khaletskii; 214000 Smolensk, ul. Oktyabrskoi Revolyutsii 1/2; tel. and fax (08100) 3-11-81; e-mail smol@ admin.smolensk.ru; internet www.admcity.smolensk.ru.

Tambov Oblast

Tambov Oblast is situated in the central part of the Oka-Don plain. It forms part of the Central Federal Okrug and the Central Chernozem Economic Area. Penza and Saratov Oblasts lie to the east, Voronezh to the south, Lipetsk to the west and Ryazan to the north. Tambov city lies 480 km (298 miles) south-east of Moscow. Its major rivers are the Tsna and the Vorona. Its territory occupies 34,300 sq km (13,240 sq miles) and measures around 250 km from south to north and 200 km from west to east. The Oblast is divided into 23 administrative districts and eight cities. According to the preliminary results of the census of 9–16 October 2002, its population was 1,179,600, giving a population density of 34.4 per sq km. At that time, 57.2% of the population inhabited urban areas. The administrative centre is at Tambov, which had a population of 294,300, according to provisional census results.

History

Tambov city was founded in 1636 as a fort to defend Moscow. The region, 'the mystical core of Russia', was the scene of an army mutiny during the anti-tsarist uprising of 1905, and came under Bolshevik control immediately after the October Revolution in 1917. None the less, numerous peasant revolts against the Bolsheviks, which were brutally suppressed by forces led by Marshal Mikhail Tukachevskii, took place in the Oblast in the early 1920s. The Oblast, which was formed on 27 September 1937, was considered part of the 'red belt' of committed communist adherence in the 1990s. The dissolution of the oblast Soviet in October 1993, and its replacement by a Regional Duma, did not ease the tension between the communist-led assembly and the regional administration. Having appointed Oleg Betin, a locally respected Governor, President Boris Yeltsin permitted a gubernatorial election in Tambov in December 1995. However, Betin lost to the Communist Party of the Russian Federation candidate, Aleksandr Ryabov, and was instead appointed as presidential representative to the region. Betin, thus, remained active in the political life of the Oblast prior to his eventual election as Governor in December 1999, with the support of two centrist movements, Fatherland and Unity. On 7 December 2003 Betin was re-elected, receiving over 75% of the votes cast. Meanwhile, in elections held to the Regional Duma in March 1998 (at which the rate of participation was just over 25%), the greatest number of seats was won by a local pro-market party, comprised largely of young directors of firms and enterprises. New elections to the Regional Duma were held in December 2001; the rate of voter participation was unexpectedly high, at some 40%.

Economy

In 2000 Tambov Oblast's gross regional product amounted to 25,871m. roubles, equivalent to 20,498 roubles per head. The region's industrial centres are at Tambov, Michurinsk, Morshansk, Kotovsk and Rasskazovo. It is situated on the ancient trading routes from the centre of Russia to the lower Volga and Central Asia, and contains several major road and rail routes. At the end of 2001 there were 746 km of railway lines and 5,365 km of paved roads in the region.

The Oblast's agriculture, which employed a relatively high proportion of the work-force (some 26.6% in 2001) consists mainly of the production of grain, sugar beet, sunflower seeds and potatoes. Animal husbandry is also important, and accounted for 39.4% of the value of agricultural production in 2001. Total agricultural output was worth 7,605m. roubles in that year. The principal industries in the Oblast are mechanical engineering, metal-working, chemicals and petrochemicals, the production of electrical energy, light manufacturing and food-processing. In 2001 18.6% of the working population were engaged in industry. Total industrial production in that year amounted to a value of 13,184m. roubles.

The economically active population stood at 543,000 in 2001, when 12.4% of the labour force were unemployed—the highest level in the Central Federal Okrug. In mid-2002 the average monthly wage in the Oblast was 3,305.6 roubles. In 2002 the region was among those with the lowest-priced foodstuffs in the Russian Federation. There was a budgetary surplus of 45m. roubles in 2001. In that year the value of external trade amounted to only US \$44.3m. in exports and \$67.1m. in imports; foreign investment in the Oblast stood at \$20.1m. At 31 December 2001 3,599 small businesses were registered in the region.

Directory

Head of the Regional Administration (Governor): OLEG I. BETIN; 392017 Tambov, ul. Internatsionalnaya 14; tel. (0752) 72-10-61; fax (0752) 72-25-18; e-mail post@regadm.tambov.ru; internet www.regadm.tambov.ru.

Chairman of the Regional Duma: VLADIMIR N. KAREV; 392017 Tambov, ul. Internatsionalnaya 14; tel. (0752) 71-23-70; fax (0752) 71-07-72.

Representation of Tambov Oblast in the Russian Federation: Moscow.

Head of Tambov City Administration (Mayor): ALEKSEI YU. ILIN; 392000 Tambov, ul. Kommunalnaya 6; tel. (0752) 72-20-30; fax (0752) 72-47-71; e-mail cvc_t@rambler.ru; internet www.cityadm.tambov.ru.

Tula Oblast

Tula Oblast is situated in the central part of the Eastern European Plain in the northern section of the Central Russian Highlands. It forms part of the Central Federal Okrug and the Central Economic Area. Tula Oblast is bordered by the Oblasts of Ryazan to the east, Lipetsk to the south-east, Orel to the south-west, Kaluga to the north-west and Moscow to the north. Tula city is 193 km (about 120 miles) south of Moscow City. The region's major rivers are the Oka, the Upa, the Don and the Osetr. The territory of the Oblast covers an area of 25,700 sq km (9,920 sq miles) and extends for 230 km from south to north and 200 km from west to east. It is divided into 23 administrative districts and 21 cities. It is a highly populated area and, according to the preliminary results of the census of 9–16 October 2002, it had a total population of 1,675,700 and a population density of 65.2 per sq km. At that time-some 81.6% of the Oblast's population inhabited urban areas. The Oblast's administrative centre is at Tula, a military town, which had a population of 472,300, according to provisional census results. Its second largest city is Novomoskovsk (with 134,000 inhabitants).

History

The city of Tula was founded in the 12th century. It became an important economic centre in 1712, with the construction of the Imperial Small Arms Factory. Tula Oblast was founded on 26 September 1937. Tula's armaments industry meant that it was closed to foreigners for most of the Soviet period.

On 7 October 1993 the Tula Regional Soviet refused to disband itself, but was subsequently dissolved and its functions transferred to the Regional Administration. A new representative body, the 48-seat Regional Duma, was later elected and remained dominated by members of the former communist nomenklatura. The

Communist Party of the Russian Federation (CPRF) remained the most widely supported party in the Oblast throughout the 1990s, receiving the largest proportion of the votes cast for any party in the State Duma elections of both 1995 and 1999. The Oblast also had a high-profile CPRF Governor, following the election of Vasilii Starodubtsev in March 1997. He had previously been known nationally as a participant in the coup organized against the Soviet leader, Mikhail Gorbachev, in August 1991. Starodubtsev's continuing reputation as a radical communist was reflected in his standing as the sole 'red belt' governor to support the candidacy of Gennadii Zyuganov in the presidential election of 26 March 2000. Starodubtsev was also elected as a CPRF member of the State Duma in the legislative election of December 1999, but he refused to take his seat as, to do so, he would have been required to relinquish his position as Governor.

Gubernatorial elections, held in two rounds in April 2001, aroused widespread controversy. One day before the first round of the elections a meeting of the electoral commission, which reportedly had been convened to consider withdrawing the right of one candidate, Andrei Samoshin, to participate in the election, was attacked by a group of men, and fighting ensued; the commission had previously accused Samoshin of misusing electoral funds and violating campaign procedures. In the event, Samoshin was permitted to participate, coming in second place, with 21.0% of the votes cast, behind Starodubtsev, with 49.4%, less than the 50% of the votes required for an outright victory. However, Samoshin withdrew his candidacy on 19 April, three days before the 'run-off' election was due to take place, citing his dissatisfaction with the conduct of the electoral commission. Despite his reluctance to participate, the commission ruled that the third-placed candidate, Viktor Soko-lovskii, was to stand against Starodubtsev in the 'run-off' election. On 22 April Starodubtsev received over 71% of the votes cast in the second round of voting, for which Sokolovskii had refused to campaign.

Economy

In 2000 Tula Oblast's gross regional product amounted to 43,722m. roubles, or 25,215 roubles per head. Its important industrial centres are at Tula, Novomoskovsk, Shchekino, Aleksin, Uzlovaya and Yefremov. At the end of 2001 there were 1,087 km of railway lines and 5,150 km of paved roads in the Oblast.

Around 73.7% of the Oblast's territory is used for agricultural purposes. Agricultural activity, in which some 10.0% of the working population were engaged in 2001, consists primarily of animal husbandry and production of grain, potatoes, fruit and vegetables, and sugar beet. Agricultural production was worth 12,917m. roubles in 2001, of which crop sales contributed 58.8% and animal husbandry 41.2%. The Oblast's main industries are mechanical engineering, metal-working, chemicals and petrochemicals, ferrous metallurgy, food-processing, the production of brown coal (lignite) and the generation of electricity. Industry employed approximately 28.4% of the working population in 2001, when total industrial production amounted to a value of 59,320m. roubles. Ferrous metallurgy, mechanical engineering and metal-working dominated exports in the region. A tourism sector is encouraged by the city's history and the Yasnaya Polyana country estate of Count Leo Tolstoy (1828–1910), the writer.

The economically active population in the Oblast numbered 828,000 in 2001, when 5.2% of the labour force were unemployed. In mid-2002 those in employment earned an average monthly wage of 3,368.1 roubles; the region was named as one of the worst for wage arrears in that year. The 2001 budget showed a deficit of 127m. roubles. The main foreign trading partners of the Oblast are Germany, Italy, the Republic of Korea (South Korea), Switzerland and the USA. In 2001 external trade comprised US $859.1m. of exports and $126.3m. of imports. Total foreign investment amounted to $43.7m. in that year. At 31 December 2001 6,492 small businesses were registered in Tula Oblast.

Directory

Head of the Regional Administration (Governor): VASILII A. STARODUBTSEV; 300600 Tula, pl. Lenina 2; tel. (0872) 27-84-36; fax (0872) 20-63-26; e-mail michel@adm.tula.ru.

Chairman of the Regional Duma: OLEG D. LUKICHEV; 300600 Tula, pl. Lenina 2; tel. (0872) 20-50-24; fax (0872) 36-47-66; e-mail oblduma@duma.tula.ru.

Representation of Tula Oblast in the Russian Federation: 127030 Moscow, Veskovskii per. 2; tel. (095) 978-14-56; fax (095) 978-06-43.

Head of Tula City Administration (Mayor): SERGEI I. KAZAKOV; Tula; tel. (0872) 27-80-85.

Tver Oblast

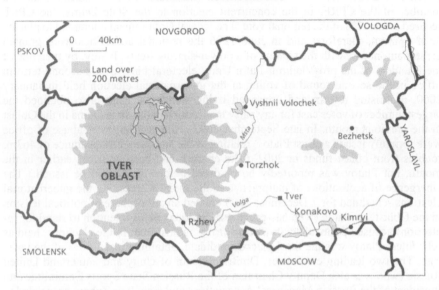

Tver Oblast (known as Kalinin from 1931 to 1990) is situated in the central part of the Eastern European Plain. It forms part of the Central Federal Okrug and the Central Economic Area. Moscow and Smolensk Oblasts lie to the south, Pskov to the west, Novgorod and Vologda to the north and Yaroslavl to the east. Its westernmost point lies some 50 km (just over 30 miles) from the border with Belarus. The major rivers in the region are the Volga, which rises within its territory, the Mologa and the Tvertsa. The Zapadnaya Dvina and the Msta rivers also have their sources in the Oblast. It has more than 500 lakes, the largest of which is the Seliger, and contains nine reservoirs. The western part of the territory is mountainous, containing the Valdai Highlands. About one-third of the territory of the Oblast is forested. It occupies 84,100 sq km (32,460 sq miles) and is divided into 36 administrative districts and 23 cities. According to the preliminary results of the census of 9–16 October 2002, the Oblast had a total of 1,472,600 inhabitants, and a population density, therefore, of 17.5 per sq km; some 73.1% of the population inhabited urban areas. The administrative centre is at Tver (formerly Kalinin), a river-port, which had a population of 409,400, according to provisional census results.

History

The city of Tver was founded as a fort in 1135 and its princes rivalled those of Moscow in the 14th and 15th centuries. The city was largely rebuilt after the great fire of 1763. The Oblast was formed in January 1935. In the 1990s the region's relations with the federal Government, led by President Boris Yeltsin, were not always cordial. In October 1993 the Tver Regional Soviet refused to disband itself, but was subsequently obliged to comply with the directives of the federal authorities and a new body, the Legislative Assembly, was elected the following year. This, too, was dominated by members of the Communist Party of the Russian Federation (CPRF) and was obstructive of executive action. Yeltsin appointed a respected local figure to head the regional administration and decided to permit a gubernatorial election in December 1995. The incumbent was defeated by Vladimir Platov, a member of the CPRF; in the concurrent election to the State Duma, the CPRF secured some 27% of the regional vote. The federal Government attempted to placate local opinion, therefore, and in June 1996 the regional authorities were granted greater autonomy, with the signing of a power-sharing treaty. Platov, by then one of the founders of the pro-Vladimir Putin Unity electoral bloc, won a second term in office in the second round of voting at the gubernatorial election held in January 2000, promising reform and improved living standards. Unity also obtained the largest number of votes cast for any party in elections to the State Duma in the Oblast in the previous month. In late September 2003 criminal charges of abuse of office were formally issued against Platov, relating to the apparent disappearance of 463m. roubles from oblast funds in 2002. (The charges had been prepared earlier in the month, but Platov was reportedly hospitalized before they could be issued.) The emergence of accusations of malpractice in the months preceding the gubernatorial elections scheduled for 7 December 2003 created an atmosphere of political tension in the Oblast, as Platov (who had previously announced his intention to stand for re-election) accused political rivals of conspiring against him. In the elections, held as scheduled, Platov was the third-placed candidate, obtaining just 12.0% of the votes cast. The two leading candidates, Dmitrii Zelenin of Unity and Fatherland-United Russia (who was also Deputy Chairman of the Russian State Sports Committee and President of the Russian Managers' Association) and Gen. Igor Zubov, proceeded to a second round of voting on 21 December. Zelenin was duly elected as Governor, securing 57.4% of the votes cast in the 'run-off' election.

Economy

In 2000 Tver Oblast's gross regional product amounted to 38,749m. roubles, equivalent to 24,338 roubles per head. Industry is the dominant branch of the Oblast's economy. The principal industrial centres are Tver, Vyshnii Volochek, Rzhev, Torzhok and Kimryi. The region is crossed by road and rail routes between Moscow and Rīga, Latvia, and a highway between Moscow and St Petersburg. At the end of 2001 the total length of railway track in the Oblast was 1,806 km, and the network of paved roads was 14,987 km long. There were 924 km of navigable waterways in the region in 1998, mainly on the Volga. There is an international airport at Tver.

Around 2.4m. ha (5.9m. acres) of the Oblast's territory is used for agricultural purposes, of which two-thirds is arable land. Agriculture in Tver Oblast, which employed around 14.5% of the work-force in 2001, consists mainly of animal husbandry and the production of vegetables, potatoes and flax (the region grows around one-quarter of the flax produced in Russia). Total agricultural output amounted to a value of 11,079m. roubles in 2001, of which crop sales accounted for 48.3% and animal husbandry for 51.7%. The region contains deposits of peat, lime and coal, and is famous for its mineral-water reserves. Its major industries are mechanical engineering, metal-working, electricity generation, food-processing and light manufacturing. In 2001 some 25.6% of the Oblast's working population were engaged in industry, and total industrial production was worth 38,174m. roubles.

The region's economically active population numbered 774,000 in 2001, when 7.8% of the labour force were unemployed. The average wage amounted to 3,413.9 roubles per month in mid-2002. The 2001 regional budget recorded a surplus of 81m.

roubles. Tver's main international trading partners were the People's Republic of China, Germany, Switzerland, Turkey and the USA. In 2001 external trade amounted to a value of US $117.2m. in exports and $156.5m. in imports. In 1998 a social and cultural development programme for Tver Oblast (for 1998–2005) was adopted by the federal Government, which gave tax incentives to foreign investors. Total foreign investment in the Oblast amounted to $24.3m. in 2001. At the end of 2001 5,725 small businesses were operating in the region.

Directory

Head of the Regional Administration (Governor): DMITRII ZELENIN; 170000 Tver, ul. Sovetskaya 44; tel. (0822) 33-10-51; fax (0822) 42-55-08; e-mail tradm@tversa .ru; internet www.region.tver.ru.

Chairman of the Legislative Assembly: MARK ZH. KHASAINOV; 170000 Tver, ul. Sovetskaya 33; tel. (0822) 32-10-11; fax (0822) 48-10-15; e-mail zsto@tdn.ru; internet www.zsto.ru.

Representation of Tver Oblast in the Russian Federation: 103246 Moscow, ul. B. Dmitrovka 26; tel. (095) 926-65-19; fax (095) 292-14-85.

Head of Tver City Administration (Mayor): OLEG S. LEVEDEV; 170640 Tver, ul. Sovetskaya 11; tel. (0822) 33-01-31; fax (0822) 42-59-39; e-mail info@www.tver .ru; internet www.tver.ru.

Vladimir Oblast

Vladimir Oblast is situated in the central part of the Eastern European Plain. It forms part of the Central Federal Okrug and the Central Economic Area. It shares borders with Ryazan and Moscow to the south-west, Yaroslavl and Ivanovo to the north and Nizhnii Novgorod to the east. The Oblast's main rivers are the Oka and its tributary, the Klyazma. Over one-half of its territory is forested. It occupies a total of 29,000 sq km (11,200 sq miles) and measures around 170 km (106 miles) from south to north and 280 km from west to east. The Oblast is divided into 16 administrative districts and 23 cities. According to the preliminary results of the census of 9–16 October 2002, the region had a total population of 1,524,900, giving a population density of 52.6 per sq km; some 79.7% of the population inhabited urban areas. The Oblast's administrative centre is at Vladimir, which had a population of 316,300, according to provisional census results. Other major cities are Kovrov (155,600) and Murom (126,800).

History

Founded in 1108 as a frontier fortress by Prince Vladimir Monomakh, after the disintegration of Kievan Rus, Vladimir city was the seat of the principality of Vladimir-Suzdal and an early Orthodox Christian bishopric. Vladimir fell under the rule of Muscovy in 1364 and was supplanted by Moscow as the seat of the Russian Orthodox patriarch, although Vladimir was chosen for the coronations of several Muscovite princes. It declined in importance from the 15th century. Vladimir Oblast was formed on 14 August 1944.

In the December 1995 parliamentary election, the Communist Party of the Russian Federation (CPRF), the nationalist Liberal Democratic Party of Russia and the pro-Government Our Home is Russia all obtained more than 10% of the votes cast, while in the December 1999 election the CPRF obtained only a slightly higher share of the votes cast than the recently formed pro-Government party, Unity. The CPRF, however, secured the election of Nikolai Vinogradov, former Chairman of the Legislative Assembly, to the post of Governor in late 1996. Vinogradov was re-elected as Governor in December 2000, with some 66% of the votes cast, defeating Yurii Glasov, who had held the post in 1991–96.

Economy

Vladimir Oblast's gross regional product in 2000 totalled 35,450m. roubles, or 22,135 roubles per head. The Oblast's main industrial centres are at Vladimir, Kovrov, Murom, Aleksandrov, Kolchugino, Vyazniki and Gus-Khrustalnyi. In 2001 there were 938 km of railway track and 5,536 km of paved roads on its territory.

Agriculture in the region, which employed 8.7% of the work-force in 2001, consists mainly of animal husbandry, vegetable production and horticulture. Total agricultural output stood at 8,206m. roubles in 2001, of which crop sales accounted for 47% and animal husbandry for 53%. Vladimir is rich in peat deposits and timber reserves, but relies on imports for around 70% of its energy supplies. The Oblast's main industries are mechanical engineering, metal-working, food-processing, the production of electrical energy, light manufacturing, chemicals, glass-making and handicrafts. Industrial output in 2001 was worth 46,182m. roubles. In that year a total of 34.2% of the working population were engaged in industry. Vladimir city's largest employer is the Vladimir Tractor Plant, which struggled to adapt to the new economic conditions from the 1990s.

Vladimir Oblast's economically active population numbered 809,000 in 2001, when 9.9% of the labour force were unemployed. The average monthly wage in the Oblast was 3,128.2 roubles in mid-2002. In 2001 there was a regional budgetary surplus of 29m. roubles. In that year external trade constituted US \$116.2m. in exports and \$195.8m. in imports; total foreign investment amounted to some \$22.7m. At 31 December 2001 6,927 small businesses were registered in the region.

Directory

Head of the Regional Administration (Governor): NIKOLAI V. VINOGRADOV; 600000 Vladimir, pr. Oktyabrskii 21; tel. (0922) 33-15-52; fax (0922) 35-34-45; e-mail post@avo.ru; internet avo.ru.

Chairman of the Legislative Assembly: ANATOLII V. BOBROV; 600000 Vladimir, Oktyabrskaya pr. 21; tel. (0922) 32-66-53; fax (0922) 23-08-06; internet www.zsvo .ru.

Representative of Vladimir Oblast in the Russian Federation: ANDREI V. YARIN; Moscow; tel. (095) 299-66-49.

Head of Vladimir City Administration: ALEKSANDR P. RYBAKOV; 600000 Vladimir, ul. Gorkogo 36; tel. (0922) 23-28-17; fax (0922) 23-85-54; e-mail mayor@ vladimir-city.ru; internet www.vladimir-city.ru.

Voronezh Oblast

Voronezh Oblast is situated in the centre of the Eastern European Plain on the middle reaches of the Volga. It forms part of the Central Federal Okrug and the Central Chernozem Economic Area. There is a short border with Ukraine in the south. Of the neighbouring Russian federal territories, Belgorod and Kursk lie to the west, Lipetsk and Tambov to the north, a short border with Saratov to the north-east, Volgograd to the east and Rostov to the south-east. The west of the territory is situated within the Central Russian Highlands and the east in the Oka-Don lowlands. Its main rivers are the Don, the Khoper and the Bityug. The Voronezh region occupies an area of 52,400 sq km (20,230 sq miles) and is divided into 32 administrative districts and 15 cities. According to the preliminary results of the census of 9–16 October 2002, the Oblast's total population was 2,379,000, and its population density was, therefore, 45.4 per sq km. Some 61.9% of the population lived in urban areas. The region's administrative centre is at Voronezh, which had a population of 848,700, according to provisional census results.

History

Voronezh city was founded in 1586 as a fortress. Tsar Petr (Peter—'the Great') founded the first units of what became the imperial Russian Navy in Voronezh in 1696. The centre of a fertile region, the city began to industrialize in the tsarist period. Voronezh Oblast was formed in June 1934.

In the immediate post-Soviet years the region remained committed to the Communist Party of the Russian Federation (CPRF), which controlled the Regional Duma. The regional legislature is among a minority in post-Soviet Russia in which there is a significant proportion (40%) of paid deputies. A CPRF member and former speaker of the oblast assembly, Ivan Shabonov, was elected Governor in December 1996. At the gubernatorial election held in December 2000 Shabonov received only 15% of the votes cast, and was defeated by Vladimir Kulakov, a general in the Federal Security Service, who obtained some 60% of the votes. Subsequently, at the regional legislative election held in March 2001 the level of CPRF representation was reduced from 23 seats to just five.

Economy

In 2000 Voronezh Oblast's gross regional product amounted to 52,100m. roubles, equivalent to 21,268 roubles per head. The important industrial centres in the Oblast are at Voronezh, Borisoglebsk, Rossosh and Kalach. At the end of 2001 the territory contained some 1,160 km (720 miles) of railway track and 9,124 km of paved roads. The road network includes sections of major routes, such as the Moscow–Rostov, Moscow–Astrakhan and Kursk–Saratov highways. There are some 640 km of navigable waterways.

Around 4.7m. ha (11.6m. acres—90% of the total) of Voronezh's territory is used for agricultural purposes, of which 3.1m. ha is arable land. In 2001 22.6% of the Oblast's working population were employed in the agricultural sector. The Oblast's agriculture consists mainly of the production of grain, sugar beet, sunflower seeds, potatoes and vegetables. Animal husbandry is also important. Total agricultural production amounted to a value of 22,300m. roubles in 2001, of which crop sales accounted for 57% and animal husbandry for 43%. The Oblast's main industries are mechanical engineering, metal-working, chemicals and petrochemicals, the production of electricity, the manufacture of building materials and food-processing. In 2001 some 19.9% of the work-force were engaged in industry, the output of which was valued at a total of 41,624m. roubles.

The Oblast's economically active population numbered 1,117,000 in 2001, when 9.6% of the labour force were unemployed. In mid-2002 the Oblast's average wage was 2.817.3 roubles per month. There was a budgetary deficit of 808m. roubles in 2001. In that year the value of external trade amounted to US $224.1m. in exports and $180.3m. in imports. Foreign investment in the region increased dramatically from the mid-1990s, and in 2001 it amounted to $29.2m., compared with $4.0m. in 1998. In 2000 there were 53 joint- or foreign enterprises, established primarily with funds from Belarus, Cyprus, Germany, the United Kingdom and the USA. At 31 December 2001 11,012 small businesses were registered in the region.

Directory

Head of the Regional Administration (Governor): VLADIMIR G. KULAKOV; 394018 Voronezh, pl. Lenina 1; tel. (0732) 55-27-37; fax (0732) 53-28-02; internet admin .vrn.ru.

Chairman of the Regional Duma: ALEKSEI M. NAKVASIN; 394018 Voronezh, ul. Kirova 2; tel. (0732) 52-21-03; fax (0732) 52-09-22; e-mail voblduma@inbox.ru.

Chief Representative of Voronezh Oblast in the Russian Federation: ALEKSANDR I. FIRSOV; 127006 Moscow, ul. M. Dmitrovka 3/10/501; tel. (095) 250-98-55; fax (095) 299-90-27.

Head of Voronezh City Administration (Mayor): YEVGENII M. SEVERGIN (acting); 394067 Voronezh, ul. Plekhanovskaya 10; tel. (0732) 55-34-20; fax (0732) 55-47-16; e-mail admin@city.vrn.ru; internet www.city.vrn.ru.

Yaroslavl Oblast

Yaroslavl Oblast is situated in the central part of the Eastern European Plain. It forms part of the Central Federal Okrug and the Central Economic Area. Ivanovo Oblast lies to the south-east, Vladimir and Moscow Oblasts in the south, Tver Oblast to the west, Vologda Oblast to the north and Kostroma Oblast to the east. Yaroslavl city, which lies on the Volga, is 282 km (175 miles) north-east of Moscow. The region has 2,500 rivers and lakes, its major two lakes being Nero and Pleshcheyevo, and there is a large reservoir at Rybinsk, formed in 1941, following the completion of a dam and a hydroelectric power plant nearby. The Volga river flows for 340 km through the region. Its territory, just over two-fifths of which is forested, covers a total area of 36,400 sq km (14,050 sq miles) and is divided into 17 administrative districts and 11 cities. According to the preliminary results of the census of 9–16 October 2002, the Oblast's total population was 1,367,700, giving a population density of 37.6 per sq km. Some 80.9% of the population inhabited urban areas at that time. The Oblast's administrative centre is at Yaroslavl, which had a population of 613,200, according to provisional census results. The second largest city in the Oblast is Rybinsk (222,800).

History

Yaroslavl city is reputed to be the oldest town on the River Volga, having been founded c. 1024. The region was acquired by the Muscovite state during the reign of Ivan III (1462–1505) and the city briefly served as the capital when Moscow was captured by Polish and Lithuanian invaders in 1610. Yaroslavl Oblast was formed in March 1936. In the 1990s the region developed a liberal and diverse political climate.

A range of interests was represented in the new, 23-seat Regional Duma elected in February 1994. Thus, in December 1995 the federal President, Boris Yeltsin, permitted his appointed Governor, Anatolii Listisyn, to contest a direct election for the post, which he won. He was re-elected for a further term on 19 December 1999, obtaining 63.9% of the votes cast. In early 2003 Listisyn announced his intention to contest the gubernatorial elections scheduled to be held on 7 December, having obtained the support of the pro-Government Unity and Fatherland-United Russia party. In the event Listisyn was re-elected, with 75.2% of the votes cast. The rate of participation by the electorate was 59.0%.

Economy

In 2000 Yaroslavl Oblast's gross regional product amounted to 46,853m. roubles, equivalent to 33,278 roubles per head. The major industrial centres in the region are at Yaroslavl itself, Rybinsk, Tutayev, Uglich and Pereslavl-Zalesskii. There are river-ports at Yaroslavl, Rybinsk and Uglich. The total length of railway track in the Oblast amounted to 650 km at the end of 2001. The Oblast lies on the main Moscow–Yaroslavl–Archangel and Yaroslavl–Kostroma highways. The total length of paved roads in the territory was 6,259 km. There are also around 789 km of navigable waterways.

The climate and soil quality in the region is not favourable to agriculture. Agricultural activity, which employed just 9.7% of the working population in 2001, consists primarily of animal husbandry and the production of vegetables, fruit and flax. Total agricultural output was worth 8,948m. roubles in 2001, of which crop sales accounted for 50.8% and animal husbandry for 49.2%. The main industries are mechanical engineering (Rybinsk Motors is Russia's largest manufacturer of aircraft engines), chemicals and petrochemicals, petroleum-refining, peat production, the production of electricity and food-processing. In 2001 industrial output in the region amounted to a value of 60,425m. roubles and industry employed some 31.6% of the work-force.

The Oblast's economically active population numbered 728,000 in 2001, when the region had an unemployment rate of 7.1%. The average wage was 3,908.4 roubles per month in mid-2002. In 2001 there was a regional budgetary deficit of 74m. roubles. In that year total foreign investment in the region amounted to US $14.1m., and external trade amounted to a value of $1,314.2m. in exports and $247.8m. in imports. At 31 December 2001 there were 7,053 small businesses registered in the Oblast.

Directory

Governor: ANATOLII I. LISITSYN; 150000 Yarovslavl, pl. Sovetskaya 3; tel. (0852) 72-81-28; fax (0852) 32-84-14; internet www.adm.yar.ru.

Chairman of the Regional Duma: ANDREI G. KRUTIKOV; 150000 Yaroslavl, pl. Sovetskaya 5; tel. (0852) 30-50-83; fax (0852) 72-76-45; e-mail duma@adm.yar.ru; internet www.adm.yar.ru/duma/index.asp.

Representation of Yaroslavl Oblast in the Russian Federation: Moscow; tel. (095) 253-45-18.

Head of Yaroslavl City Administration (Mayor): VIKTOR V. VOLONCHUNAS; 150000 Yaroslavl, ul. Andropova 6; tel. (0852) 30-46-41; fax (0852) 30-52-79; e-mail ird@gw.city.yar.ru; internet www.city.yar.ru.

NORTH-WESTERN FEDERAL OKRUG

Archangel Oblast

Archangel (Arkhangelsk) Oblast is situated in the north of the Eastern European Plain. It lies on the White, Barents and Kara Seas (parts of the Arctic Ocean) and includes the northern archipelago of Zemlya Frantsa-Iosifa and the Novaya Zemlya islands. The Oblast forms part of the North-Western Federal Okrug and the Northern Economic Area. In the north-east the Nenets Autonomous Okrug (AOk), a constituent part of the Oblast, runs eastwards along the coast to end in a short border with the Yamal-Nenets AOk (within Tyumen Oblast). The Republic of Komi lies to the south of the Nenets AOk and to the east of Archangel proper. Kirov and, mainly, Vologda Oblasts form the southern border and the Republic of Kareliya lies to the west. North-west, across the White Sea, lie the Kola Peninsula and Murmansk Oblast, while to the north there is access to the Barents Sea. The Oblast contains several large rivers (the Onega, the Severnaya Dvina and its tributary the Vaga, the Pinega, the Mezen and the Pechora) and some 2,500 lakes. Some two-fifths of its entire area are forested—much of the north-west of the territory is taiga (forested marshland)—and almost one-quarter classed as reindeer pasture. The Oblast, including the autonomous okrug, occupies an area of 587,400 sq km (226,800 sq miles) and is divided into 20 administrative districts and 14 cities. It spans three climatic zones—arctic, sub-arctic and continental. According to the preliminary results of the census of 9–16 October 2002, the Oblast's total population was 1,335,700 and its population density, therefore, stood at 2.3 per sq km; some 74.8% of the population lived in urban areas. Archangel Oblast's administrative centre is at Archangel (Arkhangelsk), which had 355,500 inhabitants, according to provisional census results. The Oblast's second city is Severodvinsk (201,500), just to the west.

History

The city of Archangel was founded in the 16th century, to further Muscovite trade. It was the first Russian seaport and the country's main one until the building of St Petersburg in 1703. The port played a major role in the attack by the Entente fleet (British and French navies) against the Red Army in 1918, and was an important route for supplies from the Allied Powers during the Second World War. Archangel Oblast was founded on 23 September 1937.

On 13 October 1993 the Archangel Regional Soviet transferred its responsibilities to the Regional Administration. Communist candidates initially formed the largest single group elected to the legislative chamber of the Regional Assembly of Deputies, although supporters of the federal Government and liberal reformists also enjoyed respectable levels of support in the cities. In March 1996 the unpopular head of the Regional Administration, Pavel Pozdeyev, a federal appointee nominated only one month previously, was forced to leave his position. Anatolii Yefremov's position as Governor was confirmed by his popular election to the post in December 1997, and by his re-election in December 2000. Legislative elections were held on 18 June 2000.

Economy

All figures in this survey incorporate data for the Nenets AOk, which is also treated separately (see below). Archangel Oblast's gross regional product totalled 58,465m. roubles in 2000, equivalent to 40,277 roubles per head. The Oblast's main industrial centres are at Archangel, Severodvinsk, Novodvinsk and, in the south-east, Kotlas. At the end of 2001 there were 1,764 km (1,096 miles) of railways and 7,228 km of paved roads on the Oblast's territory. Its main ports are Archangel, Onega, Mezen and, in the Nenets AOk, Naryan Mar (sea- and river-ports).

The Oblast's agriculture, which employed just 5.1% of the labour force in 2001, consists mainly of potato and vegetable production, animal husbandry (livestock and reindeer) and hunting. Total agricultural output in the Oblast amounted to a value of 5,274m. roubles in 2001, of which crop sales accounted for 55.3% and animal husbandry and hunting for 44.7%. The Oblast's industry, which employed 26.8% of the working population in 2001, is based on timber and timber-processing and woodworking (which accounted for 48.8% of industrial production in 2001). The territory produces a significant proportion of the Federation's timber and timber products. Other important areas of industry are the extraction of minerals (in particular, bauxite), petroleum and natural gas, electrical energy, mechanical engineering and metal-working, and the processing of fish products. In July 1998 it was announced that the federal Ministry of Finance was to allocate credit worth US $30m. for development of a diamond field in the Oblast, one of Russia's largest, run by Severoalmaz (Northern Diamonds), although repeated licensing problems delayed progress. Industrial output across the Oblast was worth 43,512m. roubles in 2001.

The Oblast's economically active population amounted to 759,000 in 2001, when 8.8% of the region's labour force were unemployed. The average monthly wage was

5,094.2 roubles in mid-2002. In 2001 the Oblast recorded a budgetary deficit of 73m. roubles. External trade in that year amounted to US $726.9m., of which $648.7m. were exports and $78.2m. were imports. Total foreign investment totalled $50.5m. in 2001. At 31 December 2001 there were 4,783 small businesses registered on the Oblast's territory.

Directory

Head of the Regional Administration (Governor): ANATOLII A. YEFREMOV; 163061 Archangel, pr. Troitskii 49; tel. (8182) 43-79-12; fax (8182) 43-21-12; internet www.arkhadm.gov.ru.

Chairman of the Regional Assembly of Deputies: VITALII S. FORTYGIN; 163061 Archangel, pl. Lenina 1; tel. (8182) 64-66-81; fax (8182) 64-66-30; e-mail ac@aosd .ru.

Chief Representative of Archangel Oblast in the Russian Federation: BORIS A. GAGARIN; 127006 Moscow, ul. M. Dmitrovka 3/10; tel. (095) 299-44-12.

Head of Archangel City Administration: OLEG V. NILOV; 163061 Archangel, pl. Lenina 5; tel. (8182) 65-64-84; fax (8182) 65-20-71; e-mail webmaster@arhcity.ru; internet www.arhcity.ru.

Nenets Autonomous Okrug

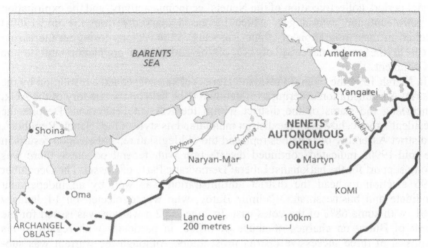

The Nenets Autonomous Okrug (AOk) is part of Archangel (Arkhangelsk) Oblast and, hence, the North-Western Federal Okrug and the Northern Economic Area. It is situated in the north-east of European Russia, its coastline lying, from west to east, on the White, Barents and Kara Seas, parts of the Arctic Ocean. Most of the territory lies within the Arctic Circle. Archangel proper lies to the south-west, but most of the Nenets southern border is with the Republic of Komi. At its eastern extremity the district touches the Yamal-Nenets AOk (part of Tyumen Oblast) and, stretching away to the north-east, the island of Novaya Zemlya, which forms a part of Archangel Oblast proper. The major river is the Pechora, which drains into the Pechora Gulf of the Barents Sea north of Naryan-Mar. The territory occupies an area of 176,700 sq km (68,200 sq miles) and extends some 300 km (190 miles) from south to north and 1,000 km from west to east. For administrative purposes it is divided into one city and two 'urban-type settlements'. According to the preliminary results of the census of 9–16 October 2002, the total population of the Nenets AOk was 41,500, giving a population density of 0.2 per sq km. Around 63.1% of the population inhabited urban areas. At 1 January 1997 estimated figures showed some 70.0% of the region's population were ethnic Russians, while 15.6% were Nenets and 9.5% Komi. The language spoken by the Nenets belongs to the Samoyedic group of Uralian languages, which is part of the Uralo-Altaic linguistic group. The district capital is at Naryan-Mar, which had an estimated population of 18,300 at 1 January 2002.

History

The Nenets were traditionally concerned with herding and breeding reindeer. A Samoyedic people, they are believed to have broken away from other Finno-Ugrian groups in around 3000 BC and migrated east where, in around 200 BC, they began to mix with Turkish-Altaic people. By the early 17th century AD their territory had come entirely under the control of the Muscovite state. The Russians established forts in the region, from which they collected fur tax.

The Nenets National Okrug was formed on 15 July 1929; in common with other national districts, it was reconstituted as an Autonomous Okrug in 1977. During the Soviet period, collectivization of the Nenets' economic activity, and the exploitation of petroleum and natural gas (which increased markedly from the mid-1960s) resulted in mass migration of ethnic Russians to the region, posing an increasing threat to the traditional way of life of the indigenous population and to the environment.

In March 1994 the federal President, Boris Yeltsin, suspended a resolution by the District Administration ordering a referendum to be held on the territory of the AOk, concerning the status of the district within the Russian Federation. Despite the President's move, however, the district maintained its style of the 'Nenets Republic'. A district Assembly of Deputies replaced the old legislature, and election results in the mid-1990s indicated continued disaffection with federal policies—there was strong support for the nationalist Liberal Democratic Party of Russia. The December 1996 election to head the district administration was won by an independent candidate and businessman, Vladimir Butov, who was re-elected on 14 January 2001, with some 68% of the votes cast. In June 2002 a warrant was issued for the arrest of Butov on charges of abuse of office, in particular with regard to his dismissal of three successive district prosecutors. Although the warrant was subsequently cancelled, a further federal arrest warrant against Butov was issued in July 2003, after he had allegedly assaulted a police-officer in St Petersburg; it was also reported that Butov had been convicted of two criminal offences prior to his being elected as governor, and that several other cases in which he was involved apparently remained unresolved. Butov also attracted criticism for his reputedly authoritarian style, while concern was repeatedly expressed during the early 2000s that he was frequently absent from the region, sometimes for several months at a time. A prominent source of opposition to Butov was believed to be the petroleum company, LUKoil, which objected to the preferable treatment granted in the Autonomous Okrug to the Nenets Oil Company (NNK), which Butov controlled.

Economy

As part of Archangel Oblast, the Nenets AOk is usually subsumed into the region's overall statistics, so few separate details are available. However, at the end of 2001 the AOk contained 167 km (103 miles) of paved roads. The AOk's major ports are Naryan-Mar and Amderma.

The territory's agriculture, which in 2001 employed 11.0% of the work-force and produced goods to a value of 206.3m. roubles, consists mainly of reindeer-breeding (around two-thirds of its territory are reindeer pasture), fishing, hunting and fur farming. (Crop sales accounted for just 8.2% of total revenue from agriculture in 2001.) There are substantial reserves of petroleum, natural gas and gas condensate in the Nenets AOk, which have yet to be fully exploited. In 1997 Exxon Arkhangelsk Ltd, an affiliate of Exxon of the USA (now ExxonMobil), purchased a 50% stake in the development of oilfields in Timan-Pechora, although it was forced to withdraw after problems with tender arrangements. In 1998 Governor Vladimir Butov gave support to plans for the construction of a petroleum transportation terminal on the Barents Sea coast, which would allow the AOk to benefit from the potential wealth to be generated by the exploitation of the Timan-Pechora oilfields. Butov's relations with the major energy companies Gazprom and LUKoil were reported to be strained during the late 1990s and early 2000s, and petroleum deposits in the region were developed only slowly, although a new sea terminal for petroleum transportation was opened at Varandei in August 2000. The annual capacity of this terminal, which was constructed by LUKoil and which was to be served by its fleet of ice-breaking tankers, was over 1m. metric tons, although this was expected to expand. Other sectors of the district's industry included the processing of agricultural products and the generation of electricity. Industry employed 16.1% of the AOk's work-force in 2001, and produced output worth 5,711m. roubles.

The economically active population in the territory numbered 24,000 in 2001, when 7.2% of the labour force were unemployed, compared with 20.0% in 1999. In mid-2002 the average monthly wage of 12,830.1 roubles was among the highest in the Russian Federation. The Nenets government budget recorded a deficit of 17m. roubles in 2001. In the late 1990s the AOk was successful in attracting foreign investment, which totalled US $346.0m. in 1999. In 2001, however, total foreign investment amounted to just $20.1m. In December 2001 there were 165 small businesses registered in the district.

Directory

Head of the District Administration: VLADIMIR YA. BUTOV; 164700 Archangel obl., Nenets AOk, Naryan-Mar, ul. Smidovicha 20; tel. (47833) 4-21-13; fax (81853) 4-22-69.

Chairman of the Deputies' Assembly: VITALINA F. GLAZUNOVA; 164700 Archangel obl., Nenets AOk, Naryan-Mar, ul. Smidovicha 20; tel. (81853) 4-21-59; fax (81853) 4-20-11; e-mail pred@atnet.ru.

Representation of the Nenets Autonomous Okrug in Archangel Oblast: Archangel.

Chief Representative of the Nenets Autonomous Okrug in the Russian Federation: TATYANA A. MALYSHEVA; 127025 Moscow, ul. Novyi Arbat 19/1120; tel. (095) 203-90-39; fax (095) 203-91-74; e-mail neninter@atnet.ru.

Head of Naryan-Mar City Administration (Mayor): YURII RODIONOVSKII; 164700 Archangel obl., Nenets AOk, Naryan-Mar, ul. Lenina 12; tel. (81853) 2-21-53; fax (095) 253-51-00.

Kaliningrad Oblast

Kaliningrad Oblast forms the westernmost part of the Russian Federation, being an exclave separated from the rest of the country by Lithuania (which borders it to the north and east) and Belarus. Poland lies to the south. The Oblast falls within the North-Western Federal Okrug and is sometimes included in the North-Western Economic Area. The city of Kaliningrad (formerly Königsberg) is sited at the mouth of the River Pregolya (Pregel), where it flows into the Vistula Lagoon, an inlet of the Baltic Sea. The other main river is the Neman (Memel). The Oblast occupies 15,100 sq km (5,830 sq miles), of which 13,300 sq km are dry land, the rest of its territory comprising the freshwater Kurshskaya (Curonian) Lagoon, in the north-east, and the Vistula Lagoon. The coastline is 140 km (87 miles) long. The Oblast is divided into 13 administrative districts and 22 cities. According to the preliminary results of the census of 9–16 October 2002, it had a total population of 955,200 and its population density was, therefore, 63.3 per sq km. Some 77.7% of the population inhabited urban areas. The Oblast's administrative centre is at Kaliningrad, which had a population of 430,300, according to provisional census results.

History

The city of Kaliningrad was founded in 1255, as Königsberg, during German expansion eastwards. The chief city of East Prussia, it was the original royal capital of the Hohenzollerns (from 1871 the German emperors). After the Second World War it was annexed by the USSR and received its current name (1945). Most of the German population was deported and the city almost completely destroyed and rebuilt. On 7 April 1946 the region became an administrative-political entity within the Russian Federation.

In mid-1993 Kaliningrad Oblast requested the status of a republic, a petition refused by the federal authorities. On 15 October the Regional Soviet was disbanded by the head of the Regional Administration for failing to support the state presidency's struggle against the federal parliament. A regional Duma was later formed. In January 1996 Yurii Matochkin was one of the first oblast governors to sign a power-sharing agreement with the federal Government. Leonid Gorbenko, an independent candidate, was elected as Governor in October.

Despite the establishment of a 'free-trade zone' in the Oblast in 1991, Kaliningrad was bedevilled by particularly high levels of corruption in the 1990s. Relations with the exclave's neighbours were also troubled at times. German groups in Russia (primarily those resident along the River Volga) and Russian ultra-nationalists made unsuccessful demands for increased German influence in the management of the Oblast. In 1998 a proposal that the region be awarded the status of an autonomous Russian Baltic republic within Russia was submitted to the Federation Council. However, Gorbenko opposed plans for greater autonomy, instead supporting the growth of closer ties with Belarus. In gubernatorial elections held in two rounds in November 2000, Gorbenko was defeated by Adm. Vladimir Yegorov, the former Commander of the Baltic Fleet. Yegorov was regarded as a pro-presidential candidate, and was elected largely on the basis of his anti-corruption campaign. In 2002, as the European Union (EU) prepared to admit several Eastern European countries, including Lithuania and Poland, in 2004, the status of Kaliningrad became an increasing source of contention; in particular, Russia initially objected to proposals that residents of Kaliningrad would require visas to travel to metropolitan Russia. In November 2002, at an EU-Russia summit meeting, held in Brussels, Belgium, Russia finally agreed to an EU proposal for simplified visa arrangements. According to the compromise accord, multiple-transit travel documentation would be made available to residents of the exclave travelling by motor vehicle; the new regulations took effect from 1 July 2003. The EU also agreed to undertake a feasibility study on the possibility of allowing high-speed, sealed trains to operate between the exclave and the remainder of the Federation, thus negating the need for transit documents. In August the oblast prosecutor's office commenced criminal proceedings against former Governor Gorbenko, on charges of abuse of office.

Economy

Kaliningrad Oblast is noted for containing more than 90% of the world's reserves of amber. Within Russia it also became noted for its reputedly flourishing parallel ('black') market, with federal officials suggesting in January 1999 that the region had become a major transhipment point for illegal drugs. Kaliningrad also suffers from a military and industrial legacy of severe pollution. In 2000 its official gross regional product totalled 26,151m. roubles, or 27,592 roubles per head—the lowest level in the North-Western Federal Okrug. Its main industrial centres are at Kaliningrad, Gusev and Sovetsk. There are rail services to Lithuania and Poland, and there were 617 km of railways on the Oblast's territory at the end of 2001. At that time Kaliningrad Oblast's road network consisted of 4,589 km of paved roads. Its main ports are at Kaliningrad and Baltiisk.

Kaliningrad Oblast's agricultural sector, which employed 10.4% of its work-force in 2001, consists mainly of animal husbandry, including fur farming, and vegetable growing and fishing. Total agricultural output was worth 4,143m. roubles in 2001, of which crop sales generated 39.2% and animal husbandry 61.8%. The Oblast has substantial reserves of petroleum (around 275m. metric tons), more than 2,500m. cu m in peat deposits and 50m. tons of coal. The industrial sector employed 19.0% of its working population and generated 18,199m. roubles in 2001. The region's main industries are mechanical engineering and metal-working, the processing of fishing and forestry products, electrical energy, and the production and processing of amber. In 2000 some 749,000 tons of petroleum were extracted. A plant to construct German BMW automobiles for the Russian market opened in 1999. The continuing strategic geopolitical situation of Kaliningrad Oblast meant that demilitarization proceeded at a much slower pace than it did elsewhere in the former USSR; in 1998 there were still around 200,000 members of military units in the Oblast.

The economically active population numbered 446,000 in 2001, when some 9.6% of the labour force were unemployed, compared with 15.4% in the previous year. The average monthly wage was 3,832.1 roubles in mid-2002. The 2001 regional budget recorded a deficit of 29m. roubles, and the region is largely dependent on federal subsidies. Foreign investment totalled US $24.6m. in that year, and there were hopes that the region would be favoured as an entry point to the Russian market. In 2001 export trade amounted to $386.8m., and imports were worth $984.4m. At 31 December 2001 there was a total of 7,576 small businesses registered in the region.

Directory

Head of the Regional Administration (Governor): Adm. VLADIMIR G. YEGOROV; 236007 Kaliningrad, ul. D. Donskogo 1; tel. (0112) 46-75-45; fax (0112) 46-38-62; e-mail egorov@gov.kaliningrad.ru; internet www.gov.kaliningrad.ru.

Chairman of the Regional Duma: VLADIMIR A. NIKITIN; 236000 Kaliningrad, ul. Kirova 17; tel. (0112) 22-84-39; fax (0112) 22-84-82; e-mail nikitin@duma .kaliningrad.org; internet duma.kaliningrad.org.

Chief Representative of Kaliningrad Oblast in the Russia Federation: YEVGENII I. IZOTOV; 114049 Moscow, ul. Zhitnaya 14/3; tel. (095) 258-44-01; e-mail rngs@ online.ru.

Head of Kaliningrad City Administration (Mayor): YURII A. SAVENKO; 236040 Kaliningrad, ul. Pobedy 1; tel. (0112) 21-14-82; fax (0112) 21-16-77; e-mail cityhall@klgd.ru; internet www.klgd.ru.

Republic of Kareliya

The Republic of Kareliya (Karelia) is situated in the north-west of Russia, on the edge of the Eastern European Plain. The Republic forms part of the North-Western Federal Okrug and the Northern Economic Area. It is bordered by Finland to the west. Murmansk Oblast lies to the north and, beyond the White Sea, to the north-east, and Archangel Oblast lies to the east, Vologda Oblast to the south-east and Leningrad Oblast to the south. Kareliya contains some 83,000 km (51,540 miles) of waterways, including its major rivers, the Kem and the Vyg, and its numerous lakes (the Ladoga—Ladozhskoye, and the Onega—Onezhskoye, being the largest and second largest lakes in Europe, respectively). A canal system 225 km long, the Belomorkanal (White Sea Canal), connects the Kareliyan port of Belomorsk to St Petersburg. One-half of Kareliya's territory is forested and much of the area on the White Sea coast is marshland. It lies, on average, 300 m–400 m above sea level. Kareliya measures some 600 km south–north and 400 km west–east and occupies an area of 172,400 sq km (66,560 sq miles). It comprises 16 administrative districts and 13 cities. According to the preliminary results of the census of 9–16 October 2002, the Republic had a total population of 716,700, giving a population density of 4.2 per sq km. Some 75.0% of the Republic's population inhabited urban areas. In 1989 some 10.0% of the population were Kareliyans (Finnish—also known as Karjala or Karyala, Korela and Karyalainen) and 73.6% Russians. The dominant religion among Kareliyans, and in the Republic as a whole, is Orthodox Christianity. The Kareliyan language consists of three dialects of Finnish (Livvi, Karjala and Lyydiki), which are all strongly influenced by Russian. In 1989, however, more than one-half of the ethnically Kareliyan population spoke Russian as their first language. The capital of Kareliya is at Petrozavodsk, with a population of 266,200, according to provisional census results.

History

Kareliya was an independent, Finnish-dominated state in medieval times. In common with much of present-day Finland, in the 16th century the area came under Swedish hegemony, before being annexed by Russia in 1721. A Kareliyan Labour Commune was formed on 8 June 1920 and became an autonomous republic within the USSR in July 1923. A Karelo-Finnish SSR (Union Republic), including territory annexed from Finland, was created in 1940. However, part of its territory was ceded to the Russian Federation in 1946; in 1956 Kareliya subsequently resumed the status of an ASSR within the Russian Federation.

The Republic declared sovereignty on 9 August 1990, and was renamed the Republic of Kareliya in November 1991; a republican Constitution was adopted in January 1994. In April elections took place to a new bicameral legislature, the Legislative Assembly (comprising a Chamber of the Republic and a Chamber of Representatives). The premier, Viktor Stepanov, who was vested with a quasi-presidential status as the republican head, was prominent in urging greater decentralization in the Russian Federation. On 17 May 1998 Stepanov was narrowly defeated in the second round of direct elections to the premiership by the former Mayor of Petrozavodsk, Sergei Katanandov. In December 2001 Stepanov (who had hitherto been widely regarded as the most popular potential challenger to the incumbent president in the forthcoming elections) was appointed as the Republic's representative to the Federation Council, the upper chamber of the Russian Federal Assembly. Katanandov was re-elected for a third term of office on 28 April 2002, receiving 54% of the votes cast. Non-partisan candidates were elected to a majority of seats in the concurrent legislative elections.

Economy

The economy of Kareliya is largely based on its timber industry. In 2000 its gross regional product was 28,509m. roubles, equivalent to 37,310 roubles per head. Its major industrial centres include those at Petrozavodsk, Sortavala and Kem. At the end of 2001 there were 2,105 km of railway lines and 6,637 km of paved roads in the Republic. In the mid-1990s Russia's first privately operated railway was constructed on Kareliya's territory. The Republic is at an important strategic point on Russia's roadways, linking the industrially developed regions of Russia with the major northern port of Murmansk. Kareliya's main port is at Petrozavodsk.

Kareliya's agriculture, which employed just 5.1% of the work-force in 2001, consists mainly of animal husbandry. In that year total production within the sector was equivalent to a value of 2,124m. roubles, of which crop sales contributed 40.9% and animal husbandry 51.1%. The Republic ranks among the leading producers of rosin and turpentine in the Russian Federation. An important agreement with the city of Moscow, which had need for construction materials, promised an increase in natural-stone production from some 3,000 cu m in 1998 to 20,000 cu m by 2002. The Republic also has important mineral reserves. Kareliya's main industries, apart from the processing of forestry products, are food-processing, ferrous metallurgy, the production of electrical energy, and the extraction of iron ore and muscovite (mica). Industry engaged some 26.2% of the Republic's labour force in 2001, when total output within the sector was worth 29,994m. roubles. The Republic's major enterprise, Segezhabumprom, is one of the world's largest pulp and paper manufacturers; it was reorganized as a joint-stock company in 1999. In the first quarter of 2000 Kareliya produced over 50% of the paper bags, over 30% of the newsprint and over 22% of all paper in the Russian Federation.

The economically active population totalled 395,000 in 2001, when 8.7% of the labour force were unemployed. The average monthly wage in the Republic was 4,613.8 roubles in mid-2002. The republican budget recorded a deficit of 130m. roubles in 2001. In that year international exports from the Republic were worth US $569.7m., and the value of imports from abroad was $117.2m. Foreign investment in Kareliya at that time amounted to $41.7m. There were 79 foreign joint enterprises in Kareliya in 2000, of which 39 had Finnish partners. At 31 December 2001 there were some 3,003 small businesses operating in the Republic.

Directory

Chairman of the Government (Head of the Republic): SERGEI L. KATANANDOV; 185028 Kareliya, Petrozavodsk, pr. Lenina 19; tel. (8142) 76-41-41; fax (8142) 76-41-48; e-mail government@karelia.ru; internet www.gov.karelia.ru.

Chairman of the Chamber of Representatives of the Legislative Assembly: NIKOLAI I. LEVIN; 185610 Kareliya, Petrozavodsk, ul. Kuibysheva 5; tel. (8142) 78-02-95; fax (8142) 78-28-27; e-mail parl@karelia.ru; internet www.gov.karelia.ru/gov/LA.

Chairman of the Chamber of the Republic of the Legislative Assembly: VLADIMIR V. SHILNIKOV; 185610 Kareliya, Petrozavodsk, ul. Kuibysheva 5; tel. (8142) 77-27-48; fax (8142) 78-28-27; e-mail parl@karelia.ru; internet www.gov.karelia.ru/gov/LA.

Chief Representative of the Republic of Kareliya in the Russian Federation: ANATOLII A. MARKOV; 101934 Moscow, per. Arkhangelskii 1; tel. (095) 207-87-24; fax (095) 208-03-18.

Head of Petrozavodsk City Administration (Mayor): VIKTOR N. MASLYAKOV; 185630 Kareliya, Petrozavodsk, pr. Lenina 2/501; tel. (8142) 78-35-70; fax (8142) 78-47-53; e-mail admcity@karelia.ru.

Republic of Komi

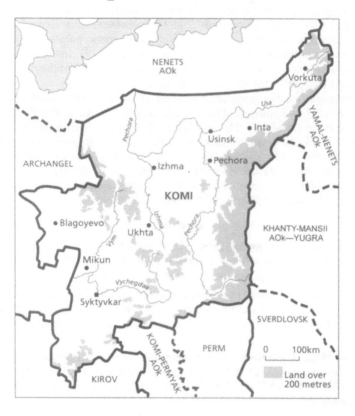

The Republic of Komi is situated in the north-east of European Russia. Its northern border lies some 50 km within the Arctic Circle. It forms part of the North-Western Federal Okrug and the Northern Economic Area. Mountains of the Northern, Circumpolar and Polar Urals occupy the eastern part of the Republic. Its major rivers are the Pechora, the Vychegda and the Mezen. Komi is bordered to the west by Archangel Oblast, to the north by Archangel's Nenets Autonomous Okrug (AOk), and to the east by Tyumen Oblast (both the Oblast proper and its two Autonomous Okrugs, those of the Khanty-Mansii—Yugra and the Yamal-Nenets). To the south Komi borders Kirov Oblast, Perm Oblast (including the Komi-Permyak AOk) and Sverdlovsk Oblast. Some 90% of its territory is taiga (forested marshland), while the extreme north-east of the Republic lies within the Arctic tundra zone. The Republic occupies an area of 415,900 sq km (160,580 sq miles), and comprises 12 administrative districts and 10 cities. According to the preliminary results of the census of 9–16 October 2002, it had a total population of 1,019,000, and a population density, therefore, of 2.5 per sq km. Some 75.3% of the population lived in urban areas. In 1989 some 23.3% of the Republic's inhabitants were Komi, a Finno-Ugrian people, and 57.7% were ethnic Russians. The predominant religion in the region is Orthodox Christianity, although among the Komi this faith is combined with strong animist traditions. There were reports of the existence in the Republic of members of the reclusive *skritniki* sect, which has links to the Orthodox Old Believers. The language of the Komi population, spoken as a native tongue by some 74%, belongs to the Finnic branch of the Uralo-Altaic family. Komi's capital is at Syktyvkar, which had a population of 230,000, according to the provisional results of the 2002 census. The Republic's second largest city is Ukhta (103,500).

History

The Komi (known historically as the Zyryans or the Permyaks) are descended from inhabitants of the river basins of the Volga, the Kama, the Pechora and the Vychegda. From the 12th century Russian settlers began to inhabit territory along the Vychegda, and later the Vym, rivers. The Vym subsequently acquired a strategic significance as the main route along which Russian colonists advanced to Siberia, and Ust-Sysolsk (now Syktyvkar), the territory's oldest city, was founded in 1586. The number of Slavs increased after the territory was annexed by Russia in 1478. The region soon acquired importance as the centre of mining and metallurgy, following the discovery of copper and silver ores in 1491. In 1697 petroleum was discovered in the territory; the first refinery was built by F. Pryadunov in 1745. The Komi were renowned as shrewd commercial traders and exploited important trade routes between Archangel and Siberia, via the Vyatka-Kama basin. Trade in fish, furs and game animals developed in the 17th century, while coal, timber, iron ore and paper became significant in the years prior to the Russian Revolution. The Komi Autonomous Oblast was established on 22 August 1921 and became an ASSR in 1931.

The Komi Republic declared its sovereignty on 30 August 1990. A new republican Constitution was adopted on 17 February 1994, establishing a quasi-presidential premier at the head of government and a State Council as the legislature; the territory became known as the Republic of Komi. In March 1996 the republican and federal Governments signed a power-sharing treaty. The Republic repudiated its declaration of sovereignty in September 2001, following a ruling of the federal Supreme Court, which stated that over one-half of the provision's declarations were in contravention of federal law. The republican presidential election, held on 16 December, was won by Vladimir Torlopov, hitherto Chairman of the republican State Council, who received 40% of the votes cast, while the incumbent, Yurii Spiridonov, received 35%. Torlopov, an ethnic Komi, received the support of the liberal Yabloko party, whereas Spiridonov's supporters included the pro-Government Unity and Father-land-United Russia party. In May 2002 Torlopov signed an agreement with federal President Vladimir Putin annulling the power-sharing treaty signed with Komi in 1996. Following legislative elections, held on 2 March 2003, repeat elections were required in six of the 30 electoral districts, in which votes 'against all candidates' had received the greatest share of votes cast. (The overall rate of participation by the electorate was 44.1%, and 27% of the votes cast were 'against all candidates'.) Only six of the incumbent legislators were returned to office. It was reported that the new State Council was dominated by representatives of business interests, particularly the energy industry; in all, some 15 corporate executives were believed to have been elected to the legislature. In April 2003 the recently appointed Presidential Representative in the North-Western Federal Okrug, Valentina Matviyenko, stated that the recent election results should serve as an indicator to the republican authorities of the need for change, stating that the economic and social situation in the republic was a great cause of concern.

Economy

The Republic of Komi is Russia's second largest fuel and energy base. Apart from a wealth of natural resources, it is strategically placed close to many of Russia's major industrial centres and has a well-developed transport network. It also contains Europe's largest area of virgin forest—approximately one-third of its massive forest stock (amounting to 2,800m. cu m) has never been cut. Komi had a high ranking within the Federation in terms of gross domestic product per head and it possessed a wealth of natural resources. However, in order to fulfil its economic potential the Republic needed to improve its export performance and diversify its economy into higher value-added activities. In 2000 gross regional product in the Republic amounted to 72,346m. roubles, equivalent to 64,068 roubles per head—one of the highest figures in Russia. Komi's major industrial centres are at Syktyvkar, Ukhta and Sosnogorsk. At the end of 2001 the Republic contained 1,692 km (1,051 miles) of railway lines and 5,345 km of paved roads. In September 2002 Russia's first privately built rail link was opened by the domestic metals producer SUAL Holding. The new, 158-km railway line connects the Sredne-Timanskoye bauxite reserves with the national railway network.

Komi's agriculture, which employed just 4.7% of the work-force in 2000, consists mainly of animal husbandry, especially reindeer-breeding. Total production within the sector amounted to a value of 3,330m. roubles in 2001, of which 46.0% was generated by crop sales and 54.0% by animal husbandry. Ore-mining was developing from the mid-1990s: the Republic contained the country's largest reserves of bauxite, titanium, manganese and chromium ore. It also accounted for around one-half of northern Europe's petroleum stock and one-third of its natural gas reserves. Total industrial production, which was based on the production and processing of petroleum and natural gas (accounting for more than 50% of output, and dominated by LUKoil), the production of coal and electrical energy, and the processing of forestry products, was worth 68,499m. roubles in 2001, when the sector employed 24.0% of the work-force. The Republic contains the Vorgashorskaya coal mine, the largest in Europe. SUAL Holding planned further to develop the aluminium industry in the Republic.

In 2001 the economically active population numbered 596,000, and 14.0% of the labour force were unemployed—the highest level in the North-Western Federal Okrug. In mid-2002 the average monthly wage in the Republic was relatively high, at 6,274.0 roubles. In 2001 there was a budgetary deficit of 50m. roubles. Foreign trade was encouraged, with, for example, an agreement being reached with Iran in December 1998. In 2001 the value of exports from the Republic amounted to US $1,009.8m., compared with $102.8m. in imports to the Republic. Foreign investment in Komi was substantial in the late 1990s, amounting to $218.1m. in 1998, although the level of investment had declined to $76.8m. by 2001. However, foreign investment was reported to have increased by more than three-fold in 2002. From the mid-1990s a number of joint ventures were established in Komi, and important foreign investors included the Finnish company Fortum Oil and Gas Oy, which established SeverTEK, a joint venture with LUKoil. In March 2002 the South African company Anglo-American purchased a majority stake in the Republic's leading paper manufacturer, Syktyvkar Forest Enterprise. At 31 December 2001 there were 3,729 small businesses in operation in the Republic.

Directory

Chairman of the Government (Head of the Republic): VLADIMIR A. TORLOPOV; 167010 Komi, Syktyvkar, ul. Kommunisticheskaya 9; tel. (8212) 28-51-05; fax (8212) 28-52-52; internet www.rkomi.ru.

Chairman of the State Council: IVAN YE. KULAKOV; 167000 Komi, Syktyvkar, ul. Kommunisticheskaya 9; tel. (8212) 28-55-08; fax (8212) 42-44-90; internet www .rkomi.ru/gossov/gossovet/gs_rk.html.

Chief Representative of the Republic of Komi in the Russian Federation: NIKOLAI N. KOCHURIN; 125367 Moscow, Volokolamskoye shosse 62; tel. and fax (095) 490-10-80.

Head of Syktyvkar City Administration: SERGEI M. KATUNIN; 167000 Komi, Syktyvkar, ul. Babushkina 22; tel. (8212) 29-44-70.

Leningrad Oblast

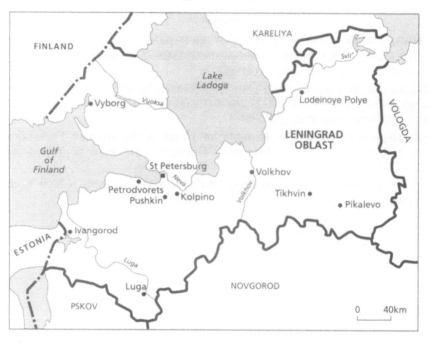

Leningrad Oblast is situated in the north-west of the Eastern European Plain. It lies on the Gulf of Finland, an inlet of the Baltic Sea, and forms part of the North-Western Federal Okrug and the North-Western Economic Area. The Republic of Kareliya (Karelia) lies to the north and the oblasts of Vologda to the east and Novgorod and Pskov to the south. There is an international border with Estonia to the west and with Finland to the north-west. Two-thirds of the Oblast are forested and over one-10th is swampland. Its main rivers are the Neva, the Sayas, the Luga and the Vuoksa. Lake Ladoga, the largest lake in Europe, with a surface area of 17,800 sq km, forms a partial border with Kareliya, and the southern tip of Lake Onega (9,700 sq km) also lies within Leningrad Oblast. The Oblast, including St Petersburg city, occupies 85,900 sq km (33,166 sq miles). It is divided into 17 administrative districts and 31 cities. According to the preliminary results of the census of 9–16 October 2002, its total population, excluding the St Petersburg city region, was 1,671,100, and some 66.4% of the population of the Oblast inhabited urban areas. Its administrative centre is in St Petersburg, now a federal city in its own right. The largest city within the Oblast proper is Gatchina (with an estimated population of 82,200 at 1 January 2002).

History

The city of St Petersburg (known as Petrograd in 1914–24 and Leningrad until 1991) was built in 1703. Leningrad Oblast, which was formed on 1 August 1927 out of the territories of five regions (Cherepovets, Leningrad, Murmansk, Novgorod and Pskov), was heavily industrialized during the Soviet period, particularly during

1926–40. The region did not change its name when the city reverted to the name of St Petersburg in October 1991.

In mid-1996 an agreement delimiting the division of powers between the federal and regional governments was signed. Later that year gubernatorial elections were held, which were won by an independent candidate, Vladimir Gustov. On 24 September 1998 the federal President, Boris Yeltsin, approved a proposal to merge the Oblast with the federal city of St Petersburg, although any immediate implementation seemed unlikely. Gustov resigned to take up the position of Deputy Prime Minister in September 1998, and his replacement, Valerii Serdyukov, confirmed his position on 5 September 1999, by securing 30% of the votes cast in an election contested by 16 candidates. The power-sharing agreement signed by the federal and regional authorities in 1996 was annulled in April 2002. In February 2003 the regional legislature approved an extension to the gubernatorial term of office from four to five years, to take effect from the forthcoming elections. Serdyukov was re-elected as Governor on 21 September 2003, receiving 56.5% of the votes cast, according to preliminary figures. Gustov was the second-placed candidate, with around 25% of the votes.

Although little formal progress towards the eventual merging of Leningrad Oblast with St Petersburg had been made by 2003, the appointment in that year of Valentina Matviyenko, known to be an enthusiastic supporter of the proposal, as Presidential Representative in the North-Western Federal Okrug, and her subsequent election, in October, as the Governor of St Petersburg, was believed likely to result in a revival of measures intended to result in the practical implementation of the scheme.

Economy

Leningrad Oblast's gross regional product amounted to 59,342m. roubles in 2000, equivalent to 35,528 roubles per head. Its main industrial centres are at St Petersburg, Vyborg (both major seaports), Sestroretsk and Kingisepp. A new port opened at Primorsk in December 2001, as part of the country's Baltic Pipeline System, to facilitate the transportation of petroleum. At the end of 2001 the region contained 2,811 km (1,747 miles) of railway track (of which 1,352 km were electrified in 1999) and 10,539 km of paved roads.

The Oblast's agriculture, which employed 12.0% of the working population in 2001, consists mainly of animal husbandry and vegetable production. Total agricultural output was worth 18,453m. roubles in 2001, of which crop sales contributed 40.1% and animal husbandry 59.9%. The region's timber reserves are estimated to cover 6.1m. ha (15m. acres). Its major industries are the processing of forestry and agricultural products, petroleum-refining and the production of electrical energy. Some 25.5% of the Oblast's work-force were engaged in industry in 2001, when industrial output amounted to a value of 74,326m. roubles.

The economically active population numbered 871,000 in 2001, when 6.9% of the labour force were unemployed—a relatively low figure compared with elsewhere in the Russian Federation, and a marked decrease compared with the figures recorded in 1998 and 1999, which had been in excess of 14%. The average monthly wage was 4,466.0 roubles in mid-2002. In 2001 the budget showed a surplus of 124m. roubles. The Oblast enjoys a relatively high level of external trade; in 2001 exports were worth US $2,115.4m., while imports amounted to $807.6m. Foreign investment amounted to $327.0m. in that year, compared with $190.7m. in 1998. In 2002 the American Chamber of Commerce in Russia, which unites US business interests, named Leningrad Oblast its 'region of the year', and annual growth of some 35.6% was reported in 2002, the highest of any federal subject. At the end of 2001 there were 9,377 small businesses registered in Leningrad Oblast.

Directory

Head of the Regional Administration (Governor): VALERII P. SERDYUKOV; 193311 St Petersburg, Suvorovskii pr. 67; tel. (812) 274-35-63; fax (812) 274-67-33; internet www.lenobl.ru.

Chairman of the Regional Legislative Assembly: VITALII N. KLIMOV; 193311 St Petersburg, Suvorovskii pr. 67; tel. (812) 274-68-73; fax (812) 274-85-39; e-mail klimov@assemblylenobl.ru; internet www.assemblylenobl.ru.

Chief Representative of Leningrad Oblast in the Russian Federation: ALEKSEI I. AKULOV; 121019 Moscow, ul. Novyi Arbat 15/1/1604; tel. (095) 291-33-55; e-mail plorf@mail.ru.

Murmansk Oblast

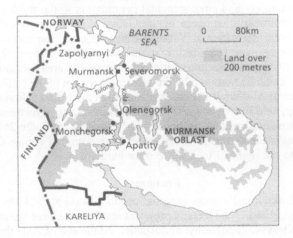

Murmansk Oblast occupies the Kola Peninsula, which neighbours the Barents Sea to the north and the White Sea to the south-east. It forms part of the North-Western Federal Okrug and the Northern Economic Area. The Oblast has international borders with Norway and Finland to the west and the Russian federal subject of Kareliya (Karelia) lies to the south. Much of its territory lies within the Arctic Circle. The major rivers in the Oblast are the Ponoi, the Varguza, the Umba, the Kola, the Niva and the Tulona. It has several major lakes, including the Imandra, Umbozero and Lovozero. The territory of the Oblast covers an area of 144,900 sq km (55,930 sq miles), extending some 400 km (250 miles) from south to north and 500 km from west to east. The climate in the Oblast is severe and changeable, influenced by cold fronts from the Arctic and warm, moist weather from the Atlantic. According to the preliminary results of the census of 9–16 October 2002, the total population of Murmansk Oblast was 893,300, giving a population density of 6.2 per sq km. Some 92.2% of the population inhabited urban areas. The Oblast is divided into five administrative districts and 16 cities. Its administrative centre is in the only large city of the region, Murmansk, a major seaport and tourist centre, which had a population of 336,700, according to provisional census results.

History

Murmansk city was founded in 1916, as a fishing port on the Barents Sea, and was known as Romanov-on-Murman (Romanov-na-Murmane) until the following year. After the Bolshevik Revolution of 1917 Murmansk region was a centre of anti-communist resistance until a peace treaty was signed with the Soviet Government on 13 March 1920. Murmansk Oblast was formed on 28 May 1938.

The development of industry in the region, particularly after the Second World War, resulted in a steady increase in population until the late 1950s. However, heavy industry, particularly the sulphurous emissions from the vast nickel-smelting works on the Kola Peninsula, was accused of causing major environmental damage by the neighbouring Nordic nations (agreement on the monitoring and limiting of this was achieved, to an extent, in mid-1996). The concentration of nuclear reactors on the

Kola Peninsula, considered to be the world's most hazardous, is also a major source of concern—in July 2002 the European Union pledged considerable funds to improving atomic safety and environmental degradation in the region.

In the 1990s political allegiances in the Oblast as a whole were fairly evenly balanced, with both the reformist Yabloko movement and the nationalist Liberal Democrats receiving over 10% of the votes cast overall in the 1995 and, more unusually, the 1999 general elections, although disparity by area was immense. Yurii Yevdokimov, a candidate favoured by the former Chairman of the National Security Council, Gen. (retd) Aleksandr Lebed, was elected in the Oblast's first direct poll to the governorship, held in November 1996. A power-sharing agreement was signed between the federal and regional authorities in November 1997. On 26 March 2000 Yevdokimov was re-elected as Governor, at a second round of voting. On 21 March 2002 elections to the regional legislature were held.

Economy

In 2000 Murmansk Oblast's gross regional product stood at 58,370m. roubles, or 59,747 roubles per head. The Oblast's principal industrial centres are at Murmansk, Monchegorsk, Kirovsk, Zapolyarnyi and Apatity. At the end of 2001 there were 891 km of railway track in the region, with Murmansk, Apatity, Olenegorsk and Kandalaksha the main railway junctions, and 2,472 km of paved roads. The port at Murmansk is Russia's sole all-weather Northern port, through which some 12m. metric tons of cargo pass every year. This is also the base for the world's only nuclear ice-breaker fleet, the Northern Fleet, and the scene of the Kursk submarine disaster in August 2000. There is an international airport at Murmansk, which operates flights to destinations in Finland, Norway and Sweden.

The Oblast's agricultural sector, which, owing to the extreme climate, employed just 1.9% of the work-force in 2001, consists mainly of fishing (the region produces 45% of the country's fish supplies), animal husbandry (livestock and reindeer) and vegetable production. In 2001 agricultural production generated a total of 1,449m. roubles, of which crop sales accounted for just 39.1%. The territory is rich in natural resources, including phosphates, iron ore and rare and non-ferrous metals. In 1985 the Shtokmanovsk gas-condensate deposit, the world's largest, was opened on the continental shelf of the Barents Sea. It was hoped that by 2005 the deposit would supply most of the north and north-west of the country. The region produces all of Russia's apatites, over 40% of its nickel, some 14% of its refined copper and about 11% of its concentrates of iron. Some 26.6% of the Oblast's working population were engaged in industry in 2001, when the industrial sector generated 51,639m. roubles. Its major industries are the production and enrichment of ores and ferrous metals, ore-mining, ferrous metallurgy, chemicals and petrochemicals, the production of electricity and food-processing. In 1999 LUKoil, the domestic petroleum producer, signed an agreement with Governor Yurii Yevdokimov, which made Murmansk a base for exploration of the Barents Sea, in association with the natural gas producer, Gazprom. LUKoil also agreed to accept payment in barter, in addition to money, for supplies of petroleum to the region. In late November 2002 LUKoil and three other large-scale domestic petroleum companies, Tyumen Oil Co (TNK— now TNK-BP), Siberian Oil Co (Sibneft) and Yukos, announced that they were to co-operate in the development of a deep-sea oil terminal in Murmansk, and connecting pipelines, at a projected cost of some US $4,500m., in an attempt to increase exports.

In 2001 the region's economically active population numbered some 577,000. Unemployment declined from the late 1990s, from 21.1% of the labour force in 1998, to 12.9% in 2001. In mid-2002 the average monthly wage in the Oblast was some 7,275.8 roubles, one of the highest in the Federation. The 2001 budget recorded a deficit of 522m. roubles. The Oblast's major exports are non-ferrous metals, fish products and apatite concentrate. In 2001 exports amounted to US $539.5m., and imports were worth $120.9m. Foreign investment totalled just $12.4m. in 2001. The Kola Centre for Business Development, employing Russian and US specialists, opened in Murmansk in 1997. It holds annual conventions bringing together companies from across and outside the Barents Region. At 31 December 2001 there were 3,186 small businesses registered in the Oblast.

Directory

Head of the Regional Administration (Governor): YURII A. YEVDOKIMOV; 183006 Murmansk, pr. Lenina 75; tel. (8152) 48-65-01; fax (8152) 45-10-04; e-mail evdokimov@murman.ru; internet gov.murman.ru.

Chairman of the Regional Duma: PAVEL A. SAZHINOV; 183016 Murmansk, ul. S. Perovskoi 2; tel. (8152) 45-36-72; fax (8152) 45-10-35; e-mail murduma@com.mels .ru.

Chief Representative of Murmansk Oblast in the Russian Federation: PETR I. ZELENOV; 103851 Moscow, ul. B. Nikitskaya 12; tel. (095) 229-69-77; fax (095) 229-53-51.

Head of Murmansk City Administration (Mayor): GENNADII G. GURYANOV; 183006 Murmansk, pr. Lenina 75; tel. (8152) 45-81-60.

Novgorod Oblast

Novgorod Oblast is situated in the north-west of the Eastern European Plain, some 500 km (just over 300 miles) north-west of Moscow and 180 km south of St Petersburg. It forms part of the North-Western Federal Okrug and the North-Western Economic Area. Tver Oblast lies to the south-east, Pskov Oblast to the south-west and Leningrad and Vologda Oblasts to the north. The territory's major rivers are the Msta, the Lovat and the outlet of Lake Ilmen, the Volkhov. Just over two-fifths of its territory is forested (either taiga—forested marshland—or mixed forest). The region contains the Valdai state national park. Novgorod territory covers an area of 55,300 sq km (21,350 sq miles) and extends 250 km from south to north and 385 km from west to east. It is divided into 21 administrative districts and 10 cities. According to the preliminary results of the census of 9–16 October 2002, the population of the Oblast was 694,700 and its population density, therefore, was 12.6 per sq km. The urban population was reckoned at 69.9% of the total. The region's administrative centre is at Great (Velikii) Novgorod, which lies on the River Volkhov, some 6 km from Lake Ilmen (the city had a population of some 217,200, according to provisional census results).

History

One of the oldest Russian cities, Great Novgorod remained a powerful principality after the dissolution of Kievan Rus, and even after the Mongol incursions further to the south-west. In 1478 Ivan III ('the Great'), prince of Muscovy and the first Tsar of All Russia, destroyed the Republic of Novgorod, a polity sometimes used as evidence for the rather spurious claim of a democratic tradition in Russia. Its wealth and importance, based on trade, declined after the foundation of St Petersburg. Novgorod Oblast was formed on 5 July 1944.

In the mid-1990s the region displayed a relatively high level of support for reformists and the centrist supporters of the federal Government of President Boris Yeltsin. The Oblast was permitted gubernatorial elections in December 1995, which were won by the pro-Yeltsin incumbent, Mikhail Prusak. Prusak's administration was characterized by his policy of pragmatic compromise with regard to the economy, spreading the region's economic benefits as widely as possible. Similar policies prevailed in the Duma, the members of which did not bear allegiance to any national political party. Prusak was re-elected for a further term of office on 5 September 1999, with approximately 90% of the votes cast. He combined demands for regional governors to be appointed rather than elected, and even for the end of direct elections to the federal presidency, with support for the purported (historical) 'Novgorod model' of federalism, property rights and subsidiarity. In May 2003 the oblast legislature voted to extend the gubernatorial term from four years to five, to take effect from the election due to be held later that year. Prusak was re-elected as Governor on 7 September, receiving 78.7% of the votes cast in a poll contested by seven candidates.

Economy

In 2000 Novgorod Oblast's gross regional product amounted to 20,920m. roubles, equivalent to 28,863 roubles per head. The Oblast's major industrial centres are at Great Novgorod and Staraya Russa (a 19th century resort town famous for its mineral and radon springs and its therapeutic mud). The major Moscow–St Petersburg road and rail routes pass through the region. At the end of 2001 there were 1,145 km (712 miles) of railways on the Oblast's territory. The road system, comprising 8,697 km of paved roads at that time, is its major transport network.

The region's agriculture, which employed 10.6% of the work-force in 2001, consists mainly of flax production and animal husbandry. Its major natural resource is timber: in the late 1990s some 2.5m. cu m were produced annually, but it was thought that there was potential for this amount to be expanded by four or five times. In 2001 total agricultural production amounted to a value of 5,320m. roubles, of which crop sales accounted for 58.6% and animal husbandry for 41.4%. The region's major industries include mechanical engineering and metal-working, chemicals and petrochemicals, wood-working, the processing of forestry and agricultural products, and electricity production. The industrial sector employed 26.2% of the working population in 2001, and generated 23,959m. roubles. Great Novgorod city is an important tourist destination, attracting around 1m. visitors annually.

The economically active population totalled 369,000 in 2001, when 6.4% of the labour force were unemployed. Those in employment in mid-2002 earned an average wage of 3,557.5 roubles per month. In 2001 the regional budget showed a deficit of 77m. roubles. In that year the external trade of the Oblast comprised US $298.4m. in exports and $113.5m. in imports. Legislative conditions for foreign investors in Novgorod Oblast were considered to be favourable in the 1990s, owing to a foreign company's exemption from all local taxes until its project returned a profit. The British-based multinational company Cadbury Schweppes invested $150m. in a chocolate factory in the region, which opened in 1996 and was the largest project the company had been involved in outside the United Kingdom. In 2001 total foreign investment in the region amounted to $50.1m. At 31 December 2001 there were 2,957 small businesses registered in the region.

Directory

Head of the Regional Administration (Governor): Mikhail M. Prusak; 173005 Velikii Novgorod, Sofiiskaya pl. 1; tel. (8162) 27-47-79; fax (8162) 13-13-30; e-mail infoserv@niac.natm.ru; internet region.adm.nov.ru.

Chairman of the Regional Duma: ANATOLII A. BOITSEV; 173005 Velikii Novgorod, Sofiiskaya pl. 1; tel. (8162) 27-47-79; fax (8162) 13-25-14.

Chief Representative of Novogorod Oblast in the Russian Federation: VLADIMIR N. PODOPRIGORA; 127006 Moscow, ul. M. Dmitrovka 3/219–220; fax (095) 299-40-04.

Head of Great (Velikii) Novgorod City Administration (Mayor): NIKOLAI I. GRAZHDANKIN; 173007 Velikii Novgorod, ul. B. Vasilyevskaya 4; tel. (81622) 7-25-40; fax (8162) 13-25-99; e-mail mayor@adm.nov.ru; internet www.adm.nov.ru.

Pskov Oblast

Pskov Oblast is situated on the Eastern European Plain. The Oblast forms part of the North-Western Federal Okrug and the North-Western Economic Area. It has international borders with Belarus to the south and Latvia and Estonia to the west. During the first half of the 1990s Estonia and Latvia questioned Russia's sovereignty of parts of Pskov Oblast and by the beginning of the 2000s there had still been no formal ratification of the now accepted border delimitations. Smolensk Oblast lies to the south-east, Tver and Novgorod Oblasts to the east and Leningrad Oblast to the north-east. Pskov's major river is the Velikaya and around two-fifths of its territory are forested. On its border with Estonia lie the Pskovskoye (Pihkva) and Chudskoye (Peipsi) lakes. Pskov Oblast covers an area of 55,300 sq km (21,350 sq miles) and is divided into 24 administrative districts and 14 cities. According to the preliminary results of the census of 9–16 October 2002, the population numbered 760,900 and the population density was, therefore, 13.8 per sq km; some 66.1% of inhabitants lived in urban areas. Around 94.3% of the territory's inhabitants were ethnic Russian in 1989. The Oblast's administrative centre is at Pskov, which had a population of 202,700 in October 2002, according to provisional census results. The second largest city is Velikiye Luki (105,000).

History

Pskov city was founded in 903, and in 1242 was the the area in which Muscovite Prince Aleksandr Nevskii defeated an army of Teutonic Knights, who sought to expand eastwards. The Muscovite state finally acquired the region in 1510. The Oblast was created on 23 August 1944. Some territory to the south of Lake Pskov was transferred from Estonia to Pskov Oblast in 1945, remaining a cause for dispute between newly independent Estonia and Russia in the 1990s. In 1995 Estonia formally renounced any territorial claim, but it remained eager to secure Russian acknowledgement of the 1920 Treaty of Tartu (by which Estonia had been awarded the disputed territory), which would render the Soviet occupation of the Baltic republic illegal.

The Oblast was a traditional bastion of support for the extreme nationalist policies of Vladimir Zhirinovskii; a gubernatorial election was held on 21 October 1996, which was won by Yevgenii Mikhailov, a former Liberal Democrat deputy. The eastward expansion of the North Atlantic Treaty Organization (NATO) was a major issue in the election campaign, as were proposals that the regional Government receive a share of the customs revenue generated by trade with the Baltic states. As Governor, Mikhailov visited both Chechnya and the Serbian province of Kosovo and Metohija in the Federal Republic of Yugoslavia (now Serbia and Montenegro), reflecting the high levels of support for him among the military (accounting for approximately one-10th of the population of Pskov Oblast). Mikhailov was re-elected as Governor in November 2000. Legislative elections were held on 31 March 2002.

Economy

In 2000 Pskov Oblast's gross regional product amounted to 17,110m. roubles, equivalent to 21,493 roubles per head. The Oblast's principal industrial centres are at Pskov and Velikiye Luki. At the end of 2001 there were 1,092 km of railway track in the region and 9,968 km of paved roads. There is an airport at Pskov, which was upgraded to international status in the late 1990s.

In 1996–98 a federal programme for the socio-economic development of Pskov Oblast invested some 1,500,000m. old roubles in the improvement of agriculture in the region. Agricultural activity, which employed 18.2% of the work-force in 2001, consists mainly of animal husbandry and the production of flax. Fishing is an important source of income in the north of the territory. Total output in the sector amounted to a value of 6,151m. roubles in 2001, of which crop sales generated 54.6% and animal husbandry 45.4%. The region's major industries are the production of electricity, mechanical engineering and metal-working, and food-processing. According to local official sources, industry in the Oblast had been completely privatized by 1995, although it was severely affected by the 1998 financial crisis, and the proportion of the working population employed in the sector declined by more than one-quarter in 1995–2000. Industry employed 20.7% of the working population in 2001, and generated 11,916m. roubles. Owing to the Oblast's three international borders, there are two representatives of foreign consulates, Latvian and Estonian, operating in the region. Pskov's main international trading partners were Estonia, Finland and Germany.

Pskov Oblast's economically active population numbered 375,000 in 2001, when 10.3% of the labour force were unemployed. In mid-2002 those in employment earned, on average, 2,954.6 roubles per month, reflecting Pskov's status as one of the poorer areas of the Russian Federation. There was a budgetary deficit of 16m. roubles in 2001. In that year external trade amounted to a value of just US $114.4m. in exports and $165.8m. in imports, while foreign investment in the region totalled just $5.2m. At 31 December 2001 2,846 small businesses were registered in the Oblast.

Directory

Head of the Regional Administration (Governor): YEVGENII E. MIKHAILOV; 180001 Pskov, ul. Nekrasova 23; tel. (8122) 16-22-03; fax (8122) 16-03-90; e-mail glava@obladmin.pskov.ru; internet www.pskov.ru.

Chairman of the Regional Assembly of Deputies: YURII A. SHCHMATOV; 180001 Pskov, ul. Nekrasova 23; tel. (8122) 16-24-44; fax (8122) 16-00-51.

Chief Representative of Pskov Oblast in the Russian Federation: IGOR P. NOVOSELOV; Moscow; tel. (095) 928-84-43; fax (095) 928-07-95.

Head of Pskov City Administration (Mayor): MIKHAIL YA. KHORONEN; 180000 Pskov, ul. Nekrasova 22; tel. (8122) 16-26-67; internet www.pskov.ellink.ru.

St Petersburg Federal City

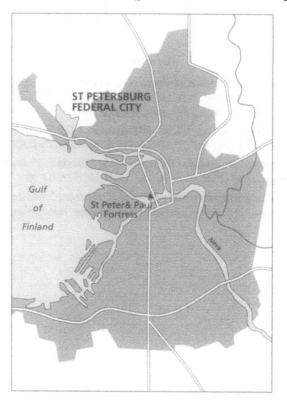

St Petersburg (Sankt-Peterburg) is a seaport at the mouth of the River Neva, which drains into the easternmost part of the Gulf of Finland (part of the Baltic Sea). St Petersburg is included in the North-Western Federal Okrug and the North-Western Economic Area. The city's territory, including a total of 42 islands in the Neva delta, occupies an area of 570 sq km (220 sq miles—making it the smallest of Russia's federal subjects), of which its waterways comprise around 10%. There are more than 580 bridges in the city and surrounding area, including 20 drawbridges. According to the preliminary results of the census of 9–16 October 2002, the population of the city was 4,669,400, making it Russia's second largest city.

History

St Petersburg was founded by Tsar Peter—Petr I ('the Great') in 1703, as a 'window on the West', and was the Russian capital from 1712 to 1918. At the beginning of the First World War, in 1914, the city was renamed Petrograd. Following the fall of the Tsar and the Bolshevik Revolution in 1917, the Russian capital was moved back to Moscow. A revolt at the naval base of Kronstadt, west of mainland Petrograd, in March 1921 presented one of the most serious challenges to the nascent Bolshevik authorities, as the island had hitherto been renowned as a stronghold of support for the Bolsheviks; the rebels, who were protesting against the steady centralization of

120   **www.europaworld.com**

powers, were quashed by troops led by Trotskii (Lev Bronstein), and several thousand deaths resulted on both sides. In 1924 the city was renamed Leningrad. During the Second World War it was besieged by German troops for 870 days, between November 1941 and January 1944. In June 1991 the citizens of the city voted to restore the name of St Petersburg, which took effect from October. On 24 September 1998 the federal President, Boris Yeltsin, approved the administrative merger of the city with Leningrad Oblast, although there was no indication when, or if, the unification (which would be subject to a referendum) would actually occur.

In June 1991 a supporter of economic reform, Anatolii Sobchak, was elected as Governor. The city Soviet was finally dissolved by presidential decree on 22 December 1993. In 1994–96 the future federal President, Vladimir Putin, was First Deputy Governor of the city Government. On 24 April 1996 Sobchak approved a draft treaty on the delimitation of powers between municipal and federal organs of government. In May 1996 another liberal, the hitherto First Deputy Mayor, Vladimir Yakovlev, was elected as Mayor, defeating Sobchak.

In the mid-1990s the reformist Yabloko bloc was the dominant political force in the city. However, a series of corruption scandals implicating the municipal authorities subsequently damaged support for Yabloko, while Yakovlev (who was elected as leader of the All-Russia grouping of regional governors in August 1999) also campaigned against the movement, notably at the December 1998 municipal legislative elections, when he sponsored his own list of candidates; following a poor performance at these elections, Yabloko went into opposition. The city legislature attracted controversy in 1999, as it attempted to bring forward the date of the gubernatorial election (as, in fact, had also happened in 1996). However, the Supreme Court ruled that attempts to hold the election earlier than originally scheduled, believed to be of benefit to Yakovlev, were invalid. None the less, Yakovlev won the election, held on 14 May 2000, obtaining 72.7% of the votes cast, having secured the support of the Communist Party of the Russian Federation and nationalist elements.

At the municipal legislative election held in December 2002 38 of the 50 incumbent deputies were re-elected to the regional Assembly, although the rate of participation in the election was only 29.4%. (Of the 50 deputies in the new assembly, 31 held no party allegiance.) In early April 2003, after several months of speculation as to whether the Governor intended to seek a change to the city Constitution to permit him to contest a third term of office, Yakovlev announced that he would not do so: Yakovlev's political position appeared to have been weakened by the formation of an anti-Governor majority in the new legislature, and, in particular, by the appointment of a close ally of Putin (who was generally regarded as an opponent of Yakovlev), Valentina Matviyenko, as Presidential Representative to the North-Western Federal Okrug in mid-March. In early June, moreover, the Chairman of the Audit Chamber, Sergei Stepashin, announced that he was to submit documents to the Office of the Prosecutor-General that apparently demonstrated the misuse of some 1,000m. roubles of public funds by the city authorities. However, it became clear that gubernatorial elections in the city were to take place ahead of schedule when, on 16 June, Putin appointed Yakovlev as a Deputy Chairman of the federal Government, with special responsibility for housing and the reform of utility services; the hitherto Vice-Governor, Aleksandr Beglov, thereby assumed the responsibilities of Governor, in an acting capacity. In mid-June Matviyenko announced her candidacy for the forthcoming gubernatorial elections; she received the support of Putin to an extent that was unprecedented for a candidate to a regional governorship. In addition, Matviyenko was supported by the liberal Union of Rightist Forces, Yabloko, the pro-Government Unity and Fatherland-United Russia, and the Communist Party of the Russian Federation, and she also received the backing of Yakovlev. In the first round of polling, on 21 September, Matviyenko received 48.7% of votes cast; she progressed, with her nearest rival, Anna Markova, Yakovlev's former Deputy Governor (with 15.8%), to a second round, on 5 October. In the 'run-off' election Matviyenko was elected as Governor, receiving around 63% of the votes cast, according to preliminary figures. The rate of participation in both rounds was around 29%.

Economy

In 2000 St Petersburg's gross regional product amounted to 205,399m. roubles, or 43,914 roubles per head, less than one-third of the per-head figure recorded in Moscow.

Industry in St Petersburg, which employed around 20.2% of its work-force in 2001 (compared with the 0.7% engaged in agriculture), consists mainly of mechanical engineering, metal-working and food-processing. Other important areas are ferrous and non-ferrous metallurgy, electricity generation, manufacture of chemicals and petrochemicals, rubber production, light manufacturing, the manufacture of building materials, timber-processing and printing. There is also a significant defence-sector industry. Total industrial production in the city amounted to a value of 175,365m. roubles in 2000. The city is also an important centre for service industries, such as tourism, financial services and leisure activities; in 2001 the services sector employed much of the city's work-force. Celebrations of the city's 300th anniversary, in 2003, which were marked by a series of festivals and special events, were expected to stimulate tourist revenues in that year.

The economically active population of St Petersburg amounted to 2.44m. in 2001, when just 3.9% of the work-force were unemployed, one of the lowest rates in Russia. In mid-2002 the average wage in St Petersburg was 5,350.0 roubles, somewhat higher than the national average. The 2001 city budget showed a surplus of 2,296m. roubles. The city is an important centre of trade: in 2001 external trade comprised some US $1,946.8m. in exports and $4,036.3m. in imports; although this figure was relatively high compared with the majority of federal subjects, it comprised only around 15% of the value of Muscovite trade in that year. In the late 1990s around 30% of Russia's imports and 20% of its exports passed through St Petersburg. In 2001 foreign investment in St Petersburg amounted to $1,171.3m., compared with $413.3m. in 1998. However, by 2002 it was not a strong commercial capital—the number of Western companies it had attracted and the extent of its property development failed to rival those of Moscow. The renationalization of the Lomonosov Porcelain Factory, which took place following a court ruling in St Petersburg in October 1999, annulled its privatization six years earlier and caused some concern to foreign investors. In 2000 there were some 1,943 joint enterprises in St Petersburg and the surrounding Leningrad Oblast, some 378 of which had Finnish partners, mainly in the Vyborg area, while 253 firms had US partners and 225 had German partners. At the end of 2001 there were some 78,599 small businesses registered in the city.

Directory

Mayor (Governor and Premier of the City Government): VALENTINA I. MATVIYENKO; 193060 St Petersburg, Smolnyi; tel. (812) 271-74-13; fax (812) 276-18-17; e-mail gov@gov.spb.ru; internet www.gov.spb.ru.

Chairman of the Legislative Assembly: VADIM A. TYULPANOV; 190107 St Petersburg, Isaakiyevskaya pl. 6; tel. (812) 319-99-31; fax (812) 319-90-01; e-mail vtulpanov@assembly.spb.ru; internet www.assembly.spb.ru.

Representation of St Petersburg City in the Russian Federation: 123001 Moscow, ul. Spiridonovka 20/1; tel. (095) 290-43-64; fax (095) 203-50-60.

Vologda Oblast

Vologda Oblast is situated in the north-west of the Eastern European Plain. It forms part of the North-Western Federal Okrug and the Northern Economic Area. It has a short border, in the north-west, with the Republic of Kareliya, which includes the southern tip of Lake Onega (Onezhskoye). Onega also forms the northern end of a border with Leningrad Oblast, which lies to the west of Vologda. Novgorod Oblast lies to the south-west and Tver, Yaroslavl and Kostroma Oblasts to the south. Kirov Oblast forms an eastern border and Archangel Oblast lies to the north. The region's main rivers are the Sukhona, the Yug, the Sheksna and the Mologa. There are three major lakes, in addition to Lake Onega—Beloye, Bozhe and Kubenskoye. Vologda Oblast occupies 145,700 sq km (56,250 sq miles) and extends for 385 km (240 miles) from south to north and 650 km from west to east. It is divided into 26 administrative districts and 15 cities. According to the preliminary results of the census of 9–16 October 2002, the Oblast's population totalled 1,270,000 and the population density was, therefore, 8.7 per sq km. Some 69.0% of the total population inhabited urban areas. The Oblast's administrative centre is at Vologda, which had a population of 292,800, according to provisional census results. Its largest major city is Cherepovets (312,200).

History

Vologda province was annexed by the state of Muscovy in the 14th century. The city was, for a time, the intended capital of Tsar Ivan IV ('the Terrible', 1533–84). Vologda Oblast was formed on 23 September 1937.

In 1991 the newly elected Russian President, Boris Yeltsin, appointed a new head of administration of Vologda Oblast. In mid-1993 the Vologda Oblast declared itself a republic, but failed to be acknowledged as such by the federal authorities. On 13 October the Regional Soviet transferred its responsibilities to the Regional Administration and elections were later held to a Legislative Assembly. In 1995 ballots implemented the Statutes of Vologda Oblast, according to which the region's Governor would lead the executive. There was a high level of support for the nationalist Liberal Democratic Party of Russia, particularly in the countryside, for much of the 1990s. In June 1996 Boris Yeltsin dismissed the local Governor, who was subsequently arrested and imprisoned on charges of corruption. His successor, Vyacheslav Pozgalev, won 80% of the votes cast in a direct election in late 1996, and was re-elected for further terms of office on 19 December 1999 and 7 December 2003, on both occasions obtaining over 80% of the votes cast. In March 2003 Pozgalev was elected to the Supreme Council of the pro-Government Unity and Fatherland-United Russia party.

Economy

In 2000 Vologda Oblast's gross regional product amounted to 68,453m. roubles, equivalent to 51,857 roubles per head. Its main industrial centres are at Vologda, Cherepovets, Velikii Ustyug and Sokol. At the end of 2001 there were 772 km of railway track in general use on its territory, as well as 11,859 km of paved roads. There are some 1,800 km of navigable waterways, including part of the Volga–Baltic route network.

Agriculture in Vologda Oblast, which employed 10.2% of the work-force in 2001, consists mainly of animal husbandry and production of flax and vegetables. The region is famous for its butter. In 2001 total agricultural output was worth 11,422m. roubles, of which 44.6% was generated by crop sales and 55.4% by animal husbandry. The territory imports around one-half of its electrical energy from other oblasts (Kostroma, Kirov, Leningrad, Tver and Yaroslavl). Its main industries are ferrous metallurgy (the region produces some 20% of Russia's iron, 19% of its rolled stock and 18% of its steel), textiles and chemicals (around 11% of the country's mineral fertilizers are manufactured in Vologda Oblast). In 2001 29.7% of the region's working population were engaged in industry. Severstal, the largest privately owned steel manufacturer in Russia, based in Cherepovets, is one of the major employers in the Oblast. The industrial sector generated a total of 88,196m. roubles in 2001.

The Oblast's economically active population numbered 665,000 in 2001, when the rate of unemployment was 8.9%. Those in employment in mid-2002 earned, on average, 4,525.8 roubles per month. The 2001 budget showed a deficit of 779m. roubles. In 2001 export trade constituted US $1,122.6m. in exports and $142.6m. in imports; total foreign investment in the Oblast in that year amounted to $29.6m. In December 2001 6,252 small businesses were registered in the region.

Directory

Governor: Vyacheslav Ye. Pozgalev; 160035 Vologda, ul. Gertsena 2; tel. (8172) 72-07-64; fax (8172) 25-15-54; e-mail governor@vologda-oblast.ru; internet www .vologda-oblast.ru.

Chairman of the Legislative Assembly: Nikolai V. Tikhomirov; 160035 Vologda, ul. Pushkinskaya 25; tel. (8172) 72-02-60; fax (8172) 25-11-33; e-mail zsvo@ vologda.ru.

Chief Representative of Vologda Oblast in the Russian Federation: Vladimir S. Smirnov; Moscow; tel. (095) 201-73-48; fax (095) 201-55-24.

Head of Vologda City Administration (Mayor): Aleksei S. Yakunichev; 160035 Vologda, ul. Kamennyi most 4; tel. (8172) 72-00-42; fax (8172) 72-25-59.

SOUTHERN FEDERAL OKRUG

Republic of Adygeya

The Republic of Adygeya (Adygheya) is situated in the foothills of the Greater Caucasus, a land-locked region in the basin of the Kuban river, surrounded by Krasnodar Krai. The Republic is in the Southern Federal Okrug and the North Caucasus Economic Area. The territory of the Republic, of which some two-fifths is forested, is characterized by open grassland, fertile soil and numerous rivers. The Republic has an area of 7,600 sq km (2,930 sq miles) and comprises seven administrative districts and two cities. According to the preliminary results of the census of 9–16 October 2002, it had 447,000 inhabitants, giving a population density per sq km of 58.8; 53.8% of the population of the Republic were urban. In 1989 of the total republican population some 68% were ethnic Russian and 22% Adyges (Lower Circassians or Kiakhs). Of the Adyge population, an estimated 95% speak the national tongue, Adyge—part of the Abkhazo-Adyge group of Caucasian languages—as their native language, although some 82% are also fluent in Russian. The dominant religion in the Republic, owing to the preponderance of Russian inhabitants, is Orthodox Christianity, but the traditional religion of the Adyges is Islam. The administrative centre of Adygeya is the only large city, Maikop, which had a total of 162,400 inhabitants in October 2002, according to provisional census results.

History

The Adyges were traditionally renowned for their unrivalled horsemanship and marksmanship. They emerged as a distinct ethnic group among the Circassians in the 13th century, when they inhabited much of the area between the Don river and the Caucasus, and the Black Sea and the Stavropol plateau. They were conquered by the Mongol Empire in the 13th century. In the 1550s the Adyges entered into an alliance with the Russian Empire, as protection against the Tatar Khanate of Crimea and against Turkic groups such as the Karachai, the Kumyks and the Nogai, which had retreated into the Caucasus from the Mongol forces of Temujin (Chinghiz or Ghengis Khan). Russian settlers subsequently moved into the Don and Kuban regions, causing unrest among the Adyges and other Circassian peoples, many of whom supported the Ottoman Empire against Russia in the Crimean War of 1853–56. The Circassians were finally defeated by the Russians in 1864. Most were forced either to emigrate or to move to the plains that were under Russian control. A Kuban-Black Sea Soviet Republic was established in 1918, but the region was soon occupied by anti-communist forces ('Whites'). Eventually the Red Army prevailed. The Adygeya Autonomous Oblast was established on 27 July 1922. From 24 August 1922 until 13 August 1928 it was known as the Adygeya (Circassian) Autonomous Oblast. The oblast was ruled from Stavropol until it was included in Krasnodar Krai, which was constituted in 1937.

Following the emergence of the policy of *glasnost* (openness) in the USSR, under Mikhail Gorbachev, the Adyge-Khase Movement was formed. This group, which demanded the formation of a national legislative council or khase, began to raise the issues of nationalism and independence in the Autonomous Oblast. Adygeya officially declared its sovereignty on 28 June 1991 and from the following year entered into co-operative agreements with several other federal subjects; an inter-parliamentary council was subsequently formed to include Adygeya and the other Circassian Republics (Kabardino-Balkariya and Karachayevo-Cherkessiya). A Constitution, which formally provided for the recognition of Adygeya as a republic, separate from the surrounding Krai, was adopted on 10 March 1995, confirming a decision of the Supreme Soviet of the RSFSR of 3 June 1991. The new Constitution provided for the institution of a bicameral legislature, the Khase (State Council), comprising a Council of Representatives and a Council of the Republic.

Although during the late 1990s the Republic remained strongly supportive of the Communist Party of the Russian Federation, the Adyge President, Aslan Dzharimov, was among those instrumental in forming the All-Russia parliamentary bloc in 1999. In an election held on 13 January 2002 Dzharimov was conclusively defeated, receiving only around 10% of the votes cast; he was succeeded by Khazrat Sovmen, the owner of a gold-mining co-operative. Following the death in April of Gen. (retd) Aleksandr Lebed, the Governor of Krasnoyarsk Krai, his former deputy, Gennadii Mikichura, who was reported to be a business associate of Sovmen, was approved by the legislature as Prime Minister of Adygeya. In August 2003 Mikichura resigned, and was replaced later in the month by Khazret Khuade, a former head of the republican customs service.

Economy

In 2000 the territory's gross regional product was 5,811m. roubles, or 12,980 roubles per head. The territory's major industrial centres are at the cities of Maikop and

Kamennomostskii. At the end of 2001 there were 148 km (92 miles) of railway track on its territory, and 1,545 km of paved roads.

Agriculture is, traditionally, the principal economic activity of Adygeya. Agricultural production consists mainly of grain, sunflowers, sugar beet, tobacco and vegetables, cucurbit (gourds and melons) cultivation and viniculture. The Republic produced over 17% of the Federation's output of grape wine in the first half of 2000. The entire sector employed some 21.0% of the working population in 2001. The decline in overall agricultural production in the Republic slowed during the mid-1990s, although animal husbandry had decreased to less than one-half of its 1991 level by 1998. Thereafter, there was some recovery in the sector. By 2001 the value of agricultural output was 2,614m. roubles (of which crop sales contributed 56.3% and animal husbandry 43.7%), compared with 995m. roubles in 1998. However, a severe drought in mid-2003 was expected to result in a marked decrease in agricultural output in that year. There is some extraction of natural gas. In industry, food-processing is particularly important, accounting for almost one-half of industrial production. Timber-processing, mechanical engineering and metal-working are also significant. Adygeya lies along the routes of the Blue Stream pipeline, completed in 2002, which delivers gas to Turkey, and planned petroleum pipelines from the Transcaucasus and Dagestan to the Black Sea ports of Novorossiisk and Tuapse. Some 15.4% of the working population were engaged in industry in 2001. Industrial production declined during the early 1990s, but began to increase from 1999. In 2001 the value of industrial production was 3,186m. roubles, compared with 1,018m. roubles in 1998.

In 2001 the economically active population in Adygeya amounted to 198,000, and some 14.1% of the labour force were unemployed, one of the highest rates in the Federation at that time. The average monthly wage was 2,625.9 roubles in mid-2002. In 2001 there was a budgetary deficit of 7m. roubles. In that year the Republic's external trade amounted to a value of US $117.6m., of which $95.6m. was accounted for by exports and $22.0m. by imports. Adygeya's main trading partners, in the mid-1990s, in terms of exports, were Belarus, France, Kazakhstan, Poland, Turkey and Ukraine. Exports consisted mainly of food products, machine-tools and petroleum and chemical products. There was relatively little foreign investment in the Republic: in 2001 it amounted to just $1.7m. At 31 December 2001 there were 2,221 small businesses registered on Adygeya's territory.

Directory

President: KHAZRAT M. SOVMEN; 352700 Adygeya, Maikop, ul. Zhukovskogo 22; tel. (87722) 7-19-01; fax (87722) 2-59-58; internet www.adygheya.ru.

Prime Minister: KHAZRET KHUADE; 352700 Adygeya, Maikop, ul. Pionerskaya 199; tel. (87722) 7-02-22; fax (87722) 2-59-58.

Chairman of the Council of Representatives of the Khase (State Council): TATYANA M. PETROVA; 352700 Adygeya, Maikop, ul. Zhukovskogo 22; tel. (87722) 2-12-61; e-mail apparat@parlament.adygheya.ru; internet www.parlament .adygheya.ru.

Chairman of the Council of the Republic of the Khase (State Council): ANATOLII G. IVANOV; 385000 Adygeya, Maikop, ul. Zhukovskogo 22; tel. (87722) 2-19-02; fax (87722) 2-19-04; e-mail apparat@parlament.adygheya.ru; internet www.parlament .adygheya.ru.

Chief Representative of the Republic of Adygeya in the Russian Federation: RUSLAN YU. GUSARUK; 115184 Moscow, per. Staryi Tolmachevskii 6; tel. (095) 230-34-01; fax (095) 230-07-48.

Head of Maikop City Administration: N. M. PIVOVAROV; 352700 Adygeya, Maikop, ul. Krasnooktyabrskaya 21; tel. (87722) 2-27-61; fax (87722) 2-63-19; e-mail priemn@admins.maykop.ru; internet www.admins.maykop.ru.

Astrakhan Oblast

Astrakhan Oblast is situated in the Caspian lowlands and forms part of the Southern Federal Okrug and the Volga Economic Area. Lying between the Russian federal subject of Kalmykiya to the south and the former Soviet state of Kazakhstan to the east, Astrakhan is a long, relatively thin territory, which flanks the River Volga as it flows out of Volgograd Oblast in the north-west towards the Caspian Sea to the south-east, via a delta at Astrakhan. The delta is one of the largest in the world and occupies more than 24,000 sq km (9,260 sq miles) of the Caspian lowlands. It gives the Oblast some 200 km (over 120 miles) of coastline. It has one major lake, the Baskunchak, measuring 115 sq km. Astrakhan Oblast occupies some 44,100 sq km (17,000 sq miles) and is divided into 11 administrative districts and six cities. According to the preliminary results of the census f 9–16 October 2002, its total population was 1,007,200 and its population density, therefore, was 22.8 per sq km. Some 67.9% of the population lived in urban areas. The Oblast's administrative centre is at Astrakhan (formerly Khadzhi-Tarkhan), which had a population of 506,400, according to provisional census results. The city lies at 22 m (72 feet) below sea level and is protected from the waters of the Volga delta by 75 km of dykes.

History

The Khanate of Astrakhan, which was formed in 1446, following the dissolution of the Golden Horde, was conquered by the Russians in 1556. The region subsequently became an important centre for trading in timber, grain, fish and petroleum. Astrakhan Oblast was founded on 27 December 1943.

There was considerable hardship in the region following the dissolution of the USSR and the economic reforms of the early 1990s. Dissatisfaction was indicated by the relatively high level of support for the nationalist Liberal Democratic Party of Russia in the 1995 State Duma elections, and by the continued pre-eminence of the Communist Party of the Russian Federation in the Oblast. The Governor, Anatolii Guzhvin, initially a federal appointee, retained his post at elections in 1997, and was re-elected for a further term of office in December 2000, receiving 81% of the votes cast. Elections to the regional legislature, the Representative Assembly, were held on 28 October 2001; in the following month the Assembly voted to rename itself the State Duma. The region continued to suffer from severe social difficulties in the early 2000s; it was reported that the operations of the Oblast's police force had been subject to criticism in a document commissioned in late 2002 by the federal Ministry of Internal Affairs. Moreover, Astrakhan was reputed to have the highest crime rate of any federal subject in the Southern Federal Okrug. Meanwhile, the municipal authorities in Akhtubinsk, the second city of the Oblast, were reported to have commenced a scheme, in accordance with which free housing was to be provided to married women who, subject to certain conditions, would agree to bear three children over the course of five years, in an attempt to combat the declining birth rate in the region.

Economy

Astrakhan Oblast's gross regional product was 32,274m. roubles in 2000, equivalent to 31,587 roubles per head—the highest level in the Southern Federal Okrug. The Oblast's main industrial centres are at Astrakhan and Akhtubinsk. At the end of 2001 there were 567 km of railways and 2,674 km of paved roads on the Oblast's territory. In October 2003 Russia's first container terminal on the Caspian Sea opened at the port of Olya, as part of work towards the construction of a 6,500 km north–south transport corridor to connect India with northern Europe, via Iran and Russia. The rise in the level of the Caspian Sea (by some 2.6 m between the late 1970s and the late 1990s) and the resulting erosion of the Volga delta caused serious environmental problems in the region. These were exacerbated by the pollution of the water by petroleum products, copper, nitrates and other substances, which frequently contributed to the death of a significant proportion of fish reserves.

The Oblast remains a major producer of vegetables and cucurbits (gourds and melons). Grain production and animal husbandry are also important. Total agricultural production amounted to a value of 3,772m. roubles in 2001, of which 47.5% was generated by crop sales and 52.5% by animal husbandry. The sector employed 15.8% of the working population at that time. The Oblast is rich in natural resources, including gas and gas condensate, sulphur, petroleum and salt. Its main industries are the production of petroleum and natural gas, food-processing (particularly fish products), mechanical engineering, ship-building and electricity production. It was anticipated that the extraction of petroleum and natural gas would improve the economic fortunes of the region from the mid-2000s. Industrial output in 2001 was worth 21,151m. roubles, and the sector employed 16.1% of the Oblast's labour force.

Regional trade was also important to the economy of Astrakhan. The Lakor freight company established important shipping links with Iran, handling around 940,000 metric tons of cargo in 1996, and in early 2000 announced plans to develop a trade route with India. In September 1997 the company, with an Iranian group, Khazar Shipping, registered the Astrakhan–Nowshahr joint shipping line. Astrakhan's exports to Iran mainly comprised paper, metals, timber, mechanical equipment, fertilizers and chemical products.

Astrakhan Oblast's economically active population numbered 512,000 in 2001, when 10.5% of the region's labour force were unemployed. The average monthly wage was 3,708.2 roubles in mid-2002. In 2001 there was a budgetary deficit of 38m. roubles. In that year export trade totalled US $449.6m., and the value of imports amounted to $48.2m. Foreign investment in the territory amounted to $1.8m., compared with $7.6m. in 1998. At 31 December 2001 there were 3,479 small businesses in operation.

Directory

Head of the Regional Administration (Governor): ANATOLII P. GUZHVIN; 414000 Astrakhan, ul. Sovetskaya 14–15; tel. (8512) 22-85-19; fax (8512) 22-95-14; e-mail ves@astrakhan.ru; internet www.gov.astrakhan-region.ru.

Chairman of the State Duma: PAVEL P. ANISIMOV; 414000 Astrakhan, ul. Volodarskogo 15; tel. (8512) 22-96-44; fax (8512) 22-22-48; e-mail ootsops@astranet.ru; internet duma.astranet.ru.

Representation of Astrakhan Oblast in the Russian Federation: 125407 Moscow, ul. 3-aya Tveskaya-Yamskaya 58/5; tel. (095) 251-07-19; fax (095) 251-06-96.

Head of Astrakhan City Administration (Mayor): IGOR A. BEZRUKAVNIKOV; 414000 Astrakhan, ul. Chernyshevskogo 6; tel. (8512) 22-55-88; fax (8512) 24-71-76; e-mail munic@astranet.ru; internet astrakhan.astranet.ru.

Chechen (Nokchi) Republic— Chechnya

The Chechen (Nokchi) Republic is located on the northern slopes of the Caucasus. It forms part of the Southern Federal Okrug and the North Caucasus Economic Area. To the east, Chechnya abuts into the Republic of Dagestan. Stavropol Krai lies to the north-west and the Republics of North Osetiya—Alaniya (Ossetia) and Ingushetiya to the west. There is an international boundary with Georgia (South Osetiya) to the south-west. The exact delimitation of the western boundary remained uncertain, awaiting final agreement between Chechnya and Ingushetiya on the division of the territory of the former Chechen-Ingush ASSR. Chechnya contains three cities and 18 administrative districts. The Republic comprises lowlands along the principal waterway, the River Terek, and around the capital, Groznyi, in the north; mixed fields, pastures and forests in the Chechen plain; and high mountains and glaciers in the south. The former Checheno-Ingush ASSR had an area of some 19,300 sq km (7,450 sq miles), most of which was allotted to the Chechens. According to the preliminary results of the census of 9–16 October 2002, the Republic had a population of 1,100,300, some 34.5% of whom lived in urban areas. However, by December 2003 more than 300,000 Chechens remained displaced from their homes, as a result of the civil conflict. The Chechens, who refer to themselves as Nokchi, are closely related to the Ingush (both of whom are known collectively as Vainakhs). They are Sunni Muslims, and their language is one of the Nakh dialects of the Caucasian linguistic family. Founded as Groznyi in 1818, the capital had a population of 223,000 in 2002, according to provisional census results, compared with a total of 405,000 in 1989.

History

In the 18th century the Russian, Ottoman and Persian (Iranian) Empires fought for control of the Caucasus region. The Chechens violently resisted the Russian forces with the uprising of Sheikh Mansur in 1785 and throughout the Caucasian War of 1817–64. Chechnya was finally conquered by Russia in 1858 after the resistance led by the ethnic Avar Imam Shamil ended. In 1865 many Chechens were exiled to the Ottoman Empire. Subsequently, ethnic Russians began to settle in the lowlands, particularly after petroleum reserves were discovered around Groznyi in 1893. Upon the dissolution of the Mountain (Gorskaya) People's Republic in 1922, Chechen and Ingush Autonomous Oblasts were established; they merged in 1934 and became the Checheno-Ingush ASSR in 1936. This was dissolved in 1944, when both peoples were deported en masse to Central Asia and Siberia. On 9 January 1957 the ASSR was reconstituted, but with limited provisions made for the restoration of property to the dispossessed Chechens and Ingush.

During 1991 an All-National Congress of the Chechen People seized effective power in the Checheno-Ingush ASSR and agreed the division of the territory with Ingush leaders. Exact borders were to be decided by future negotiation, but by far the largest proportion of the territory was to constitute a Chechen Republic. Elections to the presidency of this new polity, the Chechen Republic (Chechnya), which claimed independence from Russia, were held on 27 October, and were won by Gen. Dzhokhar Dudayev. In 1993 the territory refused to participate in the Russian general election and rejected the new federal Constitution. Dudayev's policies provoked the Chechen opposition into violent conflict from August 1994. In December federal troops entered Chechnya and, by January 1995, had taken control of the city, including the presidential palace, although fierce resistance continued throughout the Republic. In an effort to end hostilities, the federal President, Boris Yeltsin, signed an accord with the Chechen premier granting the Republic special status, including its own consulate and foreign-trade missions. None the less, in April more than 100 civilians were reported to have been killed by federal troops in a so-called 'cleansing' operation (*zachistka*) in the village of Samashki. Subsequently, in June the federal premier, Viktor Chernomyrdin, intervened in negotiations to end a siege by militants associated with the rebel Chechen leader, Shamil Basayev, who took hostage around 1,000 people in a hospital in Budennovsk, Stavropol Krai. (None the less, more than 100 people were killed during the siege, which Basayev described as an act of revenge for an attack by federal troops on the village of Vedeno in the previous month, in which 11 of his relatives had been killed.) A further large-scale hostage-taking incident conducted by Chechen militants took place in Kizlyar, Dagestan, in January 1996, increasing demands across Russia for the Government to find a settlement to the Chechen conflict; other incidences of hostage-taking attributed to supporters of Chechen independence took place in Chechnya, in other regions of Russia and, less frequently, internationally during the late 1990s and early 2000s.

In April 1996 Dudayev was killed in a Russian missile attack; he was succeeded by Zelimkhan Yandarbiyev. In May the rebel and federal authorities signed a peace agreement. However, the truce ended following Yeltsin's re-election as federal President in July. In August Chechen rebel forces led a successful assault on Groznyi, prompting the negotiation of a cease-fire by Lt-Gen. Aleksandr Lebed, the recently appointed Secretary of the Security Council. An agreement, the Khasavyurt

Accords, was signed in Dagestan on 31 August. The proposed peace settlement incorporated a moratorium on discussion of Chechnya's status for five years. An agreement on the withdrawal of all federal troops by January 1997 was signed in November 1996, signalling the end of a war that had claimed up to 100,000 lives. A formal Treaty of Peace and Principles of Relations was signed on 12 May 1997 and ratified by the Chechen Parliament the following day.

On 1 January 1997 a presidential election was held in the Republic (which subsequently renamed itself 'the Chechen Republic of Ichkeriya'), at which Khalid 'Aslan' Maskhadov, a former Chechen rebel chief of staff, obtained 64.8% of the votes cast, defeating Basayev. The main issues to dominate politics were the increasing lawlessness in the Republic and the growth of Islamist groupings, both of which served to destabilize neighbouring polities, particularly the Republic of Dagestan (q.v.). Moreover, the population of Chechnya decreased markedly following the establishment of *de facto* independence, as civilians—particularly ethnic Russians—migrated to other regions of Russia. During 1998 two incidents drew attention to the disorderly state of Chechen society: Valentin Vlasov, the federal presidential representative in Chechnya, was kidnapped in May and held hostage for six months; later in the year four engineers from the United Kingdom and New Zealand were captured, and subsequently killed. By the end of the year Groznyi was no longer secure for the Government and Maskhadov was mainly based on the outskirts of the city.

The resurgence of Chechen nationalism in the 1990s was accompanied by a renaissance for Islam. In 1997 the republican authorities announced their intention to introduce Islamic *Shari'a* law over a three-year period from 1999, in contravention of the federal Constitution. Hostilities between armed groupings in Gudermes in July 1998 resulted in the outlawing of oppositionist Islamist groups, which the federal authorities referred to as representatives of the austere Wahhabi Islamic sect, in the Republic.

In August–September 1999 Islamist factions associated with Basayev launched a series of attacks on Dagestan from Chechnya, in particular, with the aim of protecting and extending the jurisdiction of a 'separate Islamic territory' in Dagestan, over which rebels had obtained control in the previous year. (The territory was returned to federal rule in mid-September.) A series of bomb explosions in August and September in Moscow, Dagestan and Volgodonsk (Rostov Oblast), including two that destroyed entire apartment blocks, officially attributed by the Government to Chechen separatists, killed almost 300 people, prompting the redeployment of federal armed forces in the Republic from late September; the recently inaugurated premier, Vladimir Putin, presented the deployment as an 'anti-terrorist operation'. The federal regime declined requests from Maskhadov for the negotiation of a settlement, stating that it recognized only the Moscow-based State Council of the Chechen Republic, which had been formed by former members of the republican legislature.

In February 2000 federal forces took control of Groznyi and proceeded to destroy much of the city; many republican and federal administrative bodies were relocated to Gudermes. In May Putin, by this time the elected President of the Russian Federation, decreed that Chechnya would, henceforth, be ruled federally. Akhmad haji Kadyrov, a former senior mufti and a former ally of Maskhadov, was inaugurated as the Head of the Republican Administration on 20 June; Kadyrov was to be directly responsible to the federal presidential administration. In October it was announced that all Chechen ministries and government departments were to be relocated from Gudermes to Groznyi, with effect from November.

In January 2001 Putin transferred control of military operations in Chechnya from the Ministry of Defence to the Federal Security Service (FSB). The majority of troops in the region were to be withdrawn, leaving a 15,000-strong infantry division and 7,000 interior ministry troops. The FSB was to strengthen its presence in Chechnya, however, in order to combat insurgency. The local administration in Chechnya was restructured to allow it greater autonomy, and Stanislav Ilyasov, a former Governor of Stavropol Krai, was appointed as Chechen premier. Despite claims that federal military operations had effectively ended, guerrilla attacks showed no sign of abating, and concern escalated among international human rights organizations about the conduct of cleansing operations by federal troops, in which entire towns or areas were searched for rebels; in 2001–02 the discovery of a number of mass graves, containing severely mutilated corpses, prompted outrage.

In late September 2001, encountering increasing demands for a political solution to the Chechen conflict, Putin announced a 72-hour amnesty, during which rebels could surrender weapons without charge. Although only a negligible quantity of weapons were surrendered, the first official, direct negotiations to take place since the renewal of hostilities in 1999 commenced in Moscow in November 2001, between the Presidential Representative in the Southern Federal Okrug, Col-Gen. Viktor Kazantsev, and Akhmed Zakayev, deputy premier under Maskhadov. No substantive agreement was reached, however, and no further high-level negotiations took place. Putin, meanwhile, repeatedly described the conflict in Chechnya as an integral part of the 'war on terrorism' announced by US President George W. Bush in the aftermath of the suicide attacks against the US cities of New York and Washington, DC, on 11 September, and attributed to Osama bin Laden's militant Islamist al-Qa'ida (Base) network. In mid-October Kadyrov reformed the Chechen administration; although Ilyasov (who remained resident in Stavropol) was maintained as republican Prime Minister, a new, more senior position, the Chief of Staff of the Chechen Administration, was assigned to Lt-Gen. Yakov (Yan) Sergunin, hitherto responsible for the judicial system in Chechnya.

In March 2002 a newly established 'Chechen Consultative Council', comprising both Chechens supportive of, and opposed to, the independence of the Republic held its first meeting in the building of the Federal Assembly in Moscow. In April a leading Islamist commander in the conflict, who was believed to be of Jordanian or Saudi Arabian origin, Emir ibn al-Khattab, was killed by federal forces. However, rebel activity increased markedly in the months that followed; although the political authority of Maskhadov, who remained in hiding, had dwindled, his military leadership of what was known as the State Defence Committee becaming increasingly prominent as a focus for resistance to the federal troops. In July it was reported that Basayev had been appointed to a senior position on the Committee, although the exact relationship between Maskhadov and Basayev remained obscure. In mid-August federal forces experienced their single largest loss of life since the commencement of operations in 1999, when a military helicopter was shot down by rebels in Groznyi, killing 118 troops. At the end of September 2002 rebels led by Ruslan Gelayev staged incursions into Ingushetiya; at least 17 deaths were reported in fighting near the village of Galashki, in what was described as one of the largest battles in the conflict to date.

On 23–26 October 2002 over 40 heavily armed rebels, led by Movsar Barayev, the cousin of a Chechen rebel leader who had been killed by federal troops in 2001, held captive more than 800 people in a Moscow theatre, and demanded the withdrawal of federal troops from the Republic. The rebels described themselves as members of a 'suicide batallion' and, notably, included several women (referred to by the Russian authorities as 'black widows'), armed with explosive devices. The siege ended when élite federal forces stormed the theatre, having initially filled the building with an incapacitating gas. The rebels were killed, and it subsequently emerged that at least 129 hostages had died, in almost all cases owing to the toxic effects of the gas. Maskhadov issued a statement condemning the rebels' use of terrorist methods, but, despite denials by the Maskhadov-led authorities of their involvement in the incident, Zakayev was arrested on the orders of the federal Government, while attending a World Chechen Congress in Copenhagen, Denmark. (In early November Basayev announced that groups linked to him had perpetrated the hostage-taking in Moscow, and stated that Maskhadov had not known of the incident.) However, Denmark formally rejected demands for Zakayev's extradition, and he was released; he subsequently took up residence in the United Kingdom, which granted him asylum in November 2003. Meanwhile, in the aftermath of the theatre siege the federal Minister of Defence, Sergei Ivanov, announced that the Government was to intensify its military offensive in Chechnya, and that the previously planned withdrawal of troops had been cancelled. Representative offices of the 'Chechen Republic of Ichkeriya' were closed in several countries, including Azerbaijan, Georgia and Turkey, in November 2002, as the result of pressure from the Russian Government.

In mid-November 2002 Ilyasov was removed from his position as Prime Minister of Chechnya and, in what was widely perceived as a promotion, appointed as Minister without Portfolio in the federal Government, responsible for the Social and Economic Development of Chechnya; Ilyasov was succeeded as republican premier by Capt. (retd) Mikhail Babich, who had previously held senior positions in the regional administrations of Ivanovo and Moscow Oblasts. In late November Ilyasov announced that a referendum on a new draft Chechen constitution, which would, *inter alia*, determine the status of the Republic within the Russian Federation, was to be held in March 2003; this measure was confirmed by Putin in mid-December 2002. In late December at least 83 people died, and more than 150 others were injured, when suicide bombers detonated bombs in two vehicles stationed outside the headquarters of the republican Government in Groznyi; no senior officials were killed. (Basayev subsequently claimed responsibility for the attack.) By late December 2002 federal losses during the campaign, according to official figures, were put at 4,572 dead and 15,549 wounded, with 29 missing, although Chechen estimates were considerably higher. (It was also estimated that more than 14,000 rebel fighters had been killed since September 1999.) In late January Babich resigned as premier, reportedly following a disagreement with Kadyrov regarding the appointment of a republican Minister of Finance. On 10 February Anatolii Popov, the hitherto deputy chairman of the state commission for the reconstruction of Chechnya, was appointed as the new republican premier.

The referendum on the draft constitution for Chechnya, describing the republic (referred to as the Chechen—Nokchi Republic) as both a sovereign entity, with its own citizenship, and as an integral part of the Russian Federation proceeded, as scheduled, on 23 March 2003, despite concerns that the instability of the Republic would prevent the poll from being free and fair. The draft constitution also provided for the holding of fresh elections to a strengthened republican presidency and legislature. According to the official results, some 88.4% of the electorate participated in the plebiscite, of whom 96.0% supported the draft constitution. Two further questions, on the method of electing the president and the parliament of the Republic of Chechnya, were supported by 95.4% and 96.1% of participants, respectively. However, independent observers challenged the results, reporting that the rate of participation by the electorate had been much lower than officially reported. (According to official results, an identical number of valid votes had been cast in response to all three questions, while it was reported that the total number of votes cast had, in fact, been in excess of the registered electorate.)

Political violence continued to dominate Chechen affairs in the period after the referendum; in early April 2003 at least 22 people were killed in two separate incidents when their vehicles detonated landmines. In early May 2003 at least 59 people were killed when suicide bombers attacked government offices in Znamenskoye, in the north of Chechnya. Two days later another suicide bombing at a religious festival attended by Kadyrov (in his new capacity as acting President) near Gudermes resulted in at least 14 deaths, although Kadyrov escaped unhurt; Basayev claimed responsibility for the organization of both attacks.

In early June 2003 Kadyrov, using the new powers that he had been granted following the constitutional referendum, dismissed the majority of the republican Government, and the heads of every regional administration in the Republic; the vast majority were re-appointed shortly afterwards, although a new Mayor was appointed in Groznyi. On 21 June Kadyrov inaugurated an interim legislative body, the 42-member State Council, comprising the head of, and an appointed representative of, each administrative district; Khusein Isayev, hitherto head of the apparatus of the Ministry of State Property in Chechnya, was elected as Chairman of the Council. In early July Putin announced that presidential elections in Chechnya were to be held on 5 October. On 5 August Popov assumed the post of acting President, in order to permit Kadyrov to commence his electoral campaign; however, on 20 August, following a ruling by the republican electoral commission, Kadyrov was permitted to resume his former duties until 5 September.

From 1 September 2003 control of military operations in Chechnya was assumed by the federal Ministry of Internal Affairs from the FSB; it was announced that such operations were no longer regarded as having an 'anti-terrorist' character but were, rather, to form part of an 'operation to protect law and constitutional order'. Meanwhile, campaigning for the presidential elections commenced: by 20 August, when the deadline for submitting candidacies for the presidential election expired, 11 valid applications had been made; however, the withdrawal of Aslanbek Aslakhanov, a representative of the Republic in the State Duma, and the debarring of a business executive, Malik Saidullayev, both of which occured on 11 September, effectively removed any major challenges to Kadyrov's candidacy. As widely anticipated, on 5 October Kadyrov was elected as President, receiving 87.7% of votes cast, according to official figures. The rate of participation in the polls was stated to be 82.6%. In this context it remained uncertain whether Kadyrov's presidency would be regarded as legitimate within the Republic, and some commentators expressed concern that an intra-Chechen conflict could evolve. Kadyrov subsequently re-appointed Popov as premier, although on 2 December the First Deputy Chairman of the Republican Government and Minister of Finance, Eli

Isayev, was appointed acting premier, owing to Popov's ill health. Legislative elections were due to be held in the Republic in 2004.

Economy

Prior to the outbreak of armed hostilities in the region in 1994–95, Groznyi was the principal industrial centre in Chechnya. At the end of 2001 there were 304 km (189 miles) of railways and 3,057 km of paved roads on the Republic's territory. Its agriculture consisted mainly of horticulture, production of grain and sugar beet, and animal husbandry. Its main industrial activities were production of petroleum and petrochemicals, petroleum-refining, power engineering, manufacture of machinery and the processing of forestry and agricultural products. Conflict in 1994–96, and again from 1999, seriously damaged the economic infrastructure and disrupted both agricultural and industrial activity. However, future developments depended on greater stability in the territory. Another asset that could be sabotaged by, or displaced because of violence was one of Russia's major petroleum pipelines that crossed Chechnya (transit fees from Caspian hydrocarbons could be a major source of revenue). In mid-1999 the Chechen section of a petroleum pipeline from Baku, Azerbaijan, to Novorossiisk, was closed, owing to the lack of security in the region. However, attempts were being made to restore industry in the Republic; a sugar refinery and a brickworks were in operation there in 2001, and several new businesses opened thereafter. The principal petroleum company operating in the Republic in the early 2000s was Grozneftegaz, which was 51%-owned by Rosneft, and 49% by the republican Government. Output of petroleum in 2002 was estimated at approximately 1.5m. metric tons. A new polypropylene-fabric factory was constructed in Groznyi in 2002. At April 1998 around four-fifths of the Republic's population were unemployed, and the 1998 budget showed a deficit of 68m. roubles. In November 2002 it was reported that the federal budget for 2003 was to allocate some 3,500m. roubles to the Republic, under a programme that aimed to promote economic and social recovery.

Directory

President and Head of the Administration: AKHMED A. haji KADYROV; 364000 Chechnya, Groznyi, ul. Garazhnaya 10A; tel. and fax (095) 777-92-28; e-mail info@ chechnya.gov.ru; internet www.chechnya.gov.ru.

Chairman of the Republican Government (Prime Minister and First Deputy Head of the Administration): ELI ISAYEV (acting); 364000 Chechnya, Groznyi, ul. Garazhnaya 10A; tel. (8712) 22-00-01.

Chairman of the State Council: KHUSEIN ISAYEV; 364000 Chechnya, Groznyi, ul. Garazhnaya 10A.

Chief Representative of the Chechen (Nokchi) Republic in the Russian Federation: ADLAN MAGOMADOV; 127025 Moscow, ul. Novyi Arbat 19; tel. (095) 203-91-45; fax (095) 203-63-52.

Head of Groznyi City Administration (Mayor): KHOZH-AHMED ARSANOV; tel. (8712) 22-01-42.

Republic of Dagestan

The Republic of Dagestan (Daghestan) is situated in the North Caucasus on the Caspian Sea. Dagestan forms part of the Southern Federal Okrug and the North Caucasus Economic Area. It has international borders with Azerbaijan to the south and Georgia to the south-west. The Republic of Chechnya and Stavropol Krai lie to the west and the Republic of Kalmykiya to the north. Its largest rivers are the Terek, the Sulak and the Samur. It occupies an area of 50,300 sq km (19,420 sq miles) and measures some 400 km (250 miles) from south to north. Its Caspian Sea coastline, to the east, is 530 km long. The north of the Republic is flat, while in the south are the foothills and peaks of the Greater Caucasus. The Republic's lowest-lying area is the Caspian lowlands, at 28 m (92 feet) below sea level, while its highest peak is over 4,000 m high. Dagestan is made up of 41 administrative districts and 10 cities. The climate in its mountainous areas is continental and dry, while in coastal areas it is subtropical, with strong winds. According to the preliminary results of the census of 9–16 October 2002, Dagestan had a population of 2,584,200, and a population density of 51.3 per sq km; some 42.9% of the Republic's population inhabited urban areas. According to the 1989 census, some 27.5% of the population of Dagestan were Avars, 15.6% Dargins, 12.9% Kumyks, 11.3% Lezgins, 5.1% Laks, 4.3% Tabasarans, 1.6% Nogai, 0.8% Rutuls, 0.8% Aguls and 0.3% Tsakhurs, while ethnic Russians formed the fifth largest nationality, accounting for 9.2%. (However, preliminary results of the 2002 census suggested that up to one-third of those previously categorized as Avars regarded themselves as belonging to some 15 other ethnic groups.) Dagestan's capital is at Makhachkala, which had 466,800 inhabitants in October 2002, according to provisional census results. The city lies on the Caspian Sea and is the Republic's main port. Other major cities are Khasavyurt (122,000) and Derbent (100,800).

History

Dagestan formally came under Russian rule in 1723, when the various Muslim khanates on its territory were annexed from Persia (Iran). The Dagestani peoples conducted a series of rebellions, including the Murid Uprising of 1828–59, before Russian control could be established. A Dagestan ASSR was established on 20 January 1920.

The Republic of Dagestan acceded to the Federation Treaty in March 1992 and officially declared its sovereignty in May 1993. The Republic voted against the new federal Constitution in December and adopted a new republican Constitution on 26 July 1994. On 21 March 1996 the powers of the Dagestani State Council, the supreme executive body, which comprised a representative of each of the 14 largest ethnic groups in the Republic, were prolonged by a further two years. When this extra term had elapsed, the republican legislature convened as a Constituent Assembly and, on 26 June 1998, confirmed Magomedali Magomedov as the Chairman of the State Council. Parliamentary elections for a new People's Assembly were held on 7 March 1999, concurrently with a referendum to decide whether to institute an executive presidency in Dagestan; the proposal was rejected for a third time. The republican Government was widely regarded as the federal Government's closest ally, and the most active supporter of Russian territorial integrity, among the North Caucasian republics. A constitutional change of March 1998, which permitted Magomedov to serve a further term, also removed the nationality requirements for senior republican positions; this was thought to unsettle the fragile balance of power between the different ethnic groups in the Republic.

Concern was expressed at a growth in support for militant Islamist groups in Dagestan in the late 1990s, which, however, appeared to have abated somewhat by the early 2000s. In February 1998 Islamist militants seized three villages in Buinaksk district as 'a separate Islamic territory'. In May a group of 200–300 fighters belonging to the Union of Russian Muslims, a political party represented in the republican parliament and led by Nadirshakh Khachilayev, the brother of the head of the ethnic Lak community in Dagestan, occupied a government building in Makhachkala; simultaneously, 2,000 demonstrators gathered in the main city square to demand the resignation of the republican Government. (Khachilayev was assassinated in August 2003.) Meanwhile, there was increasing evidence of close ties between militant groups in Dagestan and those operating abroad, particularly in Arab countries. In 1996–97 Ayman al-Zawahiri, the leader of the militant Egyptian Islamic Jihad and a close ally of the Saudi-born leader of the Islamist al-Qa'ida (Base) organization, Osama bin Laden, was imprisoned for six months in Dagestan, after having been found guilty of entering Russia illegally.

Chechen militants, aided by Dagestani militant Islamists, invaded Dagestan on 2 August 1999 and again on 5 September; fighting ceased on 16 September, when federal troops additionally regained control over the separate Islamic territory declared in February 1998. On the same day the republican legislature approved a law prohibiting the austere Wahhabi Islamic sect. Later in the month, when the recommencement of military operations by federal troops in Chechnya appeared imminent, crowds of demonstrators prevented a planned meeting there between Magomedov, as the *de facto* representative of the federal Government, and the President of the 'Chechen Republic of Ichkeriya', Khalid Maskhadov; it was reported that the demonstrators objected to any negotiations taking place with the Chechen authorities, which they held responsible for the increasing lawlessness, and in particular the widespread incidence of hostage-taking, in Dagestan in 1996–99, including, most notoriously, an incident in January 1996, when some 2,000 hostages had been seized in the town of Kizlyar. Indeed, such was the hostility towards the rebel Chechen movement in Dagestan that the federal authorities agreed to a request from officials of the Dagestani Government that no refugees from Chechnya be accommodated in Dagestan, in contrast with most neighbouring territories.

In late September 1999, following the recommencement of military operations in Chechnya, an explosion in Buinaksk, outside accommodation used by federal troops, killed about 60 people. In 2001–03 a number of explosions in Dagestan were attributed to supporters of Chechen separatism. On 9 May 2002, during a Victory Day parade in Kaspiisk, 45 people were killed and more than 130 injured in an explosion; it was reported in June 2003 that the alleged instigator of the bombing, Rappani Khalilov, a supporter of Chechen separatism, had been killed by federal troops.

On 25 June 2002 the Constitutional Assembly voted by an overwhelming majority for Magomedov to serve for a third term as Chairman of the State Council. Elections took place on 16 March 2003, at which Magomedov was re-elected as Chairman of the State Council, and, hence, of the Government. On 10 July the republican Constitutional Assembly unanimously approved the introduction of a new republican Constitution, which implemented wide-ranging reforms to the structure of government. (The Constitution came into effect on 26 July.) Notably, a directly elected Presidency was to be established, to replace the State Council, which would be abolished following the end of its term of office in 2006; the number of parliamentary deputies was also to be reduced from 121 to 72. Meanwhile, it was reported that at least eight parliamentary deputies had been assassinated in Dagestan in 1992–2003. In late August 2003 the republican Minister for National Policy, Information and Foreign Affairs, Magomedsalikh Gusayev, was killed when a bomb was detonated by his car; Gusayev had played a particularly prominent role in combating Islamist militancy in Dagestan. In mid-December a group of militants entered Dagestani territory, reportedly from Chechnya, killing a unit of border guards and fleeing with a number of hostages. A state of emergency was declared and élite troops were dispatched to the region. Although the armed group fled, after releasing the hostages, at the end of the month it was reported that the majority of the militants had been killed and the remainder taken prisoner.

Economy

In 2000 gross regional product in the Republic of Dagestan amounted to 21,328m. roubles, or 9,885 roubles per head—one of the lowest figures among the federal units. The economic situation in the Republic was severely affected by the wars in Chechnya, mainly as a result of the transport blockade, the energy shortage and the influx of refugees. The Republic's major industrial centres are at Makhachkala, Derbent, Kaspiisk, Izberbash, Khasavyurt, Kizlyar, Kizilyurt and Buinaksk. At the end of 2001 there were 516 km of railways and 7,298 km of paved roads in the Republic. There are fishing and trading ports in Makhachkala, which is a major junction for trading routes by rail, land and sea. The major railway line between Rostov-on-Don and Baku, Azerbaijan, runs across the territory, as does the federal Caucasus highway and the petroleum pipeline between Groznyi and Baku. There is an airport some 15 km from Makhachkala. In September 1997 the federal Government announced that a new section of the petroleum pipeline from Baku would traverse the southern part of Dagestan, rather than run through Chechnya. However, the section was closed indefinitely in June 1999, following an explosion, caused by insurgents.

Owing to its mountainous terrain, Dagestan's economy is largely based on animal husbandry, particularly sheep-breeding. Its agriculture also consists of grain production, viniculture, horticulture and fishing. The agricultural sector employed around 33.7% of the Republic's work-force in 2001 (when just 14.1% worked in industry) and total output in that year amounted to a value of 13,164m. roubles (of this total, crop sales accounted for 40.3% and animal husbandry for 59.7%). Dagestan's main industries are petroleum and natural gas production, electricity generation, mechanical engineering, metal-working and food-processing. Industrial production in 2001 was worth 6,568m. roubles. The Republic's large defence-sector enterprises, such as the Dagdizel Caspian Plant, the Mogomed Gadzhiyev Plant, Aviagregat and the Dagestan Plant of Electrothermal Equipment, were operating below capacity by the mid-1990s.

Dagestan's economically active population comprised 824,000 inhabitants in 2001. In that year over one-quarter of the Republic's labour force (28.8%) were unemployed. In mid-2002 the average monthly wage was 2,188.6 roubles, the lowest recorded in the Federation. There was a budgetary surplus of 106m. roubles in 2001. Foreign investment in the territory was minimal (amounting to just US $53,000 in 1998), owing to Dagestan's proximity to Chechnya and its own incidences of insurgency and unrest. In August 1999 the federal Government approved funds of 100m. roubles in reconstruction assistance and a further 12m. roubles to aid displaced persons. There were 1,952 small businesses in Dagestan at the end of 2001.

Directory

Chairman of the State Council (Head of the Republic): MAGOMEDALI M. MAGOMEDOV; 367005 Dagestan, Makhachkala, pl. Lenina 1; tel. (8722) 67-30-59; fax (8722) 67-30-60; e-mail info@dagestan.ru; internet www.magomedov.ru.

Chairman of the Government: KHIZRI I. SHIKHSAIDOV; 367005 Dagestan, Makhachkala, pl. Lenina; tel. (8722) 67-20-17; internet www.diap.ru.

Chairman of the People's Assembly: MUKHU G. ALIYEV; 367005 Dagestan, Makhachkala, pl. Lenina; tel. (8722) 67-30-55; fax (8722) 67-30-66; internet www.rd.dgu.ru.

Chief Representative of the Republic of Dagestan in the Russian Federation: Ramazan Sh. MAMEDOV GAMZAYEV; 105062 Moscow, ul. Pokrovka 28; tel. (095) 916-15-36; fax (095) 928-41-12.

Head of Makhachkala City Administration: SAID D. AMIROV; 367025 Dagestan, Makhachkala, pl. Lenina 2; tel. (8722) 67-21-57; e-mail z999@km.ru; internet www.makhachkala.dgu.ru.

Republic of Ingushetiya

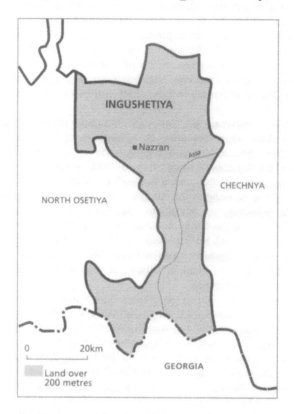

The Republic of Ingushetiya (formerly part of the Checheno-Ingush ASSR) is situated on the northern slopes of the Greater Caucasus, in the centre of the Northern Caucasus mountain ridge. It forms part of the Southern Federal Okrug and the North Caucasus Economic Area. The Republic of Chechnya borders Ingushetiya on its eastern and northern sides and the Republic of North Osetiya—Alaniya lies to the west. In the southern mountains there is an international border with Georgia. The Terek, which forms part of the northern border of Ingushetiya, the Assa and the Sunzha are the territory's main rivers. The Republic is extremely mountainous, with some peaks over 3,000 m high. The territory of the Republic occupies about 3,600 sq km (1,400 sq miles) and includes four cities. However, the border with Chechnya is not exactly determined, and the Ingush were also in dispute with North Osetiya. There were thought to be around 35,000 displaced persons from the Prigorodnyi raion of North Osetiya—Alaniya in the Republic. The number of refugees from Chechnya has fluctuated with the conflict; estimated figures in October 1999 were in the region of 155,000, but one year later the establishment of large-scale refugee camps in the Republic brought the total to around 210,000, although the number had declined to 69,000 by late November 2002, following the commencement of measures by the federal authorities to facilitate the return of refugees to Chechnya.

According to the preliminary results of the census of 9–16 October 2002, the population of the Republic had increased to 468,900, giving a population density of some 130.3 per sq km. Some 42.8% of the population lived in urban areas. The Ingush are a Muslim people closely related to the Chechens (collectively they are known as Vainakhs). They are indigenous to the Caucasus Mountains and have been known historically as Galgai, Lamur, Mountaineers and Kist. Like the Chechen language, their native tongue is a dialect of the Nakh group of the Caucasian language family. Ingushetiya's administrative centre is at Magas, a new city, opened officially in October 1998, which was named after the medieval Alanic capital believed to have been situated thereabouts. Initially the city consisted solely of a gold-domed presidential palace and government buildings, and by January 2001 its population was only about 100. The former capital of Nazran, approximately 15 miles from Magas, remained the largest city in the Republic, with a population of 126,700, according the provisional results of the 2002 census.

History

The Ingush are descended from the western Nakh people, whose different reaction to Russian colonization of the Caucasus region in the 1860s distinguished them from their eastern counterparts (subsequently known as the Chechens). The Chechens resisted the invaders violently and were driven into the mountains, while the Ingush reacted more passively and settled on the plains. Despite this, the Ingush suffered severely under Soviet rule. In 1920 their territory was temporarily integrated into the Mountain (Gorskaya) People's Republic, but became the Ingush Autonomous Oblast on 7 July 1924. In 1934 the region was joined to the Checheno-Ingush Autonomous Oblast, which was upgraded to the status of a Republic in 1936. At that time, many leading Ingush intellectuals became victims of 'purges' and the Ingush literary language was banned. In February 1944 the entire Ingush population (74,000, according to the 1939 census) was deported to Soviet Central Asia, owing to its alleged collaboration with Nazi Germany. The territory was subsequently handed over to the Osetiyans. On their return after rehabilitation in 1957 the Ingush were forced to purchase the property from Osetiyan settlers.

With the ascendancy in the ASSR of the All-National Congress of the Chechen People in 1991, a *de facto* separation between Chechen and Ingush territories was achieved. In June 1992 the Supreme Soviet of the Russian Federation formalized Ingushetiya's existence as a separate republic within the Federation, although the borders between the two new units were not delineated. In addition, the Ingush Republic claimed the eastern regions of North Osetiya and part of the North Osetiyan capital, Vladikavkaz (which had been shared until the 1930s). Prigorodnyi raion (district), with a majority of Ingush inhabitants, was at the centre of the dispute. (A federal law passed in April 1991 established the right for deported peoples to repossess their territory.) Armed hostilities between the two Republics ensued from October 1992, until a peace agreement was signed in 1994, although subsequent relations remained strained.

On 27 February 1994, alongside simultaneous parliamentary and presidential elections in the Republic, 97% of the electorate voted in favour of a draft republican constitution, which took immediate effect. At the republican presidential election, held in March 1998, Ruslan Aushev was re-elected. His popular mandate emboldened him to seek to amend federal law to conform more closely to what he termed 'national traditions', but which also incorporated aspects of *Shari'a*, or Islamic law.

Following a declaration by federal President Boris Yeltsin that a planned referendum, which sought, in particular, to pardon those charged with crimes such as revenge killings, was unconstitutional, in February 1999 Aushev signed a power-sharing agreement with the federal Government. In July Aushev issued a decree, permitting men up to four wives, in breach of the Russian Federation's family code.

The population of Ingushetiya remained generally supportive of the federal authorities, but strongly opposed federal military intervention in Chechnya—Aushev was a prominent critic of the military operations. This apparent inconsistency was reflected in the outcome of the federal presidential election of 26 March 2000; despite his leading role in recommencing armed hostilities in Chechnya, Ingushetiya awarded Vladimir Putin the largest proportion of the votes (85.4%) cast for any candidate in any federal subject. The successful implementation of a settlement between Ingushetiya and North Osetiya, signed in March 2001, according to which the Ingush could return to their former homes in Prigorodnyi and Vladikavkaz, was inhibited by logistical difficulties and protests. In November the People's Assembly voted to shorten the republican presidential term by one year, to four years, and scheduled presidential elections for March 2002. However, in December 2001 the republican Supreme Court declared these measures to be unconstitutional. In late December Aushev resigned, having announced that he would not seek re-election; in January 2002 he was appointed as Ingushetiya's representative in the Federation Council, the upper chamber of the Russian Federal Assembly. Aushev resigned from this position in April, following the disqualification of his preferred candidate for the republican presidency. After an inconclusive first round of voting on 7 April, Murat Zyazikov, the Deputy Presidential Representative in the Southern Federal Okrug (and a general in the Federal Security Service—FSB), and Alikhan Amirkhanov, a State Duma deputy, progressed to a second round. On 28 April Zyazikov was elected President, receiving 53.1% of the votes cast. In late September up to 70 deaths were reported near the village of Galashki, as Chechen rebels, who were reported to have entered the territory from the Pankisi Gorge in Georgia, clashed with federal forces; notably, rebels shot down a helicopter gunship, killing two people. In October Ingushetiya and North Osetiya signed an 'Agreement on the Development of Co-operation and Good Neighbourly Relations', which committed both sides to adopting measures to resolve their remaining differences. On 2 June 2003 Zyazikov dismissed the republican Government, and on 19 June the hitherto Deputy Chairman of the republican Government and a petroleum-industry business executive, Timur Mogushkov, was appointed as Chairman (Prime Minister). At the end of July five federal troops died after their vehicles struck a landmine near Galashki. Subsequently, in mid-September an explosive device, assembled outside the residence of Zyazikov, was successfully disabled. Later in the month three people were killed, and another 31 injured, when a truck bomb was detonated by two suicide bombers outside the offices of the FSB in Magas. At the end of September renewed clashes, apparently involving several hundred rebel fighters, in which at least 17 deaths were reported, broke out between Chechen rebels and troops and police near Galashki, although the rebels subsequently fled, allegedly returning to Chechnya. Republican legislative elections took place on 7 December, concurrently with the federal parliamentary elections.

Economy

In 2000 the gross regional product of the Republic totalled 6,021m. roubles, or 12,690 roubles per head. Essentially agricultural, Ingushetiya had hoped to benefit from the transit of Caspian hydrocarbons from the beginning of the 2000s, although continuing instability in neighbouring Chechnya and Dagestan appeared to reduce its prospects in the short term. At the end of 2001 there were 39 km (24 miles) of railways and 811 km of paved roads in the Republic.

In the early 1990s Ingushetiya's economy was largely agricultural (the sector employed only 8.2% of the Republic's work-force in 2001, compared with 28.5% in 1995), its primary activity being cattle-breeding. The serious decline in agricultural production led to intervention by the republican Government; unprofitable collective farms were converted into private enterprises and joint-stock companies. By 1 January 1997 there were over 1,000 private farms and 20 joint-stock companies in the Republic. In 2001 the value of its agricultural output was 1,217m. roubles. Of this total, crop sales (primarily of grain, fruit and vegetables) generated 42.6% and animal husbandry 57.4%. Ingushetiya's industry, which employed 14.6% of the working population in 2001, consists of electricity production, petroleum-refining and food-processing. The major petroleum company, LUKoil, was a participant in the construction of the Caspian pipeline running through the territory. Total industrial production amounted to a value of 1,028m. roubles in 2001. From the mid-1990s the services sector had also made a contribution to the economy, with the local economy receiving substantial benefits from registration fees paid by companies operating in the so-called 'offshore' tax haven that was in operation in 1994–97. At that time, the resources of this zone accounted for some 70% of the Republic's capital investments, but it was terminated following criticism by the IMF. In 2001 the economic sectors providing the largest share of employment in Ingushetiya were trade and commerce (21.0% of the total) and construction (15.9%).

In 2001 the economically active population of Ingushetiya numbered 145,000, and in that year some 34.9% of the Republic's labour force were unemployed, by far the highest level of any federal subject (excluding Chechnya, for which no figures were available). None the less, this represented a considerable improvement in comparison with the late 1990s; in 1997 as many as 58.2% of Ingushetiya's labour force were out of work, and the rate of unemployment remained in excess of 50% in 1998 and 1999. In 2002 the average monthly wage in the Republic was 3,518.8 roubles. In 2001 the regional budget showed a surplus of 51m. roubles. In that year the value of the Republic's foreign trade amounted to US $83.5m. in exports and $4.2m. in imports. At the end of 2001 there were 128 small businesses in the Republic.

Directory

President: MURAT M. ZYAZIKOV; 366720 Ingushetiya, Magas, Dom Pravitelstva; tel. and fax (87345) 5-11-55; e-mail murad@ingushetia.ru; internet ingushetia.ru.

Chairman of the Government (Prime Minister): TIMOR A. MOGUSHKOV; 366720 Ingushetiya, Magas, Dom Pravitelstva; tel. (87322) 2-56-80.

Chairman of the People's Assembly: RUSLAN S. PLIYEV; 366720 Ingushetiya, Magas, Narodnoye Sobraniye; tel. (87322) 2-61-81; fax (87322) 2-56-80.

Chief Representative of the Republic of Ingushetiya in the Russian Federation: KHAMZAT M. BELKHAROYEV; 109044 Moscow, ul. Vorontsovskaya 22/2; tel. (095) 912-93-09; fax (095) 912-92-75.

Head of Magas City Administration: ILEZ M. MIZIYEV; tel. (87322) 6-10-81.

Kabardino-Balkar Republic
(Kabardino-Balkariya)

The Kabardino-Balkar Republic is situated on the northern slopes of the Greater Caucasus and on the Kabardin Flatlands. It forms part of the Southern Federal Okrug and the North Caucasus Economic Area. The Republic of North Osetiya—Alaniya (Ossetia) lies to the east and there is an international border with Georgia in the south-west. Stavropol Krai lies to the north, with the Republic of Karachayevo-Cherkessiya to the west. Kabardino-Balkariya's major rivers are the Terek, the Malka and the Baskan. The territory of the Republic occupies an area of 12,500 sq km (4,800 sq miles), of which one-half is mountainous. The highest peak in Europe, twin-peaked Elbrus, at a height of 5,642 m (18,517 feet), is situated in Kabardino-Balkariya. The Republic consists of nine administrative districts and eight cities. According to the preliminary results of the census of 9–16 October 2002, the estimated population of the Republic was 900,500, giving a population density of 72.0 per sq km, one of the highest in the Russian Federation; 56.6% of the Republic's population lived in urban areas. Figures from the census of 1989 indicate that at that time some 48.2% of inhabitants were Kabardins, 9.4% were Balkars and 32.0% were Russian. Both the Kabardins and the Balkars are Sunni Muslims. The Kabardins' native language belongs to the Abkhazo-Adyge group of Caucasian languages. The Balkars speak a language closely related to Karachai, part of the Kipchak group of the Turkic branch of the Uralo-Altaic family. Both peoples almost exclusively speak their native tongue as a first language, but many are fluent in the official language, Russian. The capital of the Republic is at Nalchik, which had a population of 273,900 in 2002, according to provisional census results.

History

The Turkic Kabardins, a Muslim people of the North Caucasus, are believed to be descended from the Adyges. They settled on the banks of the Terek river, mixed with the local Alan people, and became a distinct ethnic group in the 15th century. The

Kabardins were converted to Islam by the Tatar Khanate of Crimea in the early 16th century, but in 1561 appealed to Tsar Ivan IV for protection against Tatar rule. The Ottoman Turks and the Persians (Iranians) also had interests in the region, and in 1739 Kabardiya was established as a neutral state between the Ottoman and Russian Empires. In 1774, however, the region once again became Russian territory under the terms of the Treaty of Kuçuk Kainavci. Although the Kabardins were never openly hostile to the Russian authorities, in the 1860s many of them migrated to the Ottoman Empire. The Balkars were pastoral nomads until the mid-18th century, when they were forced by threats from marauding tribes to retreat further into the Northern Caucasus Mountains and settle there as farmers and livestock breeders. They were converted to Islam by Crimean Tatars, followed by the Nogai from the Kuban basin, although their faith retained strong elements of their animist traditions. Balkariya came under Russian control in 1827, when it was dominated by the Kabardins. Many ethnic Russians migrated to the region during the 19th century. In 1921 autonomous Balkar and Kabardin Okrugs were created within the Mountain (Gorskaya) People's Republic (which also included present-day Chechnya, Ingush-etiya, Karachayevo-Cherkessiya and North Osetiya). In January 1922 the two former Okrugs (which had been recently separated from the Mountain Republic and reconstituted as Autonomous Oblasts) were merged into a Kabardino-Balkar Autonomous Okrug, although the progress of integrating the two polities proved difficult, and was achieved in defiance of widespread hostility from representatives of both peoples. The Kabardino-Balkar ASSR was established on 5 December 1936. In 1943 the Balkars were deported to Kazakhstan and Central Asia, in response to their alleged collaboration with German forces, and the Balkar administrative district within the Republic (which was thereby renamed the Kabardin ASSR) was dis-banded. The Balkars were not rehabilitated until 1956, when they were allowed to return to the Caucasus region; in 1957 the Republic reverted to its previous name.

Thus, although greatly outnumbered by Kabardins and Russians, the Balkars had developed a strong sense of ethnic identity. In 1991 they joined the Assembly of Turkic Peoples and on 18 November 1996 the first congress of the National Council of the Balkar People declared the sovereignty of Balkariya and the formation of a 'Republic of Balkariya' within the Russian Federation; this declaration, which reportedly had little support among the Balkar population, was, however, rescinded later in the month. Kabardino-Balkariya declared its sovereignty on 31 December 1991, and signed a bilateral treaty with the federal authorities during 1995. The Republic also developed links with its neighbours: on 21 February 1996 its President, Valerii Kokov, declared that Kabardino-Balkariya would not abide by the Commonwealth of Independent States' decision to impose sanctions on Abkhazia, Georgia, as that would run counter to a treaty between the two polities. In May 1998, at the second session of an interparliamentary council with the Republics of Adygeya and Karachayevo-Cherkessiya, a programme was adopted on the co-ordination of legislative, economic, environmental and legal activities.

Kabardino-Balkariya has an executive presidency and a bicameral Legislative Assembly or Parliament, which comprises an upper chamber, the Council of the Republic, and a lower chamber, the Council of Representatives. In the 1990s the old nomenklatura class remained firmly in control, although its allegiance was divided between the federal Government and the Communist Party. The republican leader-ship took a pragmatic approach to reform and encouraged foreign investment. A new republican Constitution was adopted in July 2001, which prevented the Republic from existing independently of the Russian Federation. In August it was reported that an attempt to stage a *coup d'état* in the Republic, and in neighbouring Karachayevo-Cherkessiya, had been prevented, and that the alleged leader of the plot, Khysyr Sallagarov, had been arrested, along with his accomplices. On 13 January 2002 the incumbent republican President, Valerii Kokov, was elected to serve a third term of office, receiving 87% of the votes cast. Revisions to the republican Constitution, implemented in mid-2002, appeared to have the effect of increasing the protection of political and civil rights in the Republic; henceforth, the ability of the republican authorities to prohibit public demonstrations, rallies and meetings was to be significantly reduced. Republican legislative elections took place on 7 December 2003, concurrently with elections to the federal State Duma.

Economy

Gross regional product in Kabardino-Balkariya amounted to 16,219m. roubles in 2000, equivalent to 20,509 roubles per head. The Republic's main industrial centres are at Nalchik, Tyrnyauz and Prokhladnyi. At the end of 2001 there were 133 km (83 miles) of railways and 2,906 km of roads in the Republic. Prokhladnyi is an important junction on the North Caucasus Railway. There is an international airport at Nalchik, from which there are regular flights to the Middle East, as well as to other cities within the Russian Federation.

Karbardino-Balkariya's main agricultural activities are the production of grain, fruit and vegetables, and animal husbandry. By 1997 there were over 600 private agricultural enterprises in the Republic, covering some 5,500 hectares. In 2001 around 26.6% of the Republic's work-force were engaged in the agricultural sector, the output of which was worth a total of 10,462m. roubles, of which 59.9% was generated by crop sales and 40.1% by animal husbandry. Like the rest of the North Caucasus region, the Republic is rich in minerals, with reserves of petroleum, natural gas, gold, iron ore, garnet, talc and barytes. The Republic's main industries, which employed some 22.0% of the work-force in 2001, are mechanical engineering, metal-working, non-ferrous metallurgy, food-processing, the production of electricity, and the production and processing of tungsten-molybdenum ores. Total industrial output in 2001 was worth 8,564m. roubles.

In 2001 the economically active population of Kabardino-Balkariya numbered 321,000, and some 16.8% of the Republic's labour force were unemployed. In mid-2002 those in employment were earning an average of 2,375.0 roubles per month. In 2001 there was a budgetary surplus of 135m. roubles. External trade is minimal, amounting to only US $9.9m. in 2001. Most of the Republic's exports (of which raw materials comprise some 70%) are to Finland, Germany, the Netherlands, Turkey and the USA. Some four-fifths of its imports are from Europe. Foreign investment in the Republic in 2000 amounted to just $244,000. At 31 December 2001 there was a total of 2,150 small businesses in operation.

Directory

President: VALERII M. KOKOV; 360028 Kabardino-Balkariya, Nalchik, pr. Lenina 27; tel. (8662) 40-41-42; fax (8662) 47-61-74; internet www.nalnet.ru.

Prime Minister: KHUSEIN D. CHECHENOV; 360028 Kabardino-Balkariya, Nalchik, pr. Lenina 27; tel. (8662) 40-29-70; fax (8662) 47-61-83.

Chairman of the Council of the Republic of the Legislative Assembly (Parliament): ZAURBI A. NAKHUSHEV; 360028 Kabardino-Balkariya, Nalchik, pr. Lenina 55; tel. (8662) 47-13-65; fax (8662) 47-27-13.

Chairman of the Council of Representatives in the Legislative Assembly: MURADIN KH. TUMENOV; 360028 Kabardino-Balkariya, Nalchik, pr. Lenina 55; tel. (86622) 40-55-79; fax (86622) 76-27-13.

Chief Representative of the Kabardino-Balkar Republic in the Russian Federation: ANATOLII M. CHERKESOV; 109004 Moscow, ul. B. Kommunisticheskaya 4; tel. (095) 911-18-52; fax (095) 912-40-53.

Head of Nalchik City Administration: MUKHAMED M. SHOGENOV; 360000 Kabardino-Balkariya, Nalchik, ul. Sovetskaya 70; tel. (86622) 2-20-04.

Republic of Kalmykiya

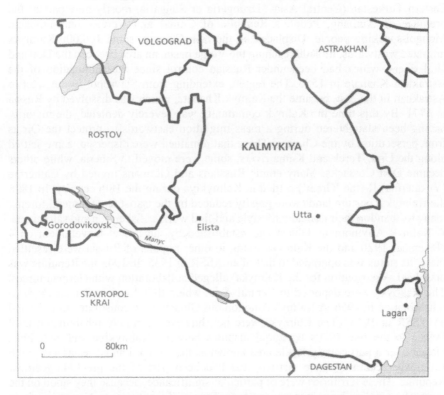

The Republic of Kalmykiya (known as the Republic of Kalmykiya-Khalmg Tangch in 1992–96) is situated in the north-western part of the Caspian Sea lowlands. It forms part of the Southern Federal Okrug and the Volga Economic Area. The south-eastern part of the Republic lies on the Caspian Sea. It has a southern border with the Republic of Dagestan and a south-western border with Stavropol Krai, while Rostov, Volgograd and Astrakhan Oblasts lie to the west, north-west and north-east, respectively. The Republic occupies an area of 75,900 sq km (29,300 sq miles), one-half of which is desert, and comprises 13 administrative districts and three cities. According to the preliminary results of the census of 9–16 October 2002, it had a total population of 292,400, giving a population density of 3.9 per sq km. Some 44.3% of the Republic's population lived in urban areas. In 1989, according to the census, some 45.4% of the total population were Kalmyks and 37.7% Russians. Unusually for Europe, the dominant religion among the Kalmyks is Lamaism (Tibetan Buddhism). Their native language is from the Mongol division of the Uralo-Altaic family and is spoken as a first language by some 90% of the indigenous population. The capital of Kalmykiya is at Elista, which had 104,300 inhabitants in 2002, according to provisional census results.

History

The Kalmyks (also known as the Kalmuks, Kalmucks, and Khalmgs) originated in Eastern Turkestan (Central Asia—Dzungaria or Sungaria, mostly now part of the province of Xinjiang, People's Republic of China) and were a semi-nomadic Mongol-speaking people. Displaced by the Han Chinese, some 100,000 Kalmyks migrated westwards, in 1608 reaching the Volga basin, an area between the Don and Ural rivers, which had been under Russian control since the subjugation of the Astrakhan Khanate in 1556. The region, extending from Stavropol in the west to Astrakhan in the east, became the Kalmyk Khanate, which was dissolved by Russia in 1771. By this time the Kalmyk community was severely depleted, the majority having been slaughtered during a mass migration eastwards to protect the Oirots from persecution by the Chinese. Those that remained were dispersed: some settled along the Ural, Terek and Kuma rivers, some were moved to Siberia, while others became Don Cossacks. Many ethnic Russians and Germans invited by Catherine (Yekaterina) II (the 'Great') settled in Kalmykiya during the 18th century. In 1806 the Kalmyks' pasture lands were greatly reduced by the tsarist Government, forcing many to abandon their nomadic lifestyle and find work as fishermen and salt miners. A Kalmyk Autonomous Oblast was established by the Soviet Government on 4 November 1920 and the Kalmyks living in other regions of Russia were resettled there. Its status was upgraded to that of an ASSR in 1935. In 1943 the Republic was dissolved as retribution for the Kalmyks' alleged collaboration with German forces. The Kalmyks were deported to Central Asia, where they lived until their *de facto* rehabilitation in 1956. A Kalmyk Autonomous Oblast was reconstituted in 1957 and an ASSR in 1958. (The Kalmyks were not, however, formally rehabilitated until 1993.) In the late 1990s territorial disputes between Kalmykiya and Astrakhan Oblast over a particularly fertile area known as the 'Black Lands' resurfaced, with Kalmykiya claiming three districts that had been part of the pre-1943 Kalmyk Republic. These territories were of particular significance, because they stood on the route of a pipeline being constructed from Tengiz, Kazakhstan, to Novorossiisk, in Krasnodar Krai.

During the late 1980s a growing Kalmyk nationalist movement began protesting against the treatment of the Kalmyks under Stalin (Iosif V. Dzhugashvili) and demanding local control of the region's mineral resources. A declaration of sovereignty by the Republic was adopted on 18 October 1990. In April 1993 a business executive, Kirsan Ilyumzhinov, was elected as President of Kalmykiya. In March 1994 Ilyumzhinov abrogated the republican Constitution and decreed that from 25 March only the Russian basic law would be valid in the Republic. However, a new republican Constitution, known as the Steppe Legislation, was adopted on 5 April 1994. The new Constitution provided for a presidential form of government, with a presidential term of seven years, and for a unicameral legislature, the People's Khural, to which deputies were to be elected for terms of four years.

In October 1995 Ilyumzhinov (who was also elected head of the International Chess Federation—FIDE in that year) was the sole, unopposed candidate in the presidential election, in contravention of federal legislation. There was little serious challenge to his rule in the second half of the decade, although he attracted increasing controversy. In early 1998 he issued a decree abolishing the republican Government, in order to reduce public spending and bureaucracy. There were repeated reports of financial irregularities on the part of the republican authorities—the federal legislature instructed the Audit Chamber to investigate the legitimacy of federal budget spending in 1996–98. Reforms to the republican Constitution, approved in mid-2002, appeared to place greater restrictions on the Kalmyk authorities than had hitherto existed; notably, elected local councils were to be established, and heads of local and city administrations to be reinstated. In the first round of presidential elections, held on 21 October, Ilyumzhinov obtained 47.3% of the votes cast. In the second round, held on 27 October, Ilyumzhinov was re-elected as President, receiving around 57% of the votes cast and defeating a banking executive, Baatyr Shondzhiyev. In April 2003 Timofei Sasykov, the republican Minister of Internal Affairs and a close ally of Ilyumzhinov, was dismissed at the instigation of the Federal Ministry of Internal Affairs. He was subsequently detained on suspicion of abuse of office, but was released in mid-July, pending further investigations by the office of the Prosecutor-General of the Southern Federal Okrug. Republican legislative elections took place on 7 December 2003, concurrently with elections to the federal State Duma.

Economy

In 2000 the Republic's gross regional product amounted to 8,845m. roubles, or 28,080 roubles per head. Kalmykiya is primarily an agricultural territory. In the 1990s much of its agricultural land suffered from desertification, a consequence of its irresponsible exploitation by the Soviet authorities during the 1950s, when the fragile black topsoil on the steppe was ploughed up or grazed all year round by sheep and cattle. Kalmykiya's major industrial centres are at Elista and Kaspiisk. At the end of 2001 there were 154 km (96 miles) of railway lines and 2,625 km of paved roads in the Republic; 65% of the road network was paved in 1998. The Republic is intersected by the Astrakhan–Kizlyar railway line. The Republic has serious problems with its water supply, with a deficit of fresh water affecting almost all regions.

Kalmykiya's agriculture consists mainly of animal husbandry. Although agricultural output declined sharply, in real terms, throughout much of the 1990s, by 2001 the sector continued to employ 28.3% of the Republic's work-force, and it generated 1,922m. roubles in that year, compared with 465m. roubles in 1998. Crop sales accounted for 41.6% of total output in 2001, while animal husbandry contributed 58.4%. The Republic's industry, which engaged just 8.2% of the working population in 2001, consists mainly of electricity production, the manufacture of building materials, and the production of petroleum and natural gas. In 2001 industrial output was equivalent to 1,804m. roubles. The Republic has major hydrocarbons reserves, the more efficient exploitation of which was named a primary objective of Aleksandr Dordzhdeyev, the premier appointed in August 1999, who aimed to increase petroleum output in the Republic to between 1.5m. and 2.0m. metric tons each year. In August 1995 Kalmykiya began negotiations with several foreign countries to build a petroleum refinery in Elista with an annual capacity of 500,000 tons. The Oman Oil Company and LUKoil (a Russian company) showed interest in exploiting the Republic's petroleum and natural gas deposits, as part of a wider programme of exploitation across the Northern Caspian region. In September 2000 discussions began on the establishment of a Kalmyk-Belarusian joint venture to extract and process crude petroleum. Despite its potential, Kalmykiya is a net importer of energy.

The economically active population in the Republic amounted to 142,000 in 2001, when some 19.1% of the Republic's labour force were unemployed. The average monthly wage in mid-2002 was 2,564.4 roubles. The cost of a minimum 'consumer basket' of foodstuffs in Elista, purchased in August 2002, was the second cheapest in the Russian Federation. There was a budgetary surplus of 58m. roubles in 2001. Measures introduced by President Kirsan Ilyumzhinov to encourage investment in the Republic (including, notably, the abolition of local taxes for companies, and their replacement with a single fee of US $300, which marked the creation of a 'special economic zone' in 1995), appeared to have little impact on improving either living standards or the republican infrastructure. In 1995 there was some US $1.64m. of foreign investment in the Republic. At the end of 2001 the Republic had 889 small businesses.

Directory

President and Chairman of the Government: Kirsan N. Ilyumzhinov; 358000 Kalmykiya, Elista, pl. Lenina, Dom Pravitelstva; tel. (84722) 6-13-88; fax (84722) 6-28-80; e-mail aris_rk@cityline.ru; internet kalm.ru.

Chairman of the People's Khural (Parliament): Vyacheslav A. Bembetov; 358000 Kalmykiya, Elista, pl. Lenina, Dom Pravitelstva; tel. (84722) 5-27-32; fax (84722) 5-03-02.

Chief Representative of the Republic of Kalmykiya in the Russian Federation: Aleksei M. Orlov; 121170 Moscow, ul. Poklonnaya 12/2; tel. (095) 291-56-72; fax (095) 249-87-41; e-mail fund@elec.ru; internet www.kalmykembassy.ru.

Head of Elista City Administration (Mayor): Radii N. Burulov; 358000 Kalmykiya, Elista, ul. Lenina 249; tel. (84722) 5-35-81; fax (84722) 5-42-56.

Republic of Karachayevo-Cherkessiya

The Republic of Karachayevo-Cherkessiya is situated on the northern slopes of the Greater Caucasus. It forms part of the Southern Federal Okrug and the North Caucasus Economic Area. Krasnodar Krai borders it to the north-west, Stavropol Krai (of which it used to form a part) to the north-east and the Republic of Kabardino-Balkariya to the east. There is an international boundary with Georgia (mainly with Abkhazia) to the south. Its major river is the Kuban. The total area of the Republic occupies some 14,100 sq km (5,440 sq miles). The territory measures 140 km (87 miles) from north to south and 160 km from west to east. Karachayevo-Cherkessiya consists of eight administrative districts and four cities. According to the preliminary results of the census of 9–16 October 2002, it had a total population of 439,700, giving a population density of 31.2 per sq km. Some 44.1% of the Republic's population inhabited urban areas and the capital city, Cherkessk, had a population of 116,400. Figures from the 1989 census showed that the Karachai accounted for 31.2% of the Republic's population, the Cherkess (Circassians) for 9.7% and ethnic Russians for 42.4%. Both the Karachai and the Cherkess are Sunni Muslims of the Hanafi school. The Cherkess speak a language close to Kabardin, from the Abkhazo-Adyge group of Caucasian languages, while the Karachais' native tongue, from the Kipchak group, is the same as that of the Balkars.

History

The Karachai, a transhumant group descended from Kipchak tribes, were driven into the highlands of the North Caucasus by marauding Mongol tribes in the 13th century. Their territory was annexed by the Russian Empire in 1828, although, like their neighbouring North Caucasian peoples, they continued to resist Russian rule throughout the 19th century. In the 1860s and 1870s many Karachai migrated to the Ottoman Empire to escape oppression by the tsarist regime. Many of the Cherkess, a Circassian people descended from the Adyges who inhabited the region between the lower Don and Kuban rivers, also fled across the Russo–Turkish border at this time. They had come under Russian control in the 1550s, having sought protection from the Crimean Tatars and some Turkic tribes, including the Karachai. Relations between the Cherkess and Russia deteriorated as many Russians began to settle in Cherkess territory. Following the Treaty of Adrianople in 1829, by which the Ottomans abandoned their claim to the Caucasus region, a series of rebellions by the Circassians and reprisals by the Russian authorities occurred. In 1864 Russia completed its conquest of the region and many Cherkess fled.

The Cherkess Autonomous Oblast was established in 1928 and was subsequently merged with the Karachai Autonomous Oblast to form the Karachayevo-Cherkess Autonomous Oblast. This represented part of Stalin—Iosif V. Dzhugashvili's policy of 'divide and conquer', by which administrative units were formed from ethnically unrelated groups (the same applied to the Kabardino-Balkar ASSR). The Karachai were deported to Central Asia in late 1943, but the Cherkess remained in the region, which was renamed the Cherkess Autonomous Oblast, until the Karachai were rehabilitated and permitted to return in 1957. Ethnic separatism in the territory, which was upgraded to republican status, and separated from Stavropol Krai, under the terms of the 1992 Federation Treaty, was, however, relatively minimal.

On 6 March 1996 a new constitutional system was adopted in the Republic, based on the results of a referendum on a republican presidency. The Republic had already, in the previous year, agreed on a division of responsibilities by treaty with the Russian Federation. The Communist Party of the Russian Federation remained the predominant party, winning 40% of the republican vote in federal parliamentary elections in late 1995. In May 1998, at the second session of an interparliamentary council with the Republics of Adygeya and Kabardino-Balkariya, a programme was adopted on the co-ordination of the Republics' legislative, economic, environmental and legal activities. The Republic's first presidential election, in 1999, provoked violence and ethnic unrest, when a second round of voting, in May, reversed the positions achieved by the 'run-off' candidates, Stanislav Derev, an ethnic Cherkess (who secured 40% of the votes in the first round and 12% in the second), and Gen. Vladimir Semonov, an ethnic Karachai and a former Commander-in-Chief of the Russian Ground Troops (who secured 18% of the votes in the first round and 85% in the second). Semonov was confirmed as the winning candidate in August and sworn in on 14 September. Derev's supporters continued to protest against the decision, and in mid-September a congress of the Republic's Cherkess and Abazin groups voted to pursue reintegration into the former Cherkess Autonomous Oblast in neighbouring Stavropol Krai. In August 2001 it was reported that an attempt to stage a *coup d'état* in the Republic, and in neighbouring Kabardino-Balkariya, had been prevented, and that the alleged leader of the plot, Khysyr Sallagarov, and his accomplices had been arrested. In the first round of presidential elections, held on 17 August 2003, and in which all five candidates were ethnic Karachai, the largest proportion of the votes cast (41.7%) was awarded to Mustafa Batdyyev, hitherto director of the republican bank; Semonov was the second-placed candidate, with 36.9%. In the run-off election, held on 31 August, Batdyyev, with 48.0% of the votes cast, narrowly defeated Semonov, with 46.4%. The rate of participation in the second round was notably high, at some 67.5%.

Economy

In 2000 gross regional product in Karachayevo-Cherkessiya totalled 5,795m. roubles, or 13,353 roubles per head. The predominant sector within the economy, in terms of volume of output and number of employees, is industry. The Republic's major industrial centres are at Cherkessk, Karachayevsk and Zelenchukskaya. At the end of 2001 it contained 51 km of railway track and 1,889 km of paved roads, including the Stavropol–Sukhumi (Georgia) highway.

Karachayevo-Cherkessiya's agriculture, which employed some 18.6% of the working population in 2001, consists mainly of animal husbandry. At 1 January 1999 there were some 133,000 cattle, 11,700 pigs and 362,800 sheep and goats in the Republic. The production of grain, sunflower seeds, sugar beet and vegetables is also important. In 2001 total agricultural production amounted to a value of 3,559m. roubles, of which crop sales accounted for 50.4% and animal husbandry for 49.6%. The Republic's main industries are petrochemicals, chemicals, mechanical engineering and metal-working, although the manufacture of building materials, food-processing and coal production are also important. In 2001 the total output of the industrial sector was equivalent to 3,985m. roubles, and it employed around 19.4% of the work-force.

In 2001 the economically active population of the Republic numbered 185,000, and 18.6% of the Republic's labour force were unemployed. The average wage was 2,596.6 roubles per month in mid-2002. In 2001 there was a balanced budget. International trade was minimal in comparison with other areas in the Federation, amounting to only US $13.0m. in 2001, and foreign investment in the Republic in that year amounted to just $3,000. At the end of that year there were 1,851 small businesses registered in the Republic.

Directory

President and Head of the Republic: MUSTAFA BATDYYEV; 357100 Karachayevo-Cherkessiya, Cherkessk, ul. Krasnoarmeiskaya 54; tel. (87822) 5-40-11; fax (87822) 5-29-80.

Chairman of the Government: RUSLAN A. KAZANOKOV; 357100 Karachayevo-Cherkessiya, Cherkess, ul. Krasnoarmeiskaya 54; tel. (87822) 5-40-08; fax (87822) 5-40-20.

Chairman of the People's Assembly: (vacant).

Chief Representative of the Republic of Karachayevo-Cherkessiya in the Russian Federation: EMMA M. KARDANOVA; Moscow; tel. (095) 959-55-15.

Head of Cherkessk City Administration (Mayor): MIKHAIL M. YAKUSH; 357100 Karachayevo-Cherkessiya, Cherkessk, pr. Lenina 54A; tel. (87822) 5-37-23; fax (87822) 5-78-43.

Krasnodar Krai

Krasnodar Krai, often known as the Kuban, is situated in the south of European Russia, in the north-western region of the Greater Caucasus and in the Kuban-Azov lowlands. The Krai forms part of the Southern Federal Okrug and the North Caucasus Economic Area. It has a short international border with Georgia (Abkhazia) in the south, while Karachayevo-Cherkessiya and Stavropol Krai lie to the east and Rostov Oblast to the north-east. The Krai's territory encloses the Republic of Adygeya (formerly an Autonomous Oblast within Krasnodar Krai). The Krai lies on the Black Sea (on the shores of which is sited the famous resort town of Sochi) in the south-west and on the Sea of Azov in the north-west. The narrow Kerch Gulf, in places only 10 km (six miles) wide, separates the western tip of the province from Crimea (under Ukrainian jurisdiction since 1954). Its major river is the Kuban. The territory of Krasnodar Krai covers 76,000 sq km (29,340 sq miles) and measures 372 km south to north and 380 km west to east. The region is divided into 38 administrative districts and 26 cities. According to the preliminary results of the census of 9–16 October 2002, Krasnodar Krai had an estimated population of 5,124,400. Its population density at that time was 67.4 per sq km, a considerably higher figure than the national average. Some 53.5% of the population lived in urban areas. Krasnodar, the Krai's administrative centre, had a population of 644,800, according to provisional census figures. Other important cities included Sochi (328,800), Novorossisk (231,900) and Armavir (193,900).

History

Krasnodar city (known as Yekaterinodar until 1920) was founded as a military base in 1793, during the campaign of Catherine (Yekaterina) II—'the Great' to win control of the Black Sea region for the Russian Empire, which was eventually achieved in 1796. Dominated by the 'Whites' in the civil wars that followed the collapse of the tsarist regime, in post-Soviet Russia the area became a stronghold of the Communist Party of the Russian Federation (CPRF). The Krai had been formed on 13 September 1937. In September 1993 the Krasnodar Provincial Soviet condemned President Boris Yeltsin's dissolution of the federal legislature. In October the Soviet refused to dissolve itself, but announced that elections would be held to a new, 32-member, provincial legislative assembly in March 1994, although this poll was subsequently postponed. CPRF leadership of the new Provincial Legislative Assembly was not seriously challenged by other forces, and the party also fared well in federal parliamentary and presidential elections in the province in 1995–96.

During 1996 the incumbent Governor, Nikolai Yegorov, attempted to use the regional courts to postpone the gubernatorial election scheduled for December. He failed, however, and Nikolai Kondratenko, a communist, and the former Chairman of the Provincial Soviet, was elected Governor by a large majority. Supporters of Kondratenko retained control of the provincial legislative assembly at elections held in November 1998. Kondratenko consistently attracted national notoriety by making overtly anti-Semitic remarks and promoting hostility towards other minority groups. Kondratenko was aided in this latter point by the establishment of a voluntary Cossack militia in the region, which was accused of persecuting minority groups. (Notably, however, more than 100,000 migrants from other regions of Russia arrived in the Krai in 1995–2000.) Following a gubernatorial election, held on 3 December 2000, Kondratenko was replaced as Governor by Aleksandr Tkachev, who obtained 82% of the votes cast. Kondratenko did not stand as a candidate in the election, citing ill health. (However, in advance of elections to the federal State Duma in December 2003, the CPRF chose Kondratenko as its second-placed candidate on its federal party list, behind the party leader, Gennadii Zyuganov.) Tkachev also became noted for his xenophobic remarks, on occasion urging various groups of non-ethnic Russians to leave the region. In March 2002, in violation of federal law, the Krai authorities declared the implementation of a 5-km 'border zone' between the Krai and Abkhazia, Georgia, with special permits required for those wishing to enter, leave, reside or work in the zone. In September the Presidential Representative in the Southern Federal Okrug, Col-Gen. Viktor Kazantsev, dismissed the deputy head of the provincial administration, Leonid Baklitskii, following his implication in the misuse of budgetary funds, although concern at the reputed prevalance of corruption in the Krai continued to be reported. At a legislative election, held in the Krai on 24 November, Kondratenko's 'Fatherland' movement (unconnected with the pro-Government Unity and Fatherland-United Russia party) won 32 of the 50 seats, with the CRPF receiving a further 13 seats.

From the late 1990s the presence of up to 21,000 Meshketian Turks—who had been exiled to the region from Georgia under Stalin (Iosif V. Dzhugashvili—1924–53), or who sought refuge in the Krai following the outbreak of inter-ethnic violence in the Fergana valley (in Kyrgyzstan, Tajikistan and Uzbekistan) in 1989 (the majority of whom were stateless)—and of several thousand Armenians in the Krai, were exploited by the chauvinist 'Fatherland' movement. In 2002 the Krai implemented legislation that restricted the granting of permanent residency permits to migrants, and also restricted access to housing and education to those without permanent residency. A new immigration service was established in the Krai in July 2003, initially on an experimental basis, in an attempt to combat the problem of illegal migration to the region. None the less, in October the US mission to the Organization for Security and Co-operation in Europe (OSCE) issued a statement which, *inter alia*, criticized the treatment of Meshketian Turks by the provincial authorities, and which urged the Russian federal authorities to intervene to ensure that full civil rights were granted to the stateless Meshketian Turks resident in Krasnodar Krai.

Meanwhile, in September 2003 work commenced to construct a causeway across the Kerch Strait, which separates the Crimea region of Ukraine from the Taman peninsula, between the Black Sea and the Sea of Azov. The regional authorities stated that the causeway was required to protect part of the Krai from environmental erosion, and Tkachev announced that the causeway could form the basis for a new transport link with Ukraine; however, Ukraine argued that the causeway would encroach on Ukrainian territory, and dispatched border troops to the nearby island of Tuzla, of which it claimed ownership. In late October, following talks between the Russian and Ukrainian Prime Ministers, Russia reportedly agreed to halt work on the causeway's construction, provided that Ukraine withdrew its troops from Tuzla, pending an agreement on the status of the Strait.

Economy

In 2000 gross regional product in Krasnodar Krai amounted to 151,405m. roubles, or 29,905 roubles per head. Krasnodar is one of the Krai's main industrial centres, as are Armavir, Novorossiisk, Kropotkin, Tikhoretsk and Yeisk. Novorossiisk, Tuapse, Yeisk, Temryuk and Port Kavkaz are important seaports. At the end of 2001 the Krai had 2,136 km of railway track and 10,654 km of paved roads.

The Krai's principal crops are grain, sugar beet, rice, tobacco, essential-oil plants, tea and hemp. Horticulture, viniculture and animal husbandry are also important. Agricultural output was worth 62,198m. roubles in 2001, when some 23.3% of the working population were engaged in agriculture. Crop sales accounted for 61.7% of total income generated from agriculture, and animal husbandry for just 38.3%. The agricultural sector of the Krai was affected by prolonged drought conditions in 2002, resulting in the loss of some 300,000 hectares of crops. Widespread, severe flooding in the previous year, in which more than 100 people died, damaged both the agricultural sector and broader infrastructure and industry of the province. There are important reserves of petroleum and natural gas in Krasnodar Krai. In 2000 around 1.7m. metric tons of petroleum were extracted, and 4.3m. tons were refined on the Krai's territory in 1996. Its main industries are food-processing (which comprised 41.9% of industrial output in 2001), electricity generation, fuel extraction, mechanical engineering and metal-working, and building materials. Total production in the sector (which employed 16.2% of the work-force) amounted to a value of 71,134m. roubles in 2001. The tourism sector is also important: the Kuban region's climate, scenery and mineral and mud springs attracted around 6m. visitors annually in the mid-1990s, when some 400,000 people were employed in tourism. The Krai contains the resort towns of Sochi, Anapa and Tuapse. The transportation and refinery of Caspian Sea hydrocarbons reserves brought economic benefits to the region, and particularly Novorossiisk, the terminus of major petroleum pipelines from Baku, Azerbaijan and Tengiz, Kazakhstan, which opened in 1997 and 2001, respectively.

In 2001 the economically active population numbered 2,290,000, and 10.7% of the labour force were unemployed. The average monthly wage was 3,483.8 roubles in mid-2002—the highest rate within the Southern Federal Okrug. In 2001 there was a budgetary surplus of 87m. roubles. In that year international trade comprised exports amounting to US $991.6m., and imports of $627.2m. The recommencement, in January 2003, of passenger rail services between Sochi and Sukhumi, in Abkhazia, for the first time since the initiation of the Abkhaz–Georgian conflict in 1992, was expected to facilitate increased international trade with the separatist region. Foreign investment amounted to $793.4m. in 2001. At 31 December 2001 there were 20,530 small businesses in operation in the Krai.

Directory

Head of the Provincial Administration: ALEKSANDR N. TKACHEV; 350014 Krasnodar, ul. Krasnaya 35; tel. (8612) 62-57-16; fax (8612) 68-25-40; e-mail registry@ kuban.ru; internet admkrai.kuban.ru.

Chairman of the Legislative Assembly: VLADIMIR A. BEKETOV; 350014 Krasnodar, ul. Krasnaya 3; tel. (8612) 68-50-07; fax (8612) 68-37-41.

Representation of Krasnodar Krai in the Russian Federation: 119180 Moscow, per. 2-i Kazachii 6; tel. (095) 238-20-28.

Head of Krasnodar City Administration (Mayor): NIKOLAI V. PRIZ; 350000 Krasnodar, ul. Krasnaya 122; tel. (8612) 55-43-48; fax (8612) 55-01-56; e-mail post@krd.ru; internet www.krd.ru.

Republic of North Osetiya—Alaniya

The Republic of North Osetiya (Severnaya Osetiya), Alaniya, is situated on the northern slopes of the Greater Caucasus and forms part of the Southern Federal Okrug and the North Caucasus Economic Area. Of the other federal subjects, Kabardino-Balkariya lies to the west, Stavropol Krai to the north, and Chechnya and Ingushetiya to the east. There is an international boundary with Georgia (specifically South Ossetia or Osetiya) in the south. Its major river is the Terek. In the north of the Republic are the steppelands of the Mozdok and Osetiyan Plains, while further south in the foothills are mixed pasture and beechwood forest (about one-fifth of the territory of the Republic is forested). Narrow river valleys lie in the southernmost, mountainous region. The territory of North Osetiya covers a total of 8,000 sq km (3,090 sq miles) and comprises eight administrative districts and six cities. According to the preliminary results of the census of 9–16 October 2002, it had a total population of 709,900, giving a population density of 88.7 per sq km. Some 65.4% of the Republic's population inhabited urban areas. In 1989 some 53.0% of the population were Osetiyans and 29.9% ethnic Russians, although around one-quarter of Russians were thought to have left North Osetiya between 1989 and 1999, largely owing to the decline of the military-industrial complex in the Republic, which had been their major employer. The Osetiyans speak an Indo-European language of the Persian (Iranian) group. According to provisional census results, in 2002 315,100 of the region's inhabitants lived in the capital, Vladikavkaz (Ordzho-nikidze 1932–44, 1954–90), situated in the east of the Republic. At the end of 1999 there were approximately 37,000 registered refugees from the armed hostilities

        www.europaworld.com

between South Ossetian and Georgian government forces, although around 1,500 others had returned to Georgia from 1997, as conditions there improved and the economy of North Osetiya deteriorated further. By the end of 1999 about 35,000 Ingush had been displaced from the Prigorodnyi raion of North Osetiya, most of whom were living in Ingushetiya.

History

The Osetiyans (Ossetins, Oselty) are descended from the Alans, a tribe of the Samartian people. The Alans were driven into the foothills of the Caucasus by the Huns in the fourth century and their descendants (Ossetes) were forced further into the mountains by Tatar and Mongol invaders. Although the Osetiyans had been converted to Orthodox Christianity in the 12th and 13th centuries by the Georgians, a sub-group, the Digors, adopted Islam from the Kabardins in the 17th and 18th centuries. Perpetual conflict with the Kabardins forced the Osetiyans to seek the protection of the Russian Empire, and their territory was eventually ceded to Russia by the Ottoman Turks at the Treaty of Kuçuk Kainavci in 1774 and confirmed by the Treaty of Iaşi (Jassy) in 1792. (Transcaucasian Osetiya, or South Ossetia—Osetiya, subsequently became part of Georgia.) The Russians fostered good relations with the Osetiyans, as they represented the principal Christian group among the Muslim peoples of the North Caucasus. Furthermore, both ends of the strategic Darial pass were situated in the region. The completion of the Georgian Military Road in 1799 facilitated the Russian conquest of Georgia (Kartli-Kakheti) in 1801.

After the Bolshevik Revolution, and having briefly been part of the Mountain (Gorskaya) People's Autonomous Republic, North Osetiya was established as an Autonomous Oblast on 7 July 1924, and as an ASSR in 1936. The Osetians were rewarded for their loyalty to the Soviet Government during the Second World War: in 1944 their territory was expanded by the inclusion of former Ingush territories to the east and of part of Stavropol Krai to the north. Furthermore, for 10 years the capital, renamed Ordzhonikidze in 1932, was known as Dzaudzhikau, the Osetian form of Vladikavkaz. The Digors, however, were deported to Central Asia, along with other Muslim peoples, in 1944.

The Republic declared sovereignty in mid-1990. From 1991 there was considerable debate about some form of unification with South Ossetia (which had, however, been deprived of its autonomous status and merged with adjoining regions by the Georgian Supreme Soviet in December 1990.) This resulted in armed hostilities between the South Ossetians and Georgian troops, during which thousands of refugees fled to North Osetiya. Meanwhile, the Republic's administration refused to recognize claims by the Ingush to the territory they were deprived of in 1944 (the Prigorodnyi raion), which led to the onset of violence in October 1992 and the imposition of a state of emergency in the affected areas (see Ingushetiya). Despite a peace settlement in 1994, the region remained unstable. Under the terms of its Constitution, adopted on 7 December 1994, the Republic's name was amended to North Osetiya—Alaniya. A power-sharing agreement was signed with the federal authorities in 1995.

The territory was a redoubt of the Communist Party of the Russian Federation during the late 1990s, although in the 2000 presidential election Vladimir Putin received the highest share of the votes cast for any candidate in the region. In January 1998 Aleksandr Dzasokhov, a former member of the Communist Party of the Soviet Union Politburo, and the chairman of the Russian delegation to the Parliamentary

Assembly of the Council of Europe, was elected as republican President, with 75% of the votes cast. Relations with Ingushetiya remained strained, and in July 1999 the President of Ingushetiya, Ruslan Aushev, announced the suspension of all negotiations with North Osetiya and proposed that direct federal rule be imposed on Prigorodnyi; in March 2000, however, Putin rejected the proposal as unconstitutional.

Instability in North Osetiya, as elsewhere in the North Caucasus, increased during 1999, as insurgency became increasingly widespread. A bomb exploded in Vladikavkaz in March, killing 42, and three further bombs exploded in military residences in May. In March 2001 three simultaneous explosions, which killed over 20, were attributed to Chechen separatists. (The trial of two Ingush residents of Prigorodnyi, on charges of perpetrating bombings in Vladikavkaz in 1999–2002, and of maintaining contacts with Chechen rebels led by Ruslan Gelayev commenced at the Supreme Court of North Osetiya—Alaniya in April 2003.) On 27 January 2002 Dzasokhov was re-elected as President, receiving 56.0% of the votes cast. Notably, 10 days before the election the republican Supreme Court had invalidated the candidacy of the former republican premier, Sergei Khetagurov; this decision was subsequently confirmed by the Federal Supreme Court. In September the power-sharing agreement of 1995 was dissolved, and in October North Osetiya and Ingushetiya signed an 'Agreement on the Development of Co-operation and Good Neighbourly Relations', which committed both sides to adopting measures to resolve remaining differences. Legislative elections were held on 11 May 2003, although repeat elections were required in 31 of the 75 electoral districts on 1 June. Of the 44 deputies elected on 11 May, some 41 were reported to be members or supporters of the pro-Government Unity and Fatherland-United Russia party, giving that party a working majority in the chamber. In early June a suicide bomber detonated explosives close to a bus carrying federal air force personnel, near Mozdok, killing 17 people; later in the month 13 police-officers were killed when their vehicle hit a landmine in the Republic. On 1 August more than 50 people were killed, and at least 100 others injured, following a suicide bombing outside a military hospital at Mozdok; both the commander of the hospital and of the military garrison were subsequently suspended by the federal Ministry of Defence, for permitting a breach of security to occur.

Economy

In 2000 gross regional product in North Osetiya—Alaniya totalled 11,691m. roubles, equivalent to 17,290 roubles per head. Its major industrial centres are at Vladikavkaz, Mozdok and Beslan. At the end of 2001 the Republic contained 144 km (89 miles) of railway track, including a section of the North Caucasus Railway. There were 2,311 km of paved roads, and one of the two principal road routes from Russia to the Transcaucasus; this route, the Transcaucasian Highway, was being upgraded in 2003 at the initiative of the North Osetiyan authorities. There is an international airport at Vladikavkaz.

Agriculture in North Osetiya, which employed 15.6% of the labour force in 2001, consists mainly of vegetable and grain production, horticulture, viniculture and animal husbandry. The rate of reform in agriculture during the 1990s was slow. In 2001 agricultural production amounted to a value of 3,893m. roubles, 41.5% of which was generated by crop sales and 58.5% by animal husbandry. In the same year industrial output was worth 7,265m. roubles, and the sector employed 17.4% of the working population. The Republic's main industries are radio-electronics (until the 1990s largely used for defence purposes), non-ferrous metallurgy and food-processing. There are also five hydroelectric power stations, with an average capacity of around 80 MWh. By the mid-1990s some 70% of industrial production within the defence sector had been converted to civilian use.

The economically active population totalled 343,000 in 2001, when some 16.7% of the labour force were unemployed. Those in employment earned an average wage of 2,522.4 roubles per month in mid-2002. The republican budget showed a surplus of 36m. roubles in 2001. In that year export and import trade together amounted to US $68.0m. Foreign investment remained deterred by the instability endemic to much of the North Caucasus region. At 31 December 2001 there were 3,729 small businesses in operation in North Osetiya.

Directory

President of the Republic: ALEKSANDR S. DZASOKHOV; 362038 North Osetiya—Alaniya, Vladikavkaz, pl. Svobody 1, Dom Pravitelstva; tel. (8672) 53-35-24; fax (8672) 74-92-48; internet president.osetia.ru.

Chairman of the Government: MIKHAIL M. SHATALOV; 362038 North Osetiya—Alaniya, Vladikavkaz, pl. Svobody 1, Dom Pravitelstva; tel. (8672) 53-35-56; fax (8672) 75-87-30.

Chairman of the Parliament: TAIMURAZ D. MAMSUROV; 362038 North Osetiya—Alaniya, Vladikavkaz, pl. Svobody 1; tel. (8672) 53-81-01; fax (8672) 53-93-46; e-mail parliament@rno-a.ru; internet parliament.rno-a.ru.

Chief Representative of the Republic of North Osetiya—Alaniya in the Russian Federation: ERIK R. BUGULOV; 109028 Moscow, per. Durasovskii 1/9; tel. (095) 916-21-47; fax (095) 916-25-22.

Head of Vladikavkaz City Administration (Mayor): MIKHAIL M. SHATALOV; 362040 North Osetiya—Alaniya, Vladikavkaz, pl. Shtyba 1; fax (8672) 75-34-35.

Rostov Oblast

Rostov Oblast is situated in the south of the Eastern European Plain, in the Southern Federal Okrug and the North Caucasus Economic Area. It lies on the Taganrog Gulf of the Sea of Azov. Krasnodar and Stavropol Krais lie to the south and the Republic of Kalmykiya to the south and east. Volgograd Oblast lies to the north-east and Voronezh Oblast to the north-west. The region has an international border with Ukraine to the west. Its major rivers are the Don and the Severnyi Donets. The Volga–Don Canal runs through its territory. Rostov Oblast covers an area of 100,800 sq km (38,910 sq miles) and consists of 43 administrative districts and 23 cities. The region is relatively densely populated—according to the preliminary results of the census of 9–16 October 2002, there was a total of 4,406,700 inhabitants, giving it a population density of 43.7 per sq km. Some 67.6% of the region's inhabitants resided in urban areas. Its administrative centre is at Rostov-on-Don (Rostov-na-Donu), which had a population of 1,070,200 in 2002, according to provisional census results. Other major cities are Taganrog (with a population of 282,300), Shakhty (220,400), Novocherkassk (170,900), Volgodonsk (166,500), Bataisk (107,300) and Novoshakhtinsk (101,200).

History

The city of Rostov-on-Don was established as a Cossack outpost in 1796. It became an important grain-exporting centre in the 19th century, and increased in economic importance after the completion of the Volga–Don Canal. Rostov Oblast was formed in September 1937. The region became heavily industrialized after 1946 and, therefore, considerably increased in population.

In the mid-1990s the liberal Yabloko bloc enjoyed its highest level of support outside the two federal cities and Kamchatka in Rostov, and it managed to obtain over 15% of the votes cast in some parts of the Oblast in elections to the State Duma in December 1999. The regional Government signed a power-sharing treaty with the federal authorities in June 1996. The Oblast directly elected the incumbent, Vladimir Chub, as Governor in September of that year. Chub was re-elected for a further term of office on 23 September 2001, as the candidate of the pro-Government Unity bloc, receiving 78% of the votes cast. (The sole opposition candidate was regarded as an obscure regional official.) Sergei Shilo, the Mayor of Taganrog, the second largest city in the Oblast, and a close ally of Chub, was murdered in October 2002; the killing was believed to be linked with a conflict of business interests. On 29 March 2003, one day before the holding of regional legislative elections, Chub was elected to the Supreme Council of the pro-Government Unity and Fatherland-United Russia (UF-UR) party. In these elections, supporters of UF-UR were successful in 39 districts, although it was reported that many of these candidates had, in fact, concealed their party allegiance; 24 of the 45 deputies elected were business executives. Moreover, the proportion of votes cast 'against all candidates' was reported to be in excess of 20% in several districts. Commentators observed that regional media legislation had resulted in severe restrictions being placed on coverage of candidates' campaigns.

Economy

In 2000 Rostov Oblast's gross regional product stood at 96,000m. roubles, or 22,090 roubles per head. The Oblast's main industrial centres are at Rostov-on-Don, Taganrog, Novocherkassk, Shakhty, Kamensk-Shakhtinskii, Novoshakhtinsk and Volgodonsk. At the end of 2001 there were 1,849 km (1,149 miles) of railways and 11,856 km of paved roads on the Oblast's territory. Its ports are Rostov-on-Don (connected by shipping routes to 16 countries) and Ust-Donetskii, both of which are river-ports.

The Oblast is one of the major grain-producing regions in Russia, with agricultural land comprising some 85% of its territory. The production of sunflower seeds, coriander, mustard, vegetables and cucurbits (gourds and melons) is also important, as are viniculture and horticulture. The sector employed some 18.4% of the working population in 2001, when total agricultural output amounted to a value of 35,452m. roubles. Of this total, 62.5% was contributed by crop sales and 37.5% by animal husbandry. The Oblast is situated in the eastern Donbass coal-mining region and contains some 6,500m. metric tons of coal, as well as significant deposits of anthracite. It is also rich in natural gas, reserves of which are estimated at 54,000m. cu m. Its other principal industries are food-processing, ferrous metallurgy, electricity generation, metal-working and mechanical engineering: Rostov-on-Don contained some 50 machine-building plants. In the early 1990s the industrial association, Rostselmash, produced 70% of all grain combines in Russia (although the quantity produced in 1999 was less than one-50th of that achieved 15 years earlier) and Krasnyi Aksai manufactured 50% of all tractor-mounted cultivators (although from 1997 it specialized in the assembly of automobiles for Daewoo of the Republic of Korea); in Novocherkassk, Krasnyi Kotelshchik produced 70% of Russia's electric locomotives, and is now a joint-stock company; and 60% of the country's steam boilers were made in Taganrog, where the largest industrial concern in the Oblast, Taganrog Metallurgical Plant (TagMet), is located. In 2001 some 19.6% of the Oblast's working population were employed in industry, and industrial production was worth 79,999m. roubles.

The economically active population numbered 2,032,000 in 2001, when 12.9% of the labour force were unemployed. In mid-2002 those in employment earned an average monthly wage of 3,115.2 roubles. The 2001 budget showed a surplus of 158m. roubles. In the same year external trade amounted to a value of US $835.3m. in exports and $647.2m. in imports; total foreign investment in the region amounted to $84.0m. At 31 December 2001 there were some 25,000 small businesses registered in the Oblast.

Directory

Head of the Regional Administration (Governor): VLADIMIR F. CHUB; 344050 Rostov-on-Don, ul. Sotsialisticheskaya 112; tel. (8632) 66-18-10; fax (8632) 65-67-43; e-mail pressa_rra@donpac.ru; internet www.donland.ru.

Chairman of the Legislative Assembly: ALEKSANDR V. POPOV; 344050 Rostov-on-Don, ul. Sotsialisticheskaya 112; tel. (8632) 40-14-47; fax (8632) 40-55-82; internet www.zsro.ru.

Chief Representative of Rostov Oblast in the Russian Federation: VIKTOR P. VODOLATSKII; 127025 Moscow, ul. Novyi Arbat 19/1909; tel. (095) 203-94-71; fax (095) 203-89-58; e-mail info@rostovregion.ru; internet www.rostovregion.ru.

Head of Rostov-on-Don City Administration (Mayor): MIKHAIL A. CHERNYSHEV; 344007 Rostov-on-Don, ul. B. Sadovaya 47; tel. (8632) 44-13-23; fax (8632) 66-62-62; e-mail meria@rostov-gorod.ru; internet www.rostov-gorod.ru.

Stavropol Krai

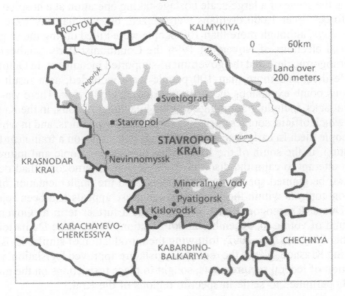

Stavropol Krai is situated in the central Caucasus region and extends from the Caspian lowlands in the east to the foothills of the Greater Caucasus Mountains in the south-west. It is part of the Southern Federal Okrug and the North Caucasus Economic Area. Krasnodar Krai lies to the west, there is a short border with Rostov Oblast in the north-west of the Krai and it shares longer borders with Kalmykiya to the north-east and Dagestan to the east. Chechnya, Ingushetiya, North Osetiya (Ossetia)—Alaniya and Kabardino-Balkariya lie to the south, and Karachayevo-Cherkessiya to the south-west. The Krai's major rivers are the Kuban, the Kuma and the Yegorlyk. Much of its territory is steppe. Its total area is 66,500 sq km (25,670 sq miles), and it is divided into 26 administrative districts and 19 cities. According to the preliminary results of the census of 9–16 October 2002, the population of Stavropol Krai numbered 2,730,500. The Krai's population density, therefore, was 41.1 per sq km; some 55.9% of the population lived in urban areas. The Krai's administrative centre is at Stavropol, which had a population of 354,600 in 2002, according to provisional census results. Other major cities are Pyatigorsk (140,300), Nevinnomyssk (132,100) and Kislovodsk (129,800).

History

Stavropol city was founded in 1777 as part of the consolidation of Russian rule in the Caucasus. The territory was created on 13 February 1924, although it was originally known as South-Eastern Oblast (when it also incorporated territories of Krasnodar Krai) and, subsequently, North Caucasus Krai. It was named Ordzhoni-kidze Krai in 1937–43, before adopting its current title. The former Karachai and Cherkess Autonomous Oblasts, which were reconstituted as the Republic of Kar-achayevo-Cherkessiya upon the adoption of the 1992 Federation Treaty, previously formed part of the Krai.

In March 1994 elections were held to a new representative body, the State Duma. In June 1995 the town of Budennovsk, situated about 150 km north of the Chechen border, was the scene of a large-scale hostage-taking operation at a hospital by rebel Chechen forces; over 1,000 civilians were seized, but the majority were released after a few days, although more than 100 people were killed during the seige. In the gubernatorial elections of November 1996 the Communist Party candidate, Aleksandr Chernogorov, defeated the government-supported incumbent. In October 2000 four people died, and more than 100 people were wounded, as a result of three simultaneous bomb explosions in Pyatigorsk and Nevinomyssk. There was a series of further attacks, including bombings and the hijacking of a bus, in the Krai during 2001–03, which official sources attributed to Chechen separatists, and in which more than 25 people died. In early December 2003 a bomb attack on a train near the town of Yessentuki, in the south of the Krai, killed at least 45 people and injured about 170. In an attempt to calm the disorder in the region, Chernogorov had demanded that the Krai be granted special territorial status and the implementation of stricter immigration controls within the Krai, although these appeals had been rejected by the State Duma. Chernogorov was re-elected for a further term as Governor in a second round of voting in December 2000. Elections to the State Duma took place in December 2001. In June 2002, following the introduction of similar legislation in neighbouring Krasnodar Krai, the regional legislature approved legislation, which, in contravention of federal requirements, sought to place restrictions on the number of immigrants permitted to settle in specific regions of the Krai.

Economy

In 2000 Stavropol Krai's gross regional product was 58,807m. roubles, or 21,884 roubles per head. Its main industrial centres are at Stavropol, Nevinnomyssk, Georgiyevsk and Budennovsk. At the end of 2001 there were 944 km (587 miles) of railway lines and 7,500 km of paved roads on the Krai's territory. In September 1997 the federal Government announced that a new section of a petroleum pipeline from Baku, Azerbaijan, was to cross Stavropol Krai, rather than run through Chechnya.

The Krai contains extremely fertile soil. Its agricultural production, which amounted to a value of 24,825m. roubles in 2001, consists mainly of grain, sunflower seeds and sugar beet and vegetables. Horticulture, viniculture, bee-keeping and animal husbandry are also important. Crop sales accounted for 58.3% of the total value of production in 2001, and animal husbandry for 41.7%. In that year the sector employed 24.5% of the working population. However, the 2003 harvest was expected to be significantly lower than usual, as a result of a prolonged drought in the region. The Krai's main industries are food-processing, mechanical engineering, production of building materials, chemicals and petrochemicals and the production of natural gas, petroleum, non-ferrous metal ores and coal, and electrical energy. Around 16.0% of the labour force worked in industry in 2001, when total industrial output was worth 37,634m. roubles.

The economically active population of Stavropol Krai numbered 1,205,000 in 2001, when 9.8% of the region's labour force were unemployed, compared with 18.5% in 1999. The average wage was 3,015.6 roubles per month in mid-2002. In 2001 there was a budgetary surplus of 174m. roubles. In that year the value of exports from the Krai amounted to US \$292.1m., and imports were worth \$112.4m. Foreign investment in the territory amounted to \$20.9m. At 31 December 2001 there were some 7,100 small businesses in operation.

Directory

Head of the Provincial Administration (Governor): ALEKSANDR L. CHERNOGOROV; 355025 Stavropol, pl. Lenina 1; tel. (8652) 35-22-52; fax (8652) 35-03-30; e-mail stavadm@stavropol.net.

Chairman of the State Duma: YURII A. GONTAR; 355025 Stavropol, pl. Lenina 1; tel. (8652) 34-82-55; fax (8652) 35-14-55.

Representation of Stavropol Krai in the Russian Federation: 127025 Moscow, ul. Novyi Arbat 19/1713; tel. (095) 203-55-36; fax (095) 203-55-39.

Head of Stavropol City Administration (Mayor): DMITRII S. KUZMIN; 355000 Stavropol, pr. K. Marksa 96/307; tel. (8652) 26-78-06; fax (8652) 26-28-23; e-mail goradm@smtn.stavropol.ru; internet www.stavropol.stavkray.ru.

Volgograd Oblast

Volgograd Oblast is situated in the south-east of the Eastern European Plain. It forms part of the Southern Federal Okrug and the Volga Economic Area. The Oblast has an international border with Kazakhstan to its east. The federal subjects of Astrakhan and Kalmykiya lie to the south-east, Rostov to the south-west, Voronezh to the north-west and Saratov to the north. The Oblast's main rivers are the Volga and the Don. Its terrain varies from fertile black earth (*chernozem*) to semi-desert. Volgograd city is the eastern terminus of the Volga–Don Canal. The region occupies an area of 113,900 sq km (43,980 sq miles) and is divided into 33 administrative districts and 19 cities. According to the preliminary results of the census of 9–16 October 2002, the Oblast had a total of 2,702,500 inhabitants, and a population density of 23.7 per sq km. Some 75.2% of the population lived in urban areas. In 1989 around 89% of the population were ethnic Russians, while 3% were Ukrainians, 2% were Kazakhs and 1% were Tatars. In the early 1990s there was an influx of immigrants to the Oblast from more unstable areas of the Caucasus. The Oblast's administrative centre is at Volgograd, which had a population of 1,012,800 in 2002, according to provisional census results. Other major cities are Volzhskii (310,700) and Kamyshin (128,100).

History

The city of Volgograd (known as Tsaritsyn until 1925 and Stalingrad from 1925 until 1961) was founded in the 16th century, to protect the Volga trade route. It was built on the River Volga, at the point where it flows nearest to the Don (the two river systems were later connected by a canal). The Oblast was formed on 10 January 1934. In 1942–43 the city was the scene of a decisive battle between the forces of the USSR and Nazi Germany.

In October 1993 the Regional Soviet in Volgograd Oblast eventually agreed to a reform of the system of government in the Oblast. It decided to hold elections to a new, 30-seat Regional Duma, which took place the following year. The Communist Party of the Russian Federation (CPRF) was the largest single party, and the continued pre-eminence of the old ruling élite was confirmed by the 27% share of the regional poll secured by the CPRF list in the 1995 election to the State Duma. Furthermore, the December 1996 gubernatorial election was won by Nikolai Maksyuta, a communist and a former Chairman of the regional assembly. In December 1998 CPRF candidates won some 23 of the 32 seats in the regional legislative elections. Maksyuta was re-elected for a second term as Governor on 19 December 1999. On 24 September 1998 the Regional Duma had voted for the principle of restoring the Oblast's previous name of Stalingrad, and this notion remained popular, among both members of the oblast legislature, and the broader populace, in the early 2000s; however, in December 2002 federal President Vladimir Putin expressed his opposition to the proposed renaming. On 7 December 2003 regional legislative elections were held, concurrently with elections to the federal State Duma.

Economy

In 2000 Volgograd Oblast's gross regional product amounted to 73,878m. roubles, or 27,680 roubles per head. Its main industrial centres are at Volgograd, Bolzhskii and Kamyshin. At the end of 2001 there were 1,618 km (1,005 miles) of railways and 8,788 km of paved roads. In 1996 construction of a road bridge across the Volga river into Volgograd began.

The region's principal agricultural products are grain, sunflower seeds, vegetables and cucurbits (gourds and melons). Horticulture, bee-keeping and animal husbandry are also important. In 2001 16.6% of the Oblast's work-force were engaged in agriculture. Total agricultural production amounted to a value of 22,684m. roubles in that year, of which crop sales accounted for 59.1% and animal husbandry for 40.9%. The Oblast's mineral reserves include petroleum, natural gas and phosphorites. The main industries in the Oblast are petroleum-refining, chemicals and petrochemicals, mechanical engineering, metal-working, ferrous metallurgy, the production of electricity, food-processing and the production of petroleum and natural gas. Industry employed 22.2% of the working population in 2001, when total industrial production was worth 70,629m. roubles.

The economically active population of the Oblast numbered 1,282,000 in 2001, when 9.8% of the labour force were unemployed—the lowest level, with that of Stavropol Krai, in the Southern Federal Okrug. The average monthly wage was 3,312.7 roubles in mid-2002. In 2001 there was a budgetary surplus of 131m. roubles. In that year external trade constituted US $735.7m. in exports and $272.1m. in imports; total foreign investment amounted to $82.8m. In 2000 there were some 94 joint foreign enterprises in the region, including 10 with investment from Cyprus and eight with investment from the United Kingdom. At the end of 2001 12,794 small businesses were registered in the region.

Directory

Head of the Regional Administration (Governor): NIKOLAI K. MAKSYUTA; 400098 Volgograd, pr. Lenina 9; tel. (8442) 33-66-88; fax (8442) 93-62-12; e-mail glava@volganet.ru; internet www.volganet.ru.

Chairman of the Regional Duma: ROMAN G. GREBENNIKOV; 400098 Volgograd, pr. Lenina 9; tel. (8442) 36-54-25; fax (8422) 36-44-03; internet duma.volganet.ru.

Representation of Volgograd Oblast in the Russian Federation: Moscow; tel. (095) 229-96-73.

Head of Volgograd City Administration (Mayor): YEVGENII P. ISHCHENKO; 400131 Volgograd, ul. Volodarskogo 5; tel. (8442) 33-50-10; fax (8442) 36-64-65; e-mail kancelyaria@volgadmin.ru; internet www.volgadmin.ru.

VOLGA FEDERAL OKRUG

Republic of Bashkortostan

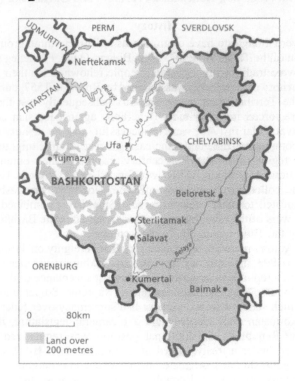

The Republic of Bashkortostan (Bashkiriya) is situated on the slopes of the Southern Urals. It forms part of the Volga Federal Okrug and the Urals Economic Area. Orenburg Oblast lies to the south and south-west of Bashkortostan, and the Republics of Tatarstan and Udmurtiya lie to the west and north-west, respectively. There are borders with Perm and Sverdlovsk Oblasts to the north and Chelyabinsk to the east. The north of the Republic (more than one-third of its land area) is forested, while the southern part is steppe. The Republic occupies an area of 143,600 sq km (55,440 sq miles) and comprises 54 administrative districts and 21 cities. According to the preliminary results of the census of 9–16 October 2002, Bashkortostan had a total population of 4,102,900, giving a population density of 28.6 per sq km. Some 64.1% of the Republic's population inhabited urban areas. The most numerous ethnic group was Russian (39% in 1989). Tatars made up 28% of the population, while Bashkirs only constituted 22%. Of the ethnic Bashkir inhabitants, some 72% spoke Bashkir as their native tongue. Bashkir is a Kipchak language closely related to that spoken by the Tatars. There are two distinct Bashkir dialects:

Kuvakan is spoken in the north of the Republic, while Yurmatin (Yurmatyn) is current in the south. The majority of Bashkirs and Tatars are Sunni Muslims of the Hanafi school, although some Bashkirs, the Nagaibak (Noghaibaq or Nogaibak), were converted to Orthodox Christianity. The Republic's administrative centre is at Ufa, which had a population of 1,042,400 in 2002, according to provisional census results. Its other major cities, with populations in excess of 100,000, are Sterlitamak (264,400), Salavat (158,500), Neftekamsk (122,300) and Oktyabrskii (108,700).

History

The Bashkirs were thought to have originated as a distinct ethnic group during the 16th century, out of the Tatar, Mongol, Volga, Bulgar, Oguz, Pecheneg and Kipchak peoples. They were traditionally a pastoral people renowned for their bee-keeping abilities. The territory of Bashkiriya was annexed by Russia in 1557, during the reign of Ivan IV—'the Terrible', and many Bashkirs subsequently lost their land and wealth and were forced into servitude. Rebellions against Russian control, most notably by Salavat Yulai in 1773, were unsuccessful, and the identity and survival of the Bashkir community came under increasing threat. A large migration of ethnic Russians to the region in the late 19th century resulted in their outnumbering the Bashkir population. A Bashkir ASSR was formed on 23 March 1919. Bashkir resistance to the collectivization policy of Stalin (Iosif V. Dzhugashvili) caused many to be relocated to other regions in the USSR. This, combined with losses during the civil wars of the revolutionary period, resulted in the Bashkirs becoming outnumbered by the Tatar population in the Republic.

The Bashkir Autonomous Republic declared its sovereignty on 11 October 1990. On 12 December 1993, the same day that Murtaza Rakhimov was elected to the new post of President, a republican majority voted against acceptance of the new federal Constitution. On 24 December the republican Supreme Soviet adopted a new Constitution, which stated that its own laws had supremacy over federal laws. The name of Bashkortostan was adopted, and a bicameral legislature, the Kurultai, established. The Republic's constitutional position was regularized and further autonomy granted under a treaty signed on 3 August 1994. By this, the federal authorities granted Bashkortostan greater independence in economic and legislative matters; the administration of the Republic, however, remained highly centralized, with the republican executive retaining extensive controls over both local govern-ment and industry, particularly the petroleum sector. A further bilateral treaty was signed in 1995. A presidential election, held on 14 June 1998, returned Rakhimov to office, his candidacy having been endorsed publicly by the federal President, Boris Yeltsin. In the State Duma elections of December 1999, the candidates of Rakhi-mov's favoured grouping, Fatherland—All Russia, were successful in the Republic; prior to the election Rakhimov was rebuked by the federal Prime Minister, Vladimir Putin, for blocking the transmission of two television channels opposed to the grouping. Commentators also observed the absence of any opposition press in Bashkortostan, and the removal from electoral lists of most of Rakhimov's oppo-nents, owing to alleged electoral violations. In the federal presidential election of 26 March 2000, Bashkortostan returned 62% of votes in favour of Vladimir Putin, well above the national average.

In May 2000 Putin ordered that Bashkortostan's Constitution be altered to conform with Russia's basic law. A new republican Constitution was introduced in November, although several articles continued to contradict federal norms. In

January 2001 one of the most significant contradictions, the statement that republican legislation should take precedence over federal law, was rescinded, and several powers formerly attributed to the republican prime minister were transferred to the republican president. In June 2002 the federal Supreme Court ruled that some 37 articles of Bashkortostan's new Constitution failed to comply with federal law, and the redaction of a further new Constitution commenced. Rakhimov declared that he wished to introduce a parliamentary system of government, and to abolish the republican presidency; in mid-November, however, this measure was rejected by the legislature, which expressed concern that the introduction of a directly elected prime minister would effectively result in the maintenance of a presidential system.

On 3 December 2002 a new Constitution was adopted, which, notably, combined the posts of president and prime minister, while maintaining a presidential system of Government. The new document removed all references to the 'sovereignty' of Bashkortostan found in its predecessors, although reference was made to the 'statehood' of the Republic. None the less, the text was widely regarded as broadly conforming with federal laws, although the future of the bilateral treaties signed between the republican and federal authorities in 1994 and 1995 remained unclear. The new Constitution also introduced a unicameral legislative assembly, which retained the name of its bicameral predecessor, the Kurultai. This new body was to have a term of five years, compared with the four-year term enjoyed by its predecessor. One of the final decisions made by the outgoing legislature, in early March 2003, was to extend Rakhimov's term of office from mid-June, when it had been due to expire, until December, in order that the republican presidential elections would be held concurrently with those to the federal State Duma.

At elections to the new Kurultai, held on 16 March 2003, the pro-Government Unity and Fatherland-United Russia (UF-UR) party obtained control of 91 of the 120 seats. Notably, Ural Rakhimov, the son of the President, who also held senior positions at three petroleum-sector companies owned by the republican Government, was elected to the Kurultai as a deputy of UF-UR. In July the federal Constitutional Court ruled that it was the sole body with the authority to determine whether the constitutions of federal subjects were in conformity with federal law; one consequence of this ruling appeared to be that a number of challenges to the former Constitutions of Bashkortostan from other bodies (such as the republican Supreme Court) were thereby effectively invalidated, and it appeared likely that measures to rewrite the new Constitution, so as to reintroduce the notion of republican sovereignity, would ensue. In the first round of the republican presidential election, held on 7 December, no candidate received an absolute majority of the votes cast. Rakhimov and the second-placed candidate, Sergei Veremeyenko, duly proceeded to a second round of voting on 21 December. Prior to the 'run-off' election, Veremeyenko announced that he had ceased campaigning, although his name remained on the ballot. This effective lack of opposition enabled Rakhimov to secure re-election, with some 78% of the votes cast. Subsequently, the third-placed candidate in the first round of voting, Relif Sarin, an outspoken opponent of Rakhimov, commenced an appeal at the republican Supreme Court to annul the results of the election, citing some 700 alleged violations of electoral legislation. On 15 January 2004 Rakhimov appointed Rafael Baidavletov as republican premier (he had previously held this position from 1999 until its abolition in 2002), following the unanimous approval of his nomination by the Kurultai.

Economy

Bashkortostan's economy is dominated by its fuel and energy and agro-industrial complexes. The Republic is one of Russia's key petroleum-producing areas and the centre of its petroleum-refining industry. It produced 4% of Russia's total petroleum output in the first six months of 2000 and accounted for around 15% of its petroleum-refining. However, the quantity of petroleum both produced and refined in the Republic declined significantly during the 1990s. In 2000 the territory's gross regional product stood at 160,751m. roubles, or 39,083 roubles per head. Amid concerns that the federal Government was seeking to gain increased control over the natural resources of the Republic, at the expense of the republican authorities, republican President Rakhimov announced, in August 2002, that several of the republican petroleum companies were to be transferred to private ownership. Bashkortostan's major industrial centres are at Ufa (at which the Republic's petroleum refineries are based), Sterlitamak, Salavat and Ishimbai. At the end of 2001 there were 1,461 km (908 miles) of railways on its territory, and 21,952 km of paved roads. Bashkir Airlines (BAL) operates air services between Ufa and major centres within Russia and elsewhere within the Commonwealth of Independent States from the Republic's international airport.

Bashkortostan's agricultural production, the value of which amounted to 36,488m. roubles in 2001 (with crop sales accounting for 44.2% and animal husbandry for 55.8%), ranks among the highest in the Russian Federation. Its main agricultural activities are grain and vegetable production, animal husbandry and bee-keeping. Some 18.0% of the Republic's work-force were employed in agriculture in 2001. As well as its petroleum resources (of which the deposits amount to 400m. metric tons), Bashkortostan contains deposits of natural gas (55m. tons), brown coal—lignite (250m. tons), iron ore, copper, gold (with reserves amounting to 32 tons in 1997, sufficient for 19 years of production), zinc, aluminium, chromium, salt (2,270m. tons), manganese, gypsum and limestone. The Republic's other industries include mechanical engineering, metal-working, electricity generation, and chemicals and petrochemicals. In 2001 industry employed 23.4% of the Republic's working population. Total industrial output was worth 157,059m. roubles in that year.

In 2001 the economically active population of the Republic amounted to 1,893,000, and 10.7% of the labour force were unemployed. The average monthly wage was 3,780.0 roubles in mid-2002. In 2001 there was a budgetary deficit of 852m. roubles. In the same year the Republic's external trade totalled US $2,489.2m., of which exports, largely comprising petroleum products and petro-chemical goods, accounted for $2,226.8m. Bashkortostan's principal trading partner is Germany. In 2001 foreign investment in the Republic amounted to some $29.6m. At the end of the year there were 14,261 small businesses registered on the Republic's territory.

Directory

President: MURTAZA G. RAKHIMOV; 450101 Bashkortostan, Ufa, ul. Tukayeva 46; tel. (3472) 50-27-24; fax (3472) 50-02-81; e-mail aprbinfo@admbashkortostan.ru; internet www.bashkortostan.ru.

Prime Minister: RAFAEL I. BAIDAVLETOV; 450101 Bashkortostan, Ufa, ul. Tukayeva 46, Dom Respubliki; tel. (3472) 50-27-24; fax (3472) 50-02-81.

Chairman of the State Assembly (Kurultai): KONSTANTIN B. TOLKACHEV; 450101 Bashkortostan, Ufa, ul. Tukayeva 46; tel. (3472) 50-19-15; fax (3472) 50-08-86; e-mail pred@kurultai.rb.ru; internet www.gs.rb.ru.

Chief Representative of the Republic of Bashkortostan in the Russian Federation: IREK YU. ABLAYEV; 103045 Moscow, Sretenskii bulv. 9/2; tel. (095) 208-46-62; fax (095) 208-39-25.

Head of Ufa City Administration (Mayor): PAVEL R. KACHKAYEV; 450098 Bashkortostan, Ufa, pr. Oktyabrya 120; tel. (3472) 79-05-79; fax (3472) 33-18-73; e-mail cityadmin@ufacity.info; internet www.ufacity.info.

Chuvash Republic (Chuvashiya)

The Chuvash Republic is situated in the north-west of European Russia. It forms part of the Volga Federal Okrug and the Volga-Vyatka Economic Area. The Republic lies on the Eastern European Plain, on the middle reaches of the Volga. Ulyanovsk Oblast neighbours it to the south, the Republic of Mordoviya to the south-west, Nizhnii Novgorod Oblast to the west and the Republics of Marii-El and Tatarstan to the north and the east, respectively. The Republic's major rivers are the Volga and the Sura, and one-third of its territory is covered by forest. It occupies 18,300 sq km (7,070 sq miles) and comprises 21 administrative districts and nine cities. The territory measures 190 km (118 miles) from south to north and 160 km from west to east. According to the preliminary results of the census of 9–16 October 2002, the Republic had a total population of 1,313,900 and a relatively high population density of 71.8 per sq km. Some 60.6% of the population lived in towns. In contrast to the native peoples in the majority of autonomous republics, the Chuvash outnumber ethnic Russians in Chuvashiya: at the census of 1989, 67.8% of inhabitants were Chuvash and 26.7% Russian. The native tongue of the Republic is Chuvash, which has its origins in the Bulgar group of the Western Hunnic group of Turkic languages and is related to ancient Bulgar and Khazar. It is spoken as a first language by an estimated 76.5% of Chuvash. The dominant religions in Chuvashiya are Islam and Orthodox Christianity. Chuvashiya's capital is at Cheboksary (Shupashkar—with a population of 440,800 in 2002, according to provisional census results). Its other major town is nearby Novocheboksarsk, with 125,900 inhabitants.

History

The Chuvash, traditionally a semi-nomadic people, were conquered by the Mongol-Tatars in the 13th century. Their territory subsequently became part of the dominion of the Golden Horde and many were converted to Islam. From the late 1430s the Chuvash were ruled by the Kazan Khanate. In 1551 Chuvashiya became a part of the Russian Empire. Despite intense Christianization and 'russification' on the part of the Russian state, the Chuvash acquired their own national and cultural identity, which had Suvar-Bulgar and Finno-Ugric components, by the end of the 15th century. The Chuvash capital was founded at Cheboksary in 1551, at the site of a settlement first mentioned in Russian chronicles in 1469. The construction of other towns and forts, intended to encourage migration into the area, followed. After 1917 the Chuvash people made vociferous demands for autonomy to the Soviet Government. A Chuvash Autonomous Oblast was established on 24 June 1920, which was upgraded to the status of an ASSR on 21 April 1925.

Chuvash nationalism re-emerged in the early 1990s: the Chuvash ASSR declared its sovereignty on 27 October 1990. It adopted the name of the Chuvash (Chavash) Republic in March 1992. In December 1993 the Republic voted against acceptance of the federal Constitution. In May 1996 the Chuvash Government signed a treaty with the Russian President, Boris Yeltsin, on the delimitation of powers. It granted the Republic greater freedom to determine policy in political, economic and social areas. Elections to the 87-seat republican legislature, the State Council, were held on 13 July 1998, with further elections for 23 unfilled seats on 1 November. In October 2001 the Chairman of the republican Council of Ministers, Enver Ablyakimov, resigned; republican President Nikolai Fedorov appointed himself to the position, announcing that combining the roles of republican president and prime minister would increase the Government's accountability. Fedorov was re-elected, with some 41% of the votes, in the presidential election held in Chuvashiya on 16 December. However, immediately following his re-election as Governor, Fedorov announced that he was to rescind his position as Chairman of the Council of Ministers (Prime Minister); Nataliya Partasova assumed this position. Elections to the republican legislature were held on 21 June 2002. In March 2003 the State Council voted to extend the term of office of deputies from four to five years.

Economy

In 2000 the Republic's gross regional product amounted to 25,189m. roubles, equivalent to 18,603 roubles per head, the lowest level in the Volga Federal Okrug. Chuvashiya's major industrial centres are at Cheboksary, Novocheboksarsk, Kanash and Alatyr. At the end of 2001 there were 396 km of railways and 4,578 km of paved roads on the Republic's territory.

Agriculture, which employed 22.3% of the work-force in 2001, consists mainly of grain, potato and hop production, and animal husbandry. The value of total agricultural output in that year amounted to 10,151m. roubles, equally divided between crop sales and animal husbandry. The Republic contains deposits of peat, sand, limestone and dolomite. Its main industries are mechanical engineering, metal-working, electricity generation, production of chemicals and petrochemicals, light industry and food-processing. The industrial sector employed 24.4% of the working population in 2001, and generated 26,127m. roubles.

The economically active population in Chuvashiya amounted to 668,000 in 2001; 9.6% of the Republic's labour force were unemployed. The average monthly wage in the territory was 2,435.3 roubles in mid-2002. In 2001 there was a budgetary surplus of 67m. roubles. In that year exports from the Republic amounted to US $71.4m., and imports to the Republic to $69.6m. Chuvashiya's major trading partners are the People's Republic of China, Finland, Germany, Italy, the Netherlands, Poland, Ukraine and the USA. Foreign investment in 2001 was worth $34.7m., compared with $1.7m. in the previous year. At 31 December 2001 there were some 4,000 small businesses operating in Chuvashiya.

Directory

President: NIKOLAI V. FEDOROV; 428004 Chuvashiya, Cheboksary, pl. Respubliki 1; tel. (8352) 62-46-87; fax (8352) 62-17-99; e-mail president@cap.ru; internet www .cap.ru.

Chairman of the Cabinet of Ministers (Prime Minister): NATALIYA YU. PARTASOVA; 428004 Chuvashiya, Cheboksary, pl. Respubliki 1; tel. (8352) 62-01-76; fax (8352) 62-31-84; e-mail partasova@chuvashia.com.

Chairman of the State Council (Parliament): MIKHAIL A. MIKHAILOVSKII; 428004 Chuvashiya, Cheboksary, pl. Respubliki 1; tel. (8352) 62-22-72; fax (8352) 62-23-15; e-mail gs@cap.ru; internet www.gs.chuvashia.com.

Chief Representative of the Chuvash Republic in the Russian Federation: GENNADII S. FEDOROV; 119017 Moscow, ul. B. Ordynka 46/1; tel. and fax (095) 953-21-59.

Head of Cheboksary City Administration (Mayor): NIKOLAI I. YEMELYANOV; 428004 Chuvashiya, Cheboksary, ul. K. Marksa 36; tel. (8352) 62-35-76; fax (8352) 62-40-50; e-mail gcheb@cap.ru; internet www.gcheb.cap.ru.

Kirov Oblast

Kirov Oblast is situated in the east of the Eastern European Plain. It forms part of the Volga Federal Okrug and the Volga-Vyatka Economic Area. It is bordered by Archangel and Komi to the north, the Komi-Permyak AOk (part of Perm Oblast) and Udmurtiya to the east, Tatarstan and Marii-El to the south, and Nizhnii Novgorod, Kostroma and Vologda to the west. Its main rivers are the Kama and the Vyatka; in addition there are almost 20,000 rivers and more than 1,000 lakes on its territory. Kirov occupies a total area of 120,800 sq km (46,640 sq miles) and measures 570 km (354 miles) from south to north and 440 km from west to east. It is divided into 39 administrative districts and 18 cities. According to the preliminary results of the census of 9–16 October 2002, the Oblast's total population numbered 1,503,600 and the population density was 12.4 per sq km. Around 71.8% of the population inhabited urban areas. At the census of 1989 ethnic Russians comprised 90.4% of the population. The Oblast's administrative centre is at Kirov (Vyatka), a river-port, which had 457,400 inhabitants in 2002, according to provisional census results.

History

The city of Khlynov was founded in 1181 as an outpost of Novgorod, and came under Muscovite rule in 1489. The city was renamed Vyatka in 1780, and Kirov in 1934, when Kirov Oblast was formed. In September 1993 a draft constitution for Kirov Oblast was prepared, which referred to the Oblast as Vyatka Krai and provided for a universally elected governor and a new legislature, a provincial duma. On 18 October the Kirov Regional Soviet voted to disband itself. The federal authorities refused to acknowledge the area's redesignation and during 1994 a Regional Duma was elected.

The most popular party in the mid-1990s was that of the nationalist supporters of Vladimir Zhirinovskii, although members of the old communist establishment were well represented in its ranks. The Communist Party of the Russian Federation candidate, Vladimir Sergeyenkov, was elected as Governor, by a narrow margin, in October 1996. In October 1997 Sergeyenkov signed a power-sharing treaty with federal President Boris Yeltsin, with the specific hope that investment in the extraction of raw materials and health care would benefit the region. Sergeyenkov was re-elected, with 58% of the votes cast, on 26 March 2000, in elections that had been brought forward by seven months to coincide with those to the federal presidency. In 2003 gubernatorial elections were again held early, on 7 December, concurrently with elections to the federal State Duma. No candidate won an overall majority of the votes cast in the first round of voting, which was not contested by Sergeyenkov. Therefore, the two leading candidates, Nikolai Shaklein and Oleg Valenchuk, proceeded to a 'run-off' election, held on 21 December, in which Shaklein was elected as Governor, securing 62.7% of the votes cast.

Economy

In 2000 the Oblast's gross regional product (GRP) stood at 38,065m. roubles, equivalent to 24,058 roubles per head. Its main industrial centres are at Kirov, Slobodskoi, Kotelnich, Omutninsk, Kirovo-Chepetsk and Vyatskiye Polyany. At the end of 2001 there were 1,098 km of railway track in the region and 8,989 km of paved roads. There are also over 2,000 km of navigable waterways on the Vyatka river. Owing to the density of rivers in the region its soil is high in mineral salts, reducing its fertility.

The Oblast's agriculture, which employed 16.5% of the working population in 2001, consists mainly of animal husbandry and the production of grain, flax and vegetables. Total output within the sector amounted to 14,016m. roubles in 2001, of which crop sales generated 48.0% and animal husbandry 52%. Kirov Oblast has significant deposits of peat, estimated at 435m. metric tons, and phosphorites, reserves of which amounted to some 2,000m. tons in the mid-1990s. Its main industries are mechanical engineering, the production of electrical energy, metal-working, chemicals and petrochemicals and the processing of agricultural and forestry products. In March 1998 the regional administration signed a protocol with the federal ministries of defence and the economy on the restructuring of the Oblast's military-industrial complex, which in 1997 accounted for just one-10th of the Oblast's GRP, despite owning 58% of its main assets. The region was also renowned for the manufacturing of toys and wood products (especially skis). Industry employed 27.5% of the work-force in 2001 and generated 35,057m. roubles.

The economically active population numbered 848,000 in 2001, when just 7.7% of the Oblast's labour force were unemployed, one of the lowest levels recorded in any federal subject. The average monthly wage was 3,105.2 roubles at mid-2002. However, in May 2003 the Oblast was named as one of the three federal subjects with the worst record on wage arrears. In 2001 the Oblast recorded a budgetary deficit of 173m. roubles. In 2001 exports amounted to a value of US $242.6m., while imports were worth $38.0m. In 2001 foreign investment amounted to $3.8m. In late 2001 there were 3,880 small businesses registered in Kirov Oblast.

Directory

Head of the Regional Administration (Governor): VLADIMIR N. SERGEYENKOV; 610019 Kirov, ul. K. Libknekhta 69; tel. (8332) 62-95-64; fax (8332) 62-89-58; e-mail region@gov-vyatka.ru; internet gov-vyatka.ru.

Chairman of the Regional Duma: ALEKSANDR N. STRELNIKOV; 610019 Kirov, ul. K. Libknekhta 69; tel. and fax (8332) 62-48-00; e-mail assembly@gov-vyatka.ru.

Representation of Kirov Oblast in the Russian Federation: 109028 Moscow, ul. Zemlyanoi Val 50/2; tel. (095) 916-69-42; e-mail kirovmos@rol.ru.

Head of Kirov City Administration (Mayor): VASILII A. KISELEV; 610000 Kirov, ul. Vorovskogo 39; tel. (8332) 62-89-40; fax (8332) 67-69-91.

Republic of Marii-El

The Republic of Marii-El is situated in the east of the Eastern European Plain in the middle reaches of the River Volga. It forms part of the Volga Federal Okrug and the Volga-Vyatka Economic Area. Tatarstan and Chuvashiya neighbour it to the south-east and to the south, respectively. Nizhnii Novgorod Oblast lies to the west and Kirov Oblast to the north and north-east. Its major rivers are the Volga, and its tributary, the Vetluga, and about one-half of its territory is forested. Marii-El measures 150 km (over 90 miles) from south to north and 275 km from west to east. It occupies an area of 23,200 sq km (9,000 sq miles) and consists of 14 administrative districts and four cities. According to the preliminary results of the census of 9–16 October 2002, the total population was 728,000, and the population density approximately 31.4 per sq km. Some 63.2% of the population inhabited urban areas. In 1989 some 43.3% of the Republic's inhabitants were Mari (also known as Cheremiss) and 47.5% ethnic Russians. Orthodox Christianity is the predominant religion in Marii-El, although many Mari have remained faithful to aspects of their traditional animistic religion. Their native language belongs to the Finnic branch of the Uralo-Altaic family. The capital of the Republic is at Yoshkar-Ola, with a population of 256,800 in 2002, according to provisional census results.

History

The Mari emerged as a distinct ethnic group in the sixth century. In the eighth century they came under the influence of the Khazar empire, but from the mid-ninth to the mid-12th century they were ruled by the Volga Bulgars. In the 1230s Mari territory was conquered by the Mongol Tatars and remained under the control of the Khazar Khanate until its annexation by Russia in 1552. Nationalist feeling on the part of the Mari did not become evident until the 1870s, when a religious movement, the Kugu Sorta (Great Candle), attacked the authority of the Orthodox Church in the region. A Mari Autonomous Oblast was established in 1920. On 5 December 1936 the territory became the Mari ASSR.

The Republic declared its sovereignty on 22 October 1990. A presidential election was held on 14 December 1991. In December 1993 elections were held to a new 300-seat parliament, the State Assembly, which was dominated by the Communist Party. The new legislature adopted the republican Constitution in June 1995, when the territory became known as the Republic of Marii-El. A power-sharing agreement between the Republic and the federal Government was signed in May 1998. At parliamentary elections held in the Republic in October 2000, left-wing and communist candidates secured the highest proportion of the votes cast. At gubernatorial elections in December the incumbent, Vyacheslav Kislitsyn, was defeated by Leonid Markelov, who represented the nationalist Liberal Democratic Party of Russia of Vladimir Zhirinovskii.

Economy

In 2000 the Republic's gross regional product amounted to 11,863m. roubles, equivalent to 15,669 roubles per head. Its major industrial centres are at Yoshkar-Ola and Volzhsk. At the end of 2001 there were 200 km of railway lines and 3,247 km of paved roads on the Republic's territory.

Marii-El's agriculture, which in 2001 employed 19.4% of the work-force, consists mainly of animal husbandry and the production of flax, vegetables, potatoes and grain. Total agricultural output in 2001 was worth 6,712m. roubles, of which crop sales accounted for 51.5% and animal husbandry for 48.5%. The Republic's main industries are mechanical engineering, metal-working, electricity production and the processing of forestry and food products. The total value of production within the industrial sector (which employed 24.5% of the work-force) was 10,631m. roubles in 2001.

In 2001 the economically active population in the Republic numbered 372,000, and 9.4% of the labour force were unemployed; in mid-2002 those in employment earned an average of 2,358.6 roubles per month. In 2001 there was a budgetary deficit of 35.0m. roubles. In that year the value of external trade with the Republic amounted to just US $46.9m. (of which exports accounted for $33.0m.). Exports primarily comprised raw materials (peat), machine parts and medical supplies, and its major international trading partners were Belarus, Finland, France, Germany, Ireland, Italy, Kazakhstan, the Netherlands, Ukraine, the United Kingdom and the USA. Foreign investment in Marii-El was minimal, amounting to just $140,000 in 2000. At 31 December 2001 some 4,100 small businesses were registered in the Republic.

Directory

President and Head of the Government: LEONID I. MARKELOV; 424001 Marii-El, Yoshkar-Ola, Leninskii pr. 29; tel. (8362) 64-15-25; fax (8362) 64-19-21; e-mail president@gov.mari.ru; internet gov.mari.ru.

Chairman of the State Assembly: YURII A. MINAKOV; 424001 Marii-El, Yoshkar-Ola, Leninskii pr. 29; tel. (8362) 64-14-13; e-mail parliament@gov.mari.ru; internet parliament.mari.ru.

Chief Representative of the Republic of Marii-El in the Russian Federation: VIKTOR P. RASSONOV; 119019 Moscow, ul. Novyi Arbat 21; tel. (095) 291-48-38; fax (095) 291-46-32.

Head of Yoshkar-Ola City Administration (Mayor): VLADIMIR V. TARKOV; 424001 Marii-El, Yoshkar-Ola, Leninskii pr. 27; tel. (8362) 55-64-01; fax (8362) 55-64-22; internet capital.mari-el.ru:8101.

Republic of Mordoviya

The Republic of Mordoviya is situated in the Eastern European Plain, in the Volga river basin. The north-west of the Republic occupies a section of the Oka-Don plain and the south-east lies in the Volga Highlands. The region forms part of the Volga Federal Okrug and the Volga-Vyatka Economic Area. The Republic of Chuvashiya lies to the north-east of Mordoviya. The neighbouring oblasts are Ulyanovsk to the east, Penza to the south, Ryazan to the west and Nizhnii Novgorod to the north. The major rivers in Mordoviya are the Moksha, the Sura and the Insar; one-quarter of its land area is forested. The territory of Mordoviya straddles the two major natural regions in Russia, forest and steppe, and occupies an area of 26,200 sq km (10,110 sq miles). The Republic consists of 22 administrative districts and seven cities. Its climate is continental, but with unpredictable levels of precipitation. According to the preliminary results of the census of 9–16 October 2002, the Republic had a population of 888,700 and a population density, therefore, of 33.9 per sq km. Some 59.8% of the Republic's population inhabited urban areas. In 1989 some 32.5% of the total population were Mordovians and 60.8% Russians. The majority of Mordovians inhabited the agricultural regions of the west and north-east. The capital, Saransk, is a major rail junction and the Moscow–Samara highway passes through the south-west of the Republic. The dominant religion among the Republic's inhabitants is Orthodox Christianity. The native tongue of the Mordovians belongs to the Finnic group of the Uralo-Altaic family, although this is spoken as a first language by less than two-thirds of the ethnic group. Mordoviya's capital is at Saransk, which lies on the River Insar and had a population of 304,900 in 2002, according to provisional census results.

History

The Mordovians (Mordvinians) first appear in historical records of the sixth century, when they inhabited the area between the Oka and the middle Volga rivers. Their territory's capital was, possibly, on the site of Nizhnii Novgorod, before it was conquered by the Russians in 1172. In the late 12th and early 13th centuries a feudal society began to form in Mordoviya. One of its most famous fiefdoms was Purgasov Volost, headed by Prince Purgas, which was recorded in the Russian chronicles. The Mordovians came under the control of the Mongols and Tatars between the 13th and the 15th centuries and, at the fall of the Khanate of Kazan in 1552, they were voluntarily incorporated into the Russian state. Many thousands of Mordovians fled Russian rule in the late 16th and early 17th centuries to settle in the Ural Mountains and in southern Siberia, while those that remained were outnumbered by ethnic Russian settlers. The region was predominantly agricultural until the completion of the Moscow–Kazan railway in the 1890s, when it became more commercial and its industry developed.

Although Mordovians had become increasingly assimilated into Russian life from the late 19th century, a Mordovian Autonomous Okrug was created in 1928, which was upgraded to an Autonomous Oblast in 1930, and to an ASSR in 1934. It declared its sovereignty on 8 December 1990. A conservative region, the territory was only renamed the Republic of Mordoviya (dispensing with the words Soviet and Socialist from the title) in January 1994. Its Constitution was adopted on 21 September 1995, establishing an executive presidency and a State Assembly as the legislature. In February 1998 President Nikolai Merkushkin was re-elected, with 96.6% of the votes cast, owing to a legislative device that disqualified all opponents other than the director of a local pasta factory, who had frequently announced his support for Merkushkin's policies. On 16 February 2003 Merkushkin was re-elected to serve a further term of office, receiving 87.3% of the votes cast in an election contested by five candidates; the rate of participation by the registered electorate was measured at 83.2%. Republican legislative elections took place on 7 December, concurrently with the elections to the federal State Duma.

Economy

In 2000 the gross regional product of Mordoviya was 24,005m. roubles, or 25,952 roubles per head. The territory's major industrial centres are at Saransk and Ruzayevka. At the end of 2001 there were 546 km (339 miles) of railway lines and 4,293 km of paved roads on the Republic's territory.

The principal crops in Mordoviya are grain, sugar beet, potatoes and vegetables. Animal husbandry (especially cattle) and bee-keeping are also important. Agriculture employed 18.1% of the working population in 2001, when total agricultural production was worth 10,175m. roubles. Of this total, crop sales accounted for 50.8%, and animal husbandry for 49.2%. Industry is the dominant sector of the economy, with output amounting to a value of 18,499m. roubles in 2001. The main industries are mechanical engineering and metal-working. There is also some production of electricity, production of chemicals and petrochemicals, and food-processing. Total employment in industry was equal to 24.9% of the Republic's work-force in 2001. Mordoviya is the centre of the Russian lighting-equipment industry and contains the Rossiiskii Svet (Russian Light) association. In December 1995 the federal Government approved a programme for the economic and social development of Mordoviya, to be implemented in 1996–2000 at a cost of around US $10,000m. The regional President, Nikolai Merkushkin, established close links and trading relationships with Moscow City under Mayor Yurii Luzhkov; the capital purchased over one-half of the Republic's output.

In 2001 the economically active population was 432,000, and 10.5% of the labour force were unemployed. The average monthly wage in the Republic was 2,346.6 roubles in mid-2002 (one of the lowest wages in the Federation and the lowest within the Volga Federal Okrug). In 2001 there was a budgetary deficit of 174m. roubles. External trade earned US $31.7m. in exports and $28.8m. in imports in that year. In 2001 foreign investment in the Republic amounted to just $1.6m. At 31 December 2001 there were some 2,500 small businesses in the Republic.

Directory

President: NIKOLAI I. MERKUSHKIN; 430002 Mordoviya, Saransk, ul. Sovetskaya 35; tel. (8342) 17-54-71; fax (8342) 17-45-26; e-mail radm@whrm.moris.ru; internet whrm.moris.ru.

Chairman of the Government (Prime Minister): VLADIMIR D. VOLKOV; 430002 Mordoviya, Saransk, ul. Sovetskaya 35; tel. (8342) 32-74-69; fax (8342) 17-36-28; e-mail pred@whrm.moris.ru.

Chairman of the State Assembly: VALERII A. KECHKIN; 430002 Mordoviya, Saransk, ul. Sovetskaya 26; tel. (8342) 32-79-50; fax (8342) 17-04-95; e-mail gsprot@whrm.moris.ru.

Chief Representative of the Republic of Mordoviya in the Russian Federation: VIKTOR I. CHINDYASKIN; 127018 Moscow, ul. Obraztsova 29; tel. (095) 219-40-49; fax (095) 218-01-42.

Head of Saransk City Administration: IVAN YA. NENYUKOV; 430002 Mordoviya, Saransk, ul. Sovetskaya 34; tel. (8342) 17-64-16; fax (8342) 17-67-70; e-mail saransk@moris.ru.

Nizhnii Novgorod Oblast

Nizhnii Novgorod Oblast is situated on the middle reaches of the Volga river. It forms part of the Volga Federal Okrug and the Volga-Vyatka Economic Area. Mordoviya and Ryazan lie to the south, Vladimir and Ivanovo to the west, Kostroma to the north-west, Kirov to the north-east and Marii-El and Chuvashiya to the east. Its major rivers are the Volga, the Oka, the Sura and the Vetluga. The terrain in the north of the Oblast is mainly low lying, with numerous forests and extensive swampland. The southern part is characterized by fertile black soil (*chernozem*). The Oblast occupies a total area of 76,900 sq km (29,690 sq miles) and measures some 400 km (250 miles) from south to north and 300 km from east to west. It is divided into 48 administrative districts and 28 cities. According to the preliminary results of the census of 9–16 October 2002, the Oblast had a total population of 3,524,000 and a population density, therefore, of 45.8 per sq km. Some 78.2% of the Oblast's inhabitants resided in urban areas. Its administrative centre is at Nizhnii Novgorod (formerly Gorkii), which lies at the confluence of the Volga and Oka rivers. The city is Russia's fourth largest, with a population of 1,311,200 in 2002, according to provisional census results. Other major cities include Dzerzhinsk (formerly Chernorech—with a population of 261,400) and Arzamas (109,500).

History

Nizhnii Novgorod city was founded in 1221 on the borders of the Russian principalities. With the decline of Tatar power the city was absorbed by the Muscovite state. The Sarov Monastery, one of Russian Orthodoxy's most sacred sites, was founded in the region. Industrialization took place in the late tsarist period. In 1905 mass unrest occurred among peasants and workers in the region, which was one of the first areas of Russia to be seized by the Bolsheviks in late 1917. Nizhnii Novgorod Oblast was formed on 14 January 1929. In 1932–90 the city and region were named Gorkii, and for much of the time the city was 'closed', owing to the importance of the defence industry.

In 1991 the Russian President, Boris Yeltsin, appointed a leading local reformer, Boris Nemtsov, as Head of the Regional Administration (Governor). Nemtsov instituted a wide-ranging programme of economic reform, which was widely praised by liberals and by the federal Government. Nemtsov secured popular election in December 1995, and was a prominent advocate of democratization and decentralization in the Federation. In June 1996 Nemtsov signed a treaty on the delimitation of powers with the federal Government, giving the Oblast greater budgetary independence and more control over its public property. In April 1997 Nemtsov was appointed to the federal Government; gubernatorial elections were subsequently held, in which the pro-Government candidate, Ivan Sklyarov (former Mayor of Nizhnii Novgorod), defeated Gennadii Khodyrev (who was supported both by the Communist Party of the Russian Federation—CPRF and the nationalist Liberal Democrats) after a 'run-off' vote in July. The Oblast's economic situation subsequently deteriorated somewhat, and the federal Government withheld funds for the continuing conversion of the Oblast's defence industry. At the second round of gubernatorial elections held in July 2001, Khodyrev, by this time a CPRF deputy in the State Duma, was elected Governor, obtaining almost 60% of the votes cast. Following his election, Khodyrev suspended his membership of the CPRF, apparently in response to allegations that the federal Government was to transfer the administrative centre of the Volga Federal Okrug to another city in the event of the election of a communist governor. In mid-September the regional Legislative Assembly voted in favour of a proposal made by Khodyrev that he act both as Governor and as Prime Minister of the Oblast. In 2001 the city of Nizhnii Novgorod became the first area in Russia to implement proposals that permitted objectors to compulsory military service to perform an alternative, civilian service; however, in early 2002 President Putin criticized these measures, and several of those undertaking civilian service were subsequently inducted into the military. Elections to the regional Legislative Assembly in March 2002 resulted in the formation of a centre-right majority in the new chamber, including many representatives of business interests in the Oblast, with Unity and Fatherland-United Russia becoming the single largest party grouping. In April the power-sharing treaty agreed in 1996 was annulled. Khodyrev finally resigned from the CPRF in May 2002, in protest at the expulsion of State Duma Chairman Gennadii Seleznev from the party. (In September 2003 Khodyrev was chosen as the first-placed candidate on the Volga inter-regional list—covering the Republic of Marii-El, the Chuvash Republic and Nizhnii Novgorod—of the pro-Government Unity and Fatherland-United Russia party, in advance of elections to the federal State Duma, scheduled to be held on 7 December.) Meanwhile, considerable controversy arose nationally, as a result of the conduct of mayoral elections in Nizhnii Novgorod, held in two rounds, in September–October 2002; the favoured candidate of both the oblast and federal authorities, Vadim Bulavinov, narrowly won the election, defeating the incumbent, Yurii Lebedev. However, the disqualification of a popular candidate, Andrei Klimentiyev, prior to the first round, was believed to be a determining factor prompting more than 28% of eligible votes, in both rounds of voting, to be cast 'against all candidates'.

Economy

In 2000 the Oblast's gross regional product amounted to 104,296m. roubles, or 28,634 roubles per head. Its principal industrial centres are at Nizhnii Novgorod, Dzerzhinsk and Arzamas. Nizhnii Novgorod contains a major river-port, from which it is possible to reach the Baltic, Black, White and Caspian Seas and the Sea of Azov. At the end of 2001 there were 13,165 km of paved roads and 1,214 km of railway track in the region. In 1985 an underground railway system opened in Nizhnii Novgorod and in 1994 an international airport was opened, from which Lufthansa (of Germany) operates flights to the German city of Frankfurt. In late 1996 plans to extend the Second Trans-European Corridor to Nizhnii Novgorod were initiated by the Russian Government and the European Union.

Reform of the farming sector in the 1990s involved extensive privatization and investment in rural infrastructure. Agriculture in the region, which employed just 8.7% of the working population in 2001, consists mainly of the production of grain, sugar beet, flax and onions and other vegetables, although the Oblast lacks many areas with the fertile black topsoil typical of the European Plain. Animal husbandry is also important. In 2001 total agricultural output was worth 18,279m. roubles, of which crop sales contributed 45.1% and animal husbandry 54.9%. As one of the three most industrially developed regions in Russia, however, it was the Oblast's industry that provided some 80% of total production (industrial output generated 125,957m. roubles in 2001). The principal industries of the Oblast include mechanical engineering and metal-working (which together accounted for 42.6% of industrial output in 2001), ferrous metallurgy, chemicals, petrochemicals and the processing of agricultural and forestry products. In 2001 some 31.5% of the working population was engaged in industry. During the Soviet period the region was developed as a major military-industrial centre, with the defence sector accounting for around three-quarters of the regional economy, and Gorkii became a 'closed' city. The Oblast also contains the secret city of Arzamas-16 (now Sarov), a centre of nuclear research. In the early 1990s much of Governor Boris Nemtsov's reform programme was aimed at the conversion of as much of the industrial base to civilian use as possible, but this process was made increasingly difficult as federal funds became less readily available. Indeed, defence-industry production in the region increased by 130% in 1999 compared with the previous year, although, overall, the Oblast was among those that dealt most successfully with the transition from military to civilian industry.

The economically active population numbered 1,841,000 in 2001, when 8.3% of the labour force were unemployed. The average monthly wage in the Oblast was 3,403.5 roubles in mid-2002. The 2001 budget recorded a surplus of 452m. roubles. In 2001 external trade in the Oblast comprised US $1,054.3m. in exports and $397.1m. in imports. The Oblast exports principally to Belarus, Belgium, France, Kazakhstan, Switzerland and the United Kingdom, and imports goods from Austria, Belarus, the People's Republic of China, Germany, Kazakhstan, the Netherlands, Ukraine and the USA. In 1997 there were 1,153 joint-stock companies in the region, as well as 34 commercial banks and 35 insurance companies. Nizhnii Novgorod Oblast was the first Russian federal subject, other than the two federal cities, to issue Eurobonds, in 1997. In 2001 foreign investment in the region totalled $20.9m. Infrastructure for small-business development had resulted in the emergence of some 13,550 small businesses by the end of 2001.

Directory

Head of the Regional Administration (Governor and Prime Minister): GENNADII M. KHODYREV; 603082 Nizhnii Novgorod, Kreml, kor. 1; tel. (8312) 39-13-30; fax (8312) 39-00-48; e-mail official@ kreml.nnov.ru; internet www.government.nnov .ru.

Chairman of the Legislative Assembly: YEVGENII B. LYULIN; 603082 Nizhnii Novgorod, Kreml, kor. 2; tel. (8312) 39-05-38; fax (8312) 39-06-29; e-mail nnovg@ duma.gov.ru.

Representation of Nizhnii Novgorod Oblast in the Russian Federation: Moscow; tel. (095) 203-77-41.

Head of Nizhnii Novgorod City Administration (Mayor): VADIM YE. BULAVINOV; 603082 Nizhnii Novgorod, Kreml, kor. 5; tel. (8312) 39-15-06; fax (8312) 39-13-02; e-mail lebedev@admgor.nnov.ru; internet www.admcity.nnov.ru.

Orenburg Oblast

Orenburg Oblast is situated in the foothills of the Southern Urals. It forms part of the Volga Federal Okrug and the Urals Economic Area. Orenburg sprawls along the international border with Kazakhstan, which lies to the south and in the east. Samara Oblast lies to the west, and in the north-west of the territory there is a short border with the Republic of Tatarstan. The Republic of Bashkortostan and Chelyabinsk Oblast neighbour the north of the Oblast. Orenburg's major river is the Ural. The region occupies a total area of 124,000 sq km (47,860 sq miles) and is divided into 35 districts and 12 cities. According to the preliminary results of the census of 9–16 October 2002, the total population of the Oblast was 2,177,500 and the population density was, therefore, 17.6 per sq km. Some 57.8% of the population lived in urban areas. The Oblast's administrative centre is at Orenburg, which had 548,800 inhabitants in 2002, according to provisional census results. Other major cities are Orsk (250,600) and Novotroitsk (106,200).

History

The city of Orenburg originated as a fortress in 1743. During the revolutionary period Orenburg was a headquarters of 'White' forces and possession of it was fiercely contested with the Bolsheviks. The city was also a centre of Kazakh (then erroneously known as Kyrgyz) nationalists and was the capital of the Kyrgyz ASSR in 1920–25. The region was then separated from the renamed Kazakh ASSR. Orenburg Oblast was formed on 7 December 1934.

The Communist Party of the Russian Federation (CPRF) remained the most popular party into the 1990s, winning 24% of the votes cast in the region at the general election of December 1995. Simultaneous elections to the post of governor, however, were won by the incumbent, Vladimir Yelagin, despite his having expressed support for the federal President, Boris Yeltsin. Yelagin was defeated in the gubernatorial elections of December 1999 by the former Chairman of the State

Duma Committee on Agrarian Issues, Aleksei Chernyshev. The region was considered strategically important, owing to its proximity to Kazakhstan, a fact that led to the signature, on 30 January 1996, of an agreement between the regional administration and Yeltsin, which defined the powers and areas of remit of the federal and local authorities. In regional legislative elections held at the end of March 1998 the CPRF maintained its relatively high level of support, but in the election of March 2002 the representation of left-wing deputies declined to just four seats. The power-sharing treaty signed in 1996 was annulled in April 2002. In June 2003 the regional legislature voted to extend the gubernatorial term of office from four years to five; it was anticipated that this measure would take effect following the gubernatorial elections scheduled to be held later that year. On 7 December Chernyshev was re-elected to the governorship, securing 65.2% of the votes cast by 54.3% of the registered electorate.

Economy

The Oblast's gross regional product was 82,646m. roubles in 2000, or 37,223 roubles per head. At the end of 2001 there were 1,652 km (1,027 miles) of railways and 13,160 km of paved roads on the Oblast's territory. Its principal industrial centres are at Orenburg, Orsk, Novotroisk, Mednogorsk, Buzuluk and Buguruslan. Owing to the region's high degree of industrialization, and that of its neighbours, Chelyabinsk and Bashkortostan, there is a high level of pollution in the atmosphere. Around 1m. metric tons of harmful substances are emitted annually, including almost 700 tons of nickel and one ton of lead. In addition, the intensive exploitation of petroleum and gas deposits have caused serious damage to the land—around 60% of arable land is eroded or in danger of suffering erosion.

Agriculture in Orenburg Oblast, which employed 20.6% of the work-force in 2001, consisted mainly of grain, vegetable and sunflower production and animal husbandry. Agricultural output in the region in 2001 amounted to a value of 23,275m. roubles, of which crop sales accounted for 57.3% and animal husbandry for 42.7%. The Oblast's major industries are ferrous and non-ferrous metallurgy, mechanical engineering, metal-working, natural gas production, electrical energy and the production of petroleum, ores, asbestos (the region produces around two-fifths of asbestos produced in Russia) and salt. In 2001 some 21.9% of the working population were engaged in industry, which generated a total of 66,707m. roubles.

The economically active population stood at 1,031,000 in 2001, when some 8.5% of the labour force were unemployed. The regional average monthly wage was 3,232.9 roubles in mid-2002. The Oblast's budget for 2001 showed a deficit of 108m. roubles, and in 2002 the region was named as one of the worst for wage arrears. In 2001 external trade comprised US $1,377.7m. in exports and $459.1m. in imports. Total foreign investment in the region in that year amounted to some $88.8m. At 31 December 2001 7,564 small businesses were registered in the Oblast.

Directory

Head of the Regional Administration (Governor): ANDREI A. CHERNYSHEV; 460015 Orenburg, Dom Sovetov; tel. (3532) 77-69-31; fax (3532) 77-38-02; e-mail office@gov.orb.ru; internet www.orb.ru.

Chairman of the Legislative Assembly: Yurii V. Trofimov; 460015 Orenburg, Dom Sovetov; tel. (3532) 77-33-20; fax (3532) 77-42-12; e-mail parlament@gov .orb.ru; internet www.parlament.orb.ru.

Chief Representative of Orenburg Oblast in the Russian Federation: Vyacheslav S. Ryabov; 127025 Moscow, ul. Novyi Arbat 19/2014; tel. (095) 203-85-32; fax (095) 203-59-76.

Head of Orenburg City Administration (Mayor): Yurii N. Mischeryakov; 461300 Orenburg, ul. Sovetskaya 60; tel. (3532) 98-70-10; fax (3532) 77-60-58; e-mail glava@admin.orenburg.ru; internet www.admin.orenburg.ru.

Penza Oblast

Penza Oblast is situated in the Volga Highlands, to the south of the Republic of Mordoviya. It forms part of the Volga Federal Okrug and the Volga Economic Area and shares borders with Ulyanovsk Oblast to the east, Saratov Oblast to the south, Tambov Oblast to the south-west and touches Ryazan Oblast in the far north-west. Penza's major river is the Sura, a tributary of the River Volga. Its territory covers an area of 43,200 sq km (16,750 sq miles) and is divided into 28 districts and 11 cities. According to the preliminary results of the census of 9–16 October 2002, the population of the Oblast was 1,453,400, giving a population density, therefore, of 33.6 per sq km. Some 65.1% of the population inhabited urban areas. The Oblast's administrative centre, Penza, had a population of 518,200 in 2002, according to provisional census results.

History

The city of Penza was founded in 1663 as an outpost on the south-eastern border of the Russian Empire. The region was annexed by Bolshevik forces in late 1917 and remained under the control of the Red Army throughout the period of civil war. Penza Oblast was formed on 4 February 1939.

Described as part of the 'red belt' of communist support in the 1990s, in 1992 the Communist Party candidate defeated the pro-Yeltsin Governor in elections to head the regional administration. The communists controlled the Legislative Assembly, elected in 1994 (although the federal presidency replaced the governor) and, almost exactly three years after the gubernatorial elections, obtained some 37% of the local vote in the federal general elections of December 1995. Although the presidentially appointed Governor, Anatolii Kovlyagin, was a member of the pro-Government movement, Our Home is Russia, he failed to give public support to the federal Government's reforms during the mid-1990s.

On 12 April 1998 a new Governor, Vasilii Bochkarev, was elected. His campaign promoted effective management and pragmatism, and he contested the election as an independent. Bochkarev was re-elected on 14 April 2002, with the support of the pro-Government Unity and Fatherland-United Russia party. The adoption, in 2002, of a new oblast flag, depicting a Russian Orthodox icon of Jesus Christ, resulted in protests in the region, particularly by representatives of the estimated 100,000-strong Muslim population of the region and communists; concern was expressed that the use of an image with religious connotations could breach the separation of religion and state guaranteed by the federal Constitution.

Economy

In 2000 Penza's gross regional product was 27,371m. roubles, or 17,961 roubles per head. The Oblast's principal industrial centres are at Penza and Kuznetsk. At the end of 2001 there were 827 km (514 miles) of railway track in the region, which included lines linking the territory to central and southern Russia as well as the Far East and Ukraine and Central Asia. Some 6,439 km of paved roads included several major highways.

Around three-quarters of the agricultural land in the Oblast consists of fertile black earth (*chernozem*). Agricultural activity, which employed 20.7% of the work-force in 2001, consists mainly of the production of grain and vegetables. Animal husbandry is also important. Total agricultural production amounted to a value of 10,254m. roubles in 2001, of which crop sales accounted for 54.5% and animal husbandry for 45.5%. The Oblast's main industries are mechanical engineering, the processing of timber and agricultural products, chemicals and petrochemicals, light manufacturing and the production of electricity. Industry employed some 22.2% of the working population in 2001, and generated 22,226m. roubles.

The economically active population in Penza Oblast numbered 746,000 in 2001, when 13.9% of the labour force were unemployed—the highest rate in the Volga Federal Okrug. Those in employment earned an average of 2,585.0 roubles per month in mid-2002. The 2001 regional budget showed a deficit of 80m. roubles. The external trade of the Oblast was relatively low, amounting to US $110.8m. in exports and $52.4m. in imports in 2001. Foreign investment in the Oblast in that year amounted to $1.7m. In 2001 there was a total of some 6,100 small businesses registered in the Oblast.

Directory

Head of the Regional Administration (Governor): Vasilii K. Bochkarev; 440025 Penza, ul. Moskovskaya 75; tel. (8412) 55-04-11; fax (8412) 63-35-75; e-mail pravobl@sura.com.ru; internet www.penza.ru.

Chairman of the Regional Legislative Assembly: Viktor A. Lazutkin; 440025 Penza, pl. Lenina, Dom Sovetov; tel. (8412) 52-22-66; fax (8412) 55-25-95; e-mail zsobl@sura.ru.

Chief Representative of Penza Oblast in the Russian Federation: Mels U. Nosinov; 127025 Moscow, ul. Novyi Arbat 19/1914; tel. (095) 203-10-75; fax (095) 203-48-93.

Head of Penza City Administration: Aleksandr S. Kalashnikov; 440064 Penza, pl. Marshala Zhukova 4, Gorodskaya Duma; tel. (8412) 66-29-85; fax (8412) 6-65-88.

Perm Oblast

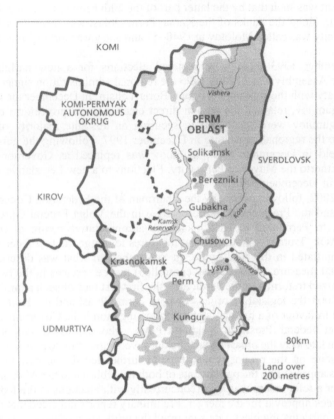

Perm Oblast is situated on the western slopes of the Central and Northern Urals and the eastern edge of the Eastern European Plain. It forms part of the Volga Federal Okrug and the Urals Economic Area. The Komi-Permyak Autonomous Okrug (AOk) forms the north-western part of the Oblast, providing part of the northern border with the Republic of Komi and most of the western border with Kirov Oblast. The Republic of Udmurtiya also lies to the west, the Republic of Bashkortostan to the south and Sverdlovsk Oblast to the east. Apart from the Kama, its major rivers are the Chusovaya, the Kosva and the Vishera. The Kamsk reservoir lies in the centre of the region. Its territory, including that of the Komi-Permyak AOk, occupies an area of 160,600 sq km (61,990 sq miles) and extends some 600 km (370 miles) from south to north and 400 km from west to east. The Oblast, excluding the AOk, is divided into 29 districts and 24 cities. According to the preliminary results of the census of 9–16 October 2002, the region's total population was 2,824,400, giving a population density of 17.6 per sq km. Some 75.2% of the population inhabited urban areas. The Oblast's administrative centre is at Perm, which had a population of 1,000,100 in 2002, according to provisional census results. Other major cities include Berezniki (with a population of 173,500) and Solikamsk (102,800).

History

Perm city was founded in 1723, with the construction of a copper foundry. Industrial development was such that by the latter part of the 20th century the city extended for some 80 km along the banks of the Kama. Perm Oblast was formed on 3 October 1938. The city was called Molotov in 1940–57 and entry was forbidden to foreigners until 1989.

In December 1993 there were regional elections for a new parliament, the Legislative Assembly. On 31 May 1996 the regional administration signed a power-sharing treaty with the Russian President, Boris Yeltsin. In December the Governor, Genadii Igumnov, retained his post in direct elections, and pro-reform candidates loyal to Igumnov were successful in securing an absolute majority of seats in elections to the regional legislature in December 1997. Following the gubernatorial election held in December 2000, Igumnov was replaced as Governor by Yurii Trutnev, hitherto the Mayor of Perm City. Elections to a new Legislative Assembly were held in December 2001.

In July 2002, following visits by the Chairman of the Federation Council, Sergei Mironov, and the Presidential Representative in the Volga Federal Okrug, Sergei Kiriyenko, to Perm and to Kudymkar, the administrative centre of the Komi-Permyak AOk, Trutnev announced that measures to merge the two federal subjects would be initiated in the near future. In September, in what was described as an experimental measure, the (federally controlled) justice services in the two regions were organized to form a unified structure, the first instance of such a unification. In February 2003 the legislative organs of both Perm Oblast and the Komi-Permyak AOk voted in favour of a merger, and the following month the Governors of the two regions met federal President Vladimir Putin, who expressed support for the proposal. In late May the oblast legislature approved legislation to permit the holding of a plebiscite on the proposed merger, and further legislation pertaining to the merger was approved by the parliaments of both the Oblast and the AOk in June. On 7 December a referendum was held (concurrently with elections to the federal State Duma) to seek approval for the merger. Preliminary reports indicated that more than 80% of the participating electorate supported the unification of the two territories to form a new political entity, Perm Krai. Elections to the leadership of the new Krai were expected to be held in December 2005, although the establishment of a single budget for the region was not anticipated before 2007.

Economy

All figures in this survey include data pertaining to the Komi-Permyak AOk, which is also treated separately (see below). In 2000 Perm Oblast's gross regional product amounted to 131,388m. roubles, or 44,424 roubles per head. Its major industrial centres are at Perm, Berezniki, Solikamsk, Chusovoi and Krasnokamsk. At the end of 2001 there were 1,493 km of railways and 10,382 km of paved roads on the Oblast's territory.

Agriculture in the Oblast, which in 2001 employed just 8.8% of the working population, consists mainly of grain and vegetable production, bee-keeping and animal husbandry. In 2001 agricultural production was worth 18,104m. roubles (of which 52.4% was generated by crop sales and 47.6% by animal husbandry), compared with a total in the industrial sector of 143,321m. roubles. The main industries are coal, petroleum, natural gas, potash and salt production, mechanical engineering, chemicals and petrochemicals, petroleum-refining and electricity generation. There is also a significant defence sector. Some 28.0% of the working population were engaged in industry in 2001.

The economically active population numbered 1,478,000 in 2001, when 6.9% of the labour force were unemployed. The average wage was above the national average and represented the highest rate in the Volga Federal Okrug, amounting to 4,375.3 roubles per month in mid-2002. In 2001 there was a budgetary deficit of 29m. roubles. In that year external trade amounted to a value of US $2,016.9m. in exports and $255.6m. in imports. The region was named as the eighth highest in Russia, in terms of investment potential, in late 1999 and in 2001 foreign investment amounted to $97.6m. At 31 December 2001 8,181 small businesses were registered in the region.

Directory

Governor: YURII P. TRUTNEV; 614006 Perm, ul. Kuibysheva 14; tel. (3422) 58-70-75; fax (3422) 34-89-52; e-mail home@trutnev.ru; internet www.trutnev.ru.

Chairman of the Legislative Assembly: NIKOLAI A. DEVYATKIN; 614006 Perm, ul. Lenina 51; tel. (3422) 58-75-55; fax (3422) 34-27-47; e-mail parliament@perm.ru; internet www.parliament.perm.ru.

Chief Representative of Perm Oblast in the Russian Federation: ALEKSANDR A. POTEKHIN; 103795 Moscow, ul. M. Dmitrovka 3; tel. (095) 299-48-36; fax (095) 209-08-97.

Head of Perm City Administration: ARKADII L. KAMENEV; 614000 Perm, ul. Lenina 15; tel. (3422) 34-33-02; fax (3422) 34-94-11; e-mail gorodperm@permregion.ru; internet www.gorodperm.ru.

Komi-Permyak Autonomous Okrug

The Komi-Permyak Autonomous Okrug (AOk) is situated in the Urals area on the upper reaches of the Kama river and forms the north-western part of Perm Oblast. The region is part of the Volga Federal Okrug and the Urals Economic Area. The other neighbouring federal territories are Komi to the north and north-west and Kirov to the west. A largely forested territory, it occupies an area of 32,900 sq km (12,700 sq miles) and comprises six administrative districts and one city. According to the preliminary results of the census of 9–16 October 2002, the region's population was 135,900, giving a population density of 4.1 per sq km; 26.3% of the population inhabited urban areas. According to the 1989 census, of the district's total population, some 60.2% were Komi Permyak and 36.1% ethnic Russian. The Komi Permyaks speak two dialects of the Finnic division of the Uralo-Altaic linguistic family. The district's administrative centre is at Kudymkar, which had a population of 34,300 at 1 January 2001.

History

The Komi Permyaks became a group distinct from the Komis in around 500, when some Komi (Zyryans) migrated from the upper Kama river region to the Vychegda basin, while the Komi Permyaks remained. The Komi-Permyak National Okrug was established on 26 February 1925, the first political entity of its kind to be established in the USSR. In 1977 the Okrug received the nominal status of an Autonomous Okrug (AOk).

The area frequently perceived the central authorities to be neglectful of their interests, and economic conditions became increasingly harsh from the late 1990s. In May 1996 the Komi-Permyak AOk's administration signed a treaty with the federal Government on the delimitation of powers between the two bodies. At a gubernatorial election held in November, the incumbent, Nikolai Poluyanov, retained his position, but was defeated by the deputy president of the audit chamber of Perm Oblast, Gennadii Savelyev, in the gubernatorial election held in December 2000. Elections to the 15-member regional Legislative Assembly took place in December 2001.

In July 2002, following visits by the Chairman of the Federation Council, Sergei Mironov, and the Presidential Representative in the Volga Federal Okrug, Sergei Kiriyenko, to the territorial capitals, the Governor of Perm Oblast, Yurii Trutnev, announced that measures to merge the two federal subjects would be initiated in the near future. In September, in what was described as an experimental measure, the (federally controlled) justice services in the two regions were reorganized to form a unified structure, the first instance of such a unification. In February 2003 the legislative organs of both territories voted to support the merger. In March Trutnev and Savelyev met federal President Vladimir Putin, who expressed support for the proposal. In late May the oblast legislature approved legislation to permit the holding of a plebiscite on the merger, and further legislation pertaining to the measure was approved by the parliaments of both administrative entities in June. On 7 December a referendum was held (concurrently with elections to the federal State Duma) to seek approval for the merger. According to preliminary results, more than 80% of those who voted supported the unification of the two territories to form a new political entity, Perm Krai. Elections to the leadership of the new Krai were expected to be held in December 2005, although a single budget was not anticipated before 2007.

Economy

In 2000 the gross regional product of the Komi-Permyak AOk stood at 2,017m. roubles. At the end of 2001 there were 1,488 km (925 miles) of paved roads in the district.

The agriculture of the territory consists mainly of grain production and animal husbandry, including fur-farming. In 2001 agriculture employed 24.3% of the workforce and produced output amounting to a value of 1,492m. roubles, of which crop sales accounted for 54.3% and animal husbandry for 45.7%. The Komi-Permyak AOk's timber reserves are estimated at 322m. cu m. There are also significant peat deposits and approximately 12.1m. metric tons of petroleum reserves. Its industry is based on the processing of forestry and agricultural products and fuel production; the sector generated 874m. roubles in 2001 and employed 18.0% of the okrug's workforce.

The economically active population numbered 63,000 in 2001, when 12.2% of the labour force were unemployed. The average monthly wage was just 2,535.9 roubles in mid-2002, and the okrug is one of the most underdeveloped and deprived European regions of Russia. The district budget showed a deficit of 38m. roubles in 2001. Figures on foreign investment in, and external trade with, the Komi-Permyak AOk were unavailable, being included with those for the Perm Oblast as a whole, but in late 2001 approximately 95 small businesses were registered in the district.

Directory

Head of the District Administration (Governor): GENNADII P. SAVELYEV; 617240 Perm obl., Komi-Permyak AOk, Kudymkar, ul. 50 let. Oktyabrya 33; tel. (34260) 4-59-03; fax (34260) 4-12-74.

Chairman of the Legislative Assembly: VALERII A. VANKOV; 617240 Perm obl., Komi-Permyak AOk, Kudymkar, ul. 50 let. Oktyabrya 33; tel. (32460) 4-24-70; fax (32460) 2-12-74.

Representation of the Komi-Permyak Autonomous Okrug in Perm Oblast: Perm.

Chief Representative of Komi-Permyak Autonomous Okrug in the Russian Federation: TAMARA A. SYSTEROVA; Moscow; tel. (095) 203-94-08.

Head of Kudymkar City Administration: ALEKSANDR A. KLIMOVICH; 617420 Perm obl., Komi-Permyak AOk, Kudymkar, ul. Gorkogo 3; tel. (34260) 2-00-47; e-mail admkud@permonline.ru; internet kudymkar.permonline.ru.

Samara Oblast

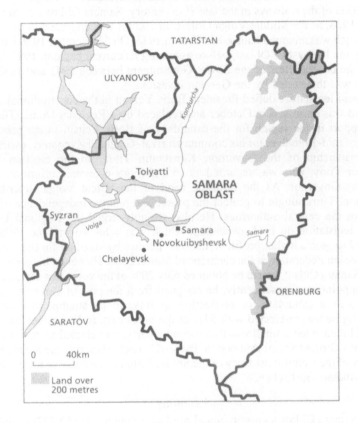

Samara Oblast is situated in the south-east of the Eastern European Plain on the middle reaches of the Volga river. It forms part of the Volga Federal Okrug and the Volga Economic Area. Its southernmost tip lies on the border with Kazakhstan. Saratov lies to the south-west, Ulyanovsk to the west, Tatarstan to the north and Orenburg to the east. The Volga snakes through the west of the territory. The Oblast's other major rivers are the Samara, the Sok, the Kunel, the Bolshoi Igruz and the Kondurcha. The region occupies an area of 53,600 sq km (20,690 sq miles). It is divided into 27 districts and 11 cities. Owing to its proximity to the Kazakhstan desert, the southernmost part of the Oblast is prone to drought. According to the preliminary results of the census of 9–16 October 2002, the region had a total population of 3,239,800, and a population density, therefore, of 60.4 per sq km. Some 80.6% of the population inhabited urban areas. The majority of the population, 83.4%, was ethnic Russian. There were also significant communities of Mordovians, Chuvash, Tatars and Ukrainians. The administrative centre is at Samara (formerly Kuibyshev), which had 1,158,100 inhabitants in 2002, according to preliminary census results. The region's second city is Tolyatti (701,900), and other major cities include Syzran (187,800) and Novokuibyshevsk (113,000).

History

Samara city was founded in 1586 as a fortress. It increased in prosperity after the construction of the railways in the late 19th century. Samara Oblast was founded on 14 May 1928, as the Middle Volga Oblast. In 1929 it was upgraded to the status of a krai, which was renamed Kuibyshev Krai in 1935. On 5 December 1936 Kuibyshev Krai became Kuibyshev Oblast, before assuming its current name in 1991. The city became the headquarters of the Soviet Government between 1941 and 1943, when Moscow was threatened by the German invasion.

The local legislature defied President Boris Yeltsin in the constitutional crisis of 1993, and was dissolved in October and replaced by a Regional Duma. There was more support in the region for the candidacy of Boris Yeltsin in the presidential election of mid-1996 than for his communist rival, Gennadii Zyuganov, owing to the strong leadership of the Governor, Konstantin Titov. In the election held in December Titov, who was regarded as an ambitious economic reformer, was re-elected as Governor. As the informal head of the 'Great Volga' inter-regional association, Titov sought to protect the power and relative independence of governors from the central authorities. He also strongly urged the Regional Duma to approve legislation on land ownership, which was achieved in June 1998. Titov attempted to gain a higher profile in national politics by standing for the presidency of the Russian Federation at the elections of March 2000. However, his performance, even in Samara Oblast, where he obtained only 20% of the votes cast and came third, was disappointing. Consequently, he resigned from the post of Governor in April, but stood as a candidate for re-election in July, in an attempt to confirm his legitimacy; he was re-elected with 53% of the votes cast. In November 2001 Titov, who had hitherto led a small social-democratic party, was elected as co-chairman of the recently formed Social Democratic Party of Russia, alongside the former General Secretary of the Communist Party of the Soviet Union and executive President of the USSR, Mikhail Gorbachev.

Economy

In 2000 Samara Oblast's gross regional product amounted to 155,732m. roubles, or 47,339 roubles per head. The Oblast's major industrial centres are at Samara, Tolyatti, Syzran and Novokuibyshevsk. At the end of 2001 there were 1,377 km (856 miles) of railways and 7,455 km of paved roads in the region.

Agriculture in the Oblast, which employed just 7.6% of the working population in 2001, consists mainly of animal husbandry, bee-keeping and the production of grain, sugar beet and sunflower seeds. Total agricultural production in 2001 was worth 20,752m. roubles, of which 58.8% was generated by crop sales and 41.2% by animal husbandry. There are some reserves of petroleum and natural gas in the region. Its main industries are mechanical engineering, metal-working, petroleum-production and -refining, food-processing, and chemicals and petrochemicals. The Oblast's principal company is AvtoVAZ (Volga Automobile Plant), manufacturer of the Lada automobile, accounting for over 40% of industrial output in the region, and the largest automobile manufacturer in Russia. In 2002, as part of a joint venture with the US corporation, General Motors, AvtoVAZ also began to manufacture Chevrolet Niva automobiles and sports-utility vehicles. In 2001 some 28.4% of the region's work-force were engaged in industry, which generated 213,881m. roubles.

The economically active population of Samara Oblast numbered 1,715,000 in 2001, when just 6.0% of the labour force were unemployed, the lowest rate in the

Volga Federal Okrug. In mid-2002 those in employment earned an average wage of 4,317.7 roubles per month, well above the national average. In 2001 the regional budget recorded a deficit of 216m. roubles. In December 2001 the Oblast's Governor, Konstantin Titov, issued a decree introducing state control over the finances of Samara city and two rural districts of the Oblast, the debts of which exceeded 10% of their total consolidated budgets. In 2001 total foreign investment in the region amounted to US $260.4m. By 1998 some 300 foreign companies, including some of the world's largest, such as Coca-Cola and General Motors of the USA and Nestlé of Switzerland, had invested in the region, attracted by its technologically advanced industrial base and well-educated, urbanized labour force. In 2001 the external trade of the region amounted to some $3,600.5m. in exports and $655.7m. in imports, representing one of the highest levels of trade in any federal subject. At 31 December 2001 there were 27,566 small businesses in operation.

Directory

Governor: KONSTANTIN A. TITOV; 443006 Samara, ul. Molodogvardeiskaya 210; tel. (8462) 32-22-68; fax (8462) 32-13-40; e-mail governor@samara.ru; internet www .adm.samara.ru.

Chairman of the Regional Duma: VIKTOR F. SAZANOV; 443110 Samara, ul. Molodogvardeiskaya 187; tel. (8462) 32-75-06; fax (8462) 42-38-08; e-mail samgd@duma.sam-reg.ru; internet www.duma.sam-reg.ru.

Representative of Samara Oblast in the Russian Federation: VIKTOR B. LEON-TYEV; 103030 Moscow, per. Veskovskii 2; tel. (095) 973-19-95; fax (095) 973-05-54; e-mail tradoc@samarapostpred.ru.

Head of Samara City Administration (Mayor): GEORGII S. LIMANSKII; 443010 Samara, ul. Kuibysheva 135/137; tel. (8462) 32-20-68; fax (8462) 33-67-41; e-mail city@vis.infotel.ru.

Saratov Oblast

Saratov Oblast is situated in the south-east of the Eastern European Plain. It forms part of the Volga Federal Okrug and the Volga Economic Area. On the international border with Kazakhstan (to the south-east), the federal territories adjacent to Saratov are Volgograd (south), Voronezh and Tambov (west), and Penza, Ulyanovsk and Samara (north). Its main river is the Volga. The west of the Oblast (beyond the left bank of the Volga) is mountainous, the east low-lying. The region's territory occupies an area of 100,200 sq km (38,680 sq miles). It comprises 38 districts and 18 cities. According to the preliminary results of the census of 9–16 October 2002, Saratov Oblast had a total of 2,669,300 inhabitants, and a population density of 26.6 per sq km. Some 73.6% of the Oblast's population inhabited urban areas. Its administrative centre is at Saratov, a major river-port on the Volga, with a population of 873,500 in 2002, according to preliminary census results. Other major cities are Balakovo (200,600) and Engels (193,800).

History

Saratov city was founded in 1590 as a fortress city, to protect against nomad raids on the Volga trade route. Strategically placed on the Trans-Siberian Railway, it was seized by Bolshevik forces in late 1917 and remained under communist control, despite attacks by the 'White' forces under Adm. Aleksandr Kolchak in 1918–19. The Oblast was formed in 1936, having been part of a Saratov Krai from 1934. The region became heavily industrialized in the Soviet period, before the Second World War.

Saratov remained an important centre for the military and for communist support into the 1990s. However, in September 1996 Dmitrii Ayatskov, a presidential appointment, retained his post heading the regional administration, having secured 81.4% of the popular vote to become the first popularly elected regional leader in Russia. He was re-elected for a further term in April 2000, amid accusations of electoral manipulation, which removed all other serious candidates from the contest, and press censorship. As Governor, Ayatskov carried out extensive reform to the region's agro-industrial sector, which culminated, in November 1997, in the passing in the Oblast of the first law in Russia to provide for the purchase and sale of agricultural land. The law greatly diminished the power base of communists and nationalists in the region, and by April 1998 land sales had already generated 3m. roubles for the regional economy. A series of bilateral trade agreements signed with the Mayor of Moscow, Yurii Luzhkov, in August 1996, also benefited the economy of Saratov Oblast.

Legislative elections, held in August 2002, were dominated by nominally inde-pendent candidates and by supporters of the pro-Government Unity and Fatherland-United Russia. In February 2003 the former oblast Minister of Culture, Yurii Grishchenko, was sentenced to two years' imprisonment by the regional court, on charges of accepting bribes during his tenure as minister, becoming one of the highest-ranking state officials to be subject to such punishment. (The sentence, however, was regarded as relatively mild, and significantly below that which was provided for by law.) Grishchenko was additionally to be prohibited from being employed by any government body for a period of one year after his release.

Economy

In 2000 Saratov Oblast's gross regional product totalled 67,908m. roubles, equiva-lent to 25,103 roubles per head. The region's major industrial centres are at Saratov, Engels and Balakovo. In 2001 there were 2,296 km (1,427 miles) of railways and 10,231 km of paved roads on the Oblast's territory. It was the major Soviet/Russian arsenal for chemical weapons, provoking some local concern. In January 1996 it was announced that chemical weapons stored near the village of Gornyi would be destroyed, in accordance with international agreements. A new chemicals-weapons processing plant, at Gornyi, commenced operations in December 2002.

The Oblast's agriculture, which employed some 19.7% of the working population in 2001, consists primarily of animal husbandry and the production of grain (the Oblast is one of Russia's major producers of wheat) and sunflower seeds. In 2001 total agricultural production amounted to a value of 25,512m. roubles, of which crop sales accounted for 52.5% and animal husbandry for 47.5%. The Oblast's main industries are mechanical engineering and metal-working, the production of elec-tricity, petroleum-refining, chemicals and petrochemicals, food-processing and the production of petroleum and natural gas. In the late 1990s the region produced over 30% of the cement and 20% of the mineral fertilizer produced in the Volga Economic Area. Total industrial production was worth 55,840m. roubles in 2001, and some 20.2% of the work-force was engaged in industry at that time.

The region's economically active population numbered 1,309,000 in 2001, when 10.0% of the labour force were unemployed. In mid-2002 the average wage in the Oblast was 2,796.3 roubles per month. The regional budget for 2001 showed a deficit of 41m. roubles. In that year the value of external trade amounted to US $403.1m. in exports and $161.9m. in imports. Foreign investment amounted to $8.9m. in 2001, when 48 joint enterprises were registered in the region; of these, 10 involved partners from Cyprus, and nine involved partners from Germany. At 31 December 2001 there were some 10,850 small businesses registered in the region.

Directory

Head of the Regional Administration (Governor): DMITRII F. AYATSKOV; 410042 Saratov, ul. Moskovskaya 72; tel. (8452) 27-20-86; fax (8452) 72-52-54; e-mail governor@gov.saratov.ru; internet www.gov.saratov.ru.

Chairman of the Regional Duma: SERGEI A. SHUVALOV; 411031 Saratov, ul. Radishcheva 24A; tel. (8452) 27-99-80; fax (8452) 27-53-31; e-mail post@srd.ru; internet www.srd.ru.

Representation of Saratov Oblast in the Russian Federation: 109028 Moscow, per. Podkopayevskii 7/3; tel. and fax (095) 917-05-19.

Head of Saratov City Administration (Mayor): YURII N. AKSENENKO; 410600 Saratov, ul. Pervomaiskaya 78; tel. (8452) 23-77-78; fax (8452) 27-84-44; e-mail mayor@admsaratov.ru; internet www.admsaratov.ru.

Republic of Tatarstan

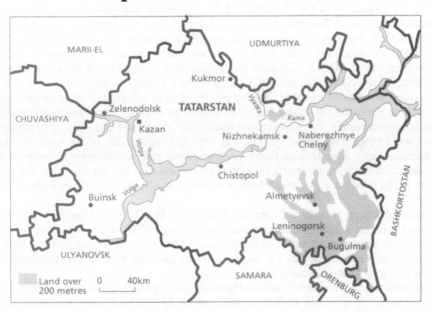

The Republic of Tatarstan is situated in the east of European Russia and forms part of the Volga Federal Okrug and the Volga Economic Area. It neighbours several other Republics: Bashkortostan to the east; Udmurtiya to the north; Marii-El to the north-west; and Chuvashiya to the west. The Oblasts of Ulyanovsk, Samara and Orenburg lie to the south, and that of Kirov to the north (between Udmurtiya and Marii-El). The Republic's major rivers are the Volga and the Kama, and one-fifth of its total territory of 67,836 sq km (26,260 sq miles) is forested. It measures 290 km (180 miles) from south to north and 460 km from west to east. The Republic is divided into 43 administrative districts and 20 cities. According to the preliminary results of the census of 9–16 October 2002, it had an estimated population of 3,779,800 and, therefore, a population density of 55.7 per sq km. Some 73.8% of the Republic's population inhabited urban areas. In 1989 some 48.5% of the total population were Tatars and 43.3% ethnic Russians. Tatarstan's capital is Kazan, which lies on the River Volga and had a population of 1,105,300 in 2002, according to preliminary census results. Other major cities include Naberezhnye Chelny (formerly Brezhnev—with a population of 510,000), Nizhnekamsk (225,500), Almetyevsk (140,500) and Zelenodolsk (100,100).

History

After the dissolution of the Mongol Empire the region became the Khanate of Kazan, the territory of the Golden Horde. Kazan was conquered by Russian troops, led by Tsar Ivan IV—'the Terrible' in 1552. Some of the Muslim Tatars succumbed to Russian pressures to convert to Orthodox Christianity (the Staro-Kryashens—'Old-Baptized' still exist, using Tatar as their spoken and liturgical tongue), but most did not. A modernist school of thought in Islam, Jadidism, originated among the Volga

Tatars, who attained an exceptionally high cultural level in the 19th-century Russian Empire. A Tatar ASSR was established on 27 May 1920.

On 31 August 1990 the Chairman of the republican Supreme Soviet, Mintimer Shamiyev, declared Tatarstan a sovereign republic. In 1991 Shamiyev was elected as republican President. Apart from secessionist Chechnya, Tatarstan was the only Republic to reject the Federation Treaty and adopt its own Constitution on 6 November 1992, which provided for a presidential republic with a bicameral legislature, the State Council. In February 1994 Shamiyev won important concessions from Russia's central Government by signing a treaty that ceded extensive powers to Tatarstan, including full ownership rights over its petroleum reserves and industrial companies, the right to retain most of its tax revenue and the right to pursue its own foreign-trade policy. This was the first agreement of its kind in the Federation and, despite significant contradictions and weaknesses, it became a model for other federal subjects seeking to determine their relations with the federal centre. The division of responsibilities was confirmed by treaty with the Federation in 1995.

In a republican presidential election, held on 24 March 1996, Shamiyev was re-elected, winning some 93% of the votes cast. During 1999 Shamiyev was one of the regional governors most active in the creation of the new All Russia political bloc. Republican parliamentary by-elections in March gave the President's supporters a clear majority in the legislature.

In 2000 federal President Vladimir Putin offered Shamiyev the post of presidential envoy to the new Volga Federal Okrug, which he declined, amid constitutional uncertainty regarding the legitimacy of Shamiyev's intention to contest a third term of office as Governor. In the event, Shamiyev was permitted to compete in the election in March 2001, when he obtained some 80% of the votes cast, becoming the first Governor of any federal subject in the Russian Federation to be elected three times to that post.

As Putin's administration, from mid-2000, sought to harmonize federal legislation with that of the constituent units of the Russian Federation, Tatarstan (along with neighbouring Bashkortostan) became one of the principal regions in which the republican authorities demonstrated sustained resistance to these measures. In May 2001 the federal Supreme Court declared that some 42 articles of the Republic's Constitution were at variance with federal law (a ruling by the republican Supreme Court confirmed these findings in October). Despite federal government demands that the inconsistencies be removed, in July Shamiyev signed an agreement with the Presidential Representative to the Volga Federal Okrug, Sergei Kiriyenko, which permitted the continued operation of various practices that contradicted federal practice; in particular, a highly centralized system of local governance was to be retained in Tatarstan. The text of a new Constitution, which was intended to comply with federal law, was none the less approved by the republican State Council in late February 2002; the new Constitution took effect from 19 April. Although the new document referred to Tatarstan being subject to the Constitution and laws of the Russian Federation, it continued to declare the 'limited' and 'residual' sovereignty of the Republic of Tatarstan and preserved the notion of Tatar citizenship. Consequently, in June the office of the federal Prosecutor-General demanded that several articles of the Constitution be amended, issuing a complaint to both the republican legislature and republican Supreme Court. However, in mid-September the State Council rejected any notion that the constitutional text was in breach of federal law, and instead referred the matter to both the republican and federal Constitutional Courts. Eventually the threat of the office of the Prosecutor-General to disband the State Council was rescinded, but the tensions between the federal and republican authorities remained largely unresolved. (These tensions were further heightened by federal legislation, approved by Putin in November 2002, that demanded that all state languages of federal subjects be written in Cyrillic on official documents—the republican authorities had, in 2000, begun to implement a programme to re-introduce the Latin script for the Tatar language.) In July 2003 the federal Constitutional Court ruled that it was the sole body with the authority to determine whether the constitutions of federal subjects were in conformity with federal law; one consequence of this ruling appeared to be that a number of challenges to the Constitution of Tatarstan from other bodies (including the federal Supreme Court) were declared invalid.

Economy

In 2000 the Republic's gross regional product totalled 202,734m. roubles, or 53,695 roubles per head, the highest level in the Volga Federal Okrug. The territory is one of the most developed economic regions of the Russian Federation and has vast agricultural and industrial potential. Its main industrial centres are Kazan, Naberezhnye Chelny, Zelenodolsk, Nizhnekamsk, Almetyevsk, Chistopol and Bugulma. Kazan is the most important port on the Volga and a junction in the national rail, road and air transport systems. Russia's second primary petroleum export pipeline to Europe starts in Almetyevsk. At the end of 2001 there were 865 km of railway lines and 12,641 km of paved roads on the Republic's territory.

Tatarstan's agriculture, in which some 14.3% of the work-force were engaged in 2001, consists mainly of grain production, animal husbandry, horticulture and bee-keeping. Total output in this sector amounted to a value of 40,214m. roubles in 2001, to which crop sales contributed 55.9% and animal husbandry 44.1%. Mineral natural resources are more important, and the Republic has significant reserves of hydrocarbons reserves. The region is an important industrial centre, and industry accounted for 25.7% of employment in 2001. The Republic's capital, Kazan, and the neighbouring towns of Zelendolsk and Vasilyevo are centres for light industry, the manufacture of petrochemicals and building materials, and mechanical engineering. The automobile and petroleum industries are major employers in the region. Kazanorgsintez, a petrochemicals giant, is the largest polyethylene producer in Russia. Industries connected with the extraction, processing and use of petroleum represent around one-half of the Republic's total industrial production, which was worth 215,251m. roubles in 2001. In the mid-1990s the US automobile company, General Motors, signed a contract to manufacture 50,000 automobiles per year at the Yelabuga plant, which later became the centre of a zone offering special tax incentives. In April 1996 a programme, drafted with French and US assistance, which envisaged the transformation of Tatarstan's economy from a military to a socially orientated system, was adopted by the Council of Ministers.

The economically active population in the Republic amounted to 1,823,000 in 2001, when just 6.3% of the labour force were unemployed. The average monthly wage was 3,866.4 roubles in mid-2002. The 2001 budget recorded a surplus of 1,065m. roubles. Tatarstan also fared well in terms of trade; the value of exports amounted to US $2,826.8m. in 2001, and imports to $346.9m. In the same year foreign investment in the Republic amounted to $651.0m. In 2000 there were 93 foreign joint-stock enterprises in Tatarstan, 20 of which received financing from the USA, while 13 received financing from Germany, 10 from the United Kingdom and seven from Cyprus. By the beginning of 1997 over 1,000 large and medium-sized enterprises in Tatarstan had been privatized; at 31 December 2001 there were 16,521 small businesses.

Directory

President: MINTIMER SH. SHAIMIYEV; 420014 Tatarstan, Kazan, Kreml; tel. (8432) 92-74-66; fax (8432) 91-78-66; e-mail secretariat@tatar.ru; internet www.tatar.ru.

Prime Minister: RUSTAM N. MINNIKHANOV; 420060 Tatarstan, Kazan, pl. Svobody 1; tel. (8432) 64-15-51; fax (8432) 36-28-24.

Chairman of the State Council: FARID KH. MUKHAMETSHIN; 420060 Tatarstan, Kazan, pl. Svobody 1; tel. (8432) 64-15-00; fax (8432) 36-88-45; e-mail gossov@ kabmin.tatarstan.ru; internet www.gossov.tatarstan.ru.

Chief Representative of the Republic of Tatarstan in the Russian Federation: NAZIF M. MIRIKHANOV; 107813 Moscow, per. 3-i Kotelnicheskii 13–15/1; tel. (095) 915-05-02; fax (095) 915-06-10; e-mail adm@msk.tatarstan.ru.

Head of Kazan City Administration: KAMIL SH. ISKHAKOV; 420014 Tatarstan, Kazan, ul. Kremlevskaya 1; tel. (8432) 92-38-38; fax (8432) 92-76-72; e-mail kanc@kazan.gov.tatarstan.ru; internet www.kazan.org.ru.

Udmurt Republic (Udmurtiya)

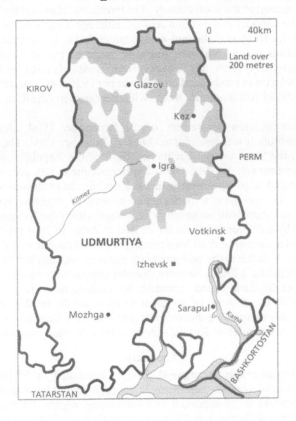

The Udmurt Republic occupies part of the Upper Kama Highlands. It forms part of the Volga Federal Okrug and the Urals Economic Area. Tatarstan lies to the south, Bashkortostan to the south-east, Perm to the east and Kirov to the north and west. Its major river is the Kama, dominating the southern and eastern borderlands, while the Vyatka skirts the territory in the west. About one-half of its territory is forested. Its total area covers some 42,100 sq km (16,250 sq miles). The Republic consists of 25 administrative districts and six cities. According to the preliminary results of the census of 9–16 October 2002, Udmurtiya had a total population of 1,570,500, and a population density, therefore, of 37.3 per sq km. Some 69.7% of the population inhabited urban areas. In 1989 some 30.9% of the total population were Udmurts and 58.9% ethnic Russians. The dominant religion in the Republic is Orthodox Christianity. The 1989 census showed that some 70% of Udmurts spoke their native tongue, from the Permian group of the Finnic branch of the Uralo-Altaic family, as their first language. The capital of Udmurtiya is at Izhevsk (formerly Ustinov), which had a population of 632,100 in 2002, according to preliminary census results. Other major towns in the region are Sarapul (103,200) and Glazov (100,900).

History

The first appearance of the Votyaks (the former name for Udmurts) as a distinct ethnic group occurred in the sixth century. The territories inhabited by Votyaks were conquered by the Khazars in the eighth century, although Khazar influence gave way to that of the Volga Bulgars in the mid-ninth century. In the 13th century the Mongol Tatars occupied the region, but were gradually displaced by the Russians from the mid-15th century. By 1558 all Votyaks were under Russian rule. A Votyak Autonomous Oblast was established on 4 November 1920. On 1 January 1932 it was renamed the Udmurt Autonomous Oblast, which became an ASSR on 28 December 1934.

The Republic declared sovereignty on 21 September 1990, although a new republican Constitution was not adopted until 7 December 1994. The Chairman of the legislature, the State Council, remained head of the Republic, and a premier chaired the Government. In 1996 the Udmurt parliament was accused of having virtually eliminated local government in the Republic, in contravention of federal law. Measures to introduce a presidential system of regional government in Udmurtiya, in common with most other Republics within the Russian Federation, were endorsed by a referendum held on 26 March 2000. In June the Udmurt State Council adopted a number of draft laws transferring the Republic to presidential rule. Aleksandr Volkov, hitherto the parliamentary speaker, was elected President on 15 October. The Republic's Prime Minister, Nikolai Ganza, who was supported by the Unity party, was the third-placed candidate; he resigned three days later.

From the 1990s the disposal of chemical weapons on the territory of Udmurtiya proved to be a serious social and ecological problem—the Republic was thought to contain around one-quarter of Russia's entire arsenal of such weapons.

Economy

In 2000 the Republic's gross regional product amounted to 55,766m. roubles, equivalent to 34,216 roubles per head. Udmurtiya possesses significant hydro-carbons reserves and is an important arms-producing region. Its major industrial centres are at Izhevsk, Sarapul and Glazov. Its main river-ports are at Sarapul and Kambarka. In 2001 there were 768 km (477 miles) of railway track and 5,652 km of paved roads on its territory. In 1998 there were 178 km of navigable waterways. Twelve major gas pipelines and two petroleum pipelines pass through the Udmurt Republic.

Udmurtiya's agriculture employed 14.3% of the working population in 2001 and consists mainly of animal husbandry and grain and potato production. Total agricultural production in 2001 was worth 13,369m. roubles, of which crop sales accounted for 42.9% and animal husbandry for 57.1%. There are substantial reserves of coal and of petroleum (prospected resources are estimated at 379,543m. metric tons), which in the late 1990s the Republic hoped to exploit with the aid of foreign investment. In 2001 some 28.9% of the Republic's working population were engaged in industry. The main industries in Udmurtiya, apart from the manufacture of weapons, are mechanical engineering (in the first half of 2000 the Republic produced some 89% of all the motorcycles manufactured in Russia), metal-working, metallurgy, food-processing, petroleum production and the production of peat. Total industrial output in 2001 amounted to a value of 59,314m. roubles.

In 2001 the economically active population amounted to 800,000, and 7.5% of the labour force were unemployed; in mid-2002 those in employment earned an average monthly wage of 3,475.8 roubles. The republican budget recorded a surplus of 297m. roubles in 2001, when there was foreign investment in the Republic of US $6.8m. External trade in 2001 amounted to $751.2m., of which exports accounted for $658.1m. The principal exports are metallurgical products, engines and machinery, and rifles. In the late 1990s the Republic had particularly active trade links with Germany. At 31 December 2001 there were approximately 7,950 small businesses registered in the Republic.

Directory

President: ALEKSANDR A. VOLKOV; 426074 Udmurtiya, Izhevsk, pl. 50 let Oktyabrya 15; tel. and fax (3412) 49-70-10; e-mail president@ udmurt.ru.

Chairman of the Government: YURII S. PITKEYVICH; 426007 Udmurtiya, Izhevsk, ul. Pushkinskaya. 214; tel. (3412) 25-50-89; fax (3412) 25-50-17; e-mail premier@ udmurt.ru.

Chairman of the State Council (Legislature): IGOR N. SEMENOV; 426074 Udmurtiya, Izhevsk, ul. 50 let Oktyabrya 15; tel. (3412) 75-34-98; fax (3412) 75-29-87; e-mail premier@udmurt.ru.

Chief Representative of the Udmurt Republic in the Russian Federation: ANDREI V. SAKOVICH; 127025 Moscow, ul. Novyi Arbat 19; tel. (095) 203-53-52; fax (095) 203-91-47.

Head of Izhevsk City Administration (Mayor): VIKTOR V. BALAKIN; 426070 Udmurtiya, Izhevsk, ul. Pushkinskaya 276; tel. (3412) 22-45-90; fax (3412) 22-84-94; e-mail izhevsk@izh.ru; internet www.izh.ru.

Ulyanovsk Oblast

Ulyanovsk Oblast is situated in the Volga Highlands. It forms part of the Volga Federal Okrug and the Volga Economic Area. The Republics of Mordoviya and of Chuvashiya and Tatarstan lie to the north-west and to the north, respectively. There are also borders with Samara Oblast in the south-east, Saratov Oblast in the south and Penza Oblast in the south-west. The region's major river is the Volga. The region occupies an area of 37,300 sq km (14,400 sq miles) and is divided into 21 administrative districts and six cities. According to the preliminary results of the census of 9–16 October 2002, the total population of the Oblast was 1,382,300, and the population density, therefore, was 37.1 per sq km. Some 73.2% of the population inhabited urban areas. The administrative centre at Ulyanovsk (formerly Simbirsk) had a population of 635,600 in 2002, according to provisional census results. The other major city in the region is Dimitrovgrad (130900).

History

Simbirsk city was founded in 1648. Lenin (Vladimir Ulyanov) was born there in 1870, and it was his home until 1887. The city assumed his family name following his death in 1924. Ulyanovsk Oblast, which was formed on 19 January 1943, formed part of the 'red belt' of communist support in post-Soviet Russia. Thus, it refused to revert to its old name and also gave the Communist Party of the Russian Federation (CPRF) 37% of the regional votes cast in the 1995 elections to the federal State Duma. In December 1996 the CPRF-backed candidate, Yurii Goryachev, won the election to the governorship of the Oblast.

Goryachev, whose support came largely from the Oblast's rural community, banned local privatization and collective-farm reforms, imposed restrictions on imports and exports, and subsidized bread prices until early 1997. Goryachev was defeated in the gubernatorial elections held in December 2000, and replaced by Lt-Gen. Vladimir Shamanov. In June 2002 the national power company, Unified

Energy System of Russia (RAO EES Rossii), announced its intention to appeal to the federal authorities for the direct imposition of federal rule over Ulyanovsk Oblast, owing to the region's debts to that company, which had been permitted to accrue in the period prior to Shamanov's election. In early 2003 widespread protests followed the announcement that electricity tariffs in the Oblast were to increase by 43%, in order to repay the debts over a period of 15 years. In response to the protests, in April tariffs were increased by just 14%. On 7 December regional legislative elections took place, concurrently with the elections to the federal State Duma.

Economy

In 2000 Ulyanovsk Oblast's gross regional product amounted to 32,860m. roubles, or 22,462 roubles per head. The Oblast's major industrial centres are at Ulyanovsk and Melekess. At the end of 2001 there were 716 km (445 miles) of railway lines and 4,343 km of paved roads on the Oblast's territory.

Around 1.5m. ha of its territory is used for agricultural purposes, of which over four-fifths is arable land. Agriculture in the region, which employed some 15.7% of the working population in 2001, consists primarily of animal husbandry and the production of grain, sunflower seeds and sugar beet. Total agricultural production amounted to a value of 9,916m. roubles in 2001, of which crop sales generated 54.1% and animal husbandry 45.9%. The Oblast's main industries are mechanical engineering, food-processing and electrical energy. The region's major companies included the UAZ automobile plant and the Aviastar aeroplane manufacturer (both of which were operating at 50% capacity in the late 1990s). In late 2002 Aviastar signed a contract, reportedly worth US $335m., to construct 25 TU-204-120 jets, following the acquisition of a 25% stake (less one share) in the firm by the Egyptian concern Sirocco Aerospace International; the Chairman of Sirocco, Ibrahim Kamel, expressed the intention of further developing the capacities of the Aviastar plant. Industry employed 28.9% of the working population in 2001, and generated some 32,579m. roubles.

The economically active population numbered 687,000 in 2001, when 9.0% of the labour force were unemployed. Those in employment earned an average of 2,907.5 roubles per month in mid-2002. In mid-2003 the region was named as one of the three worst regions for public-sector wage arrears, which were reported to amount to some 125m. roubles. The recently appointed Deputy Chairman of the federal Government, responsible for Social Affairs, Galina Karelova, visited Ulyanovsk in June, and announced that a special commission was to be established to investigate the situation. There was a budgetary deficit of 49m. roubles in 2001. In that year external trade constituted US $111.0m. in exports and $48.4m. in imports; total foreign investment in the Oblast amounted to $2.2m. At 31 December 2001 4,822 small businesses were registered in the region.

Directory

Head of the Regional Administration (Governor): Lt-Gen. VLADIMIR A. SHA-MANOV; 432970 Ulyanovsk, pl. Lenina 1; tel. (8422) 41-38-22; fax (8422) 41-48-12; e-mail admobl@mv.ru; internet www.ulyanovsk-adm.ru.

Chairman of the Legislative Assembly: BORIS I. ZOTOV; 432700 Ulyanovsk, ul. Radishcheva 1; tel. and fax (8422) 41-34-52; internet zsuo.ru.

Representative of Ulyanovsk Oblast in the Russian Federation: GENNADII V. SAVINOV; 119002 Moscow, per. Denezhnyi 12; tel. (095) 241-31-42; fax (095) 241-38-99.

Head of Ulyanovsk City Administration (Mayor): PAVEL ROMANENKO; 432700 Ulyanovsk, ul. Kuznetsova 7; tel. (8422) 41-45-08; fax (8422) 41-40-20; e-mail meria@mv.ru; internet www.ulmeria.ru.

URALS FEDERAL OKRUG

Chelyabinsk Oblast

Chelyabinsk Oblast is situated in the Southern Urals, in the Transural (Asian Russia). It forms part of the Urals Federal Okrug and the Urals Economic Area. Orenburg Oblast lies to the south, the Republic of Bashkortostan to the west, Sverdlovsk Oblast to the north and Kurgan Oblast to the east. There is an international border with Kazakhstan in the south-east. Much of the region lies on the eastern slopes of the Southern Ural Mountains. The major rivers in the Oblast are the Ural and the Miass. It has over 1,000 lakes, the largest of which are the Uvildy and the Turgoyak. The Oblast covers an area of 87,900 sq km (34,940 sq miles) and is divided into 24 administrative districts and 30 cities. According to the preliminary results of the census of 9–16 October 2002, Chelyabinsk Oblast had a population of 3,606,100, giving a population density of 41.0 per sq km. At that time some 81.8% of the population inhabited urban areas. The Oblast's administrative centre is at Chelyabinsk, a city with a population of 1,078,300. Other major cities are Magnitogorsk (419,100), Zlatoust (194,800) and Miass (158,500).

History

Chelyabinsk city was established as a Russian frontier post in 1736, but was deep within Russian territory by the 19th century. The Oblast was created on 17 January 1934. The region was heavily industrialized during the Soviet period and remained dominated by communist cadres following the disintegration of the USSR.

In December 1992, at elections for the head of the regional administration, the incumbent Governor, a supporter of Boris Yeltsin, the Russian President, was defeated. Yeltsin re-established his authority in late 1993 and required the election of a Duma during 1994. Both in this body, and in the local results of the general election of 1995, pro-Yeltsin and reformist forces obtained significant levels of support. In the gubernatorial election of late 1996, however, Petr Sumin was returned to power. Sumin, a communist, had been removed as head of the regional administration following the attempted coup of August 1991. Sumin's pro-communist movement also won an absolute majority of seats in the legislature in the local elections held in December 1997. Sumin was re-elected as Governor in December 2000.

Economy

In 2000 the gross regional product of the Oblast amounted to 136,063m. roubles, equivalent to 37,131 roubles per head. The region's major industrial centres are at Chelyabinsk, Magnitogorsk, Miass, Zlatoust and Kopeisk. Although output declined by one-half between 1989 and 1997, Magnitogorsk remains well known as the city that produced the steel for over one-half of the tanks used by Soviet troops in the Second World War, and as the largest iron and steel production complex in the world. The Oblast is a major junction of the Trans-Siberian Railway. At the end of 2001 there were 1,793 km (1,114 miles) of railway track in the Oblast and 8,707 km of paved roads.

The Oblast's agriculture, which employed just 9.1% of the working population in 2001, consists mainly of animal husbandry, horticulture and the production of grain. Total agricultural output in 2001 was worth 15,696m. roubles, of which 47.4% was generated by crop sales and 52.6% by animal husbandry. The Oblast is one of the most polluted in the Federation; in particular, high rates of disease and environmental despoliation resulted from the Kyshtym nuclear accident of 1957, in the north of the region, when up to three times the levels of radiation emitted at the Chornobyl (Chernobyl) disaster in Ukraine in 1986 were released into the surrounding area. Approximately 180 sq km of agricultural land remained out of use because of radioactivity, and water supplies in many parts of the region were also unsafe. Chelyabinsk Oblast became one of the most industrialized territories of the Russian Federation, following the reconstruction of plants moved there from further west during the Second World War. In 2001 industry employed some 31.5% of the economically active population. The Oblast's main industries are ferrous and non-ferrous metallurgy (which accounted for a total of 64.6% of industrial activity in 2001), ore-mining, mechanical engineering, metal-working, and fuel and energy production. In the north-west, the closed city of Ozersk (formerly Chelyabinsk-40) is a major plutonium-processing and -storage site, while in the west are centres for weapons manufacturing and space technology. The conversion of former military plants to civilian use in the 1990s meant that the former tank factory at Magnitogorsk began to produce tractors, and the Mayak nuclear armament plant (the location of the

1957 disaster) sought to become a recycling plant for foreign nuclear waste. In 2001 the industrial sector generated 170,723m. roubles.

The economically active population numbered 1,711,000 in 2001, when 8.7% of the labour force were unemployed. At mid-2002 those in employment earned an average wage of 3,953.7 roubles per month. The 2001 budget recorded a deficit of 939m. roubles. Export trade amounted to US $1,721.3m. in 2001, when imports were worth $692.0m. Attempts to attract foreign investment in the Oblast from the mid-1990s were largely successful: foreign capital amounted to $767.1m. by 2001, compared with $59.1m. in 1998. In 2000 there were some 119 enterprises with foreign capital in the Oblast. At 31 December 2001 there were 20,438 small businesses registered on the Oblast's territory.

Directory

Governor: PETR I. SUMIN; 454009 Chelyabinsk, ul. Tsvillinga 28; tel. (3512) 63-92-41; fax (3512) 63-12-83; internet www.ural-chel.ru.

Chairman of the Legislative Assembly: VIKTOR F. DAVYDOV; 454009 Chelyabinsk, ul. Kirova 114; tel. (3512) 65-78-26; fax (3512) 63-63-79; e-mail zscr@chel.surnet .ru; internet www.ural-chel.ru/gubern/zaksob/index.html.

Chief Representative of Chelyabinsk Oblast in the Russian Federation: OLEG N. ANDREYEV; 127422 Moscow, Dmitrovskii pr. 4A; tel. (095) 210-88-59; fax (095) 977-08-35.

Head of Chelyabinsk City Administration (Mayor): VYACHESLAV M. TARASOV; 454113 Chelyabinsk, pl. Revolyutsii 2; tel. (3512) 33-38-05; fax (3512) 33-38-55.

Kurgan Oblast

Kurgan Oblast is situated in the south of the Western Siberian Plain. It forms part of the Urals Federal District and the Urals Economic Area. Chelyabinsk Oblast lies to the west, Sverdlovsk Oblast to the north and Tyumen Oblast to the north-east. There is an international border with Kazakhstan to the south. The main rivers flowing through Kurgan Oblast are the Tobol and the Iset and there are numerous lakes (more than 2,500) in the south-east of the region. The Oblast occupies 71,000 sq km (27,400 sq miles) and measures 290 km (180 miles) from south to north and 430 km from east to west. It is divided into 24 administrative districts and nine cities, and had a total population of 1,019,900 in mid-October 2002, according to preliminary census results, giving a population density of 14.4 per sq km. At that time some 56.3% of the population inhabited urban areas, the lowest proportion of any region in the Urals Federal Okrug. Its administrative centre is at Kurgan, which had a population of 345,700, according to the provisional results of the census.

History

The city of Kurgan was founded as a tax-exempt settlement in 1553, on the edge of Russian territory. Kurgan Oblast was formed on 6 February 1943. The Communist Party of the Russian Federation (CPRF) was the largest party in the Regional Duma elected on 12 December 1993, and remained the most popular party in the Oblast at elections to the State Duma in 1995. The CPRF candidate, Oleg Bogomolov, hitherto speaker of the Regional Duma, was elected as Governor in late 1996, running unopposed in the second round of the election after his opponent stood down. Bogomolov was re-elected in December 2000. The agricultural policies of the federal Government were a focus for political protest in Kurgan in the early 2000s, as a result of the increasing economic difficulties faced by farmers in the Oblast. Concern was also expressed about the economic viability of Kurgan Oblast as a political entity, giving rise to suggestions that the region be merged with one or more of its neighbours, although by late 2003 no definite proposals had been established to that end.

Economy

Kurgan Oblast, with its fertile soil and warm, moist climate, is the agricultural base of the Urals area, producing around one-10th of the region's grain, meat and milk. In 2000 its gross regional product amounted to 19,941m. roubles, equivalent to 18,246 roubles per head, the lowest figure in the Urals Federal Okrug. The Oblast's main industrial centres are at Kurgan, a river-port in the south-east of the region, and Shadrinsk, on the Iset. At the end of 2001 there were 748 km of railways and 6,411 km of paved roads on the Oblast's territory. The Trans-Siberian Railway passes through the Oblast, as do several major petroleum and natural gas pipelines.

The Oblast's important agricultural sector employed 24.7% of the work-force in 2001 and consists mainly of grain production and animal husbandry. Total agricultural production in the region was worth 10,111m. roubles in 2001, of which crop sales contributed 52.9% and animal husbandry 47.1%. The Oblast's main industries are mechanical engineering, metal-working, electricity production and food-processing. The industrial sector employed 21.1% of the working population and generated 16,320m. roubles in 2001.

The economically active population numbered 494,000 in 2001. The rate of unemployment increased from the late 1990s, reaching 13.3% of the labour force by 2001. This represented the highest level of any territory in the Urals Federal Okrug. Those in employment earned, on average, just 3,030.1 roubles per month in mid-2002. There was a budgetary deficit of 282m. roubles in 2001, when foreign investment totalled US $889,000. In 2001 external trade amounted to a value of $163.5m., while imports totalled $50.3m. The economic situation of the region deteriorated markedly from the late 1990s, and in mid-2002 it was reported that up to 60% of the Oblast's budget comprised transfers from the federal Government, and that around 60% of the region's population lived in conditions of, or approaching, poverty. In late 2001 there were 2,981 small businesses registered in the Oblast.

Directory

Head of the Regional Administration (Governor): OLEG A. BOGOMOLOV; 640024 Kurgan, ul. Gogolya 56; tel. (3522) 41-70-30; fax (3522) 41-71-32; e-mail kurgan@ admobl.kurgan.ru; internet www.admobl.kurgan.ru.

Chairman of the Regional Duma: VALERII Z. PONOMAREV; 640024 Kurgan, ul. Gogolya 56; tel. (3522) 41-72-17; fax (3522) 41-88-91.

Chief Representative of Kurgan Oblast in the Russian Federation: OLEG YE. PANTELEYEV; 103798 Moscow, ul. M. Dmitrovka 3; tel. (095) 200-39-78; fax (095) 299-33-67.

Head of Kurgan City Administration (Mayor): ANATOLII F. YELCHANINOV; 640000 Kurgan, pl. Lenina; tel. (3522) 46-22-25; fax (3522) 41-70-40; e-mail inform@ munic.kurgan.ru; internet www.munic.kurgan.ru.

Sverdlovsk Oblast

Sverdlovsk Oblast is situated on the eastern, and partly on the western, slopes of the Central and Northern Urals and in the Western Siberian Plain. It forms part of the Urals Federal Okrug and the Urals Economic Area. Tyumen Oblast lies to the east (with its constituent Khanty-Mansii AOk—Yugra to the north-west); there is a short border with the Republic of Komi in the north-west and Perm Oblast lies to the west. To the south are Bashkortostan, Chelyabinsk and Kurgan. The region's major rivers are those of the Ob and Kama basins. The west of the region is mountainous, while much of the eastern part is taiga (forested marshland). The territory of the Oblast covers an area of 194,800 sq km (75,190 sq miles) and is divided into 30 administrative districts and 47 cities. According to the preliminary results of the census of 9–16 October 2002, the population totalled 4,489,800, and the population density was 23.0 per sq km. As many as 87.9% of the region's inhabitants lived in urban areas at that time. The Oblast's administrative centre is at Yekaterinburg (formerly Sverdlovsk), which had a population of 1,293,000, according to provisional census results. Other major cities are Nizhnii Tagil (390,600), Kamensk-Uralskii (186,300), Pervouralsk (132,800) and Serov (100,300).

History

Yekaterinburg city was founded in 1821 as a military stronghold and trading centre. Like the Oblast (formed on 17 January 1934) it was named Sverdlovsk in 1924 but, unlike the Oblast, reverted to the name of Yekaterinburg in 1991. The city was infamous as the location where the last Tsar, Nicholas II, and his family were assassinated in 1918. The region became a major industrial centre after the Second World War.

Following the disintegration of the USSR, Sverdlovsk Oblast was among the most forthright in demanding the devolution of powers from the centre. In September 1993 the Regional Soviet adopted a draft constitution for a 'Ural Republic', which was officially proclaimed on 27 October by the Regional Soviet and the head of the regional administration, Eduard Rossel. The 'Ural Republic' was dissolved by presidential decree, however, and Rossel was dismissed on 9 November. In 1994 elections were held to a Regional Duma. In August 1995 Rossel was reinstated as Governor, having won the direct election to head the regional administration. His popularity enabled him to establish an independent Transformation of the Urals Movement that eclipsed support for the national parties in the region in the federal elections of December 1995.

As Governor, Rossel continued to strive for more autonomy for the Oblast, one of the most powerful and potentially most prosperous regions in the Federation. In January 1996 Rossel signed an agreement on the division of powers and spheres of competence between federal and regional institutions. This accord was the first of its kind to be signed with a federal territory that did not have republican status. In April elections were held to the oblast Legislative Assembly, one of the few bicameral legislatures among the Oblasts of the Russian Federation, and also one of the few regional legislatures that makes no provision for the formation of groupings of deputies. Less than one-third of the electorate participated, but some 35% voted for Rossel's Transformation bloc. Subsequently, however, the Governor's popularity began to decline: in April 1998 the Transformation bloc won just 9.3% of the votes to the regional legislature and claimed just two seats in the lower house, the Regional Duma (where it had previously held a majority). Nevertheless, Rossel was re-elected as Governor of Sverdlovsk Oblast on 12 September 1999.

It was claimed that the Urals Federal Okrug, formed in mid-2000 by President Vladimir Putin, incorporated several regions traditionally regarded as part of Siberia, while excluding other regions that were included in the Urals Economic Area, so as to inhibit any revival of an appeal for a 'Ural Republic'. Rossel subsequently adopted a less oppositional stance towards the federal authorities, and became a member of the pro-Government Unity and Fatherland-United Russia (UF-UR); he was elected to the Supreme Council of the party in March 2003. On 21 September Rossel was re-elected as Governor of the Oblast, receiving 55.5% in a 'run off' election against Anton Bakov, of Gennadii Seleznev's Party of the Rebirth of Russia. Later in the month Rossel was appointed as the leader of the UF-UR list in Sverdlovsk Oblast for the elections to the federal State Duma, which took place on 7 December.

Economy

Sverdlovsk Oblast is a leading territory of the Russian Federation in terms of industry; the concentration of industry in the Oblast is around four times the average for a federal unit. In 2000 the territory's gross regional product amounted to 165,761m. roubles, equivalent to 36,056 roubles per head. Its most important industrial centres are at Yekaterinburg, Nizhnii Tagil, Pervouralsk, Krasnouralsk, Serov, Alapayevsk and Kamensk-Uralskii. At the end of 2001 there were 3,569 km (2,218 miles) of railway lines and 10,576 km of paved roads on the Oblast's territory. There is an international airport, Koltsovo, outside Yekaterinburg.

The Oblast's agriculture, which employed just 6.6% of its work-force in 2001, consists mainly of grain production and animal husbandry. Total agricultural output in 2001 was worth 21,644m. roubles, of which crop sales accounted for 49.1% and animal husbandry for 50.9%. There is some extraction of gold and platinum in the Oblast. Its main industries are ferrous and non-ferrous metallurgy, the production of electrical energy, mechanical engineering (the most important plant being the Yekaterinburg-based Uralmash), food-processing and the production of copper and other ores, bauxite, asbestos, petroleum, peat and coal. There is also a significant defence sector. Industry employed some 32.3% of the working population in 2001 and generated 209,753m. roubles. The services sector was also of increasing significance in the regional economy; the Oblast was given approval to issue US $500m.-worth of Eurobonds.

Sverdlovsk's economically active population numbered 2,322,000 in 2001, when 7.7% of the labour force were unemployed. The average monthly wage in the region was 4,731.5 roubles in mid-2002. The 2001 budget showed a deficit of 44m. roubles, and total foreign investment in that year was US $747.8m.; international trade amounted to some $2,912.8m. in exports and $747.5m. in imports. At 31 December 2001 there were 21,580 small businesses registered in the region.

Directory

Chairman of the Administration (Governor): EDUARD E. ROSSEL; 620031 Sverdlovsk obl., Yekaterinburg, pl. Oktyabrskaya 1; tel. (3432) 51-13-65; fax (3432) 70-54-72; e-mail press-center@midural.ru; internet www.rossel.ru.

Chairman of the Government: ALEKSEI P. VOROBEV; 620031 Sverdlovsk obl., Yekaterinburg, pl. Oktyabrskaya 1; tel. (3432) 71-79-20; fax (3432) 77-17-00; internet www.midural.ru.

Chairman of the House of Representatives of the Legislative Assembly: VIKTOR V. YAKIMOV; 620031 Sverdlovsk obl., Yekaterinburg, pl. Oktyabrskaya 1; tel. (3432) 78-91-08; fax (3432) 71-80-48; e-mail duma@midural.ru; internet www.duma .midural.ru.

Chairman of the Regional Duma of the Legislative Assembly: NIKOLAI A. VORONIN; 620031 Sverdlovsk obl., Yekaterinburg, pl. Oktyabrskaya 1; tel. (3432) 78-91-08; fax (3432) 71-80-48; e-mail duma@midural.ru; internet www.duma .midural.ru.

Chief Representative of Sverdlovsk Oblast in the Russian Federation: VLADIMIR S. MELENTIYEV; 121019 Moscow, ul. Novyi Arbat 21; tel. and fax (095) 291-90-72.

Head of Yekaterinburg City Administration (Mayor): ARKADII M. CHERNETSKII; 620014 Sverdlovsk obl., Yekaterinburg, pr. Lenina 24; tel. (3432) 56-29-90; fax (3432) 71-79-26; e-mail glava@sov.mplik.ru.

Tyumen Oblast

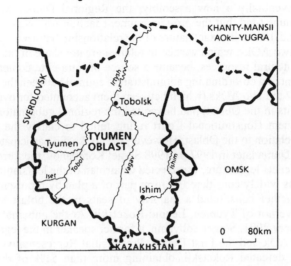

Tyumen Oblast is situated in the Western Siberian Plain, extending from the Kara Sea in the north to the border with Kazakhstan in the south. It forms part of the Urals Federal Okrug and the Western Siberian Economic Area. Much of its territory comprises the Khanty-Mansii—Yugra and Yamal-Nenets Autonomous Okrugs (AOks). To the west (going south to north) lie Kurgan, Sverdlovsk, Komi and the Nenets AOk—part of Archangel Oblast; to the east lie Omsk, Tomsk and Krasnoyarsk—in the far north the border is with Krasnoyarsk's Taimyr AOk. The region has numerous rivers, its major ones being the Ob, the Taz, the Pur and the Nadym. Much of its territory is taiga (forested marshland). The territory of the Oblast, including that of the AOks, occupies an area of 1,435,200 sq km (554,130 sq miles) and is divided into 38 administrative districts and 28 cities. The Oblast, in particular that section within the Khanty-Mansii—Yugra and the Yamal-Nenets AOks, is a sparsely populated region: according to the preliminary results of the census of 9–16 October 2002, the total population was 3,265,700, and the population density was 2.3 per sq km. When the area of the AOks is excluded, the area of the Oblast is 161,800 sq km, and the population of this area was 1,325,200, giving a population density of 8.2 per sq km. The Oblast, excluding the AOks, is divided into 22 administrative districts and five cities. Some 77.4% of the entire Oblast's inhabitants lived in urban areas. The Oblast's administrative centre is at Tyumen, which had a population of 510,700, according to provisional census results.

History

Tyumen city was founded in 1585 on the site of a Tatar settlement. It subsequently became an important centre for trade with the Chinese Empire. Tyumen Oblast was formed on 14 August 1944. The region became industrialized after the Second World War.

On 21 October 1993 the Regional Soviet in Tyumen Oblast repealed its earlier condemnation of government action against the federal parliament but refused to disband itself. Legislative elections were held in the Oblast in March 1994, but the results in several constituencies were declared invalid, owing to a low level of participation. Eventually a new assembly, the Regional Duma, was elected. It remained communist-led, but the pro-Government faction was well represented.

During the mid-1990s the exact nature of the relationship between Tyumen Oblast proper and the two AOks, which wished to retain a greater share of the income from their wealth of natural resources, became a source of intra-élite contention, despite the establishment of a co-ordinating administrative council between the three entities in 1995. In 1997 the two AOks (which between them accounted for over 90% of the output and profits in the Oblast) had boycotted the regional gubernatorial elections, while a subsequent Constitutional Court ruling failed to clarify the status of the autonomies in relation to the Oblast. However, the AOks did participate in elections to the Regional Duma later in 1997. In 1998 Sergei Korepanov, the former Chairman of the Yamal-Nenets legislature, was elected Chairman of the legislature of Tyumen Oblast. This was widely considered to form part of a plan by representatives of the AOks (who together constituted a majority of seats in the oblast legislature) to remove the Governor of Tyumen, Leonid Roketskii. At the gubernatorial election held on 14 January 2001, Sergei Sobyanin, a former speaker in the legislature of the Khanty-Mansii AOk and the First Deputy Presidential Representative in the Urals Federal Okrug, defeated Roketskii, obtaining more than 51% of the votes cast. Sobyanin consistently stated his opposition to any reabsorption of the two AOks into Tyumen Oblast, emphasizing his belief that a successful balance of powers and distribution of financial resources had been attained between the three political entities.

Economy

All figures in this survey include data for the two AOks, which are also treated separately (see below). In the mid-1990s Tyumen Oblast was considered to have great economic potential, owing to its vast hydrocarbons and timber reserves (mainly located in the Khanty-Mansii—Yugra and Yamal-Nenets AOks). In 2000 its gross regional product amounted to 618,032m. roubles, equivalent to 191,412 roubles per head (by far the highest figure in the Russian Federation). Its main industrial centres are at Tyumen, Tobolsk, Surgut, Nizhnevartovsk (the last two in the Khanty-Mansii AOk—Yugra) and Nadym (Yamal-Nenets AOk). At the end of 2001 there were 2,451 km (1,523 miles) of railway lines and 9,717 km of paved roads on the Oblast's territory.

The Oblast's agriculture, which employed just 5.9% of its work-force in 2001, consists mainly of animal husbandry (livestock- and reindeer-breeding and fur-farming), and the production of grain, potatoes and vegetables. In 2001 agricultural production was worth 15,778m. roubles; of this total, crop sales accounted for 47.7% and animal husbandry for 52.3%. The production of alcoholic beverages, particularly vodka, increased markedly in the early 2000s, and by 2003 the region was one of the seven principal regions active in the sector. In the late 1990s the Oblast's reserves of petroleum, natural gas and peat were estimated at 60%, 90% and 36%, respectively, of Russia's total supply. The Tyumen Oil Company (TNK), formed in 1995 from nine other companies, was among the largest petroleum companies in Russia. From 1997, when the state's share in the company was reduced to less than one-half, TNK became increasingly market-driven. In 2003 TNK merged with Sidanco and the Russian interests of British Petroleum, and was renamed TNK-BP. Overall petroleum output in the region totalled 213m. metric tons in 2000. The Oblast's other major industry is the production of electrical energy. Industry employed some 22.1% of the Oblast's working population in 2001 and generated a total of 559,081m. roubles, by far the highest level of any federal subject.

The economically active population totalled 1,734,000 in 2001, when 10.4% of the work-force were unemployed. The average monthly wage was 12,400.9 roubles in mid-2002, among the highest wages in the Federation. The budget for 2001 recorded a deficit of 5,293m. roubles. Trade figures for 2001 showed the Oblast to have generated some US $15,153.1m. in exports and to have purchased $830.2m. of imports. Total foreign investment in the Oblast amounted to $284.4m. in that year. At the end of 2001 11,317 small businesses were registered in the region.

Directory

Governor: SERGEI S. SOBYANIN; 625004 Tyumen, ul. Volodarskogo 45; tel. (3452) 46-77-20; fax (3452) 46-55-42; internet www.adm.tyumen.ru.

Chairman of the Regional Duma: SERGEI YE. KOREPANOV; 625018 Tyumen, ul. Respubliki 52, Dom Sovetov; tel. (3452) 45-50-81; e-mail tyumduma@tmn.ru; internet www.tmn.ru/~tyumduma.

Chief Representative of Tyumen Oblast in the Russian Federation: VLADIMIR M. GORYUNOV; 119017 Moscow, ul. Pyatnitskaya 47/2; tel. and fax (095) 291-71-94.

Head of Tyumen City Administration: STEPAN M. KIRICHUK; 625036 Tyumen, ul. Pervomaiskaya 20; tel. (3452) 24-67-42; fax (3452) 46-42-72; e-mail ves@ tyumen-city.ru; internet www.tyumen-city.ru.

Khanty-Mansii Autonomous Okrug— Yugra

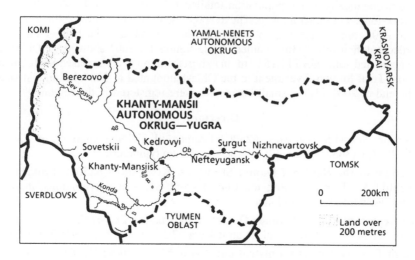

The Khanty-Mansii Autonomous Okrug (AOk)—Yugra is situated in the Western Siberian Plain and the Ob-Irtysh river basin. The district forms part of the Urals Federal Okrug and the Western Siberian Economic Area, and lies within the territory of Tyumen Oblast. The other autonomous okrug within Tyumen Oblast, the Yamal-Nenets AOk, lies to the north, while to the south of the district's centre lies the region of Tyumen proper. The Republic of Komi is to the west and Sverdlovsk to the south-west; to the south-east lies Tomsk and to the east Krasnoyarsk. Apart from the Ob and the Irtysh, the district's major rivers are the Konda, the Sosva, the Vakh, the Agan and the Bolshoi Yugan. It has numerous lakes, and much of its territory is Arctic tundra (frozen steppe) and taiga (forested marshland). More than one-third of the territory of the Khanty-Mansii district is forested. It occupies a total of 523,100 sq km (201,970 sq miles) and measures about 900 km (560 miles) from south to north and 1,400 km from east to west. There are nine administrative districts and 16 cities. According to the preliminary results of the census of 9–16 October 2002, the AOk had a total of 1,433,100 inhabitants, giving a population density of 2.7 per sq km. At that time as many as 90.9% of the population lived in urban areas. Ethnic Khants and Mansi, collectively known as Ob-Ugrian peoples, are greatly out-numbered by ethnic Russians in the district: the census of 1989 found that some 66.3% of total inhabitants were Russians, 11.6% Ukrainians, 7.6% Tatars, 2.4% Bashirs and 2.2% Belarusians, compared with just 0.9% Khants and 0.5% Mansi. The Khanty and the Mansii languages are grouped together as an Ob-Ugrian sub-division of the Ugrian division of the Finno-Ugrian group. The Autonomous Okrug's administrative centre is at the town of Khanty-Mansiisk, which had 39,700 inhab-itants at 1 January 2001. Other major, and larger, cities in the Okrug are Surgut (285,500, according to provisional results of the 2002 census), Nizhnevartovsk (239,000) and Nefteyugansk (107,800).

History

The Khanty-Mansii region, known as Yugra in the 11th–15th centuries, came under Russian control in the late 16th and early 17th centuries, as Russian fur traders established themselves in western Siberia. Attempts were made to assimilate the Khants and Mansi into Russian culture, and many were forcibly converted to Orthodox Christianity. The modern territory was created in December 1930, as the East Vogul (Ostyako-Vogulskii) National Autonomous Okrug (becoming known as Khanty-Mansii Autonomous Okrug—AOk in 1943).

From about the time of the Second World War the district became heavily industrialized, causing widespread damage to fish catches and reindeer pastures. In 1996 the okrug authorities appealed to the Constitutional Court against Tyumen Oblast's attempt to legislate for district petroleum and natural gas reserves, and a protracted dispute ensued. As in the neighbouring Yamal-Nenets AOk, the exact nature of the constitutional relationship between the Khanty-Mansii AOk and Tyumen Oblast remained obscure. This dispute partly reflected the domination of different interest groups in the two administrations—the district authorities favoured the federal Government and the energy industry, while the Communist Party of the Russian Federation retained support in Tyumen Oblast.

Aleksandr Filipenko, the head of the district administration, was returned to power in the gubernatorial election held in late 1996. He was re-elected, with 91% of the votes cast, in an election held simultaneously with the federal presidential election of 26 March 2000, in which he was a vocal supporter of Vladimir Putin's candidacy. Legislative elections were held on 14 January 2001; the district legislature, notably, incorporated a four-member Assembly of Representatives of Native Small Peoples of the North, with a particular remit to settle disputes over land use. In February 2003 the district legislature amended the charter of the Khanty-Mansii AOk, formally appending the name Yugra; in July federal President Putin signed a decree, in accordance with which the new name (Khanty-Mansii AOk—Yugra) was officially incorporated into the federal Constitution.

Economy

The AOk's economy is based on industry, particularly on the extraction and refining of petroleum. In the late 1990s it produced around 5% of Russia's entire industrial output and over 50% of its petroleum. The AOk's main industrial centre is at the petroleum-producing town of Surgut. Its major river-port is at Nizhnevartovsk. At the end of 2001 there were 1,073 km of railway track and 1,895 km of paved roads, many of which were constructed during the 1990s. In September 2000 a long-awaited road bridge across the River Ob was opened.

Agriculture in the Khanty-Mansii AOk, which employed just 1.5% of the work-force in 2001, consists mainly of fishing, reindeer-breeding, fur-farming, hunting and vegetable production. Total agricultural output in that year was worth 2,118m. roubles, while industrial production amounted to a value of some 429,997m. roubles. Industry, which employed some 25.6% of the work-force in 2001, is based on the extraction of petroleum and natural gas and the production of electricity. In 2002 55 companies in the Khanty-Mansii AOk accounted for 57.3% of the petroleum produced in Russia. The most significant producers of petroleum in the region were Surgutneftegaz (SNG) Oil Co, LUKoil-Western Siberia and Yuganskneftegaz, a subsidiary of Yukos Oil Co. Yukos assisted in the construction of housing and leisure facilities and in the operation of educational establishments during the early 2000s.

The economically active population of the okrug numbered 785,000 in 2001, when 11.0% of the labour force were unemployed. The average monthly wage was some 15,183.9 roubles in mid-2002. In 2001 the local budget recorded a surplus of 6,895m. roubles. There was considerable foreign investment in the okrug from the late 1990s, and it totalled US $201.0m. in 2001. Data for external trade, although substantial, are included within the aggregate figures for Tyumen Oblast (q.v.). On 31 December 2001 4,385 small businesses were registered in the Khanty-Mansii AOk.

Directory

Governor (Chairman of the Government): ALEKSANDR V. FILIPENKO; 628007 Tyumen obl., Khanty-Mansii AOk, Khanty-Mansiisk, ul. Mira 5; tel. (34671) 3-20-95; fax (34671) 3-34-60; e-mail kominf@hmansy.wsnet.ru; internet www.hmao.wsnet.ru.

Chairman of the District Duma: VASILII S. SONDYKOV; 628007 Tyumen obl., Khanty-Mansii AOk, Khanty-Mansiisk, ul. Mira 5; tel. (34671) 3-06-01; fax (34671) 3-16-84; e-mail dumahmao@hmansy.wsnet.ru.

Chief Representative of the Khanty-Mansii Autonomous Okrug—Yugra in Tyumen Oblast: NIKOLAI M. DOBRYNIN; 626002 Tyumen, ul. Komsomolskaya 37; tel. (3452) 46-67-79; fax (3452) 46-00-91; e-mail hmaoda@tmn.ru.

Chief Representative of the Khanty-Mansii Autonomous Okrug—Yugra in the Russian Federation: VLADIMIR A. KHARITON; 119002 Moscow, Starokonyushennyi per. 10/10/2; tel. (095) 920-42-38; fax (095) 291-17-62; e-mail ugra_msk@dial.cnt.ru.

Head of Khanty-Mansiisk City Administration (Mayor): VALERII M. SUDEIKIN; 626200 Tyumen obl., Khanty-Mansii AOk, Khanty-Mansiisk, ul. Dzerzhinskogo 6; tel. (34671) 3-20-70; fax (34671) 3-21-74; e-mail ugo@admhmansy.ru; internet www.admhmansy.ru.

Yamal-Nenets Autonomous Okrug

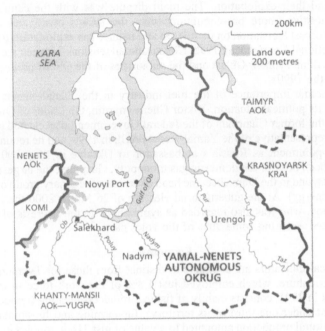

The Yamal-Nenets Autonomous Okrug (AOk) is situated on the Western Siberian Plain on the lower reaches of the Ob river. It forms part of Tyumen Oblast and, therefore, the Urals Federal Okrug and the Western Siberian Economic Area. The territory lies on the Asian side of the Ural Mountains and has a deeply indented northern coastline, the western section, the Yamal Peninsula, being separated from the eastern section by the Gulf of Ob. The rest of Tyumen Oblast, including the Khanty-Mansii AOk—Yugra, lies to the south. To the west lie the Nenets AOk (within Archangel Oblast) and the Republic of Komi, to the east Krasnoyarsk Krai (including the Taimyr AOk in the north-west). Apart from the Ob, the Yamal-Nenets district's major rivers are the Nadym, the Taz and the Pur. Around one-10th of its area is forested. The territory of the Yamal-Nenets AOk occupies 750,300 sq km (289,690 sq miles). It comprises seven administrative districts and seven cities. According to the preliminary results of the census of 9–16 October 2002, it had a total population of 507,400 inhabitants, and a population density of 0.7 per sq km. At that time some 83.4% of the population inhabited urban areas. In the 1989 census, ethnic Russians represented some 59.3% of the population, Ukrainians 17.2% and Tatars 5.3%, while Nenets represented just 4.2%, although the proportion of Nenets was thought to have increased subsequently. The district administrative centre is at Salekhard, which had a population of 34,100 in January 2001.

History

The Nenets were traditionally a nomadic people, who were totally dominated by Russia from the early 17th century. The Yamal-Nenets AOk was formed within Tyumen Oblast on 10 December 1930. Environmental concerns provoked protests in the 1980s and 1990s, and prompted the local authorities (comprising an administration and, from 1994, an elected Duma) to seek greater control over natural resources and their exploitation. The main dispute was with the central Tyumen Oblast authorities (more pro-communist than the AOk's own), and the AOk's rejection of oblast legislation on petroleum and natural gas exploitation first reached the Constitutional Court during 1996. Constitutional tensions between the two AOks contained within Tyumen Oblast and the authorities of the Oblast proper continued throughout the 1990s.

The economic importance of the fuel industry in the Yamal-Nenets AOk was reflected in its political situation. Viktor Chernomyrdin, the leader of Our Home Is Russia and the former Chairman of the federal Government, was elected to the State Duma as a representative of the Yamal-Nenets AOk in 1998, and he retained his seat until his appointment as Russia's ambassador to Ukraine in May 2001. He had previously been head of the domestic gas monopoly, Gazprom, the largest employer in the district, and in the Duma became head of an inter-factionary group of deputies, Energiya (Energy). At the gubernatorial election of 26 March 2000 the incumbent, Yurii Neyelov, who was also regarded as sympathetic to the interests of Gazprom, was re-elected, securing some 90% of the votes cast.

Economy

Few statistical indicators are available as distinct from those for Tyumen Oblast in general. Agriculture, which employed just 1.3% of the work-force in the Yamal-Nenets AOk in 2001, consists mainly of fishing, reindeer-breeding (reindeer pasture occupies just under one-third of its territory), fur-farming and fur-animal hunting. Total agricultural production amounted to a value of just 316m. roubles in 2001. The AOk's main industries are the production of natural gas and petroleum and the production of electricity. In 2001 the industrial sector employed 23.4% of the work-force and generated a total of some 104,915m. roubles, a considerably larger amount than that generated by many oblasts or republics in the Russian Federation. The potential wealth of the district generated foreign interest. In January 1997 a loan of US $2,500m. to Gazprom was agreed by the Dresdner Bank group (of Germany), to support construction of the 4,200-km (2,610-mile) Jagal pipeline from the Autonomous Okrug to Frankfurt-an-der-Oder on the German border with Poland. This was to be the world's largest gas-transport project and was expected to be fully operational by 2005.

The economically active population numbered 305,000 in 2001, when 7.1% of the labour force were unemployed. In 2001 the district government budget showed a surplus of 1,401m. roubles. These statistics, like the high average monthly wage of 15,374.2 roubles (the highest in the Russian Federation) in mid-2002, have far more in common with those of the Khanty-Mansii AOk than those of Tyumen Oblast as a whole. As mentioned above, the Yamal-Nenets AOk has also been successful in attracting foreign investment, receiving US $73.2m. in 2001. No separate details for external trade are available, although it was believed to be substantial. At 31 December 2001 there were some 2,190 small businesses registered in the district.

Directory

Governor: YURII V. NEYELOV; 626608 Tyumen obl., Yamal-Nenets AOk, Salekhard, ul. Respubliki 72; tel. (34922) 4-46-02; fax (34922) 4-52-89; e-mail yanao@ salekhard.ru; internet www.yamal.ru.

Chairman of the District State Duma: SERGEI N. KHARYUCHI; 629000 Tyumen obl., Yamal-Nenets AOk, Salekhard, ul. Respublika 72; tel. and fax (34591) 4-51-51.

Chief Representative of Yamal-Nenets Autonomous Okrug in Tyumen Oblast: FUAT G. SAIFITDINOV; 625048 Tyumen, ul. Kholodilnaya 136/1; tel. (3422) 27-32-11; fax (3422) 40-24-80.

Chief Representative of Yamal-Nenets Autonomous Okrug in the Russian Federation: NIKOLAI A. BORODULIN; 101000 Moscow, per. Arkhangelskii 15/3; tel. (095) 924-67-89; fax (095) 925-83-38.

Head of Salekhard City Administration: ALEKSANDR M. SPIRIN; 629000 Tyumen obl., Yamal-Nenets AOk, Salekhard, ul. Respubliki 72; tel. (34922) 4-50-67; fax (34922) 4-01-82; e-mail press@ytc.ru.

SIBERIAN FEDERAL OKRUG

Altai Krai

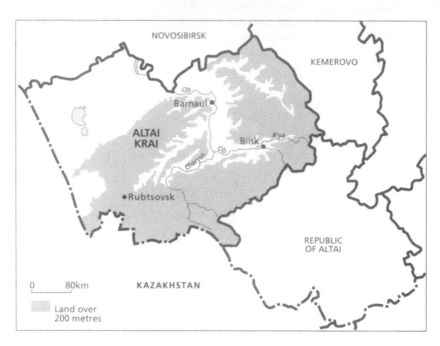

Most of Altai Krai lies within the Western Siberian Plain. Part of the Siberian Federal Okrug and the Western Siberian Economic Area, it has an international boundary to the south with Kazakhstan. To the north lies the federal subject of Novosibirsk Oblast, with Kemerovo Oblast to the north-east and the Republic of Altai (formerly the Gorno-Altai Autonomous Oblast, then a constituent part of the Krai) to the south-east. Its major river is the Ob, which has numerous tributaries (there are altogether some 17,000 rivers within the territory). There are many thousands of lakes, about one-half of which are fresh water. About one-third of its total area is forested. In the east of the Krai are mountains, in the west steppe. The Krai occupies an area of 169,100 sq km (65,290 sq miles). It is divided into 60 administrative districts and 12 cities. According to the preliminary results of the census of 9–16 October 2002, it had a total population of 2,607,200, giving a population density of 15.4 per sq km. At that time some 53.2% of the population lived in urban areas. In 1996 ethnic Russians comprised an estimated 90.3% of the population, Germans 4.8%, Ukrainians 2.4% and Altais just 0.1%. The Krai's administrative centre is at Barnaul, which had a population of 603,500, according to the provisional results of the 2002 census. Other major cities are Biisk (218,600) and Rubtsovsk (163,100).

History

The territory of Altai Krai was annexed by Russia in 1738 (for more on the Altais, see the Republic of Altai below). The region was heavily industrialized during the Soviet period, particularly in 1926–40. The current Altai Krai was formed on 28 September 1937, at which time it already included the territory of what is now the Republic of Altai. Gornyi Altai, officially an autonomous oblast, declared its sovereignty in 1990 and was formally recognized as a separate republic from the Krai in 1992.

On 13 March 1994, in accordance with a federal presidential decree of October 1993, a new provincial legislature, the Legislative Assembly, was elected, in place of the Provincial Soviet. The new legislature was bicameral, comprising a lower chamber of 25 deputies and an upper chamber of 72 deputies (one from each district in the Krai). The Chairman of the Provincial Council of People's Deputies, Aleksandr Surikov, a communist, defeated the incumbent Governor, Lev Korshunov, in the gubernatorial election of November 1996. Surikov retained his post in the election of 26 March 2000, obtaining 77% of the votes cast. In the early 2000s proposals for the reunification of Altai Krai with the Altai Republic became increasingly popular, with the most prominent proponent of reunification being the Krai's legislative Chairman, Aleksandr Nazarchuk, who repeatedly called for a referendum to be held concerning the proposed merger. However, despite the close political allegiances of Nazarchuk and the Governor of the Republic of Altai elected in December 2001, Mikhail Lapshin'(both of whom were prominent members of the Agrarian Party of Russia), the authorities in the Republic reportedly opposed any merger, fearing that such a measure would result in the former autonomous oblast returning to a subordinate status within the Krai.

Economy

Altai Krai's gross regional product totalled 48,691m. roubles in 2000, equivalent to 18,391 roubles per head. Its main industrial centres are at Barnaul, Biisk, Rubtsovsk, Novoaltaisk and Slavgorod. There are major river-ports at Barnaul and Biisk. The Krai has well-developed transport networks—1,803 km (1,067 miles) of railway lines at the end of 2001, and 14,461 km of paved roads. About one-quarter of its territory is served by water transport, which operates along a network of some 1,000 km of navigable waterways. There are five airports, including an international airport at Barnaul, with a service to Düsseldorf, Germany. The Krai is bisected by the main natural gas pipeline running from Tyumen to Barnaul via Novosibirsk.

The Krai's principal crops are grain, flax, sunflowers and sugar beet. Animal husbandry, including fur-farming and bee-keeping, is also important. In 2001 some 23.2% of its work-force were engaged in agriculture, and total production in the sector amounted to 31,591m. roubles. Of this total, crop sales accounted for 61.0% and animal husbandry for 39.0%. The Krai contains substantial mineral resources, including salt, iron ore, soda and precious stones, most of which are not industrially exploited. Its main industries are mechanical engineering (including tractor-manufacturing, primarily by the Rubtsovsk tractor plant), food-processing (the Krai's agro-industrial complex is one of the largest in the country), metal-working, electricity production, and chemicals and petrochemicals. In addition, Barnaul contains one of the largest textiles enterprises in Russia, producing cotton fibre and yarn for cloth. Industry employed 19.3% of the population in 2001, when total production in the sector amounted to a value of 39,009m. roubles.

In 2001 the economically active population of Altai Krai totalled 1,237,000, and 9.9% of the Krai's labour force were unemployed. The average monthly wage was 2,558.8 roubles in mid-2002. Living costs are low in the region: in August 2002 a 'consumer basket' of basic foodstuffs purchased in Barnaul was found to be the lowest-priced in the Russian Federation. In 2001 the local budget showed a deficit of 623m. roubles. External trade amounted to a value of US $274.8m. in exports and $144.0m. in imports. In that year foreign investment in the territory totalled $1.5m. At 31 December 2001 there were 12,250 small businesses registered in the Krai.

Directory

Head of the Provincial Administration (Governor): ALEKSANDR A. SURIKOV; 656035 Altai Krai, Barnaul, pr. Lenina 59; tel. (3852) 35-69-35; e-mail glava@ alregn.ru; internet www.altairegion.ru.

Chairman of the Provincial Council of People's Deputies: ALEKSANDR G. NAZA-RCHUK; 656035 Altai Krai, Barnaul, pr. Lenina 59; tel. (3852) 35-69-86; fax (3852) 22-85-42; e-mail press@alregn.ru.

Chief Representative of Altai Krai in the Russian Federation: TEIMURAZ S. BABLUMYAN; 109017 Moscow, per. B. Tolmachevskii 5/9; tel. (095) 953-36-83; fax (095) 953-01-84; e-mail altaypred@mail.ru.

Head of Barnaul City Administration: VLADIMIR N. KOLGANOV; 656099 Altai Krai, Barnaul, pr. Lenina 18/16; tel. (3852) 39-32-72; e-mail info@bar.alt.ru; internet barnaul.altai.ru.

Republic of Altai

The Republic of Altai (Gornyi Altai—Mountainous Altai) is situated in the Altai Mountains, in the basin of the Ob river. The Republic forms part of the Siberian Federal Okrug and the West Siberian Economic Area. It has international borders with Kazakhstan in the south-west, a short border with the People's Republic of China to the south, and with Mongolia to the south-east. Kemerovo Oblast lies to the north, the Republics of Khakasiya and Tyva to the north-east, and the Altai Krai, of which the Republic formerly constituted a part, to the north-west. The Republic includes the highest peak in Siberia, Belukha, at 4,506 m (14,783 feet), and about one-quarter of its territory is forested. Its major rivers, apart from the Ob, are the Katyn and the Biya, and it has one large lake, Teletskoye. It contains one of Russia's major national parks, Altai State National Park, covering an area of some 9,000 sq km (3,475 sq miles). The Republic occupies 92,600 sq km and comprises 10 administrative districts and one city. Its climate is continental, with short summers and long, cold winters. According to the preliminary results of the census of 9–16 October 2002, the Republic had a population of 202,900 and a population density, therefore, of only 2.2 per sq km. Of its inhabitants, 26.4% resided in urban areas. The census of 1989 put the number of Russians at some 60% of the total and of ethnic Altais at 31%, while some 5.6% of the population were Kazakh. The Altai people can be divided into two distinct groups: the Northern Altai, or Chernnevye Tatars, consisting of the Tubalars, the Chelkans or Leberdin and the Kumandins; and the Southern Altai, comprising the Altai Kizhi, the Telengit, the Telesy and the Teleut. The language spoken by both groups is from the Turkish branch of the Uralo-Altaic family: that of the Northern Altais is from the Old Uigur group, while the language of the Southern Altais is close to the Kyrgyz language and is part of the Kipchak group. Over 84% of Altais speak one or other language as their native tongue, and some 62% of the Altai population is fluent in Russian. Although the traditional religion of the Altai was animist or Lamaist, many were converted to Christianity, so the dominant religion in the Republic is Russian Orthodoxy. The Republic's administrative centre is at Gorno-Altaisk (known as Ulala until 1932, then as Oirot-Tura until 1948), which had a population of 52,700 at 1 January 2001.

History

From the 11th century the Altai peoples inhabited Dzungaria (Sungaria—now mainly in the north-west of the People's Republic of China). The region was under Mongol control until 1389, when it was conquered by the Tatar forces of Tamerlane (Tamberlane or Timur 'the Lame'); it subsequently became a Kalmyk confederation. In the first half of the 18th century many Altais moved westwards, invading Kazakh territory and progressing almost as far as the Urals. In 1758, however, most of Dzungaria was incorporated into Xinjiang (Sinkiang), a province of the Chinese Empire. China embarked on a war aimed at exterminating the Altai peoples. Only a few thousand survived, finding refuge in the Altai Mountains or in Russian territory. In the 19th century Russia began to assert its control over the region, which was finally annexed in 1866. In the early 1900s Burkhanism or White Faith, a nationalist religious movement, emerged. The movement was led by Oirot Khan, who claimed to be a descendant of Chinghiz (Genghis) Khan and promised to liberate the Altais from Russian control. However, in February 1918 it was a secular nationalist leader, B. I. Anuchin, who convened a Constituent Congress of the High Altai and demanded the establishment of an Oirot Republic—to include the Altai, the Khakassians and the Tyvans. In partial recognition of such demands, on 1 July 1922 the Soviet Government established an Oirot Autonomous Oblast in a wider Altai province. In 1948 the region was renamed the Gorno-Altai Autonomous Oblast, in an effort to suppress nationalist sentiment.

In the late 1980s nationalism re-emerged in response to Mikhail Gorbachev's policy of *glasnost* (openness). Renamed the Altai Republic, the region formally became an autonomous republic, independent of Altai Krai, at the signing of the Russian Federation Treaty in March 1992, having adopted its State Sovereignty Declaration on 25 October 1990. A resolution adopted on 14 October 1993 provided for the establishment of a State Assembly (El Kurultai), which comprised 27 deputies and represented the highest body of power in the Republic. The Altai Republic was one of only four subjects of the Russian Federation to award the communist candidate, Gennadii Zyuganov, a higher proportion of the votes than Vladimir Putin in the presidential election of 26 March 2000. In February 2001 several amendments to the republican Constitution were approved by the El Kurultai, to bring them into conformity with the fundamental laws of the Russian Federation, as had been demanded by the federal Constitutional Court. A provision that had forbidden persons of the same nationality from simultaneously occupying the posts of chairman of the republican government and parliamentary speaker was one of those to be removed.

Following an inconclusive first round of voting in the election to the post of Chairman of the Government held in the Republic on 16 December 2001, the incumbent, Semen Zubakin, and Mikhail Lapshin, the leader of the Agrarian Party of Russia (APR), progressed to a second round, held on 20 January 2002. On that occasion Lapshin decisively defeated Zubakin, receiving 68% of the votes cast, according to preliminary results. Notably, Lapshin received the support of the pro-Government Unity and Fatherland-United Russia party in the second round, in addition to that of the Communist Party of the Russian Federation. Legislative elections were held in the Republic in December. In the early 2000s proposals for the reunification of the Republic of Altai with Altai Krai were led by the Krai's legislative Chairman, Aleksandr Nazarchuk. Although Nazarchuk, like Lapshin, was a prominent member of the APR, the authorities in the Republic reportedly opposed any merger, fearing that such a measure would result in Gornyi Altai returning to a subordinate status within the Krai.

Economy

The Republic of Altai is predominantly an agricultural region. Its gross regional product amounted to 4,027m. roubles in 2000, or 19,625 roubles per head. The main industrial centre in the Republic is at its capital, Gorno-Altaisk. Owing to its mountainous terrain, at the end of 2001 the Republic contained just 2,797 km (1,738 miles) of paved roads, including a section of the major Novorossiisk–Biisk–Tashanta highway. There are no railways or airports. In March 1996 the Russian Government allocated some 1,800m. old roubles to alleviate the effects in the Republic of the nuclear tests conducted at Semipalatinsk, Kazakhstan, in 1949–62. However, in the early 2000s further concern was expressed about the negative effect of frequent rocket launches from the Baikonur Cosmodrome in Kazakhstan on both the health of the residents of the Republic and the surrounding environment.

Agriculture in the Republic of Altai, which employed 26.1% of the working population in 2001, consists mainly of livestock-breeding (largely horses, deer, sheep and goats). The export of the antlers of Siberian maral and sika deer, primarily to South-East Asia, is an important source of convertible currency to the Republic. In 2001 the total value of agricultural output was 1,869m. roubles. The Republic's mountainous terrain often prevents the easy extraction or transport of minerals, but there are important reserves of manganese, iron, silver, lead and wolfram (tungsten), as well as timber. Stone, lime, salt, sandstone, gold, mercury and non-ferrous metals are also produced. There are also food-processing and construction materials industries. Industry employed just 7.6% of the working population in 2001, and the value of industrial production amounted to 526m. roubles.

In 2001 a total of 90,000 of the Republic's inhabitants were economically active, and some 9.7% of the labour force were unemployed, compared with 17.5% in the previous year. The average monthly wage was 3,160.6 roubles in mid-2002. There was a budgetary surplus of 122m. roubles in 2001. In that year the value of the Republic's exports was US $42.0m., and its imports were equivalent to around $138.0m. The level of foreign investment was very low, amounting to just $99,000 in 2000. At December 2001 there were 884 small businesses registered in the Republic.

Directory

Chairman of the Government: MIKHAIL I. LAPSHIN; 659700 Altai Republic, Gorno-Altaisk, ul. Kirova 16; tel. (38822) 2-26-30; e-mail root@apra.gorny.ru; internet www.altai-republic.com.

Chairman of the El Kurultai (State Assembly): IGOR E. YAIMOV; 659700 Altai Republic, Gorno-Altaisk, ul. Erkemena Palkina 1; tel. (38822) 2-26-18; fax (38822) 9-51-65; e-mail root@altek.gorny.ru.

Chief Representative of the Altai Republic in the Russian Federation: SERGEI D. KONCHAKOVSKII; 103795 Moscow, ul. M. Dmitrovka 3/221; tel. (095) 299-41-94; fax (095) 299-81-97.

Head of Gorno-Altaisk City Administration: VIKTOR A. OBLOGIN; 659700 Altai Republic, Gorno-Altaisk, pr. Kommunisticheskii 18; tel. (38822) 2-23-40; fax (38822) 2-25-59.

Republic of Buryatiya

The Republic of Buryatiya is situated in the Eastern Sayan Mountains of southern Siberia and forms part of the Siberian Federal Okrug and the Eastern Siberian Economic Area. It lies mainly in the Transbaikal region to the east of Lake Baikal, although it also extends westwards along the international boundary with Mongolia in the south, to create a short border with the Russian federal territory of Tyva in the extreme west. Irkutsk Oblast lies to the north and west, and Chita Oblast to the east. Buryatiya's rivers mainly drain into Lake Baikal, the largest being the Selenga, the Barguzin and the Upper Angara, but some, such as the Vitim, flow northwards into the Siberian plains. The Republic's one lake, Baikal, forms part of the western border of the Republic. Baikal is the oldest and deepest lake in the world, possessing over 80% of Russia's surface freshwater resources and 20% of the world's total. Considered holy by the Buryats, until the 1950s it was famed for the purity of its waters and its unique ecosystem. Intensive industrialization along its shores threatened Baikal's environment, and only in the 1990s were serious efforts made to safeguard the lake. Some 70% of Buryatiya's territory, including its low mountains, is forested, and its valleys are open steppe. The Republic's territory covers 351,300 sq km (135,640 sq miles) and comprises a total of 21 administrative districts and six cities. The winter is protracted but sees little snow, with the average temperature in January falling to –27.1°C; the average temperature in July is 16.0°C. According to the preliminary results of the census of 9–16 October 2002, Buryatiya had a population of 981,000, and a population density of 2.8 per sq km. Around 59.6% of the population inhabited urban areas. In 1989 some 70% of the inhabitants were ethnic Russians and 24% Buryats. The industrial areas of the Republic are mainly inhabited by ethnic Russians. The Buryats are a native Siberian people of Mongol descent. The majority of those inhabiting the Republic are Transbaikal Buryats, as distinct from the Irkutsk Buryats, who live west of Lake Baikal. The Buryats' native tongue is a Mongol dialect. Some Buryats are Orthodox Christians, but others still practise Lamaism (Tibetan Buddhism), which has been syncretized with the region's traditional animistic shamanism. The Pandito Hambo Lama, a Buddhist spiritual leader, resides in Buryatiya's capital, Ulan-Ude, which had a population of 359,400 in October 2002, according to provisional census results.

History

Buryatiya was regarded as strategically important from the earliest years of the Muscovite Russian state, as it lay on the Mongol border. Russian influence reached the region in the 17th century and Transbaikal was formally incorporated into the Russian Empire by the Treaties of Nerchinsk and Kyakhta in 1689 and 1728, respectively. The latter agreement ended a dispute over the territory between the Russian and the Chinese Manzhou (Manchu) Empires. Many ethnic Russians subsequently settled in the region, often inhabiting land confiscated from the Buryats, many of whom were 'russified'. Other Buryats, however, strove to protect their culture, and there was a resurgence of nationalist feeling in the 19th century. Jamtsarano, a prominent nationalist, following a series of congresses in 1905 demanding Buryat self-government and the use of the Buryat language in schools, led a movement that recognized the affinity of Buryat culture to that of the Mongols, most of whom were ruled from China. Russia's fears about the Buryats' growing allegiance to its eastern neighbour were allayed, however, after a formal treaty signed with Japan in 1912 recognized Outer Mongolia (Mongolia) as a Russian sphere of influence.

With the dissolution of the Far Eastern Republic (based at Chita), a Buryat-Mongol ASSR was established on 30 May 1923. In the early 1930s, following Stalin—Iosif V. Dzhugashvili's policy of collectivization, many Buryats fled the country or were found guilty of treason and executed. In 1937 the Soviet Government considerably reduced the territory of the Republic, transferring the eastern section to Chita Oblast and a westerly region to Irkutsk Oblast. Furthermore, the Buryat language's Mongolian script was replaced with a Cyrillic one. In 1958 the Buryat-Mongol ASSR was renamed the Buryat ASSR, amid suspicions of increasing co-operation between the Mongolian People's Republic (Mongolia) and the People's Republic of China. The territory declared its sovereignty on 10 October 1990, and was renamed the Republic of Buryatiya in 1992.

In March 1994 the republican legislature, the Supreme Soviet, adopted a Constitution, providing for an executive presidency. The hitherto Chairman of the Supreme Soviet, Leonid Potapov, became the Republic's first President, and the legislature was redesignated the People's Khural. A bilateral treaty on the division of powers was signed with the Federation Government in 1995. On 21 June 1998 presidential and legislative elections were held in the Republic, and Potapov was re-elected President. In October 2000 the People's Khural approved several amendments to Buryatiya's Constitution, but rejected the implementation of several proposed amendments required by federal legislation, including, notably, the abolition of the requirement that presidential candidates know both state languages, Russian and Buryat. In early 2002 Potapov resigned from the Communist Party of the Russian Federation. In April he threatened to dissolve the Khural if it opposed the cancellation of the declaration of sovereignty issued in 1990; the declaration of sovereignty was consequently rescinded. On 23 June Potapov was re-elected for a third term as President of the Republic, receiving 68% of the votes cast. The pro-Government Unity and Fatherland-United Russia party (UF-UR) chose to support Potapov, in preference to his closest electoral opponent, Bato Semenov, a representative of the UF-UR in the State Duma. Notably, in the period preceding the election, three of the four independent radio stations in Ulan-Ude had their operations suspended by the republican State Communications Inspectorate.

Economy

In 2000 Buryatiya's gross regional product amounted to 22,479m. roubles, equivalent to 21,782 roubles per head. Its major industrial centre is at Ulan-Ude, which is on the route of the Trans-Siberian Railway. At the end of 2001 there were 1,199 km (745 miles) of railways on Buryatiya's territory, and 6,238 km of paved roads.

The Republic's agriculture, which employed around 14.1% of the work-force in 2001, consists mainly of animal husbandry (livestock and fur-animal breeding) and the production of grain, vegetables and potatoes. Total agricultural production in 2001 was worth 5,384m. roubles, of which crop sales accounted for 30.0% and animal husbandry for 70.0%. The Republic is rich in mineral resources, including gold, uranium, coal, wolfram (tungsten), molybdenum, brown coal, graphite and apatites. Its main gold-mining enterprise, Buryatzoloto, operates two mines near Lake Baikal. In 1996 its reserves were estimated at 3.2m. troy ounces (almost 100 metric tons). Apart from ore-mining and the extraction of minerals, its main industries are mechanical engineering, metal-working, food-processing, timber production and wood-working. The Republic is also a major producer of electrical energy. The industrial sector employed 18.7% of the Republic's work-force in 2001, and its total output in that year was worth 16,046m. roubles. The services sector with the most potential is tourism, owing to the attractions of Lake Baikal.

Buryatiya's economically active population totalled 456,000 in 2001, but some 18.5% of the Republic's labour force were unemployed. The average monthly wage in the Republic was 4,088.4 roubles in mid-2002. In 2001 there was a budgetary deficit of 306m. roubles. Foreign trade in that year comprised US $141.8m. in exports and $30.2m. in imports; the Republic had over 50 trading partners, although in 1999 over one-half of its international trade was with the People's Republic of China. Foreign investment in Buryatiya amounted to just $180,000 in 2001. At 31 December 2001 there were 3,983 small businesses registered in the Republic.

Directory

President and Chairman of the Government: LEONID V. POTAPOV; 670001 Buryatiya, Ulan-Ude, ul. Sukhe-Batora 9; tel. (3012) 21-51-86; fax (3012) 21-28-22; e-mail pres_rb@icm.buryatia.ru; internet president.buryatia.ru.

Chairman of the People's Khural: ALEKSANDR G. LUBSANOV; 670001 Buratiya, Ulan-Ude, ul. Sukhe-Batora 9; tel. (3012) 21-31-57; fax (3012) 21-49-61; e-mail kontup01@icm.buryatia.ru; internet chairman.buryatia.ru.

Chief Representative of the Republic of Buryatiya in the Russian Federation: INNOKENTII N. YEGOROV; 107108 Moscow, ul. Myasnitskaya 43/2; tel. (095) 925-95-00; fax (095) 923-60-46.

Head of Ulan-Ude City Administration (Mayor): GENNADII A. AYDAYEV; 670000 Buryatiya, Ulan-Ude, ul. Lenina 54; tel. (3012) 21-57-05; fax (3012) 26-32-44; internet www.ulan-ude.ru.

Chita Oblast

Chita Oblast is situated in Transbaikal, and forms part of the Siberian Federal Okrug and the Eastern Siberian Economic Area. Buryatiya lies to the west, Irkutsk Oblast to the north, Sakha (Yakutiya) and Amur to the east. To the south there are international borders with the People's Republic of China and Mongolia. The Aga-Buryat Autonomous Okrug (AOk) lies within the Oblast, in the south. The western part of the region is situated in the Yablonovii Khrebet mountain range. Chita Oblast's major rivers are those in the Selenga, the Lena and the Amur basins. More than one-half of the Oblast's territory is forested. Excluding the Aga-Buryat AOk, the Oblast covers an area of 412,500 sq km (159,300 sq miles) and is divided into 28 districts and 10 cities. According to the preliminary results of the census of 9–16 October 2002, the population of the Oblast, excluding the Aga-Buryat AOk, was 1,084,000, and its population density was 2.6 per sq km (less than one-third of the national average). Some 65.9% of the region's inhabitants lived in urban areas. The Oblast's administrative centre is at Chita, which had a population of 317,800, according to provisional census results.

History

The city of Chita was established by the Cossacks in 1653, at the confluence of the Chita and Ingoda rivers. It was named Ingodinskoye Zirnove for a time. Chita was pronounced the capital of the independent, pro-Bolshevik Far Eastern Republic upon its establishment in April 1920. It united the regions of Irkutsk, Transbaikal, Amur and the Pacific coast (Maritime Krai, Khabarovsk Krai, Magadan and Kamchatka), but merged with Soviet Russia in November 1922. Chita Oblast was founded on 26 September 1937.

A new Regional Duma was elected in 1994. The Communists and the nationalist Liberal Democrats were the most popular parties in the mid- and late 1990s. In a gubernatorial election held on 29 October 2001 the incumbent, Ravil Genialutin, was re-elected with 57.4% of the votes cast. Elections to the regional legislature were held concurrently. In July 2003 one of the Oblast's vice-governors, Aleksandr Shapnevskii, was murdered, in what was suspected to be a contract killing.

Economy

All figures in this survey incorporate data for the Aga-Buryat AOk, which is also treated separately (see below). Chita Oblast's gross regional product amounted to 31,549m. roubles in 2000, equivalent to 25,154 roubles per head. The region's main industrial centres are at Chita, Nerchinsk, Darasun, Olovyannaya and Tarbagatai. In 2000 there were some 2,399 km (1,490 miles) of railway track in the territory, including sections of the Trans-Siberian and the Far Eastern (Baikal–Amur) Railways. There were also 9,769 km of paved roads, and in 1998 there were 1,000 km of navigable waterways. The Chita–Khabarovsk highway (forming part of a direct route between Moscow and Vladivostok) opened in September 2003.

Chita Oblast's agriculture, which employed some 13.5% of its working population in 2001, consists mainly of animal husbandry (livestock- and reindeer-breeding) and fur-animal hunting. In that year total agricultural output amounted to a value of 6,229m. roubles, of which crop sales accounted for 33.1% and animal husbandry for 66.9%. The region's major industries are non-ferrous metallurgy, electrical energy, fuel extraction (including uranium), food-processing and ore-mining. Industry employed some 13.8% of the work-force in 2001, when total industrial production was worth 12,000m. roubles. Coal-mining in the Oblast was centred around the Vostochnaya mine; gold- and tin-mining were based at Sherlovaya Govra; and lead- and zinc-ore mines are situated at Hapcheranga, 200 km south-east of Yakutsk. In 1992 it was revealed that thorium and uranium had been mined until the mid-1970s at locations just outside Balei. The resulting high levels of radiation had serious consequences among the town's population, with abnormally high incidences of miscarriages and congenital defects in children. The regional Government lacked sufficient funds to relocate Balei's inhabitants and reduce radiation in the area. In 1997, however, the Australian mining company, Armada Gold, announced that it planned to seal the abandoned mines and exploit the nearby gold deposits. A 'Chinese market' in Chita city reflects the importance of the People's Republic of China as a major trading partner of the Oblast, in particular as a source of imports. In common with other regions neighbouring China, Chita suffered short-term economic disruption in May–June 2003, when cross-border travel was restricted, as a result of an outbreak of Severe Acute Respiratory Syndrome (SARS) in China and elsewhere in the Far East.

The territory had an economically active population of 543,000 in 2001, when 17.0% of the labour force were unemployed; the average monthly wage was 4,378.4 roubles in mid-2002. In 2001 the budget showed a deficit of 257m. roubles. In that year the Oblast's exports, largely comprising timber, metals and radioactive chemicals, amounted to US $85.4m., and imports amounted to $263.3m. For much of the 1990s and into the 2000s foreign investment in the Oblast remained low, and it totalled $6.0m. in 2001. At 31 December 2001 a total of 2,923 small businesses were in operation in Chita Oblast.

Directory

Head of the Regional Administration (Governor): RAVIL F. GENIALUTIN; 672021 Chita, ul. Chaikovskogo 8; tel. (3022) 23-34-93; fax (3022) 26-33-19; internet www .adm.chita.ru.

Chairman of the Regional Duma: ALESKANDR F. EPOV; 67021 Chita, ul. Chaikovskogo 8; tel. (3022) 23-58-59.

Representation of Chita Oblast in the Russian Federation: 127025 Moscow, ul. Novyi Arbat 19/2001; tel. (095) 203-33-28; fax (095) 203-45-39.

Head of Chita City Administration (Mayor): ANATOLII D. MIKHALEV; 672090 Chita, ul. Butina 39; tel. (3022) 23-24-07; fax (3022) 32-06-85; e-mail info@admin .chita.ru.

Aga-Buryat Autonomous Okrug

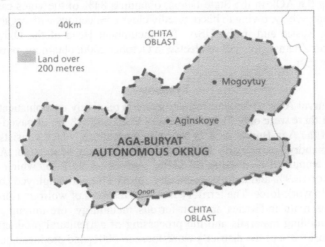

The Aga-Buryat Autonomus Okrug (AOk) is situated in the south-east of Trans-baikal, within the southern part of Chita Oblast. It forms part of the Siberian Federal Okrug and the East Siberian Economic Area. Its major rivers are the Aga, the Onon and the Ingoda, and about one-third of its territory is forested. Aginskoye is about 550 km (just under 350 miles) to the east of Ulan-Ude, the capital of Buryatiya (which lies to the west of Chita Oblast) and 130 km from Chita city. The district contains varied terrain, ranging from desert to forest-steppe. The Aga-Buryat AOk occupies a total of 19,000 sq km (7,340 sq miles) and extends for about 250 km from south to north and 150 km from west to east. It has three administrative districts and four 'urban-type settlements'. Its climate is severe and annual precipitation is as little as 250mm–380 mm (about 100 inches–150 inches) per year. According to the preliminary results of the census of 9–16 October 2002, the Aga-Buryat AOk's population was 72,200, giving a population density, therefore, of 3.8 per sq km. Just 35.3% of the population inhabited urban areas. In 1989 ethnic Buryats were found to make up some 54.9% of the population, and ethnic Russians 40.8%. The Buryats inhabiting the district are Transbaikal Buryats, who are more closely related to their Mongol ancestors than their western counterparts, the Irkutsk Buryats. The administrative centre is at Aginskoye, which had a population of just 9,500 in January 2001.

History

The Aga-Buryat-Mongol AOk was created on 26 September 1937, as part of Stalin—Iosif Dzhugashvili's policy of dispersing the Buryat population, whom he perceived as a threat because of their ethnic and cultural links with the Mongolian People's Republic (Mongolia). Its formation occurred as part of the division of the Eastern Siberian Oblast into Chita and Irkutsk Oblasts (the former of which it became a part). It assumed its current name on 16 September 1958. Under the Federation Treaty of March 1992, the Aga-Buryat AOk was recognized as one of the constituent units of the Russian Federation.

The district attracted some notoriety in 1997, when Iosif Kobzon, a popular singer frequently referred to as the 'Russian Frank Sinatra', won a by-election for a seat representing the AOk in the State Duma, obtaining 84% of the votes cast. Kobzon attracted controversy, owing to his reputedly close connections with organized crime both within Russia and in the USA. The incumbent Head of the Okrug Administration, Bair Zhamsuyev, was re-elected in October 2000, obtaining more than 89% of the votes cast.

Economy

The Aga-Buryat AOk's transport infrastructure is relatively unsophisticated—at the end of 2001 there were only 71 km of railway track and 898 km of paved roads. The economy of the Aga-Buryat AOk is based on agriculture, which consists mainly of animal husbandry (particularly sheep-rearing) and grain production. Agricultural production amounted to a value of 624m. roubles in 2001 (of which crop sales accounted for 18.9% and animal husbandry for 81.1%) and employed some 33.4% of the AOk's work-force. The territory is rich in reserves of wolfram (tungsten) and tantalum. Its main industries are non-ferrous metallurgy, ore-mining, the manufacture of building materials and the processing of agricultural products. Industry employed just 9.3% of the district's work-force in 2001, and produced output worth 67m. roubles. The transport, trade and services sectors were fully privatized by 1995. The Aga-Buryat AOk is one of the most underdeveloped federal territories in terms of its health and social-security provision and educational establishments.

In 2001 the economically active population of the Aga-Buryat AOk numbered 32,000, and from the mid-1990s, when separate figures for the district began to become available, it was consistently among those federal subjects with the highest levels of unemployment. In 1998 some 35.2% of the labour force were unemployed, although by 2001 the rate had declined to 23.0%. The average monthly wage was just 2,524.6 roubles in mid-2002. The 2001 district budget showed a surplus of 11m. roubles. The main foreign trading partners are the People's Republic of China and Mongolia. Some 140 small businesses were registered in the territory at late 2001.

Directory

Head of the District Administration: Bair B. Zhamsuyev; 674460 Chita obl., Aga-Buryat AOk, PGT. Aginskoye, ul. Bazara Rinchino 92; tel. (30239) 3-41-52; fax (30239) 3-46-91; e-mail abao@aginskchita.ru.

Chairman of the District Duma: Dashi Ts. Dugarov; 674460 Chita obl., Aga-Buryat AOk, PGT Aginskoye, ul. Bazara Rinchino 92; tel. (30239) 3-44-81; fax (30239) 3-45-95; e-mail duma@agatel.ru.

Representation of the Aga-Buryat Autonomous Okrug in Chita Oblast: Chita.

Chief Representative of the Aga-Buryat Autonomous Okrug in the Russian Federation: Vladimir D. Shoizhilzhapov; 103025 Moscow, ul. Novyi Arbat 19; tel. (095) 203-95-09; fax (095) 203-80-14; e-mail postpredstvo@hotmail.ru.

Irkutsk Oblast

Irkutsk Oblast is situated in eastern Siberia in the south-east of the Central Siberian Plateau. The Oblast forms part of the Siberian Federal Okrug and the Eastern Siberian Economic Area. The Republic of Sakha (Yakutiya) lies to the north-east, Krasnoyarsk Krai (including the Evenk AOk) to the north-west and Tyva to the south-west. Most of the long south-eastern border is with Buryatiya and, in the east, Chita. Irkutsk Oblast includes the Ust-Orda Buryat Autonomous Okrug (AOk). Lake Baikal is the deepest in the world, possessing over 80% of Russia's, and 20% of the world's, surface freshwater resources. The Oblast's main rivers are the Angara (the only river to drain Lake Baikal), the Nizhnyaya Tunguska, the Lena, the Vitim and the Kirenga. More than four-fifths of the region's territory is covered with forest (mainly coniferous). The total area of the Oblast, excluding that of the Ust-Orda Buryat AOk, is 745,500 sq km (287,838 sq miles) and stretches 1,400 km (850 miles) from south to north and 1,200 km west to east. The Oblast proper is divided into 27 administrative districts and 22 cities. According to the preliminary results of the census of 9–16 October 2002, the Oblast's total population, excluding the AOk, was 2,446,300, giving a population density of 3.3 per sq km. Some 83.7% of the total population lived in urban areas. The Oblast's administrative centre is at Irkutsk, which had a population of 593,400 in 2002, according to provisional census results.

Other major cities in the region include Bratsk (259,200), Angarsk (247,100) and Ust-Ilimsk (100,600).

History

The city of Irkutsk was founded as an ostrog (military transit camp) in 1661, at the confluence of the Irkut and Angara rivers, 66 km to the west of Baikal. Irkutsk became one of the largest economic centres of eastern Siberia. After the collapse of the Russian Empire, the region was part of the independent, pro-Bolshevik Far Eastern Republic (based in Chita), which was established in April 1920 and merged with Soviet Russia in November 1922. On 26 September 1937 an Irkutsk Oblast was formed.

In late 1993, following the federal presidency's forcible dissolution of parliament, the executive branch of government secured the dissolution of the Regional Soviet, and in 1994 a Legislative Assembly was elected in its place. As a 'donor region' to the Russian Federation, central-regional relationships in Irkutsk Oblast were frequently strained. In May 1996 the regional and federal authorities signed a power-sharing agreement. Following the resignation of the Governor, Yurii Nozhikov, in April 1997, the government-supported candidate, Boris Govorin (who also received Nozhikov's endorsement), was elected as his successor, receiving 50.3% of the votes cast. At the gubernatorial election held in August 2001 Govorin was re-elected for a further term of office; however, the relatively high proportion of votes awarded to the Communist Party candidate, Sergei Levchenko, who received 45.4% (compared with the 47.5% received by Govorin), appeared to reflect increasing dissatisfaction with the economic situation in the region. In March 2002 the Chairman of the Legislative Assembly, Viktor Borovskii, who had been regarded as the leading opponent of Govorin in the region, was removed from office, and replaced by a loyalist, Sergei Shishkin. In late May 2003 the Legislative Assembly approved legislation providing for the extension of the terms of office of both the regional governor and regional deputies, from four years to five years. In both cases these extensions were to apply from the next elections, scheduled to take place in 2005 and 2004, respectively.

During the early 2000s proposals to unite the Ust-Orda Buryat AOk and Irkutsk Oblast became increasingly popular and appeared to be supported by the authorities in both territories; moreover, in September 2002 the Chairman of the Federation Council, Sergei Mironov, stated that the two federal subjects already satisfied the prerequisites for becoming a single unit. However, only very limited progress towards the merging of the two political entities was subsequently reported.

Economy

Irkutsk Oblast is one of the most economically developed regions in Russia, largely owing to its significant fuel, energy and water resources, minerals and timber, and its location on the Trans-Siberian Railway. All figures in this survey incorporate data for the Usta-Orda Buryat AOk, which is also treated separately (see below). In 2000 the Oblast's gross regional product totalled 106,909m. roubles, or 38,999 roubles per head. The region's main industrial centres are at Irkutsk, Bratsk, Ust-Ilimsk and Angarsk. The Oblast, which is traversed by the Trans-Siberian and the Far Eastern (Baikal–Amur) Railways, contained 2,479 km of railway track at the end of 2001. There were almost 12,272 km of paved roads in the region, which carried some 40m. metric tons of freight annually in the late 1990s. The Oblast has two international airports, at Irkutsk and Bratsk, from which there are direct and connecting flights to Japan, the People's Republic of China, the Republic of Korea (South Korea), Mongolia and the USA. In the late 1990s approximately one-10th of the region's freight was transported by river—there are two major river-ports on the Lena river, at Kirensk and Osetrovo (Ust-Kut). These are used to transport freight to Sakha (Yakutiya) and the northern seaport of Tiksi.

The Oblast's agriculture, which employed just 8.6% of its work-force in 2001, consists mainly of grain and potato production, animal husbandry (fur-animal-, reindeer- and livestock-breeding), hunting and fishing. Total agricultural production in the territory generated 16,216m. roubles in 2001, of which 48.2% was generated by crop sales and 51.8% by animal husbandry. The region contains the huge Kovytkinskoye oilfield, which was awaiting an international consortium with the resources to construct an export pipeline across the People's Republic of China. In the late 1990s more than 45% of the Oblast's fixed assets were in the industrial sector, which engaged some 25.2% of the working population in 2001. The main industries are non-ferrous metallurgy, the processing of forestry products, mining (coal, iron ore, gold, muscovite or mica, gypsum, talc and salt), mechanical engineering, metal-working and electricity generation. In 2001 the total value of manufactured goods in the Oblast was 105,129m. roubles, of which the non-ferrous metallurgy industry contributed 27% and the timber and timber-processing industries 22%.

The economically active population in Irkutsk Oblast totalled 1,359,000 in 2001, when 10.9% of the labour force were unemployed. For those in employment, the average wage amounted to 4,966.2 roubles per month in mid-2002. In 2001 there was a budgetary deficit of 109m. roubles. In that year the value of exports from the territory amounted to some US $3,144.6m., while imports were worth $434.5m. Foreign investment in the territory was worth some $101.1m. At 31 December 2001 there were 13,964 small businesses registered in the Oblast.

Directory

Governor: BORIS A. GOVORIN; 664047 Irkutsk, ul. Lenina 1A; tel. (3952) 20-00-15; fax (3952) 24-33-40; internet www.admirk.ru.

Chairman of the Legislative Assembly: SERGEI I. SHISHKIN; 664047 Irkutsk, ul. Lenina 1A; tel. (3952) 24-17-60; fax (3952) 20-00-27; internet irk.gov.ru.

Chief Representative of Irkutsk Oblast in the Russian Federation: TATYANA I. RYUTINA; 109028 Moscow, per. Durasovskii 3/2; tel. (095) 916-17-08; fax (095) 915-70-58.

Head of Irkutsk City Administration (Mayor): VLADIMIR V. YAKUBOVSKII; 664025 Irkutsk, ul. Lenina 14; tel. (3952) 24-37-04.

Ust-Orda Buryat Autonomous Okrug

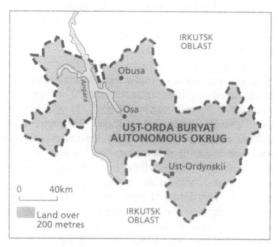

The Ust-Orda Buryat Autonomous Okrug (AOk) is situated in the southern part of the Lena-Angara plateau. The district forms part of Irkutsk Oblast and, hence, the Siberian Federal Okrug and the Eastern Siberian Economic Area. It lies to the north of Irkutsk city, west of Lake Baikal. Its major rivers are the Angara and its tributaries, the Osa, the Ida and the Kuda. Most of its terrain is forest-steppe. It occupies an area of 22,400 sq km (8,650 sq miles) and comprises six administrative districts. According to the preliminary results of the census of 9–16 October 2002, the Ust-Orda Buryat AOk's estimated population was 135,500 and its population density stood at 6.0 per sq km. In 1992, the last year for which comprehensive demographic statistics were available, just 18.3% of the population of the district lived in urban areas. According to the 1989 census, some 56.5% of the population were ethnic Russians and 36.3% were western or Irkutsk Buryats. The capital is at Ust-Ordynskii, which had a population of 13,600 in 2001.

History

The Buryat-Mongol Autonomous Soviet Socialist Republic (BMASSR), created in 1923, was restructured by Stalin (Iosif Dzhugashvili) in September 1937. Anxious to discourage nationalism and links with Mongolia, Stalin had resolved to divide the Buryat peoples administratively. The Ust-Orda Buryat AOk, which represented the four western counties of the BMASSR, was established within the territory of Irkutsk Oblast.

The Communist Party of the Russian Federation remained the most popular party in the Legislative Assembly (which replaced the District Soviet in 1994). In 1996 the federal President, Boris Yeltsin, had signed an agreement with the Ust-Orda Buryat AOk's administration on the delimitation of powers between the federal and district authorities. Later that year an independent candidate, Valerii Maleyev, was elected Governor, and was re-elected in November 2000.

In October 1999 the Governor of Irkutsk Oblast, Boris Govorin, stated that the district (70% of the budget of which comprised federal transfers) should be reincorporated into the Oblast proper, as the Oblast provided fuel and other resources to the AOk and there were concerns that Buryat nationalists might seek to unite the three nominally Buryat federal subjects. During the early 2000s proposals to unite the Ust-Orda Buryat AOk and Irkutsk Oblast became increasingly popular and appeared to be supported by officials in both territories. Moreover, in September 2002 the Chairman of the Federation Council, Sergei Mironov, stated that the two federal subjects already possessed the necessary preconditions for becoming a single unit, but subsequent progress was limited.

Economy

Statistical information for Irkutsk Oblast generally includes data on the Ust-Orda Buryat AOk, so separate figures are limited. At the end of 2001 there were 2,189 km (1,360 miles) of paved roads on the AOk's territory.

Agriculture consists mainly of grain and potato production and animal husbandry. In 2001 some 48.0% of the AOk's working population were engaged in agriculture (by far the highest proportion of any federal subject), and production in that year was valued at 3,463m. roubles, of which crop sales accounted for 38.1% and animal husbandry for 61.9%. The Ust-Orda Buryat AOk's main industries are the processing of agricultural and forestry products and the production of coal and gypsum. Industry generated 290m. roubles in 2001 and employed just 7.0% of the work-force.

The economically active population numbered 61,000 in 2001, when 14.2% of the labour force were unemployed. In mid-2002 the average monthly wage was just 2,336.7 roubles—the lowest figure for any territory within the Siberian Federal Okrug. There was a budgetary deficit of 44m. roubles in 2001. In that year around 100 small businesses were registered in the Ust-Orda Buryat AOk.

Directory

Head of the District Administration (Governor): VALERII G. MALEYEV; 666110 Irkutsk obl., Ust-Orda Buryat AOk, pos. Ust-Ordynskii, ul. Lenina 18; tel. (39541) 2-10-62; fax (39541) 2-25-93; e-mail okrug@irmail.ru; internet www.ust-orda.ru.

Chairman of the District Duma: ALEKSEI P. KHORINOYEV; 669001 Irkutsk obl., Ust-Orda Buryat AOk, pos. Ust-Ordynskii, ul. Lenina 18; tel. (39541) 2-16-87; fax (39541) 2-26-71.

Chief Representative of the Ust-Orda Buryat Autonomous Okrug in Irkutsk Oblast: SERGEI V. DOLGOPOLOV; 626002 Tyumen, ul. Komsomolskaya 37; tel. (3952) 57-17-14.

Chief Representative of the Ust-Orda Buryat Autonomous Okrug in the Russian Federation: OLEG B. BATOROV; 127025 Moscow, ul. Novyi Arbat 19; tel. and fax (095) 203-52564; fax (095) 203-64-04.

Kemerovo Oblast

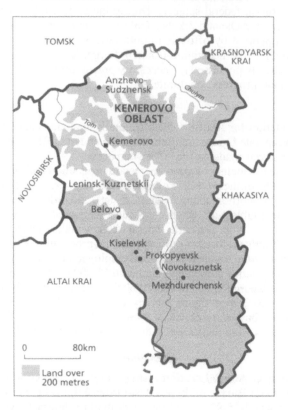

Kemerovo Oblast, also known as the Kuzbass, is situated in southern central Russia and forms part of the Siberian Federal Okrug and the Western Siberian Economic Area. Krasnoyarsk Krai and the Republic of Khakasiya lie to the east, Tomsk to the north, Novosibirsk to the west and the Altai Krai and the Republic of Altai to the south-west. The region lies in the Kuznetsk basin, the area surrounding its main river, the Tom. The territory of the Oblast occupies 95,500 sq km (36,870 sq miles) and is divided into 19 administrative districts and 20 cities. According to the preliminary results of the census of 9–16 October 2002, the total population numbered 2,900,200 and the population density in the region was 30.4 per sq km. Some 86.7% of the population inhabited urban areas. The region's administrative centre is at Kemerovo, which had a population of 485,000 in 2002, according to provisional census results. Other major cities are Novokuznetsk (550,100), Proko-pevsk (224,600), Leninsk-Kuznetskii (112,300), Kiselevsk (106,400) and Mezhdur-echensk (102,000).

History

Kemerovo (formerly Shcheglovsk) was founded in 1918 and became the admin-istrative centre of the Oblast at its formation on 26 January 1943. The city is at the centre of Russia's principal coal-mining area. In July 1997 the Governor, Mikhail

Kislyuk, a former head of the Kuzbass coal workers, was dismissed by President Boris Yeltsin, as the result of a dispute over unpaid pensions arrears. Kislyuk had earned criticism, as had the federal authorities, for refusing to schedule elections to a new Duma (to replace the bicameral Regional Assembly—elected in March 1994; its activities were suspended in 1995).

In the December 1995 federal general election, the Communist Party of the Russian Federation won 48% of the regional votes cast, its second highest proportion in any constituent unit of the Federation. Much of this support was secured because of the popular leadership of Amangeldy Tuleyev, speaker of the suspended local assembly. Tuleyev contested the federal presidency in 1991, 1996 and 2000, and spent 11 months in 1996–97 as the Minister for Co-operation with Members of the CIS. Having been appointed Governor by Yeltsin, following the removal of Kislyuk, Tuleyev's position was confirmed by an overwhelming victory in popular elections to the post in October 1997 (he received 94.6% of the votes cast).

In May 1998 widespread industrial action by coal-miners over wage arrears threatened to bring the regional administration into direct confrontation with the federal Government. The workers blockaded a section of the Trans-Siberian Railway, seriously affecting rail transportation throughout the country, and the strike did not end until late July. At this time Tuleyev's administration signed a framework agreement with the federal Government on the delimitation of powers, and accompanied by 10 accords aimed at strengthening the economy of the region. Despite the economic situation, Tuleyev was widely considered to be Russia's most popular regional leader and, when he stood for the presidency of the Russian Federation in March 2000, Tuleyev received 51.6% of the votes cast in Kemerovo Oblast, more than twice the number of votes cast there for Vladimir Putin. In January 2001 Tuleyev announced his resignation, thus bringing forward the gubernatorial election to April of that year, several months earlier than previously scheduled. His opponents criticized this decision as a tactic to ensure his re-election, as the Governor had widespread popular support at that time. In the election, held on 22 April, Tuleyev received 93.5% of the votes cast. In March 2003 Tuleyev was appointed to the Supreme Council of the generally pro-Government Unity and Fatherland-United Russia (UF-UR) party. Supporters of Tuleyev, comprising the oblast organizations of the UF-UR and the People's Party of the Russian Federation, united in the 'I Serve the Kuzbass!' (Sluzhu Kuzbassu!) electoral bloc, won an overwhelming majority in oblast legislative and municipal elections held on 20 April 2003; the bloc obtained 34 seats in the 35-member legislature, and obtained control of 11 of 12 municipalities where elections were held. Moreover, at the end of May federal President Vladimir Putin appointed Tuleyev to serve for a six-month term of office on the rotating presidium of the consultative State Council.

Economy

The economy of Kemerovo Oblast is based on industry. It is rich in mineral resources and contains the Kuzbass basin, one of the major coal reserves of the world. The region produced over 35% of Russia's coal in the late 1990s, but intensive mining in the Soviet period had resulted in severe environmental degradation. In 2000 Kemerovo's gross regional product amounted to 93,636m. roubles, equivalent to 31,448 roubles per head. The Oblast's main industrial centres are at Kemerovo, Novokuznetsk, Prokopevsk, Kiselevsk and Leninsk-Kuznetskii. At the end of 2001 the region had 1,728 km (1,074 miles) of railway track and 5,742 km of paved roads on its territory.

Kemerovo Oblast's agriculture, which employed just 5.4% of the work-force in 2001, consists mainly of potato and grain production, animal husbandry and bee-keeping. The value of agricultural output in 2001 was 10,821m. roubles, of which crop sales accounted for 52.3% and animal husbandry for 47.7%. In the mid-1990s reserves of coal to a depth of 1,800 m (5,900 feet) were estimated at 733,400m. metric tons. In the same period deposits of iron ore were estimated at 5,250m. tons. Production of complex ores, ferrous metallurgy and electricity generation are also important industries in the region. The industrial sector as a whole employed 31.1% of the working population in 2001 and generated 124,888m. roubles.

The economically active population numbered 1,439,000 in 2001, when 10.0% of the labour force were unemployed. The average monthly wage was 4,345.0 roubles in mid-2002. The 2001 regional budget registered a surplus of 130m. roubles. In that year export trade totalled US $2,102m., and imports were worth $181m. From the mid-1990s foreign investors showed some interest in exploiting the region's coal reserves. Total foreign investment in the Oblast in 2001 amounted to $33.9m. in 2001, compared with $5.1m. in the previous year. By 1995 some 61% of employees were working in the private sector. In the late 1990s the regional Government aimed to promote small businesses, of which 13,911 were registered at 31 December 2001.

Directory

Head of the Regional Administration (Governor): AMANGELDY M. TULEYEV; 650099 Kemerovo, pr. Sovetskii 62; tel. (3842) 36-43-33; fax (3842) 36-34-09; e-mail postmaster@ako.kemerovo.su; internet www.kemerovo.su.

Chairman of the Regional Council of People's Deputies: GENNADII T. DYUDYAYEV; 650099 Kemerovo, pr. Sovetskii 58; tel. (3842) 58-41-42; fax (3842) 58-54-51.

Chief Representative of Kemerovo Oblast in the Russian Federation: SERGEI V. SHATIROV; 115184 Moscow, ul. B. Tatarskaya 5/14/9; tel. and fax (095) 953-54-89.

Head of Kemerovo City Administration (Mayor): VLADIMIR V. MIKHAILOV; 650099 Kemerovo, pr. Sovetskii 54; tel. (3842) 36-46-10; fax (3842) 58-18-91; e-mail sityadm@kuzbass.net; internet kemerovo.rosemis.ru.

Republic of Khakasiya

The Republic of Khakasiya is situated in the western area of the Minusinsk hollow, on the left bank of the River Yenisei, which flows northwards towards, ultimately, the Arctic Ocean. In the heart of Eurasia, it lies on the eastern slopes of the Kuznetsk Alatau and the northern slopes of the Western Sayan Mountains. It comprises part of the Siberian Federal Okrug and the Eastern Siberian Economic Area. The Republic of Tyva lies to the south-east and the Republic of Altai to the south-west. To the west is Kemerovo Oblast, while Krasnoyarsk Krai lies to the north and east. Its major rivers are the Yenisei and its tributary, the Abakan. Khakasiya occupies 61,900 sq km (23,900 sq miles) and comprises eight administrative regions and five cities. According to the preliminary results of the census of 9–16 October 2002, the Republic had a total population of 546,100 and a population density, therefore, of 8.8 per sq km. Some 70.8% of the population lived in urban areas. In 1989 ethnic Khakasiyans numbered 11.1% of the population, and Russians 79.5%. At that time over 76% of the Khakass spoke the national language—primarily derived from the Uigur group of Eastern Hunnic languages of the Turkic family—as their native tongue. Khakasiya's capital is at Abakan, with 165,200 inhabitants in 2002, according to provisional census results.

History

The Khakass or Khakasiyans were traditionally known as the Minusinsk (Minusa), the Turki, the Yenisei Tatars or the Abakan Tatars. They were semi-nomadic hunters, fishermen and livestock-breeders. Khakasiya was a powerful state in Siberia, owing to its trading links with Central Asia and the Chinese Empire. Russian settlers began to arrive in the region in the 17th century and their presence was perceived as valuable protection against Mongol invasion. The annexation of Khakasiyan territory by the Russians was eventually completed during the reign of Peter (Petr) I—'the Great', with the construction of a fort on the River Abakan. The Russians subsequently imposed heavy taxes, seized the best land and imposed Orthodox Christianity on the Khakasiyans. After the construction of the Trans-Siberian Railway in the 1890s the Khakasiyans were heavily outnumbered. Following the Bolshevik Revolution a Khakass National Uezd (district) was established in 1923, becoming an okrug in 1925, and the Khakass Autonomous Oblast on 20 October 1930, within Krasnoyarsk Krai. In 1992 it was upgraded to the status of an Autonomous Republic under the terms of the Federation Treaty, having declared its sovereignty on 3 July 1991.

The Communist Party remained the most popular political grouping in the Republic in the early 1990s, and the nationalist ideas of Vladimir Zhirinovskii (leader of the Liberal Democratic Party of Russia) also enjoyed significant support. On 25 May 1995 the Republic adopted its Constitution. Aleksei Lebed, an independent candidate and younger brother of the politician and former general, Aleksandr Lebed (Governor of Krasnoyarsk Krai from May 1998 until his death in 2002), was elected to the presidency of the Republic in December 1996, when elections were also held for a new republican legislature. A former representative of the Republic in the State Duma, Aleksei Lebed had based his electoral campaign on the issues of administrative, budgetary, social and economic reform. Lebed was re-elected as Chairman of the Government, receiving 72% of the votes cast, in December 2000.

Economy

Khakasiya's gross regional product amounted to 17,441m. roubles in 2000, or 30,036 roubles per head. Khakasiya's major industrial centres are at Abakan, Sorsk, Sayanogorsk, Chernogorsk and Balyksa. At the end of 2001 there were 642 km (399 miles) of railway lines and 2,498 km of paved roads in the Republic.

The Republic's agriculture, which employed around 10.2% of the working population in 2001, consists mainly of potato and vegetable production and animal husbandry. Total agricultural production in 2001 was worth 3,594m. roubles, of which 50.5% was generated by crop sales and 49.5% by animal husbandry. The Republic's main industries are ore-mining, electricity production and non-ferrous metallurgy. The territory is also renowned for its handicrafts (wood-carving and embroidery). In 1997 Khakasiya was estimated to have reserves of 36,000m. metric tons of coal and 1,500m. tons of iron ore. Other mineral reserves included molybdenum, lead, zinc, barytes, aluminium and clay. There was also the potential for extraction of petroleum and natural gas. In 2001 the Republic's industrial output amounted to a value of 14,621m. roubles, and the industrial sector employed 22.8% of the work-force.

The Republic's economically active population numbered 269,000 in 2001, when 8.8% of the labour force were unemployed. The average monthly wage stood at

4,146.5 roubles in mid-2002. The republican budget for 2001 showed a surplus of 29m. roubles. Foreign investment in Khakasiya was minimal: the highest level recorded was US $2.3m., in 1996, and such investment totalled just $78,000 in 2001. However, external trade was somewhat more substantial; in 2001 exports amounted to a value of $360.8m. and imports amounted to $169.6m. At 31 December 2001 there were 1,522 small businesses registered in the Republic.

Directory

Chairman of the Government: ALEKSEI I. LEBED; 655019 Khakasiya, Abakan, pr. Lenina 67; tel. (39022) 6-33-22; fax (39022) 6-50-96; e-mail pressa@khakasnet.ru; internet www.gov.khakassia.ru.

Chairman of the Supreme Council: VLADIMIR N. SHTYGASHEV; 655019 Khakasiya, pr. Lenina 67; tel. (39022) 6-74-00; fax (39022) 6-82-81; e-mail info@vskhakasia .ru; internet www.vskhakasia.ru.

Chief Representative of the Republic of Khakasiya in the Russian Federation: VIKTOR K. BABAKHIN; 127025 Moscow, ul. Novyi Arbat 19/830; tel. (095) 203-83-41; fax (095) 203-83-45.

Head of Abakan City Administration: NIKOLAI G. BULAKIN; 655000 Khakasiya, Abakan, ul. Shchetinkina 10A/6, POB 6; tel. and fax (39022) 6-37-91; internet meria .abakan.ru.

Krasnoyarsk Krai

Krasnoyarsk Krai occupies the central part of Siberia and extends from the Arctic Ocean coast in the north to the Western Sayan Mountains in the south. The Krai forms part of the Siberian Federal Okrug and the Eastern Siberian Economic Area. It is bordered by the Republic of Sakha (Yakutiya) and Irkutsk Oblast to the east and the Republic of Tyva to the south. To the west lie the Republic of Khakasiya, the Oblasts of Kemerovo and Tomsk, as well as Tyumen Oblast's Khanty-Mansii—Yugra and Yamal-Nenets AOks. Its major river is the Yenisei, one of the longest in Russia, measuring 4,102 km (2,549 miles). Most of its area is covered by taiga (forested marshland). The Krai, including its two autonomous okrugs (Evenk and Taimyr—Dolgano-Nenets), covers a total area of 2,339,000 sq km (902,850 sq miles), the second largest federal unit in Russia, or 710,000 sq km (274,133 sq miles) when those districts are excluded. Krasnoyarsk Krai measures almost 3,000 km from south to north. In the Krai proper there are 42 administrative districts and 24 cities. The Krai lies within three climatic zones—arctic, sub-arctic and continental. According to the preliminary results of the census of 9–16 October 2002, it had a total population of 2,966,200 at mid-October 2002, and a population density of 1.3 per sq km. Some 75.7% of the population inhabited urban areas. The Krai's administrative centre is at Krasnoyarsk, which had a population of 911,700 in 2002, according to provisional census results. Other major cities include Norilsk

(135,100—which is considered an integral part of the Krai, and not part of Taimyr, which surrounds it), Achinsk (118,700) and Kansk (103,100).

History

The city of Krasnoyarsk was founded in 1628 by Cossack forces as an ostrog (military transit camp) during the period of Russian expansion across Siberia (1582–1639). The region gained importance after the discovery of gold, and with the construction of the Trans-Siberian Railway. The Krai was formed on 7 December 1934. During the Soviet era the region was closed to foreigners, owing to its nuclear-reactor and defence establishments.

A gubernatorial election in December 1992 was won by Valerii Zubov (the incumbent, a supporter of federal President Boris Yeltsin), and elections to a new parliament, the Legislative Assembly, were held on 6 March 1994. In the mid-1990s Zubov's regime proved to be increasingly ineffectual, and by 1997 the region had one of the worst records for wage arrears in the country. This largely contributed to the victory in the 1998 gubernatorial election of Gen. (retd) Aleksandr Lebed, the former secretary of the National Security Council, who was perceived by many as a suitably strong leader to rule a region of such economic and political significance. Lebed died in a helicopter crash on 28 April 2002. An election to appoint a successor, held on 8 September, and contested by 14 candidates, proved inconclusive; the Chairman of the provincial legislature, Aleksandr Uss, whose campaign was supported by the company Russian Aluminium (RusAl), received 27.6% of the votes cast, closely followed by the Governor of Taimyr and the former General Director of Norilsk Nickel, Aleksandr Khlopanin, with 25.2%. These two candidates proceeded to a second round. In third place, with an unexpected 21.4%, was Sergei Glazyev, who was supported by the Communist Party of the Russian Federation (CPRF), but who had served as Minister of External Economic Relations in the 'reform' Government of 1992–93. In the 'run-off' election, held on 22 September, Khlopanin was the first-placed candidate, winning 48.1% of the votes cast, compared with the 41.8% of the votes received by Uss. However, at the end of September the Krai's electoral commission annulled the results of the election, citing irregularities in the conduct of Khlopanin's campaign. On 1 October a court in Krasnoyarsk overturned the decision of the commission, and two days later federal President Vladimir Putin appointed Khlopanin to serve as acting Governor; on the following day the central electoral commission confirmed Khlopanin as elected Governor, and Khlopanin was inaugurated shortly afterwards. The Supreme Court confirmed the validity of the election results in November, and at the end of January 2003 a provincial court agreed to the request of central electoral commission that the Krai's electoral commision be disbanded.

A new electoral commission, containing none of the former members, was inaugurated in mid-May 2003. Meanwhile, in March Khlopanin was elected to the Supreme Council of the pro-Government Unity and Fatherland-United Russia, although he was not formally a member of that party. Following his inauguration as Governor of Krasnoyarsk Krai, Khlopanin was thereby obliged to resign as Governor of the Taimyr AOk. Although Khlopanin emphasized that he did not intend to transfer officials from Taimyr administration to the Krai, his success appeared to heighten speculation that the two federal subjects (and potentially the third constituent part of the Krai, the Evenk AOk) would eventually merge to form a single unit. (A proposed referendum on such a merger had been cancelled in 2002, following the death of Lebed.) In February 2003 the Governors of Krasnoyarsk Krai and the two AOks signed a protocol of intent to establish a Council of Governors, to facilitate joint decision-making in social, economic and cultural areas of policy; a council of the legislative assemblies of the three entities was subsequently established, although it was emphasized that there would be no expedited measures towards the merging of the territories.

Economy

Krasnoyarsk Krai is potentially one of Russia's richest regions, containing vast deposits of minerals, gold and petroleum, although, particularly since the late 1990s, it has experienced serious economic problems, many of them typical of northern regions. All of the figures included in this survey include figures for the two autonomous okrugs, which are also considered separately (see below). In 2000 the Krai's gross regional product amounted to 217,292m. roubles, equivalent to 71,730 roubles per head, by far the highest level in the Siberian Federal Okrug. The Krai's major industrial centres are at Krasnoyarsk, Norilsk, Achinsk, Kansk and Minusinsk. In 2001 there were 2,069 km of railway track and 12,711 km of paved roads on the Krai's territory.

The principal crops are grain, potatoes and vegetables. Animal husbandry and bee-keeping are also important. The agricultural sector employed 10.0% of the working population in 2001, when total output within the sector was worth 21,792m. roubles. Of this total, crop sales accounted for 56.7% and animal husbandry for 43.3%. The Krai's main industries are non-ferrous metallurgy (which accounted for 72.5% of total output in 2001), electricity production and ore-mining (particularly bauxite, for aluminium). Industry employed 24.6% of the work-force in 2001, when the industrial output of Krasnoyarsk Krai amounted to a value of 187,094m. roubles. The Krai contains the world's second largest aluminium smelter, Krasnoyarsk Aluminium, which forms part of the Krasnoyarsk Metallurgical Plant (KraMZ), 28% of which was owned by RusAl in 2003.

In 2001 the territory's economically active population totalled 1,539,000, and 9.7% of the labour force were unemployed. The average monthly wage in the Krai was 5,971.7 roubles in mid-2002, somewhat in excess of the national average. In 2001 the local budget showed a deficit of 2,373m. roubles. In that year export trade amounted to US $2,859.5m., and imports to $610.6m. Foreign investment totalled $30.1m. in 2001. At the end of the year there were 9,188 small businesses in Krasnoyarsk Krai.

Directory

Head of the Provincial Administration (Governor): ALEKSANDR G. KHLOPANIN; 660009 Krasnoyarsk, pr. Mira 110; tel. (3912) 22-22-63; fax (3912) 22-11-63; e-mail klimik@krskstate.ru; internet www.krskstate.ru.

Chairman of the Legislative Assembly: ALEKSANDR V. USS; 660009 Krasnoyarsk, pr. Mira 110; tel. (3912) 22-33-87; fax (3912) 22-22-24; internet www.legis.krsn.ru.

Representation of Krasnoyarsk Krai in the Russian Federation: 107996 Moscow, ul. Gilyarovskogo 31/2; tel. (095) 284-86-56; fax (095) 284-82-41.

Head of Krasnoyarsk City Administration (Mayor): PETR I. PIMASHKOV; 660049 Krasnoyarsk, ul. K. Marksa 93; tel. (3912) 22-22-31; fax (3912) 22-25-12; e-mail webmaster@admkrsk.ru; internet www.admkrsk.ru.

Evenk Autonomous Okrug

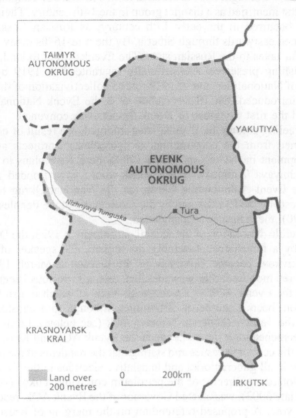

The Evenk Autonomous Okrug (AOk) is a land-locked territory situated on the Central Siberian Plateau. It is part of the Siberian Federal Okrug and the Eastern Siberian Economic Area. The district forms the central-eastern part of Krasnoyarsk Krai, with the core territories of the province lying to the west and south and the other autonomous okrug, the Taimyr (Dolgano-Nenets) AOk, to the north. Sakha (Yakutiya) adjoins to the east, and Irkutsk to the south-east. The district has numerous rivers, the largest being the Nizhnyaya Tunguska and the Podkammenaya Tunguska, both tributaries of the Yenisei. The Evenk AOk occupies a total area of 767,600 sq km (296,370 sq miles), of which almost three-quarters is forested, and comprises three administrative districts and one 'urban-type settlement'. According to the preliminary results of the census of 9–16 October 2002, the total population was 17,700. Its population density, of 0.02 per sq km, was the lowest in the Federation. Some 32.8% of the population inhabited urban areas. According to the 1989 census, ethnic Russians comprised 67.5% of the district's population and ethnic Evenks 14.0%. The Evenks' native tongue is part of the Tungusic group of the Tungusic-Manuchu division of the Uralo-Altaic language family. The region's administrative centre is at Tura, which had just 5,300 inhabitants on 1 January 2001.

History

The Evenks, who are thought to be descended from a mixture of Tungus and Yukagir culture, were first identified as a distinct group in the 14th century. Their first contact with Russians occurred in the early 17th century, as Russian Cossacks and fur trappers advanced eastwards through Siberia. By the mid-1620s many Evenks were forced to pay fur taxes to the Russian state. The Evenks' right to land, pasture, and hunting and fishing preserves was officially guaranteed in 1919 by the Soviet Commissariat of Nationalities, but in 1929 forced collectivization of their economic activities was introduced. On 10 December 1930 the Evenk National Okrug was established and the first Congress of Evenk Soviets was convened.

Nationalist feeling among the Evenks later emerged as a result of environmental damage sustained from the construction of hydroelectric projects and extensive mineral development in the region. In the 1980s there were plans to build a dam across the Nizhnyaya Tunguska river, which would have flooded much of the territory of the Event Autonomous Okrug (as the National Okrug had become). Following protests by the Evenks, and by the Association of the Peoples of the North (formed in 1990), the project was abandoned.

After the forcible dissolution of the federal parliament in 1993, the District Soviet was replaced by a Legislative Assembly or Suglan. The speaker of the Suglan, Aleksandr Bokivkov, became Governor of the district in March 1997, after an election held three months earlier was annulled, owing to various irregularities. The relationship of the Evenk AOk to Krasnoyarsk Krai, of which it also forms a part, has, on occasion, been a source of difficulties, although to a considerably lesser extent than in the Taimyr (Dolgano-Nenets) AOk (see below). From June 1997 a number of agreements were signed between the Evenk AOk and Krasnoyarsk Krai, regulating specific economic issues and stating that the residents of the district would participate fully in all gubernatorial and legislative elections in the Krai. On 8 April 2001 Boris Zolotarev, a director of the petroleum company, Yukos (which merged with Sibneft in late 2003), was elected Governor of the Evenk AOk, receiving 51.8% of the popular vote. A proposed referendum on the merging of Krasnoyarsk Krai with both of its constituent AOks was cancelled, following the death of Krasnoyarsk Krai Governor Aleksandr Lebed in 2002. However, in February 2003 the Governors of Krasnoyarsk Krai and the two AOks signed a protocol of intent to establish a Council of Governors, to facilitate joint decision-making in social, economic and cultural areas of policy; a council of the legislative assemblies of the three entities was subsequently established, although it was emphasized that there were no immediate plans for union.

Economy

Despite its size and, indeed, its potential wealth, the Evenk AOk remains an undeveloped and economically insignificant producer. In 2001 9.3% of its working population were occupied in agriculture, producing total output worth 68m. roubles. The district's agriculture consists mainly of fishing, hunting, reindeer-breeding and fur-farming. The estimated combined hydroelectric potential of the district's two major rivers is 81,300m. kWh. Its main industries otherwise are the production of petroleum, natural gas, graphite and Iceland spar, and food-processing. In 2001 industry employed just 3.3% of the Evenk AOk's work-force, and generated 135m. roubles.

The economically active population of the Evenk AOk numbered 11,000 in 2001, when the rate of unemployment, at 2.9%, was the second lowest in the Russian Federation (after Moscow City). The average monthly wage was some 7,898.1 roubles in mid-2002—the highest level in the Siberian Federal Okrug. The 2001 budget showed a deficit of 896m. roubles. At 31 December 2001 just nine small businesses were registered in the district.

Directory

Head of the District Administration (Governor): BORIS N. ZOLOTAREV; 648000 Krasnoyarsk Krai, Evenk AOk, PGT Tura, ul. Sovetskaya 2; tel. (3912) 63-63-55; fax (3912) 63-63-56; e-mail zolotarevbn@tura.evenkya.ru; internet www.evenkya .ru.

Chairman of the District Legislative Assembly (Suglan): ANATOLII YE. AMOSOV; 648000 Krasnoyarsk Krai, Evenk AOk, PGT Tura, ul. Sovetskaya 2; tel. (3912) 63-63-73; fax (39113) 2-26-31; e-mail amosovae@tura.evenkya.ru.

Representation of the Evenk Autonomous Okrug in Krasnoyarsk Krai: 660097 Krasnoyarsk, pr. Mira 36/719; tel. and fax (3912) 26-34-55.

Chief Representative of the Evenk Autonomous Okrug in the Russian Federation: GALINA F. SEMENOVA; 127025 Moscow, ul. Novyi Arbat 19/1531; tel. (095) 956-19-00; fax (095) 207-75-94.

Taimyr (Dolgano-Nenets) Autonomous Okrug

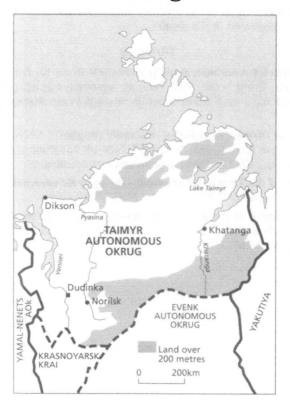

Taimyr (Dolgano-Nenets) Autonomous Okrug (AOk) is situated on the Taimyr Peninsula, which abuts into the Arctic Ocean, separating the Kara and Laptev Seas. The district comprises the northern end of Krasnoyarsk Krai and, in common with its south-eastern neighbour, the Evenk AOk, forms part of the Siberian Federal Okrug and the Eastern Siberian Economic Area. The Yamal-Nenets AOk, in Tyumen Oblast, lies to the west and the Republic of Sakha (Yakutiya) is located to the south-east. Taimyr district's major rivers are the Yenisei (which drains into the Kara Sea in the west of the region), the Pyasina and the Khatanga. The district is mountainous in the south and in the extreme north, and just under one-half of it is forested. It has numerous lakes, the largest being Lake Taimyr. The territory occupies a total area of 862,100 sq km (332,860 sq miles), which is divided into three administrative districts and one city. The climate in Taimyr is severe, with snow for an average of 280 days per year. According to the preliminary results of the census of 9–16 October 2002, the Taimyr AOk had a population of 39,800. Its population density, therefore, was 0.05 per sq km. Some 66.3% of the total population inhabited urban areas. In 1989 67.1% of the district's inhabitants were ethnic Russians, 8.8% Dolgans, 8.6% Ukrainians and 4.4% Nenets. The AOk's administrative centre is at

Dudinka, which had a population of 26,700 in 2001. The city of Norilsk, east of Dudinka, which had a population of 135,100 in 2002, according to provisional census results, does not form part of the AOk, being considered for administrative purposes a part of Krasnoyarsk Krai proper.

History

The territory of the Taimyr district was first exploited by Russian settlers in the 17th century. An autonomous okrug for the Dolgans and Nenets was founded on 10 December 1930, as part of Krasnoyarsk Krai. In 1993, following Russian President Boris Yeltsin's forcible dissolution of the Russian parliament, on 18 October the Dolgano-Nenets or Taimyr District Soviet voted to disband itself and a new District Duma was subsequently elected. The administration was generally supportive of the federal authorities, but there was also significant popular support for the nationalist Liberal Democratic Party of Russia.

Tensions arose between Taimyr and Krasnoyarsk Krai over the division of authorities between the two federal subjects, the exact relationship of which remained constitutionally obscure. In October 1997 Yeltsin and first deputy premier Boris Nemtsov signed a power-sharing treaty with the leaders of the Taimyr AOk, Krasnoyarsk Krai and the other autonomous okrug within the Krai, the Evenk AOk. The first of its kind, this treaty clearly delineated authority between the national, krai and okrug authorities, and ensured that some of the wealth generated by the local company, Norilsk Nickel, the world's largest producer of nickel, went to pay salaries and other benefits within Taimyr. None the less, the attitudes of Taimyr leaders towards the Krai were variable; the AOk did not participate in elections to the Krai legislature in 1997 or 2000, although it did participate in the gubernatorial election of the Krai in April 1998. The victor in that election, Gen. (retd) Aleksandr Lebed, unilaterally cancelled the previous power-sharing agreement in October 1999, fuelling suspicions that he wished the Krai to reimpose greater control over its districts.

At the gubernatorial election held in the AOk on 28 January 2001, Aleksandr Khlopanin, hitherto the General Director of Norilsk Nickel, the major employer in the region, was elected as Governor, with some 63% of the votes cast. However, following Khlopanin's election as Governor of Krasnoyarsk Krai (q.v.) in September 2002, he was obliged to resign as Governor of the AOk; his deputy, Sergei Nauman, assumed the governorship in an acting capacity. Gubernatorial elections, held on 26 January 2003, and contested by seven candidates, were won by Oleg Budargin, hitherto the Mayor of Norilsk and a former senior manager at Norilsk Nickel, with 69.1% of the votes cast. Although Budargin had contested the election as an independent, he was regarded as the preferred candidate of both Khlopanin and Norilsk Nickel.

In February 2003 the Governors of Krasnoyarsk Krai and the two autonomies signed a protocol of intent to establish a Council of Governors, and a council of the legislative assemblies of the three entities was subsequently established. No immediate proposals for a union had been suggested since the cancellation of a referendum on merger, following Lebed's death in 2002.

Economy

As with most of the autonomous okrugs, separate economic data on the Taimyr (Dolgano-Nenets) AOk are scarce, the district being part of Krasnoyarsk Krai. The major ports in the AOk are Dudinka, Dikson and Khatanga. There is limited transport—only the Dudinka–Norilsk railway line (89 km, or 55 miles, long) operates throughout the year. The district's roads, which totalled 112 km in length at the end of 2001, are concentrated in its more populous areas.

Agricultural production was valued at just 44m. roubles in 2001, mainly provided by fishing, animal husbandry (livestock- and reindeer-breeding) and fur-animal hunting. In that year agriculture employed just 7.7% of the Taimyr AOk's work-force. There are extensive mineral reserves, however, including petroleum and natural gas. The main industries are ore-mining (coal, copper and nickel), electricity generation and food-processing (which accounted for 59.0% of the territory's industrial output in 2001). In that year industry provided employment to some 20.7% of the work-force and produced output equivalent to 200m. roubles. Norilsk Nickel accounted for some 20% of the world's, and 80% of Russia's, nickel output in the mid-1990s. The plant also produced 19% of the world's cobalt (70% of Russia's), 42% of the world's platinum (100% of Russia's) and 5% of the world's copper (40% of Russia's). Its activity, however, caused vast environmental damage to its surroundings, in the form of sulphur pollution.

The economically active population numbered 26,000 in 2001, when only 7.3% of the labour force were unemployed. The average monthly wage in the region was some 10,736.2 roubles in mid-2002. The district administrative budget for 2001 showed a deficit of 16m. roubles. At the end of 2001 there were 30 small businesses registered in the AOk.

Directory

Head of the District Administration (Governor): OLEG M. BUDARGIN; 663210 Krasnoyarsk Krai, Taimyr (Dolgano-Nenets) AOk, Dudinka, ul. Sovetskaya 35; tel. (39111) 2-11-60; fax (39111) 2-33-17; e-mail atao@taimyr.ru; internet www.taimyr.ru.

Chairman of the District Duma: VIKTOR V. SITNOV; 647000 Krasnoyarsk Krai, Taimyr (Dolgano-Nenets) AOk, Dudinka, ul. Sovetskaya 35; tel. (39111) 2-37-37; fax (39111) 2-29-39; e-mail dudinka@dumatao.krasnoyarsk.su; internet www.dumatao.ru.

Representation of the Taimyr (Dolgano-Nenets) Autonomous Okrug in Krasnoyarsk Krai: Krasnoyarsk.

Chief Representative of the Taimyr (Dolgano-Nenets) Autonomous Okrug in the Russian Federation: OLEG YE. MORGUNOV; Moscow; tel. (095) 120-45-36.

Head of Dudinka City Administration: SERGEI M. MOSHKIN; 663210 Krasnoyarsk Krai, Taimyr (Dolgano-Nenets) AOk, Dudinka, ul. Sovetskaya 35; tel. (39111) 2-13-30; fax (39111) 2-55-52.

Novosibirsk Oblast

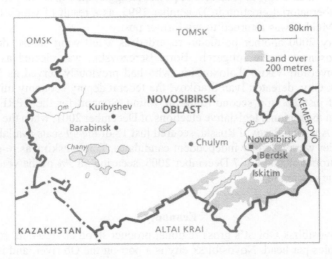

Novosibirsk Oblast is situated in the south-east of the Western Siberian Plain, at the Ob-Irtysh confluence. The Oblast forms part of the Siberian Federal Okrug and the Western Siberian Economic Area. Its south-western districts lie on the international border with Kazakhstan. The neighbouring federal territories are Omsk Oblast to the west, Tomsk Oblast to the north, Kemerovo Oblast to the east and Altai Krai to the south. The region's major rivers are the Ob and the Om. The Oblast has around 3,000 lakes, the four largest being Chany, Sartlan, Ubinskoye and Uryum. About one-third of its territory is swampland. It occupies a total area of 178,200 sq km (68,800 sq miles) and measures over 400 km (250 miles) from south to north and over 600 km from west to east. It is divided into 30 administrative districts and 14 cities. According to the preliminary results of the census of 9–16 October 2002, the Oblast had a population of 2,692,200, and a population density, therefore, of 15.1 per sq km. At that time some 75.1% of the population inhabited urban areas. There is a small German community in the Oblast, constituting 2.2% of its population in 1989. Just over one-half of the region's inhabitants live in its administrative centre, Novosibirsk, which had a population of 1,425,600 at mid-October 2002, according to provisional census results.

History

The city of Novosibirsk (known as Novonikolayevsk until 1925) was founded in 1893, during the construction of the Trans-Siberian Railway. It became prosperous through its proximity to the Kuznetsk coal basin (Kuzbass—see Kemerovo Oblast). The Oblast, which was formed on 28 September 1937, increased in population throughout the Soviet period as it became heavily industrialized, and was a major centre of industrial production during the Second World War.

In October 1993 the federal President, Boris Yeltsin, dismissed the head of the Regional Administration, Vitalii Mukha. In 1994 elections were held to a new representative body, which was dominated by the Communist Party of the Russian Federation (CPRF), after the elections in both 1994 and 1998; the regional legislature was constantly in dispute with the executive, the head of which was a presidential appointment. In an effort to resolve this power struggle, the President permitted the Oblast a gubernatorial election in December 1995, as a result of which the CPRF candidate, Mukha, was returned to his former post.

In January 2000 another politician regarded as a left-wing statist, despite his reported closeness to the 'oligarch' Boris Berezovskii, was elected as the new regional Governor. Viktor Tolokonskii, who had previously served as Mayor of Novosibirsk City, defeated Ivan Starikov, the federal deputy economy minister, by a margin of just 2% in a second round of voting. Support for the CPRF declined somewhat in the regional legislative elections of December 2001, when the party and its ally, the Agrarian Party of Russia, secured just 18 of the 49 seats available, while the remainder were filled by independent candidates. Tolokonskii was re-elected in the gubernatorial election of 7 December 2003, securing 58.3% of the votes cast by 55.4% of the electorate.

Economy

In 2000 Novosibirsk Oblast's gross regional product stood at 76,948m. roubles, or 28,093 roubles per head. Novosibirsk city is a port on the Ob river, and is also the region's principal industrial centre. At the end of 2001 there were 1,530 km of railways and 9,613 km of paved roads on the Oblast's territory. There are 12 airports in the region, including Tolmachevo, an international airport.

The Oblast's agriculture employed 14.8% of its working population in 2001 and consists mainly of animal husbandry, bee-keeping and the production of grain, vegetables, potatoes and flax. Agriculture generated 25,402m. roubles in 2001, of which crop sales accounted for 54.9% and animal husbandry for 45.1%. In the same year a total of 48,953m. roubles was contributed by the industrial sector. Extraction industries involved the production of coal, petroleum, natural gas, peat, marble, limestone and clay. Manufacturing industry includes non-ferrous metallurgy, mechanical engineering, metal-working, electricity generation and food-processing. Industry employed some 19.0% of the region's work-force in 2001. In the mid-1990s the region's defence industry was largely converted to civilian use—by 1999 only 15% of the output from the former military-industrial complex was for military purposes.

The Oblast's economically active population totalled 1,308,000 in 2001, when 12.4% of the labour force were unemployed. The average monthly wage in the region was 3,892.7 roubles in mid-2002. The 2001 budget showed a deficit of 1,396m. roubles. In 2001 the Oblast's external trade comprised US $502.3m. in exports and $326.8m. in imports. In the same year foreign investment in the Oblast totalled some $103.9m. roubles. At the end of the year there were some 23,725 small businesses registered in the region, one of the largest figures in any federal subject outside Moscow and St Petersburg.

Directory

Head of the Regional Administration (Governor): VIKTOR A. TOLOKONSKII; 630011 Novosibirsk, Krasnyi pr. 18; tel. (3832) 23-08-62; fax (3832) 23-57-00; internet www3.adm.nso.ru.

Chairman of the Regional Council of Deputies: VIKTOR V. LEONOV; 630011 Novosibirsk, ul. Kirova 3; tel. (3832) 23-62-52; fax (3832) 23-23-78; internet www .sovet.nso.ru.

Chief Representative of Novosibirsk Oblast in the Russian Federation: NINA M. PIRYAZEVA; Moscow; tel. (095) 203-27-20.

Head of Novosibirsk City Administration (Mayor): VLADIMIR F. GORODETSKII; 630099 Novosibirsk, Krasnyi pr. 34; tel. (3832) 22-49-32; fax (3832) 22-08-58; e-mail cic@admnsk.ru.

Omsk Oblast

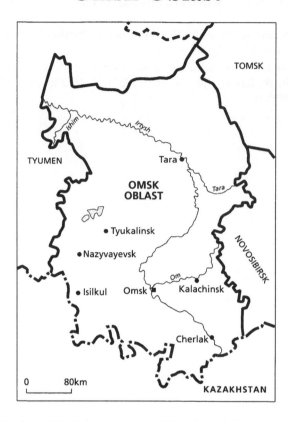

Omsk Oblast is situated in the south of the Western Siberian Plain on the middle reaches of the Irtysh river. Kazakhstan lies to the south. Other federal subjects that neighbour the Oblast are Tyumen to the north-west and Tomsk and Novosibirsk to the east. Omsk forms part of the Siberian Federal Okrug and the Western Siberian Economic Area. The major rivers are the Irtysh, the Ishim, the Om and the Tara. Much of the territory is marshland and about one-quarter is forested. The total area of Omsk Oblast covers some 139,700 sq km (53,920 sq miles). It measures some 600 km (370 miles) from south to north and 500 km from west to east and is divided into 32 administrative districts and six cities. According to the preliminary results of the census of 9–16 October 2002, the region had a total population of 2,079,200 and a population density, therefore, of 14.9 per sq km. Of the Oblast's inhabitants, some 68.7% lived in urban areas. Its administrative centre is at Omsk, which lies at the confluence of the Ob and Irtysh rivers and had a population of 1,133,900 in 2002, according to provisional census results.

History

The city of Omsk was founded as a fortress in 1716. In 1918 it became the seat of Adm. Aleksandr Kolchak's 'all-Russian Government'. However, Omsk fell to the

Bolsheviks in 1919 and Kolchak 'abdicated' in January 1920. Omsk Oblast was formed on 7 December 1934.

In the 1990s the region was generally supportive of the Communist Party of the Russian Federation (CPRF), although the nationalist Liberal Democrats also enjoyed a significant level of popularity. The regional Governor, Leonid Polezhayev, although a supporter of the federal state President, Boris Yeltsin, was well respected locally and was re-elected in December 1995. In May 1996 the regional and federal administrations signed a treaty on the delimitation of powers. Legislative elections were held in the Oblast on 22 March 1998, in which the CPRF and other leftist candidates won 30 assembly seats and a majority of seats on Omsk city council. Polezhayev was re-elected in September 1999, defeating the regional leader of the CPRF, Aleksandr Kravets. Nevertheless, Omsk was one of only four regions in which the CPRF candidate, Gennadii Zyuganov, received a larger proportion of the votes cast than Vladimir Putin in the federal presidential election of March 2000. The Oblast abolished its power-sharing treaty with the federal Government in mid-2001. At elections to the Legislative Assembly on 24 March 2002 supporters of Pole-zhayev, including, notably, members of the Unity and Fatherland-United Russia party, obtained control of the Assembly. Polezhayev was re-elected as Governor on 7 September 2003, receiving 57% of the votes cast.

Economy

In 2000 Omsk Oblast's gross regional product amounted to 48,704m. roubles, equivalent to 22,608 roubles per head. Omsk is one of the highest-ranking cities in Russia in terms of industrial output. The region lies on the Trans-Siberian Railway and is a major transport junction. At the end of 2001 it contained 775 km of railway track and 7,735 km of paved roads. There are also some 1,250 km of navigable waterways on the Oblast's territory and some 580 km of pipeline, carrying petroleum and petroleum products. There are two airports—a third, international airport was under construction in the late 1990s.

The Oblast's soil is the fertile black earth (*chernozem*) characteristic of the region. Its agriculture, which generated a total of 23,742m. roubles in 2001 (with crop sales accounting for 49.2% of the total and animal husbandry for 50.8%) and employed some 18.9% of the work-force, consists mainly of the production of grain, and animal husbandry (including fur-farming) and hunting. The region's mineral reserves include clay, peat and lime. There are also deposits of petroleum and natural gas. Industry employed 18.4% of the work-force in 2001. The Oblast's main industries are electricity generation, fuel, chemical and petrochemical production, mechanical engineering, petroleum-refining and food-processing. Total industrial production amounted to a value of 37,376m. roubles in 2001. The Omsk petroleum refinery, one of Russia's largest and most modern, formed part of Sibneft (Siberian Oil Co), one of the country's newer, vertically integrated petroleum companies. The region's exports primarily comprise chemical, petrochemical and petroleum prod-ucts. The defence sector is also significant to the economy of the region.

The economically active population numbered 979,000 in 2001, when 10.0% of the region's labour force were unemployed. In mid-2002 the average wage in the Oblast was 3,464.0 roubles per month, although it was named as one of the worst regions in Russia for wage arrears. The region was, however, among those with the cheapest prices for foodstuffs in that year. The 2001 budget recorded a deficit of 106m. roubles. In that year external trade comprised US $809.7m. in exports and

$163.8m. in imports. The Oblast's main foreign trading partners include the People's Republic of China, Cyprus, Germany, Kazakhstan, Spain, Switzerland and the United Kingdom. In 2001 foreign investment in the region totalled some $925.2m. In 2000 there were some 74 enterprises in the Oblast with foreign capital. At 31 December 2001 there was a total of 10,856 small businesses registered in the region.

Directory

Head of the Regional Administration (Governor): LEONID K. POLEZHAYEV; 644002 Omsk, ul. Krasnyi Put 1; tel. (3812) 24-14-15; fax (3812) 24-23-72; e-mail teleomsk@echo.ru; internet www.omskportal.ru.

Chairman of the Regional Legislative Assembly: VLADIMIR A. VARNAVSKII; 640002 Omsk, ul. Krasnyi Put 1; tel. (3812) 24-23-33; fax (3812) 23-24-66; e-mail root@topos.omsk.ru.

Representation of Omsk Oblast in the Russian Federation: 107078 Moscow, per. B. Kozlovskii 14–15/1; tel. (095) 921-65-54; fax (095) 921-21-57.

Head of Omsk City Administration (Mayor): YEVGENII I. BELOV; 644099 Omsk, ul. Gagarina 34; tel. (3812) 24-30-33; fax (3812) 24-49-34; e-mail media@grad .omsk.ru; internet www.omsk.ru.

Tomsk Oblast

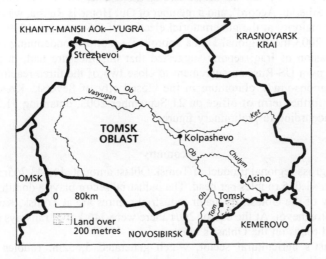

Tomsk Oblast is situated in the south-east of the Western Siberian Plain. It forms part of the Siberian Federal Okrug and the Western Siberian Economic Area. Kemerovo and Novosibirsk Oblasts lie to the south, Omsk to the south-west, the Khanty-Mansii AOk—Yugra (part of Tyumen Oblast) to the north-west and Krasnoyarsk Krai to the east. The major rivers are the Ob, the Tom, the Chulym, the Ket, the Tym and the Vasyugan. The Ob flows for about 1,000 km (almost 400 miles) from the south-east to the north-west of the territory. The largest lake is the Mirnoye. Almost all the Oblast's territory is taiga (forested marshland), and over one-half of its total area is forested. It occupies 316,900 sq km (122,320 sq miles) and is divided into 16 administrative districts and six cities. According to the preliminary results of the census of 9–16 October 2002, the total population was 1,046,000, giving a population density of only 3.3 per sq km. Some 68.4% of the population inhabited urban areas. Around 88.2% of the population were ethnically Russian, 2.6% Ukrainian and 2.1% Tatar. The administrative centre of the Oblast is at Tomsk, which had a population of 487,700 in 2002, according to provisional census results. The other major city in the region is Seversk (formerly the closed city known as Tomsk-7—115,700), 15 km downriver from Tomsk city.

History

Tomsk city was founded as a fortress in 1604. It was a major trading centre until the 1890s, when the construction of the Trans-Siberian Railway promoted other centres. Tomsk Oblast was formed on 13 August 1944.

In 1993 the Regional Soviet was initially critical of President Boris Yeltsin's forcible dissolution of the federal parliament. It too, therefore, was disbanded, and replaced by a Regional Duma. The Communist Party of the Russian Federation remained the most popular party in the region, securing 19% of the votes cast in elections to the federal State Duma in 1995. However, in a simultaneous gubernatorial election for the Oblast, the pro-Yeltsin incumbent, Viktor Kress, won the popular mandate to head the regional administration. In elections to the regional legislature in January 1998, independent candidates fared well, with the business lobby winning 30 of the 42 seats. Kress, the Chairman of the inter-regional association 'Siberian Accord', and a member of Our Home is Russia, was re-elected with a clear majority at the gubernatorial election of 5 September 1999.

In March 2003 the Regional Duma approved a motion condemning the US-led military invasion of Iraq; reports suggested that this measure had, in part, been precipitated by a US-Russian agreement to close two of the three reactors used to produce weapons-grade plutonium in the closed city of Seversk. Kress was re-elected to a further term of office on 21 September 2003, obtaining 71.2% of the votes cast, according to preliminary figures.

Economy

In 2000 the gross regional product of Tomsk Oblast amounted to 43,765m. roubles, equivalent to 41,055 roubles per head. The industrial sector plays a dominant role in the economy of the Oblast. Its major industrial centres are at Tomsk, Kolpashevo, Asino and Strezhevoi. At the end of 2001 there were 346 km of railways and 3,553 km of paved roads on the Oblast's territory.

The Oblast's agricultural sector, which generated 5,662m. roubles in 2001, consists mainly of animal husbandry and the production of grain, vegetables and potatoes. Of the total value of agricultural output, crop sales accounted for 41.5%, and animal husbandry for 58.5%. Some 8.5% of the Oblast's working population was engaged in agriculture in 2001. Around 1.4m. ha (3.4m. acres) of the Oblast's territory was used for agricultural purposes, of which one-half was arable land. The Oblast has substantial reserves of coal, as well as of petroleum and natural gas (estimated at 333.7m. metric tons and 300,000m. cu m, respectively). Its other main industries are mechanical engineering, metal-working, chemicals and petrochemicals, non-ferrous metallurgy and electricity generation. Industry employed 20.7% of the working population in 2001, and industrial output amounted to a value of 33,716m. roubles in that year.

The economically active population of Tomsk Oblast numbered 534,000 in 2001, when 9.8% of the labour force were unemployed. The average monthly wage was 5,508.4 roubles in mid-2002. There was a budgetary deficit of 1,058m. roubles in 2001. The Oblast's most significant partners in international trade are the USA and the Republic of Korea (South Korea), with the chemicals industry accounting for the majority of this activity. In 2001 the value of external trade amounted to US $630.9m. in exports and $63.3m. in imports. In that year total foreign investment amounted to $24.6m. At 31 December 2001 6,920 small businesses were registered in the region.

Directory

Head of the Regional Administration (Governor): VIKTOR M. KRESS; 634050 Tomsk, pl. Lenina 6; tel. (3822) 51-05-05; fax (3822) 51-03-23; e-mail ato@tomsk .gov.ru; internet www.tomsk.gov.ru.

Chairman of the Regional Duma: BORIS A. MALTSEV; 634050 Tomsk, pl. Lenina 6; tel. (3822) 51-01-47; fax (3822) 51-06-02; e-mail duma@tomsk.gov.ru; internet duma.tomsk.gov.ru.

Chief Representative of Tomsk Oblast in the Russian Federation: ALEKSANDR N. CHEREVKO; 103030 Moscow, ul. Dolgorukovskaya 38/1/406; tel. (095) 973-31-21; fax (095) 299-37-95; e-mail tomskadm@chat.ru.

Head of Tomsk City Administration (Mayor): ALEKSANDR S. MAKAROV; 634050 Tomsk, pr. Lenina 73; tel. (3822) 52-68-99; fax (3822) 52-68-60; e-mail pmayor@ admin.tomsk.ru; internet admin.tomsk.ru.

Republic of Tyva

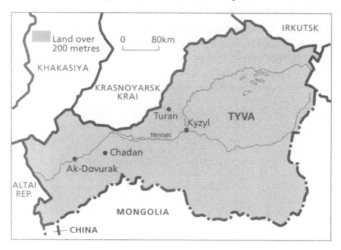

The Republic of Tyva (Tuva) is situated in the south of eastern Siberia in the Sayan Mountains. It forms part of the Siberian Federal Okrug and the Eastern Siberian Economic Area. Tyva has an international border with Mongolia to the south and a very short one with the People's Republic of China in the far south-west. The Republic of Altai lies to the west, the Republic of Khakasiya to the north-west and Krasnoyarsk Krai to the north. Irkutsk Oblast lies to the north-east and the Republic of Buryatiya forms part of the eastern border. Tyva's major river is the Yenisei, which rises in the Eastern Sayan range. The territory of the Republic consists of a series of high mountain valleys. One-half of this area is forested. The Republic has numerous waterways, including over 12,000 rivers and 8,400 freshwater lakes. Tyva occupies 170,500 sq km (65,830 sq miles) and consists of 16 administrative districts and five cities. According to the preliminary results of the census of 9–16 October 2002, Tyva had a total population of 305,500 and a population density of only 1.8 per sq km. Some 51.7% of the population lived in urban areas. In 1989 some 64.3% of inhabitants were Tyvans (Tuvinians) and 32.0% Russians. Lamaism (Tibetan Buddhism) is the predominant religion in the Republic. The Tyvan language belongs to the Old Uigur (Uygur) group of the Turkic branch of the Uralo-Altaic linguistic family. The capital of Tyva is at Kyzyl, which had a population of 104,100 in mid-October 2002, according to provisional census results.

History

The Tyvans (known at various times as Soyons, Soyots and Uriankhais) emerged as an identifiable ethnic group in the early 18th century. The territory of what is now Tyva was occupied in turn between the sixth and the ninth centuries by the Turkish Khanate, the Chinese, the Uigurs and the Yenisei Kyrgyz. The Mongols controlled the region from 1207 to 1368. In the second half of the 17th century the Dzungarians (Sungarians) seized the area from the Altyn Khans. In 1758 the Manzhous (Manchus) annexed Dzungaria and the territory thus became part of the Chinese Empire. Russian influence dates from the Treaty of Peking (Beijing) of 1860, after which trade links were developed and a number of Russians settled there. One year after the Chinese Revolution of 1911 Tyva declared its independence. In 1914, however, Russia established a protectorate over the territory, which then became the Tannu-Tuva People's Republic. This was a nominally independent state until October 1944, when it was incorporated into the USSR as the Tuvinian Autonomous Oblast. It became an ASSR on 10 October 1961, within the Russian Federation.

The Republic declared sovereignty on 11 December 1990 and renamed itself the Republic of Tuva in August 1991. On 21 October 1993 the Tyvan Supreme Soviet resolved that the Republic's name was Tyva (as opposed to the russified Tuva) and adopted a new Constitution. The Constitution provided for a legislature, the Supreme Khural, and a supreme constitutional body, the Grand Khural. The new parliament was elected on 12 December. On the same day the new Constitution was approved by 62.2% of registered voters in Tyva. Only 32.7%, however, voted in favour of the Russian Constitution. The victory of a nationalist Liberal Democratic candidate, Aleksandr Kashin, in the April 1998 mayoral elections in Kyzyl was, perhaps, a sign of intolerance with the reformism of the federal Government (particularly among the predominantly ethnic Russian population of the city). Apathy was also a likely cause, as a low rate of participation in the general election of the same month meant that only 21 of the 38 seats in the Supreme Khural were filled. Further rounds later in the year failed to resolve the situation and, indeed, for two months in 1998–99 the assembly was rendered inquorate by the death of a deputy.

In 2000 the Grand Khural was obliged to make 26 amendments to the republican Constitution, in order to comply with the All-Russian Constitution. A new Constitution, which removed Tyva's right to self-determination and to secede from the Federation, was approved by referendum in May 2001. In early March 2002 various amendments to the Constitution were approved, in order to bring it more closely into compliance with federal norms. Notably, the Supreme Khural was reconstituted as a bicameral legislature, comprising an upper chamber, the 130-member Chamber of Representatives, and a lower chamber, the 32-member Legislative Chamber. On 17 March the incumbent President, Sherig-ool Oorzhak, was elected to serve a third term of office, receiving 53% of the votes cast. Elections to the bicameral legislature were held on 2 June; the overall rate of participation by the electorate was 52%, although repeat elections were required to elect 40 members of the Chamber of Representatives and nine members of the Legislative Chamber.

Economy

Tyva's economy is largely agriculture-based. In 2000 its gross regional product stood at 3,761m. roubles, or 12,081 roubles per head, the lowest level of any territory in the Siberian Federal Okrug. The Republic's main industrial centres are at Kyzyl and Ak-Dovurak. There are road and rail links with other regions, although the distance from Kyzyl to the nearest railway station is over 400 km (250 miles). At the end of 2001 there were 2,518 km of paved roads in the Republic.

Tyva's agriculture, which employed 15.1% of the work-force in 2001, consists mainly of animal husbandry, although forestry and hunting are also important. Total agricultural production in 2001 amounted to a value of 1,752m. roubles. At 1 January 1999 there were some 670,400 sheep and goats, 140,100 cattle and 19,200 pigs in the Republic. Gold extraction was developed from the mid-1990s; in 1996 it amounted to almost one metric ton. Tyva's main industries were ore-mining (asbestos, coal, cobalt and mercury), production of electricity, food-processing and non-ferrous metallurgy. In 2001 industry employed 9.1% of the working population and total production within the sector was worth just 934m. roubles.

The economically active population of Tyva totalled 120,000 in 2001, when 23.9% of the labour force were unemployed—the highest rate of unemployment of any territory outside the Southern Federal Okrug. In mid-2002 the average monthly wage in the Republic was 3,870.5 roubles, somewhat lower than the national average. Moreover, in the late 1990s the Republic was one of the areas of the Russian Federation worst affected by wage arrears and most dependent on federal transfers. In September 2000 the federal Government arranged to pay wage arrears amounting to 216.7m. roubles in Tyva, in addition to providing for improvements to educational and medical services in the Republic. The 2001 budget showed a surplus of 66m. roubles. Foreign investment in the Republic was minimal, and amounted to just US $381,000 in 2000. At 31 December 2001 a total of 619 small businesses were registered in Tyva.

Directory

President (Chairman of the Government): SHERIG-OOL D. OORZHAK; 667000 Tyva, Kyzyl, ul. Chulduma 18, Dom Pravitelstva; tel. (39422) 1-12-77; fax (39422) 3-74-59; e-mail tuva@tuva.ru; internet gov.tuva.ru.

President of the Chamber of Representatives of the Supreme Khural: DANDYR-OOL K.-KH. OORZHAK; 667000 Tyva, Kyzyl, ul. Lenina 32; tel. (39422) 1-31-79; fax (39422) 3-33-71; e-mail parliament@tuva.ru; internet gov.tuva.ru/gosvo/predct_p .htm.

President of the Legislative Chamber of the Supreme Khural: VASILII M. OYUN; 667000 Tyva, Kyzyl, ul. Lenina 32; tel. (39422) 3-74-78; fax (39422) 1-16-32; e-mail parliament@tuva.ru; internet gov.tuva.ru/gosvo/zakdat_p.htm.

Chief Representative of the Republic of Tyva in the Russian Federation: ORLAN O. CHOLBENEI; 119049 Moscow, ul. Donskaya 8/2; tel. (095) 236-48-01; fax (095) 236-45-53.

Head of Kyzyl City Administration (Mayor): DMITRII K. DONGAK; 667000 Tyva, Kyzyl, ul. Lenina 32; tel. (39422) 3-50-55.

FAR EASTERN FEDERAL OKRUG

Amur Oblast

Amur Oblast is situated in the south-east of the Russian Federation, to the west of Khabarovsk Krai. It forms part of the Far Eastern Federal Okrug and the Far Eastern Economic Area. The Jewish (Birobidzhan) Autonomous Oblast lies to the south-east, Chita Oblast to the west and the Republic of Sakha (Yakutiya) to the north. Southwards it has an international border with the People's Republic of China. The Oblast's main river is the Amur, which is 2,900 km (1,800 miles) long in total, and here forms the international border with China, where it is known as the Heilong Jiang. A large reservoir, the Zeya, is situated in the north of the region. A little under three-quarters of the Oblast's territory is forested. Its total area occupies 363,700 sq km (140,430 sq miles) and measures 750 km south to north and 1,150 km south-east to north-west. It is divided into 20 administrative districts and nine cities. According to the preliminary results of the census of 9–16 October 2002, the territory's inhabitants numbered 902,500, and the population density was, therefore, 2.5 per sq km. Most people (65.8%) lived in urban areas. Amur Oblast's administrative centre is at Blagoveshchensk, near the Chinese border, which had a population of 218,800 in 2002, according to provisional census results.

History

The Amur region was first discovered by European Russians in 1639 and came under Russian control in the late 1850s. Part of the pro-Bolshevik Far Eastern Republic (based in Chita) until its reintegration into Russia in 1922, Amur Oblast was formed on 20 October 1932.

In the first year of post-Soviet Russian independence, the federal President, Boris Yeltsin, called for a gubernatorial election to be held in the region in December 1992. However, his appointed head of the administration was defeated. In July 1993 Amur Oblast declared itself a republic, a measure that was not recognized by the federal authorities. The Governor was subsequently dismissed and the Regional Soviet dissolved. In January 1996 the Regional Administration brought action against the Regional Assembly for adopting a Charter, a republican constitution, some of the clauses of which ran counter to federal laws and presidential decrees. In the same month, in accordance with the Charter, the Assembly changed its name to the Council of People's Deputies. In elections to the new legislature, held in March, Communist Party of the Russian Federation (CPRF) candidates won up to 40% of the votes cast. In June President Yeltsin again dismissed the Governor, and appointed Yurii Lyashko, formerly the chief executive of Blagoveshchensk city, in his place. A further gubernatorial election was held on 22 September. It was won by the CPRF candidate, Anatolii Belonogov, by a narrow margin, but the results were subsequently annulled because of alleged irregularities. Belonogov succeeded in securing a clear majority in the repeat election held in March 1997. In gubernatorial elections held in two rounds in March–April 2001 Belonogov was defeated by Leonid Korotkov, hitherto a deputy in the State Duma, and a member of the CPRF until 1999. Legislative elections were held on 25 March 2001. In May–June 2003, in response to the outbreak of Severe Acute Respiratory Syndrome (SARS) in the People's Republic of China and other countries in the Far East, border crossings between the Oblast and China were temporarily closed, causing particular short-term economic disruption to the Oblast. It was also reported in May by the federal Ministry of Health that a hospital patient in Blagoveshchensk had been diagnosed with the disease. Meanwhile, in June Amur Oblast was named by the federal First Deputy Minister of Finance as one of the three federal subjects worst affected by public-sector wage arrears, with delays of more than half a month reported.

Economy

Amur Oblast's gross regional product (GRP) was 26,954m. roubles in 2000, equivalent to 26,908 roubles per head. Its main industrial centres are at Blagoveshchensk, Belogorsk, Raichikhinsk, Zeya, Shimanovsk and Svobodnyi. At the end of 2001 there were 6,975 km of paved roads in the Oblast. There were 2,934 km of railway track, including sections of two major railways, the Trans-Siberian and the Far Eastern (Baikal–Amur). There are five river-ports, at Blagoveshchensk, Svobodnensk, Poyarkovsk, Amursk (all of which transport cargo to and from the People's Republic of China) and Zeisk. There is an international airport at Blagoveshchensk, which serves flights to Japan, the Democratic People's Republic of Korea (North Korea) and the Republic of Korea (South Korea), and (on a charter basis) to Turkey.

Agriculture in Amur Oblast, which employed 9.5% of the work-force in 2001, just over one-half the number employed in the sector in 1995, consists mainly of grain and vegetable production, animal husbandry (including reindeer- and fur-animal-breeding) and bee-keeping. The soil in the south of the region is particularly fertile—in 1998 Amur Oblast contained 57% of the arable land in the Russian Far East and produced 30% of its agricultural output. In 2001 agricultural output in Amur Oblast amounted to 7,940m. roubles, of which crop sales generated 69.3% and animal husbandry 30.7%. In 1998 timber reserves were estimated at 2,000m. cu m. The region is rich in mineral resources, but by the end of the 1990s it was estimated that only around 5% of these resources were being exploited. None the less, the mining sector produced around 15% of GRP in the late 1990s. In the late 1990s around 10–12 metric tons of gold were extracted annually, making the Oblast the third largest producer of gold in Russia. The eventual liberalization of the artisanal sector, which was reported to be supported by the regional authorities in the early 2000s, subject to the approval of the federal parliament, could be expected to increase the output of gold appreciably. Other raw-material deposits in the Oblast include bituminous coal, lignite (brown coal) and kaolin. There are also substantial reserves of iron, titanium and silver ores. In addition, coal-mining is important, as are mechanical engineering, electricity generation, electro-technical industry and the processing of agricultural and forestry products. In 2001 15.8% of the Oblast's work-force were employed in industry, and total output in the sector amounted to a value of 11,704m. roubles. The region contains the Amur Shipbuilding Plant (which in 1997 was contracted to build a 111-sq-km steel platform for a foreign consortium, intended to exploit the petroleum and natural gas fields of Sakhalin Oblast) and produces nuclear-powered submarines. There is a hydroelectric power plant at Zeya, with a reservoir of 2,400 sq km. Two units of another power station, at Bureya, commenced operations in 2003; a third unit was expected to begin operations in 2004.

Amur's economically active population numbered 486,000 in 2001, when 12.2% of the region's labour force were unemployed. Those in employment earned, on average, 4,882.6 roubles per month in mid-2002. There was a budgetary deficit of 317m. roubles in 2001. In that year export trade amounted to a value of US $96.5m., and import trade totalled $21.6m. The Oblast's main trading partners include the People's Republic of China, Japan and North Korea. Foreign investment totalled just $203,000 in 2001. At 31 December 2001 there were 3,829 small businesses registered in the Oblast.

Directory

Head of the Regional Administration: Leonid V. Korotkov; 675023 Amur obl., Blagoveshchensk, ul. Lenina 135; tel. (4162) 44-03-22; fax (4162) 44-62-01; e-mail glava@amurobl.ru; internet www.amurobl.ru.

Chairman of the Regional Council of People's Deputies (Regional Council): Stanislav I. Goryanskii; 675023 Amur obl., Blagoveshchensk, ul. Lenina 135; tel. (4162) 42-46-75; fax (4162) 44-38-58.

Representation of Amur Oblast in the Russian Federation: 127006 Moscow, ul. M. Dmitrovka 3; tel. (095) 299-38-63; fax (095) 299-42-02.

Head of Blagoveshchensk City Administration (Mayor): Aleksandr M. Kolyagin; 675023 Amur obl., Blagoveshchensk, ul. Lenina 133; tel. (4162) 42-49-85.

Chukot Autonomous Okrug

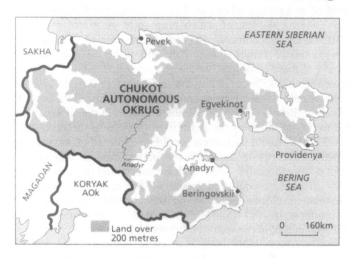

The Chukot Autonomous Okrug (AOk—Chukotka) is situated on the Chukotka Peninsula and an adjacent section of the mainland. The Okrug forms part of the Far Eastern Federal Okrug and the Far Eastern Economic Area. It is the easternmost part of Russia and faces the Eastern Siberian Sea (Arctic Ocean) to the north and the Bering Sea to the south; the Anadyr Gulf, part of the Bering Sea, cuts into the territory from the south-east. The USA (Alaska) lies eastwards across the Bering Straits. The western end of the district borders the Republic of Sakha (Yakutiya) to the west, and Magadan Oblast to the south. Also to the south lies the Koryak AOk (within Kamchatka Oblast). The district's major river is the Anadyr, the area around its estuary being low marshland. The Chukot (sometimes Chukchi) AOk occupies an area of 737,700 sq km (284,830 sq miles), of which approximately one-half lies within the Arctic Circle, and is divided into eight administrative districts and three cities. Its climate is severe; the average temperature in January is –29.2°C, and in July it is 9.4°C. The AOk is a sparsely populated area. According to the preliminary results of the census of 9–16 October 2002, it had a total of 53,600 inhabitants, and a population density of 0.07 per sq km. Approximately 66.4% of the territory's population inhabited urban areas. Around 80,000 people left the AOk between 1991 and 2002, reducing the population by about one-half. According to the census of 1989, ethnic Russians represented 66.1% of the region's total population, while only 7.3% were Chukchi. The Chukchi speak the Chukotic language as their native tongue, which belongs to the Paleo-Asiatic linguistic family. Until the 20th century the Chukchi (who call themselves the Lyg Oravetlyan, and are also known as the Luoravetlan, Chukcha and Chukot) could be subdivided into several distinct tribal groups. Traditionally they were also divided into two economic groups, the nomadic and semi-nomadic reindeer herders (the Chavchu or Chavchuven), and the coastal dwellers (known as the An Kalyn). The district's administrative centre is at Anadyr, which had an estimated population of 12,000 in 2001, compared with 17,000 in 1989.

History

Russian settlers first arrived in the territories inhabited by Chukchi tribes in the mid-17th century. Commercial traders, fur trappers and hunters subsequently established contact with the Chukchi, many of whom were forcibly converted to Orthodox Christianity and enserfed. Economic co-operation continued to expand and reached its height in 1905, with the construction of the Trans-Siberian Railway. A Chukot national okrug was created within Magadan Oblast by the Soviet Government on 10 December 1930, as part of its policy to incorporate the peoples of the north of Russia into the social, political and economic body of the USSR. (It acquired nominally autonomous status in 1980.) Simultaneously, collectivization was introduced into the district. Throughout the 1950s and 1960s eastern Siberia was rapidly industrialized, resulting in extensive migration of ethnic Russians to the area and a drastic reduction of the territory available to the Chukchi for herding reindeer. Many abandoned their traditional way of life to work in industry.

In March 1990 the Chukchi participated in the creation of the Association of the Peoples of the North. They also campaigned for the ratification of two international conventions, which would affirm their right to the ownership and possession of the lands they traditionally inhabited. In February 1991 the legislature of the Chukot AOk seceded from Magadan Oblast and declared the territory the Chukot Soviet Autonomous Republic (the word 'Soviet' was removed from the district's title following the disintegration of the USSR in December). This measure failed to be recognized by the federal Government, although the district was acknowledged as a constituent member of the Federation by the Treaty of March 1992 and, subsequently, as free from the jurisdiction of Magadan Oblast.

At the gubernatorial election held in December 2000, the incumbent Governor, Aleksandr Nazarov, withdrew his candidacy. Roman Abramovich, an 'oligarch' associated with the petroleum company Sibneft (Siberian Oil Co), was elected in his place, receiving 91% of the votes cast. Although Abramovich was generally regarded as a popular Governor in the region, owing largely to improvements to public services and utilities implemented in the Okrug after his election, by 2003 he had made it known that he did not intend to stand for re-election in 2004. Meanwhile, Abramovich sought to cultivate closer ties between the region and the nearby US state of Alaska. The first Alaska-Chukotka summit was held in Nome, Alaska, in mid-2001 to that end; it was intended that this summit would henceforth be an annual occurrence. Following the 2002 summit Abramovich and the Governor of Alaska, Tony Knowles, signed a document that provided for the eventual establishment of regular air services between Nome and Anadyr and for the promotion of co-operation in areas including education, health care, economic development and environmental protection.

Economy

Alone among the autonomous okrugs, Chukotka is no longer included in a larger territory and there has been, therefore, fuller coverage of it in official statistics. In 2000 the AOk's gross regional product amounted to 4,129m. roubles, equivalent to 58,520 roubles per head. Although relatively high, this level of regional wealth was highly dependent on federal transfers. At the end of 2001 the territory had 1,330 km (826 miles) of paved roads and a relatively undeveloped infrastructure. Anadyr is one of the district's major ports, the others being Pevek, Providenya, Egvekinot and Beringovskii.

The AOk's agricultural sector, which employed 8.8% of the work-force in 2001, consists mainly of fishing, animal husbandry (especially reindeer-breeding) and hunting. Total agricultural production was worth 108m. roubles in 2001. In 1992 it was estimated that some 500,000 reindeers were raised in state-controlled breeding areas. The region contains reserves of coal and brown coal (lignite), petroleum and natural gas, as well as gold, tin, wolfram (tungsten), copper and other minerals. It is self-sufficient in energy, containing two coal-mines, six producers of electricity and one nuclear power station. Its main industries are ore-mining, non-ferrous metallurgy (which accounted for 56.3% of total industrial output in 2001), electricity generation and food-processing. Industry employed some 22.1% of the district's working population in 2001 and generated 2,929m. roubles.

The AOk's economically active population numbered 44,000 in 2001. The rate of unemployment has been relatively low, compared with other regions in the Far East of Russia; in 2001 7.4% of the labour force were unemployed. Those in employment in mid-2002 earned an average of 12,195.5 roubles per month, well above the national average, although this was counterbalanced by some of the highest living costs in the Federation; in August 2002 a typical 'consumer basket' cost about three times as much in Anadyr as the national average and, indeed, considerably more than elsewhere in the Russian Far East. The 2001 district government budget showed a surplus of 75m. roubles, representing a considerable improvement compared with earlier years; in 1994 and 1995 the deficit had exceeded the entire gross output of the district. The external trade of the district is minimal, and in 2001 exports amounted to only US $0.1m. and imports to $2.2m. At 31 December 2001 there were 86 small businesses registered in the AOk; an extra-budgetary fund was created for the support and development of small business during 1996 and 1997, although little success was evident.

Directory

Head of the District Administration (Governor): ROMAN A. ABRAMOVICH; 689000 Chukot AOk, Anadyr, ul. Beringa 20; tel. (42722) 2-90-13; fax (42722) 4-24-66; internet www.chukotka.org.

Chairman of the District Duma: VASILII N. NAZARENKO; 689000 Chukot AOk, Anadyr, ul. Otke 29; tel. (42722) 2-25-24; fax (42722) 2-44-70; e-mail dumachao@ mail.ru.

Chief Representative of the Chukot Autonomous Okrug in the Russian Federation: ALEKSANDR V. MOSKALENKO; 119034 Moscow, per. Kursovoi 4; tel. (095) 502-97-30; fax (095) 925-82-27.

Head of Anadyr City Administration: VIKTOR A. KHVAN; 689000 Chukot AOk, Anadyr, ul. Beringa 45; tel. (41361) 2-04-38; fax (41361) 4-22-16.

Jewish Autonomous Oblast

The Jewish Autonomous Oblast (Yevreiskaya AOb—Birobidzhan) is part of the Amur river basin, and is included in Russia's Far Eastern Federal Okrug and Far Eastern Economic Area. It is situated to the south-west of Khabarovsk Krai, on the international border with the People's Republic of China. There is a border with Amur Oblast in the north-west. Apart from the River Amur (Heilong Jiang), which is frozen for around five months of the year, the region's major river is the Tungusk. Forest, which is particularly concentrated in the north-west, covers more than one-third of its territory. Around one-half is mountainous, with the south and east occupying the western edge of the Central Amur Lowlands. It occupies 36,000 sq km (13,900 sq miles) and has five administrative districts and two cities. According to the preliminary results of the census of 9–16 October 2002, the Jewish AOb had a population of 190,900, and a population density, therefore, of 5.3 per sq km. Around 67.3% of its population inhabited urban areas. The census of 1989 found that, according to official declaration of nationality, ethnic Russians accounted for some 83.2% of the Jewish AOb's population and Jews for 4.2% (although this figure can be expected to have decreased subsequently; in the early 1950s Jews had constituted around one-quarter of the population of the region). Indeed, in 1990 alone, around 1,000 of the 9,000 resident in the oblast in the previous year whose nationality was officially registered as Jewish emigrated to Israel. The regional capital is at Birobidzhan, which had an estimated population of 78,400 in January 2001.

History

The majority of Russian Jews came under Russian control following the Partitions of Poland in 1772–95. Attempts by the Soviet authorities in the 1920s to create nominally Jewish regions in Ukraine and Crimea were largely unsuccessful, because of hostility on the part of the local population in these regions, although some nominally Jewish adminstrative sub-districts existed in southern Ukraine prior to the Nazi German invasion of the USSR in 1941. The Soviet regime established a national Jewish district at Birobidzhan in 1928, but it never became the centre of

Soviet (or Russian) Jewry, largely because of its remote location and the absence of any prior Jewish settlement there. (In Imperial Russia, between 1835 and 1917, Jews were required to receive special permission to live outside the 'Pale of Settlement' in the south-west of the Empire, which constituted territories largely in present-day Belarus, Lithuania, Poland and Ukraine.) This province received the status of an Autonomous Oblast in May 1934 and formed part of Khabarovsk Krai until 25 March 1991.

In the early post-Soviet period the region remained a redoubt of communist support. Despite the advice of the Russian President, Boris Yeltsin, at a session on 14 October 1993 the Regional Soviet announced that it would not disband itself. Subsequently, however, the council was replaced by a new body, the Legislative Assembly, elections to which confirmed Communist Party domination. A gubernatorial election held on 20 October 1996 was won by the incumbent, Nikolai Volkov; he was re-elected with 57% of the votes cast on 26 March 2000.

Economy

In 2000 the Jewish AOb's gross regional product stood at 3,824m. roubles, equivalent to 19,282 roubles per head—the lowest level in the Far Eastern Federal Okrug. Birobidzhan is the region's main industrial centre. At the end of 2001 there were 309 km (192 miles) of railway track, including a section of the Trans-Siberian Railway, and 1,615 km of paved roads on the region's territory. In February 2000 the opening of a bridge across the Amur river provided improved road and rail links with the city of Khabarovsk and the People's Republic of China. There are around 600 km of navigable waterways in the south of the Jewish AOb.

Agriculture, which employed 13.3% of the region's work-force in 2001, and generated a total of 1,232m. roubles in that year, consists mainly of grain, soybean, vegetable and potato production, and animal husbandry. (Of the total value of agricultural production in 2001, crop sales accounted for 63.2% and animal husbandry for 36.8%.) From the late 1990s the oblast authorities encouraged Chinese farmers to undertake agricultural activity (both arable and livestock) in the region; greater diversity of crops, as well as an improvement in productivity, resulting in part from a higher level of farming technology, were reported as a result, although concern was expressed in early 2003 about the number of illegal immigrants in the region. There are major deposits of coal, peat, iron ore, manganese, tin, gold, graphite, magnesite and zeolite, although they are largely unexploited. The main industries are mechanical engineering and metal-working, the manufacture of building materials, the production of electricity, wood-working and light manufacturing. Industry employed around 15.7% of the Jewish AOb's working population and generated a total of 1,269m. roubles in 2001. In the mid-1990s the region's foreign economic activity was largely concentrated in the Far East, including the People's Republic of China and Japan.

In 2001 the Jewish AOb's economically active population numbered 94,000. Although more than one-quarter of the labour force were unemployed in 1997, by 2001 the unemployment rate had declined to 9.5%. In mid-2002 the average monthly wage in the Birobidzhan region was 4,254.2 roubles. The 2001 budget showed a surplus of 36m. roubles. In that year external trade amounted to a value of US $16.7m. in exports and $4.0m. in imports. In 2001 foreign investment amounted to just $9,000; five of the seven foreign- or jointly owned enterprises operating in the territory had Chinese partners. At 31 December 2001 571 small businesses were registered in the region.

Directory

Head of the Regional Administration (Governor and Chairman of the Government): NIKOLAI M. VOLKOV; 682200 Jewish AOb, Birobidzhan, pr. 60-letiya SSSR 18; tel. and fax (42622) 6-04-89; e-mail gov@eao.ru; internet www.eao.ru.

Chairman of the Legislative Assembly: ANATOLII F. TIKHOMIROV; 682200 Jewish AOb, Birobidzhan, pr. 60-letiya SSSR 18; tel. (42622) 6-44-27; fax (42622) 6-04-78; e-mail press-zs@eao.ru; internet www.eao.ru/?p=22.

Representation of the Jewish Autonomous Oblast in the Russian Federation: Moscow.

Head of Birobidzhan City Administration: ALEKSANDR VINNIKOV; Jewish AOb, 682200 Birobidzhan, ul. Lenina 29; tel. (42622) 6-22-02; fax (42622) 4-04-93.

Kamchatka Oblast

Kamchatka Oblast occupies the Kamchatka Peninsula in the easternmost part of Russia and is, therefore, part of the Far Eastern Federal Okrug and the Far Eastern Economic Area. The Peninsula, some 1,600 km (1,000 miles) in length and 130 km in width, separates the Sea of Okhotsk, in the west, from the Bering Sea, in the east. The Oblast also includes the Karaginskiye and Komandorskiye (Commander) Islands and the southernmost part of the Chukotka Peninsula. In the latter area there are land borders with other Russian federal territories, the Chukot Autonomous Okrug (AOk) to the north and Magadan Oblast to the west. This part of the Oblast, together with the northern section of the Kamchatka Peninsula, comprises the Koryak AOk (see separate chapter below). The region is dominated by the Sredinnyi Khrebet mountain range, which is bounded to the west by a broad, poorly drained coastal plain, and to the east by the Kamchatka river valley. The territory's other main river is the Avacha. Two-thirds of its area is mountainous (including the highest point in the Russian Far East, Mt Klyuchevskaya, at 4,685 m—15,961 feet) and it contains many hot springs. Kamchatka Oblast covers an area of 472,300 sq km (182,350 sq miles), including the autonomous okrug, but only 170,800 sq km (65,946 sq miles), excluding the Koryak AOk. The Oblast, excluding the AOk, is divided into seven administrative districts and four cities. There is a high annual rate of precipitation in the region, sometimes as much as 2,000 mm, and temperatures vary considerably according to region. The average temperature for January is −16.4°C, while that for July is 13.0°C. According to the preliminary results of the census of 9–16 October 2002, the total population of the region (excluding the Koryak AOk) was 333,800 and the population density, therefore, was 2.0 per sq km (including the okrug, the density was only 0.8 per sq km); some 85.2% of the region's population inhabited urban areas. The Oblast's administrative centre is at Petropavlovsk-Kamchatskii, in the south-east, which was inhabited by 198,200 people in 2002, according to provisional census results.

History

The Kamchatka Peninsula was first sighted in 1697 and was annexed by Russia during the 18th century. Petropavlovsk came under Russian control in 1743. After the Soviet Revolution Kamchatka was part of the short-lived Far Eastern Republic. A distinct Kamchatka Oblast was formed on 20 October 1923, but as part of Khabarovsk Krai until 23 January 1956.

Following the dissolution of the USSR in 1991, Kamchatka tended to be supportive of the federal Government. In the general election of December 1995, however, the most successful party was the liberal Yabloko, which obtained 20% of the votes cast in the Oblast (a higher proportion than the reformists obtained even in the great cities). This success was largely because the local candidate, Mikhail Zadornov, was a popular figure, who was subsequently appointed as the federal Minister of Finance in 1997. Yabloko repeated this success in the oblast legislative elections of December 1997, in which it won nine seats, coming second only to the Communist Party of the Russian Federation (CPRF), with 10. However, as the Oblast continued to suffer from economic and social hardship, support for the CPRF and its left-wing supporters experienced a resurgence. At the gubernatorial election held in December 2000, the CPRF candidate, Mikhail Mashkovtsev, was elected Governor; the incumbent, Vladimir Biryukov, had declined to stand.

A particular source of tension in the region in the early 2000s was the accumulation of debts by Petropavlovsk-Kamchatskii municipality (headed by Mayor Yurii Golenishchev) to energy companies, and the consequent disruption to power supplies in the oblast capital. In mid-December 2003 the Petropavlovsk-Kamchatskii municipal court ruled that Golenishchev be suspended, pending the conclusion of a criminal investigation into allegations that he had misused budgetary funds and failed to provide adequate heating to city residents.

Economy

The waters around Kamchatka Oblast (the Sea of Okhotsk, the Bering Sea and the Pacific Ocean) being extremely rich in marine life, fishing, especially of crabs, is the dominant sector of Kamchatka Oblast's economy, accounting for over 90% of its trade in the mid-1990s. The region's fish stocks comprise around one-half of Russia's total. All figures in this survey incorporate data for the Koryak AOk, which is also treated separately (see below). In 2000 the Oblast's gross regional product amounted to 18,348m. roubles, or 48,190 roubles per head. Petropavlovsk is one of two main industrial centres and ports in the territory, the other being Ust-Kamchatka. There is an international airport, Yelizovo, situated 30 km from Petropavlovsk-Kamchatskii. In 2000 there were 1,338 km of paved roads in the Oblast.

Apart from fishing, agriculture in Kamchatka Oblast consists of vegetable production, animal husbandry (livestock, reindeer, mostly in the Koryak AOk, and fur animals) and hunting. Just 4.2% of the working population were employed in agriculture in 2001, when agricultural output amounted to 1,724m. roubles (of which crop sales accounted for 63.5% and animal husbandry for 36.5%). There are deposits of gold, silver, natural gas, sulphur and other minerals in Kamchatka Oblast, which by the early 2000s had been explored and were in the process of development. The relatively limited industrial sector, which employed 23.0% of the work-force in 2001, is based on the processing of agricultural products, non-ferrous metallurgy and coal and electricity production. The first geothermal energy plant in Russia, at Mutnovo, commenced operations in October 2002; by 2003 the plant was expected to produce annual output of 50 MW, representing one-quarter of the Oblast's energy requirements. Total industrial output was worth 19,978m. roubles in 2001.

The economically active population of Kamchatka Oblast numbered 232,000 in 2001, when 14.5% of the labour force were unemployed—the highest rate of unemployment within the Far Eastern Federal Okrug. Those in employment earned an average of 8,177.6 roubles per month in mid-2002, a relatively high wage compared with the rest of the Russian Federation, but one balanced by the high cost of living in the Oblast (in that year the cost of a 'consumer basket' of foodstuffs in Petropavlovsk-Kamchatskii was the second highest in the Federation, behind Anadyr, the capital of the remote Chukot AOk). Moreover, wage arrears prompted municipal workers in Petropavlovsk-Kamchatskii to observe a widespread strike from late November. There was a budgetary deficit of 620m. roubles in 2001. Foreign investment in the Oblast amounted to US $78.4m. in that year, although international trade was limited, amounting to just $155.4m. in exports and $46.7m. in imports. With trade dominated by the fishing industry, one of the Oblast's main foreign markets was Japan. At 31 December 2001 there were 1,576 small businesses registered in the region.

Directory

Governor: MIKHAIL B. MASHKOVTSEV; 683040 Kamchatka obl., Petropavlovsk-Kamchatskii, pl. Lenina 1; tel. (4152) 11-20-96; fax (4152) 11-20-96; e-mail kra@svyaz.kamchatka.su.

Chairman of the Legislative Assembly: NIKOLAI YA. TOKOMANTSEV; 683040 Kamchatka obl., Petropavlovsk-Kamchatskii, pl. Lenina 1; tel. (4152) 11-27-61; fax (4152) 11-26-95.

Chief Representative of Kamchatka Oblast in the Russian Federation: MIKHAIL M. SITNIKOV; 119002 Moscow, Denezhnyi per. 12/16; tel. (095) 241-03-13; fax (095) 241-35-46.

Head of Petropavlovsk-Kamchatskii City Administration (Mayor): (vacant); 683040 Kamchatka obl., Petropavlovsk-Kamchatskii, ul. Leninskaya 14; tel. (41522) 2-49-13; e-mail citiadm@svyaz.kamchatka.su.

Koryak Autonomous Okrug

The Koryak Autonomous Okrug (AOk) comprises the northern part of the Kamchatka Peninsula and the adjacent area of mainland. It forms part of the Far Eastern Federal Okrug and the Far Eastern Economic Area, and of Kamchatka Oblast. Its eastern coastline lies on the Bering Sea, and its western shores face the Shelekhov Gulf (Sea of Okhotsk). South of the district lies the rest of Kamchatka Oblast. In the north it is bordered by the Chukot AOk and Magadan Oblast, to the north and to the west, respectively. The Koryak AOk occupies 301,500 sq km (116,410 sq miles) and is divided, for administrative purposes, into four districts and two 'urban-type settlements'. According to the preliminary results of the census of 9–16 October 2002, its total population was 25,000, and its population density, therefore, stood at just 0.08 per sq km. Just 26.0% of the population inhabited urban areas. The 1989 census showed that 62.0% of the AOk's population were ethnically Russian, 7.2% were Ukrainian, 16.4% Koryak, 3.6% Chukchi and 3.0% Itelmeni. The administrative centre of the district is at Palana, which had a population of just 4,100 at 1 January 2001.

History

The area was established as a territorial unit within Kamchatka Oblast on 10 December 1930. Like the Chukchi, the Koryaks comprise nomadic and semi-nomadic hunters and more sedentary coastal dwellers. They first encountered ethnic Russians in the 1640s, when Cossacks, commercial traders and fur trappers arrived in the district. The Soviet Government attempted to collectivize the Koryaks' economic activity, beginning with the fishing industry in 1929 and continuing with reindeer hunting in 1932, a measure that was violently opposed by the Koryak community. After the Second World War large numbers of ethnic Russians moved to the area, which was becoming increasingly industrialized. The resultant threat to the Koryaks' traditional way of life, and environmental deterioration, became a source of contention between the local community and the federal Government during the period of *glasnost* (openness) in the late 1980s. In the first years of independence, however, the local élite were sufficiently placated to be generally supportive of both the federal Government and, indeed, of the reformists.

An independent candidate, Valentina Bronevich, was elected Governor in late 1996, the first woman to head the administration of a territorial unit in the Russian Federation. On 5 May 1999 Bronevich signed a co-operation agreement with the Governor of Kamchatka Oblast. On 3 December 2000 a local businessman, Vladimir Loginov, defeated Bronevich in a gubernatorial election, receiving 51% of the votes cast. The okrug Duma is the only legislative body of any federal subject, apart from those of the two cities of federal status, to consist in its entirety of paid deputies.

Economy

Much economic data on the Koryak AOk is incorporated into the figures for Kamchatka Oblast, although certain indicators are available. Fishing is the most important economic activity in the district, contributing 60% of total industrial output.

The district's agriculture, which employed just 8.8% of the work-force in 2001, consists mainly of reindeer-breeding, fur-farming and hunting. Total agricultural output was worth 69m. roubles in that year. The main industries are the production of non-ferrous metals (primarily palladium and platinum) and food-processing (which in 2001 accounted for 41.9% and 52.1% of total output, respectively) and the extraction of brown coal (lignite). Industry employed 27.3% of the work-force and generated a total of 4,155m. roubles in 2001.

The economically active population numbered 17,000 in 2001, when 15.2% of the labour force were unemployed. The average monthly wage was some 8,223.9 roubles in mid-2002. The budget recorded a deficit of 109m. roubles in 2001. By the early 2000s the okrug remained impoverished and dependent on federal subsidies; in 1999 it had been named as being among the federal subjects with the highest rates of inflation and the least promising opportunities for investment, and in 2002 was identified as one of the worst regions for wage arrears. In 2001 the region attracted foreign investment worth US $4.3m. At the end of that year 43 small businesses were registered in the territory.

Directory

Governor: VLADIMIR A. LOGINOV; 684620 Kamchatka obl., Koryak AOk, PGT Palana, ul. Porotova 22; tel. (41543) 3-13-80; fax (41543) 3-13-70.

Chairman of the District Duma: VLADIMIR I. ZUYEV; 684620 Kamchatka obl., Koryak AOk, PGT Palana, ul. Porotova 22; tel. (41543) 3-10-30.

Representation of the Koryak Autonomous Okrug in Kamchatka Oblast: Kamchatka obl., Petropavlovsk-Kamchatskii.

Chief Representative of the Koryak Autonomous Okrug in the Russian Federation: IRINA V. YEVDOKIMOVA; Moscow; tel. (095) 921-90-96.

Khabarovsk Krai

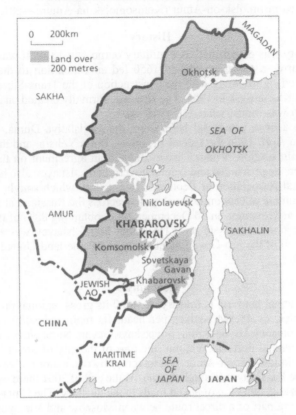

Khabarovsk Krai is situated in the Far East, on the Sea of Okhotsk and the Tatar Strait. The region forms part of the Far Eastern Federal Okrug and the Far Eastern Economic Area. Maritime Krai lies to the south, the Jewish Autonomous Oblast (Birobidzhan—part of the Krai until 1991) is to the south-west, Amur Oblast lies to the west, the Republic of Sakha (Yakutiya) to the north-west and, in the north of the province, Magadan Oblast lies to the east. The island of Sakhalin (part of Sakhalin Oblast) lies off shore to the east, across the Tatar Strait. There is a short international border with the People's Republic of China in the south-west. Khabarovsk's main river is the Amur (Heilong Jiang), which rises near the Russo–Chinese border and flows into the Tatar Strait at the town of Nikolayevsk-on-Amur (Nikolayevsk-na-Amure). More than one-half of the Krai's total area of 788,600 sq km (304,400 sq miles) is forested and almost three-quarters comprises mountains or plateaux. The territory, one of the largest in the Federation, measures 1,780 km (1,105 miles) south to north and 7,000 km west to east. Its coastline is 2,500 km long. It is divided into 17 administrative districts and seven cities. The climate is monsoon-like in character, with hot, humid summers. Annual average precipitation in mountain areas can be as much as 1,000 mm (40 inches), while in the north it averages 500 mm. According to the preliminary results of the census of 9–16 October 2002, the total population of Khabarovsk Krai was 1,435,400; the population density was 1.8 per sq km. Some

80.6% of the population lived in urban areas. Khabarovsk Krai's administrative centre is at Khabarovsk, which had a population of 582,700. The Krai's second largest city is Komsomolsk-on-Amur (Komsomolsk-na-Amure—281,000).

History

Khabarovsk city was established as a military outpost in 1858. It was named after Yerofei Khabarov, a Cossack, who in 1650 led an expedition to the region. The region prospered significantly with the construction of the Trans-Siberian Railway, which reached Khabarovsk in 1905. The Krai was formally created on 20 September 1938. The area was industrialized in 1946–80.

Elections to a new, provincial legislature, the Legislative Duma, were held in March 1994. In April 1996 the federal President, Boris Yeltsin, and the head of the provincial administration, Viktor Ishayev, signed an agreement on the division of powers between the provincial and federal governments. Ishayev also headed the Far East-Transbaikal Association of Economic Interaction, which sought to promote a coherent programme of economic development across the Russian Far East. Ishayev was re-elected as Governor on 10 December 2000, obtaining 88% of the votes cast. Legislative elections were held on 9 December 2001. Ishayev was elected to the Supreme Council of the pro-Government Unity and Fatherland-United Russia party in March 2003.

Economy

The Krai's principal land use is forestry. In 2000 its gross regional product totalled 68,684m. roubles, or 45,424 roubles per head. Its main industrial centres are at Khabarovsk, Komsomolsk-on-Amur, Sovetskaya Gavan, Nikolayevsk-on-Amur and Amursk. Its principal ports are Vanino (the port of the city of Sovetskaya Gavan), Okhotsk and Nikolayevsk-on-Amur. It is traversed by two major railways, the Trans-Siberian and the Far Eastern (Baikal–Amur). At the end of 2001 there were 2,307 km of railway lines and 4,953 km of paved roads in the territory. The Chita–Khabarovsk highway (forming part of a direct route between Moscow and Vladivostok) opened in September 2003. A ferry service runs between the Krai and Sakhalin Oblast. The Krai is the most important Far Eastern territory in terms of its national and international air services, which connect Moscow and other European cities with Japan.

Agriculture, which employed just 4.1% of the working population in 2001 and generated 5,167m. roubles, consists mainly of the production of grain, soybeans, vegetables and fruit, animal husbandry (including reindeer breeding) and hunting. Of the total value of production in 2001, crop sales generated 60.9% and animal husbandry 39.1%. Hunting is practised on about 97.5% of the Krai's territory. The Krai's main industries are mechanical engineering, electricity production, metal-working, non-ferrous and ferrous metallurgy, food-processing, the processing of forestry products, extraction of coal (2.0m. metric tons of which were mined in 2000), ores and non-ferrous metals, shipbuilding (including oil rigs) and petroleum-refining. Some 21.9% of the territory's work-force were engaged in industry in 2001, when total industrial output amounted to a value of 69,444m. roubles.

Khabarovsk Krai's economically active population numbered 776,000 in 2001, when 10.3% of the labour force were unemployed. In mid-2002 the average monthly wage was 5,639.5 roubles. In 2001 the provincial administration recorded a budgetary deficit of 403m. roubles. In the 1990s the territory began to develop its trade links with 'Pacific Rim' nations apart from Japan (with which it had a long trading history), such as Canada, the People's Republic of China, the Democratic People's Republic of Korea (North Korea) and the Republic of Korea (South Korea), Australia, New Zealand, Singapore and the USA. Its exports largely consisted of raw materials (timber, petroleum products, fish and metals). External trade amounted to a value of some US $2,352.1m. in exports and $145.9m. in imports in 2001. In common with other regions of the Russian Far East, economic activity was disrupted in early 2003 by the outbreak of Severe Acute Respiratory Syndrome (SARS) in China and other countries of the Far East, and border crossings were temporarily closed in May–June. In 2001 total foreign investment amounted to $19.9m. According to the regional foreign investment promotion agency, in January 2000 731 joint ventures were registered in the territory. At 31 December 2001 8,256 small businesses were in operation.

Directory

Head of the Provincial Administration (Governor): VIKTOR I. ISHAYEV; 680000 Khabarovsk, ul. K. Marksa 56; tel. (4212) 33-55-40; fax (4212) 33-87-56; internet www.adm.khv.ru.

Chairman of the Provincial Legislative Duma: YURII I. ONOPRIYENKO; 680002 Khabarovsk, ul. Muravyeva-Amurskogo 19; tel. (4212) 32-52-19; fax (4212) 32-44-57; e-mail duma@duma.khv.ru; internet www.duma.khv.ru.

Chief Representative of Khabarovsk Krai in the Russian Federation: ANDREI B. CHIRKIN; 127025 Moscow, ul. Novyi Arbat 19; tel. (095) 203-41-28; fax (095) 203-83-25; e-mail khab.rep@g23.relcom.ru; internet www.khabrep.ru.

Head of Khabarovsk City Administration (Mayor): ALEKSANDR N. SOKOLOV; 680000 Khabarovsk, ul. K. Marksa 66; tel. (4212) 23-58-67; fax (4212) 33-53-46; internet www.khabarovsk.kht.ru.

Magadan Oblast

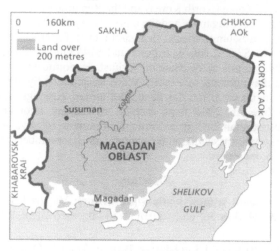

Magadan Oblast is situated in the north-east of Russia and forms part of the Far Eastern Federal Okrug and the Far Eastern Economic Area. To the north-east, on the Chukotka Peninsula, lies the Chukot Autonomous Okrug (AOk), which, until 1992, formed part of Magadan Oblast. The rest of its border with territory on Chukotka is with the Koryak AOk (Kamchatka Oblast), which lies to the east. Magadan has a coastline on the Sea of Okhotsk in the south-east. Khabarovsk Krai lies to the south-west of the region and the Republic of Sakha (Yakutiya) to the north-west. Its main river is the Kolyma, which flows northwards and drains into the Arctic Ocean by way of Sakha. A considerable proportion of the territory of the region is mountainous, whereas the south is dominated by larch forests and coastal marshland. Much of the Oblast is tundra or forest-tundra. The Oblast occupies a total area of 461,400 sq km (178,150 sq miles—much reduced from when it included the Chukot AOk). It is divided into six administrative districts and two cities. The climate in the region is severe, with winters lasting from six to over seven months. The average temperature in January is –29.4°C, while that in July is 14.4°C. According to the preliminary results of the census of 9–16 October 2002, the Oblast had a total population of 182,700. It is one of the most sparsely populated regions, with a population density of just 0.4 per sq km. The majority of the population (92.3%) inhabited urban areas. The Oblast's administrative centre is at the only large city in the Oblast, Magadan, which had an estimated population of 120,600 in 2001.

History

Russians first reached the Magadan region in the mid-17th century. At the beginning of the Soviet period it was in the Far Eastern Republic, which in 1922 was reintegrated into Russia. The region held many penal establishments of the GULAG (State Corrective Camp) system established during the regime of Stalin—Iosif Dzhugashvili (1924–53). Magadan Oblast was formed on 3 December 1953, after the death of Stalin, although it then included the Chukot national district. The successful rejection of Magadan's jurisdiction over the Chukot AOk (as it had by then become—acknowledged by the federal authorities in 1992) significantly reduced Magadan's territory.

Deteriorating social conditions contributed to local feeling of remoteness and of neglect by the centre in the 1990s. Thus, in the elections to the State Duma held in December 1995, candidates of the nationalist Liberal Democratic Party of Russia secured 22% of the votes cast in the region and remained relatively popular there during the late 1990s. The gubernatorial election of 3 November 1996 was won by a gold-mine proprietor, Valentin Tsvetkov, who was backed by the communist-dominated Popular-Patriotic Union. In May 1999 a special economic zone was created in the Oblast, in the hope that investors would facilitate the exploitation of the region's rich natural resources. Tsvetkov was re-elected as Governor in November 2000; however, in mid-October 2002 he was shot and killed in Moscow, in an apparent contract killing. He was succeeded, on an acting basis, by Nikolai Dudov, hitherto First Vice-Governor of the Oblast. Following the first round of gubernatorial elections, held on 2 February 2003 and contested by 12 candidates, Dudov, who received 26.0% of the votes cast, and Nikolai Karpenko, the Mayor of Magadan (who was supported by the pro-Government Unity and Fatherland-United Russia party), with 37.6%, proceeded to a second round, held on 16 February. In this poll Dudov obtained 50.4% of the votes cast, thereby being elected as Governor.

Economy

Magadan Oblast is Russia's principal gold-producing region. In 2000 its gross regional product amounted to 12,760m. roubles, equivalent to 55,480 roubles per head. The Oblast's main industrial centres are at Magadan and Susuman. Magadan and Nagayevo are its most important ports. There are no railways in the territory, but there were 2,231 km (1,386 miles) of paved roads at the end of 2001. There is an international airport at Magadan.

The region's primary economic activities are fishing, animal husbandry and hunting. These and other agricultural activities, which employed 3.2% of the region's work-force, generated just 419m. roubles in 2001. Ore-mining is important: apart from gold, the region contains considerable reserves of silver, tin and wolfram (tungsten). It is also rich in peat and timber. In early 1998 the regional Government hired a prospecting company to explore offshore petroleum deposits in the Sea of Okhotsk, in a zone thought to hold around 5,000m. metric tons of petroleum and natural gas. The Kolyma river is an important source of hydroelectric energy. In 1997 the Pan American Silver Corporation of Canada purchased a 70% stake in local company ZAO Dukat, to reopen a defunct silver mine in the Oblast, which contained an estimated 477m. troy ounces of silver and 1m. troy ounces of gold. However, licensing and other bureaucratic obstacles delayed operations. Other industry includes non-ferrous metallurgy (which accounted for 57.1% of total industrial output in 2001), food-processing, electricity generation, mechanical engineering and metal-working. In 2001 23.2% of the working population were engaged in industry, and industrial output amounted to a value of 12,334m. roubles. Construction is a significant source of employment, engaging 10.6% of the labour force in 2001.

The economically active population of the Oblast numbered 138,000 in 2001, when 11.7% of the labour force were unemployed. The average monthly wage was some 7,101.1 roubles in mid-2002, one of the highest figures in the Federation, although the region was also among those with the highest cost of living. In 2001 the budget recorded a deficit of 243m. roubles, and throughout the 1990s persistent deficit problems, not helped by high wages, led to continuing problems with payment arrears. The value of external trade was relatively low; in 2001 exports were worth only US $2.8m., while imports amounted to $55.4m. Foreign investment in the Oblast amounted to $26.4m. in 2001. At 31 December 2001 there were some 2,900 small businesses registered in the Oblast.

Directory

Governor: Nikolai N. Dudov; 685000 Magadan, ul. Gorkogo 6; tel. (41322) 2-31-34; fax (41322) 2-04-25; e-mail info@magadan.ru; internet www.magadan.ru.

Chairman of the Regional Duma: Stanislav A. Yeliseikin; 685000 Magadan, ul. Gorkogo 6; tel. (41322) 2-31-00; fax (41322) 2-55-12.

Representation of Magadan Oblast in the Russian Federation: 103025 Moscow, ul. Novyi Arbat 19; tel. (095) 203-92-74.

Head of Magadan City Administration (Mayor): Nikolai B. Karpenko; 685000 Magadan, pl. Gorkogo 1; tel. (41300) 2-50-47; fax (41322) 2-49-40; e-mail admin@cityadm.magadan.ru; internet www.cityadm.magadan.ru.

Maritime (Primorskii) Krai

Maritime (Primorskii) Krai—Primorye is situated in the extreme south-east of Russia, on the Tatar Strait and the Sea of Japan. The province is part of the Far Eastern Federal Okrug and the Far Eastern Economic Area. Its only border with another federal subject is with Khabarovsk Krai to the north. There is an international border with the People's Republic of China to the west and a short border with the Democratic People's Republic of Korea (North Korea) in the south-west. The province's major river is the Ussuri. The territory occupies 165,900 sq km (64,060 sq miles), more than two-thirds of which is forested. It is divided into 24 administrative districts and 12 cities. According to the preliminary results of the census of 9–16 October 2002, the total number of inhabitants in the territory was 2,068,200 and the population density was, therefore, 12.5 per sq km. Some 78.3% of the population lived in urban areas. Maritime Krai's administrative centre is at Vladivostok, which had 591,800 inhabitants in 2002. Other major cities are Ussuriisk (formerly Voroshilov—157,800) and Nakhodka (149,300).

History

The territories of the Maritime Krai were recognized as Chinese possessions by Russia in the Treaty of Nerchinsk in 1687. They became part of the Russian Empire in 1860, however, being ceded by China under the terms of the Treaty of Peking (Beijing), and the port of Vladivostok was founded. Along with other Transbaikal and Pacific regions of the former Russian Empire, the territory was part of the Far Eastern Republic until its reintegration into Russia under Soviet rule in 1922. Maritime Krai was created on 20 October 1938.

The territory declared itself a republic in mid-1993, but was not recognized as such by the federal authorities. In 28 October 1993 the provincial Governor disbanded the Soviet. Elections for a provincial Governor, set for October 1994, were cancelled by presidential decree, after alleged improprieties by the incumbent, Yevgenii Nazdratenko, during his election campaign. Nazdratenko was elected, however, in December 1995, with 76% of the votes cast, and was re-elected by a similar majority in December 1999. His populist style of government and control of the local media reinforced his position.

The Governor's disputes with the central Government continued after his election—in October 1996 the head of the Presidential Administration, Anatolii Chubais, publicly blamed Nazdratenko for the serious energy crisis in the region, citing his failure to introduce market reforms. The ongoing energy crisis, owing to non-payment of bills, finally forced the resignation of Nazdratenko (officially on health grounds) in February 2001, whereupon he was appointed Chairman of the federal State Committee for Fisheries. (He was suspended in February 2002, following a dispute over regional quotas, and dismissed in April, whereupon he was appointed as Deputy Secretary of the Security Council.) In gubernatorial elections held in May–June 2001, Sergei Darkin, a local businessman, who was intitially regarded as Nazdratenko's preferred successor, was elected Governor in the second round of voting, with 40% of the votes cast. He defeated Gennadii Apanasenko, the deputy presidential representative to the region; Viktor Cherepkov, the former Mayor of Vladivostok, who had taken second place in the first round of voting, behind Darkin, was barred from standing as a candidate in the second round of the elections by the provincial court, which cited irregularities in his campaign. Cherepkov encouraged his supporters to vote against all candidates in the 'run-off' election, and 33.7% of voters did so.

Regional legislative elections, held in December 2001, were declared invalid for 18 of the 39 seats, as the rate of voter participation was lower than the 25% required to legitimize the results, particularly in the large cities. Repeat elections, in which the majority of votes were cast by supporters of Nazdratenko, were held in June 2002; although the rate of participation by the electorate was just 18%, the elections were declared valid, as the 25% threshold had been abolished. Between mid-2001 and late 2002 there were reported to have been more than 30 contract killings, mostly of businessmen, in the region; consequently the security services of the Krai were placed under special federal supervision.

Economy

Maritime Krai's gross regional product totalled 66,342m. roubles in 2000, equivalent to 30,628 roubles per head. Its major industrial centres are at Vladivostok, the terminus of the Trans-Siberian Railway, Ussuriisk, Nakhodka, Dalnegorsk and Lesozavodsk. The Krai's most important ports are at Vladivostok, Nakhodka and Vostochnyi (formerly Vrangel). Vessels based in these ports comprise around four-fifths of maritime transport services in the Far East. In late 2003 there were indications that the Russian Government might agree to a Japanese proposal to construct an export pipeline to transport petroleum from Siberia to Nakhodka. Maritime Krai has rail links with Khabarovsk Krai and, hence, other regions, as well as international transport links with North Korea and the Republic of Korea (South Korea). At the end of 2001 there were 1,553 km (965 miles) of railway lines and 7,076 km of paved roads on the Krai's territory.

The Krai's agricultural sector, which employed 8.3% of the labour force in 2001, consists mainly of grain, vegetable and soybean production, animal husbandry (including fur-farming), bee-keeping and fishing. Total agricultural output in 2001 amounted to a value of 6,752m. roubles, of which crop sales accounted for 63.8% and animal husbandry for 36.2%. Illicit agricultural activities were also thought to include the cultivation of marijuana, particularly in the Khankai district. The Krai contains some 1,200m. metric tons of coal reserves. The hydroelectric-energy potential of the region's rivers is estimated at 25,000m. kWh, and timber reserves are estimated at 1,500m.–1,800m. cu m. Its main industries are food-processing (which accounted for 40.6% of industrial production in 2001), fuel and electrical-energy production, ore-mining, the processing of fish and forestry products, mechanical engineering and ship repairs, metal-working and timber processing. Total industrial production was worth 44,889m. roubles in 2001, when the sector employed 20.4% of the working population. Energy production in the Krai was hindered by political mismanagement from the mid-1990s. Dalenergo, its electricity-generation monopoly, was notorious as one of the worst-performing utilities in the country, unable to collect accounts, service debts or pay for fuel, which led to fuel shortages and frequent strikes by its workers. The territory is ideally placed, in terms of its proximity to the Pacific nations, for international trade, although the perception of widespread corruption restrained its development. A new railway crossing into the People's Republic of China at Makhalino-Hunchun, which was expected to carry an eventual 3m. tons of cargo annually, opened in August 1998. The construction of a cross-border trade and economic centre, uniting the city of Pogranichnyi, in the Krai, with Suifenhe, in China, commenced in early 2003, and was due for completion in 2005. In common with other areas of the Russian Far East, restrictions on cross-border travel were implemented in May–June 2003, during the outbreak of Severe Acute Respiratory Syndrome (SARS) in China and other countries of the region.

The economically active population of Maritime Krai numbered 1,142,000 in 2001, when 8.6% of the labour force were unemployed. The average monthly wage was 4,573.2 roubles in mid-2002—the lowest figure of any territory within the Far Eastern Federal Okrug. In 2001 there was a budgetary deficit of 295m. roubles. External export trade amounted to US $1,146m. in that year, when imports totalled $466.1m. According to the European Bank for Reconstruction and Development, the Krai had huge investment potential; foreign investment totalled $108.6m. in 2001. In August 1997 Hyundai (of South Korea), opened a $100m. hotel and business centre in Vladivostok. South Korea also planned to create an industrial park for high-technology industries over an 11-year period in the free economic zone of Nakhodka, although some analysts doubted the practicality of the project. At 31 December 2001 there were 16,068 small businesses registered in the territory.

Directory

Head of the Provincial Administration (Governor): SERGEI M. DARKIN; 690110 Maritime Krai, Vladivostok, ul. Svetlanskaya 22; tel. (4232) 22-38-00; fax (4232) 22-52-77; e-mail gubernator@primorsky.ru; internet www.primorsky.ru.

Chairman of the Provincial Duma: SERGEI A. SOPCHUK; 690110 Maritime Krai, 690110 Vladivostok, ul. Svetlanskaya 22; tel. (4232) 22-35-70; fax (4232) 26-90-32; e-mail predsedatel@duma.primorsky.ru; internet www.primorsky.ru/prim/duma.

Chief Representative of Maritime (Primorskii) Krai in the Russian Federation: MIKHAIL N. MALGINOV; 123100 Moscow, pr. 1-i Krasnogvardeiskii 9/22/315; tel. (095) 255-82-14; fax (095) 255-82-13.

Head of the Vladivostok City Administration (Mayor): Yurii M. Kopylov; 690600 Maritime Krai, Vladivostok, Okeanskii pr. 20; tel. (4232) 22-30-16; fax (4232) 22-68-40.

Republic of Sakha (Yakutiya)

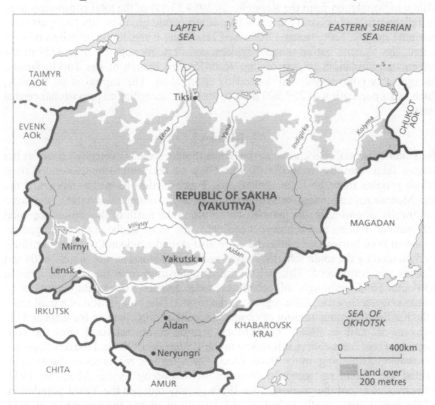

The Republic of Sakha (Yakutiya) is situated in eastern Siberia on the Laptev and Eastern Siberian Seas. Some two-fifths of the Republic's territory lies within the Arctic Circle. It forms part of the Far Eastern Federal Okrug and the Far Eastern Economic Area. To the west it borders Krasnoyarsk Krai (the Taimyr and Evenk Autonomous Okrugs—AOks), while Irkutsk and Chita Oblasts lie in the south-west, Amur Oblast to the south and Khabarovsk Krai and Magadan Oblast along the south-east. In the north-eastern corner of the territory there is a border with the Chukot AOk. The main river is the Lena, which drains into the Laptev Sea via a large swampy delta; other important rivers are the Lena's tributaries, the Aldan, the Viliyuy and the Olenek, as well as the Yana, the Indigirka and the Kolyma. Apart from the Central Yakut Plain, the region's territory is mountainous and four-fifths is taiga (forested marshland). Sakha is the largest federal unit in Russia, occupying an area of 3,103,200 sq km (1,198,150 sq miles), making it larger than Kazakhstan, itself the second largest country, after Russia, in Europe or the former USSR. The Republic consists of 33 administrative districts and 13 cities. Its climate, owing to its size, is varied: the north lies within the arctic zone whereas the south has a more temperate climate. The average temperature in January is as low as −35.6°C, and the average temperature in July is around 13.3°C. According to the preliminary results of the census of 9–16 October 2002, the Republic had a total population of 948,100, and a population density, therefore, of 0.3 per sq km. Some 64.2% of the population inhabited urban areas. In the late 1990s and early 2000s there was a continuous outflow of population from the Republic. In 1989 33.4% of the total population were the indigenous Yakuts (who represent the largest ethnic group in Siberia, apart from Russians) and 50.3% Russians. Orthodox Christianity is the dominant religion in the region. The Yakuts' native tongue, spoken as a first language by over 93% of the indigenous population, is part of the North-Eastern branch of the Turkic family, although it is considerably influenced by Mongolian. The capital is at Yakutsk, which had a population of 209,500 in October 2002, according to provisional census results.

History

The Yakuts (Iakuts), also known as the Sakha (Saka), were historically known as the Tungus, Jekos and the Urangkhai Sakha. They are believed to be descended from various peoples from the Lake Baikal area, Turkish tribes from the steppe and the Altai Mountains, and indigenous Siberian peoples, including the Evenks. They were traditionally a semi-nomadic people, with those in the north of the region occupied with hunting, fishing and reindeer-breeding, while those in the south were pastoralists who bred horses and cattle and were also skilled blacksmiths. Their territory, briefly united by the toion (chief), Tygyn, came under Russian rule in the 1620s and a fur tax was introduced. This led to violent opposition from the Yakuts between 1634 and 1642, although all rebellions were crushed. Increasing numbers of Russians began to settle in the region, as the result of the completion of a mail route to the Far East, the construction of camps for political opponents to the tsars and the discovery of gold in 1846. The territory became commercialized after the construction of the Trans-Siberian Railway in the 1880s and 1890s and the development of commercial shipping on the River Lena. The economic resources of the territory enabled the Yakut to secure a measure of autonomy as an ASSR in 1922. Collectivization and the purges of the 1930s greatly reduced the Yakut population, and the region was rapidly industrialized, largely involving the extraction of gold, coal and timber.

Nationalist feeling re-emerged during the period of *glasnost* (openness) in the late 1980s. Cultural, ecological and economic concerns led to the proclamation of a Yakut-Sakha SSR on 27 April 1990. The republican Supreme Soviet declared a Yakut Republic on 15 August 1991, and demanded republican control over the reserves of gold, diamonds, timber, coal, petroleum and tin located on its territory. On 22 December elections for an executive presidency were held, and were won by the former Chairman of the Supreme Soviet, Mikhail Nikolayev. The Republic was renamed the Republic of Sakha (Yakutiya) in March 1992 and a new Constitution was promulgated on 27 April. On 12 October 1993 the Supreme Soviet dissolved itself and set elections to a 60-seat bicameral legislature for 12 December. On 26 January 1994 the new parliament named itself the State Assembly; it comprised an upper Chamber of the Republic and a lower Chamber of Representatives. Although support for the Communist Party of the Russian Federation was relatively high in Sakha, the federal Government's willingness to concede a significant degree of local control over natural resources ensured that it too enjoyed some confidence. Native languages were designated official in certain areas and attempts to protect traditional lifestyles even involved the restoration of land. Thus, a Yeven-Bytantai Okrug was established on traditional Yeven territory in the mid-1990s. In June 1997 the

Republic was honoured at a UN special session on the environment held in New York, USA, for its commitment to preserving its natural heritage (around one-quarter of its territory had been set aside as protected areas).

Meanwhile, in December 1996 Nikolayev was re-elected President by an overwhelming majority and continued his efforts to win greater autonomy from the centre, including the maintenance (in breach of federal law) of gold and hard-currency reserves and, from August 1998, a ban on the sale of gold outside the republican Government. A power-sharing agreement with the federal Government in June 1995 was followed, in March 1998, by a framework agreement on co-operation for five years, which provided for collaboration on a series of mining and energy projects.

In May 2001 over 5,000 people were adversely affected by particularly severe flooding in the Republic. In December the federal Audit Chamber announced that an investigation was to take place into the alleged misspending by the republican Government of funds allocated for restoration work. In the same month Nikolayev withdrew his candidacy from the forthcoming gubernatorial elections, and urged voters to transfer their support to Vyacheslav Shtyrov, the head of the local diamond-producing joint-stock company, Almazy Rossii-Sakha—Alrosa, who was the candidate of the pro-presidential Unity and Fatherland-United Russia party. In the first round of voting, held on 23 December, Shtyrov received 45% of the votes cast, more than any other candidate, but fewer than the 50% required to secure an outright victory. Shtyrov subsequently received 59% of the votes in the second round, held on 13 January 2002, defeating businessman Fedot Tumusov. The election, in particular the second round, was characterized by widespread allegations of malpractice.

Also in 2002 controversy ensued with regard to discrepancies between the republican and federal Constitutions; in March the approval by the republican legislature of amendments to 11 articles of Sakha's Constitution was reportedly supposedly as insufficiently rigorous by the federal authorities. It was reported that the Republic's Chief Prosecutor was to recommend that President Shtyrov dissolve the legislature. Elections to the new, unicameral, 70-member legislature were held on 29 December; some 33 business executives were among the deputies elected, and 14 employees of Alrosa and its subsidiaries were elected.

Economy

Owing to the Republic's wealth of mineral reserves, its gross regional product in 2000 was 81,919m. roubles, equivalent to 84,011 roubles per head, the third highest figure in the Russian Federation, after the city of Moscow and Tyumen Oblast. The Republic's major industrial centres are at Yakutsk, Mirnyi, Neryungri, Aldan and Lensk. Its main port is Tiksi. At the end of 2001 there were 165 km (103 miles) of railways in the Republic. During the 1990s the extent of paved roads increased by more than two-fold, reaching some 7,339 km by December 2001.

Sakha's agriculture, in which 10.1% of the working population was engaged in 2001, consists mainly of animal husbandry (livestock- and reindeer-breeding), hunting and fishing. Grain and vegetable production tends to be on a small scale. Total agricultural output in 2001 was worth 7,044m. roubles (compared with a figure of 80,594m. roubles for the industrial sector). Industry employed 17.5% of the Republic's working population in 2001: its main industries are non-ferrous metallurgy (which accounted for 74.4% of output in 2001), ore-mining (gold—Sakha produced approximately 25% of the Russian Federation's output in the first half of the 1990s; diamonds—of which Sakha is the second largest producer and exporter in the world; also tin, muscovite—mica, antimony and coal), the production of electricity and natural gas production. Both industrial output and foreign trade in Sakha increased throughout the 1990s. In September 1997 Alrosa signed a preliminary one-year trade accord with the South African diamond producer, De Beers. The accord was subsequently extended until 2001, and De Beers was to purchase US $550m. worth of raw diamonds during this period. Alrosa also diversified its operations into polishing and selling its gems. A new, five-year agreement was signed with De Beers in December 2001.

The economically active population of the Republic amounted to 489,000 in 2001, and some 8.2% of the labour force were unemployed. The social situation in Sakha from the mid-1990s was typical of the northern regions of the Russian Federation. Growth in the cost of goods and services was compounded by a weak economic structure, poorly developed social services and inappropriate conditions for people to grow their own food. In 1999, in terms of a 'consumer basket', the Republic was one of the most expensive regions in the country. The average monthly wage was 8,357.8 roubles in mid-2002 (considerably higher than the national average, but offset by the high cost of living). During the late 1990s the Republic maintained consistently large budgetary deficits; in 1998 the deficit amounted to 2,238m. roubles. However, in 2001 the republican budget recorded a surplus of 2,263m. roubles. In the same year the value of export trade amounted to some US $331.1m., compared with imports of $999.0m. Foreign investment in Sakha amounted to $144.5m. in 2001. At 31 December 2001 there were 2,284 small businesses registered on its territory.

Directory

President: Vyacheslav A. Shtyrov; 677012 Sakha (Yakutiya), Yakutsk, ul. Kirova 11; tel. (4112) 43-50-50; fax (4112) 24-06-24; internet www.sakha.gov.ru.

Chairman of the Government: Yegor A. Borisov; 677000 Sakha (Yakutiya), Yakutsk, ul. Kirova 11; tel. (4112) 43-55-55; fax (4112) 24-06-07; internet www .sakha.gov.ru/main.asp?c=1476.

Chairman of the State Assembly (Il Tumen): Nikolai I. Solomov; 677022 Sakha (Yakutiya), Yakutsk, ul. Yaroslavskogo 24/1; tel. (4112) 43-53-88; internet www .sakha.gov.ru/main.asp?c=10.

Chief Representative of the Republic of Sakha (Yakutiya) in the Russian Federation: Andrei V. Krivoshapkin; 107078 Moscow, Myasnitskii pr. 3/26; tel. (095) 925-52-81; fax (095) 928-42-21.

Head of Yakutsk City Administration (Mayor): Ilya F. Mikhalchuk; 677000 Sakha (Yakutiya), Yakutsk, ul. Kirova 11; tel. (4112) 42-30-20; fax (4112) 42-48-80; e-mail erb@yacc.yakutia.su.

Sakhalin Oblast

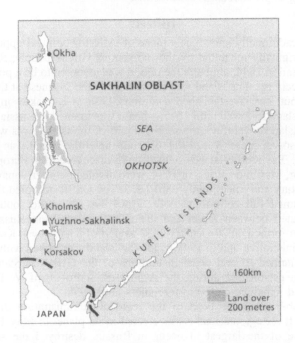

Sakhalin Oblast comprises the island of Sakhalin and the Kurile (Kuril) Islands in the Pacific Ocean. It forms part of the Far Eastern Federal Okrug and the Far Eastern Economic Area. The island of Sakhalin lies off the coast of Khabarovsk Krai, separated from the mainland by the Tatar Strait. Eastward lie the Kurile Islands (annexed by the USSR in 1945, but claimed by Japan), which are an archipelago of some 56 islands extending from the Kamchatka Peninsula in the north-east, to Hokkaido Island (Japan) in the south-west. Sakhalin Island is 942 km (just over 580 miles) in length and contains two parallel mountain ranges running north to south and separated by a central valley. The highest peaks on the island, both belonging to the eastern range of mountains, are Lopatin (1,609 m or 5,281 feet) and Nevelskogo (1,397 m). The north-west coast of the island is marshland, and much of its area is forested. The Kurile Islands are actively volcanic and contain many hot springs. There are some 60,000 rivers on Sakhalin Island, the major ones being the Poronai (350 km in length), the Tym (330 km), the Viakhtu (131 km) and the Lyutoga (130 km), all of which are frozen during the winter months (December–April/May). The Kurile Islands contain around 4,000 rivers and streams and the largest waterfall in the Russian Federation, Ilya Muromets. Sakhalin Oblast covers a total area of 87,100 sq km (33,620 sq miles) and is divided into 17 administrative districts and 18 cities. According to the preliminary results of the census of 9–16 October 2002, the Oblast's total population was 546,500, the region's population density being 6.3 per sq km. Some 86.7% of the region's total population resided in urban areas. The population of the Oblast declined during the 1990s, largely reflecting migration from the region as a result of the decline of its industrial base. The Oblast's administrative centre is at Yuzhno-Sakhalinsk, which had 174,700 inhabitants in mid-October 2002, according to provisional census results.

History

Sakhalin was traditionally known as a place of exile for political opponents to the tsars. It was originally inhabited by the indigenous Gilyak people; Russians first reached the island in 1644, although the region was assumed to be a peninsula until the early 19th century. The island was conquered by the Japanese at the end of the 18th century, but Russia established a military base at Korsakov in 1853. Joint control of the island followed until 1875, when it was granted to Russia in exchange for the Kurile Islands. Karafuto, the southern part of the island, was won by Japan during the Russo–Japanese War (1904–05), but the entire island was ceded to the USSR in 1945. The Kurile Islands, which were discovered for Europeans by the Dutch navigator, Martin de Vries, in 1634, were divided between Japan and Russia in the 18th century and ruled jointly until 1875. The USSR occupied the islands in 1945 and assumed full control in 1947. From the 1990s the southern Kuriles remained disputed between Japan and the newly independent Russia. Sakhalin Oblast had been formed on 20 October 1932 as part of Khabarovsk Krai. It became a separate administrative unit in 1947, when the island was united with the Kuriles. The region contained several penal institutions of the GULAG (State Corrective Camps) system established during the regime of Stalin—Iosif V. Dzhugashvili (1924–53)—and remained closed to foreigners until 1990.

On 16 October 1993 the head of the regional administration disbanded the Regional Soviet; a Regional Duma was elected in its place. In May 1995 a major earthquake, one of the largest to occur in Russia, destroyed the settlement of Neftegorsk in the north of the region, and killed an estimated 2,000 people. In May 1996 the federal President, Boris Yeltsin, signed a power-sharing treaty with the regional Government. The gubernatorial elections of October 1996 and October 2000 were won by the incumbent, Igor Farkhutdinov. In 1998 Russia and Japan agreed to attempt to settle their territorial dispute by 2000. However, in September 2000 federal President Vladimir Putin rejected continuing Japanese demands for the sovereignty of four of the Southern Kuriles (known as the 'Northern Territory' to Japan), and the continuing dispute meant that the two countries had still to sign a peace treaty officially marking the end of the Second World War.

In December 1998 the Oblast authorities signed a friendship and economic co-operation accord with the Japanese province of Hokkaido, and a further agreement was signed in January 2000. A special economic zone in the Southern Kuriles was established in the late 1990s, in order to encourage foreign investment. Increasingly, concerns about the high levels of organized crime in the Oblast, and the illicit smuggling of fish and fish produce, notably to Japan, were expressed from the late 1990s. These concerns were believed to have contributed to the introduction by the federal authorities of restrictions on movement on Sakhalin Island (and other border regions of the Russian Federation) from March 2003; henceforth, both foreign citizens and Russian citizens resident outside the Oblast were required to obtain permits before travelling beyond Yuzhno-Sakhalinsk.

On 20 August 2003 Farkhutdinov and several senior officials of Sakhalin Oblast were killed in a helicopter crash. The first round of voting in a gubernatorial election was held on 7 December (concurrently with elections to the federal State Duma). Acting Governor Ivan Malakhov and Fedor Sidorenko, the two leading candidates, proceeded to a second round of voting, held on 21 December, in which Malakhov emerged as the victor, with some 53% of the votes cast.

Economy

In 2000 Sakhalin Oblast's gross regional product amounted to 36,376m. roubles, or 61,208 roubles per head. The Oblast's principal industrial centres are at Yuzhno-Sakhalinsk, Kholmsk, Okha (the administrative centre of the petroleum-producing region), Nevelsk, Dolinsk and Poronaisk. At the end of 2001 there were 957 km of railways and 812 km of paved roads in the Oblast. Its ports are Kholmsk (from where the Kholmsk-Vanino ferry connects Sakhalin Island with the mainland) and Korsakov. There are flights to Moscow, Khabarovsk, Vladivostok, Petropavlovsk-Kamchatskii and Novosibirsk, and international services to Alaska, USA, the Republic of Korea (South Korea) and Japan.

Agriculture in the region is minimal, owing to its unfavourable climatic conditions—agricultural land occupies only 1% of its territory. It employed just 4.2% of the working population in 2001, and consists mainly of potato and vegetable production and animal husbandry (largely comprising reindeer-breeding and fur-farming). Total agricultural production amounted to a value of 2,890m. roubles in 2001, of which crop sales generated 69.4% and animal husbandry 31.6%. Annual catches of fish and other marine life amount to around 400,000 metric tons. Fishing and fish-processing is the major traditional industry. The entire industrial sector employed some 24.3% of the region's work-force and generated 32,892m. roubles in 2001. There is some extraction of coal and, increasingly, petroleum and natural gas in, and to the north of, Sakhalin Island. Some petroleum is piped for refining to a plant in Komsomolsk-on-Amur (Khabarovsk Krai), although from 1994 the Oblast had its own refinery, with a capacity of some 200,000 tons per year. Coal was the region's primary source of energy, but in the late 1990s a gradual conversion to gas was initiated. The further development of Sakhalin's rich hydrocarbons reserves was the subject of negotiations between a number of Russian and foreign companies in the mid-1990s, and by the end of the 1990s four major consortia had been formed. Sakhalin-1, a project to produce petroleum on the continental shelf of Sakhalin Island comprises ExxonMobil of the USA (30%), Japan's Sodeco consortium (involving Itochi, Japan National Oil Company, Japex and Marubeni, 30%), Rosneft (of which Sakhalinmorneftegaz is a local subsidiary, with 20%) and India's Oil and Natural Gas Corporation (20%). Sakhalin-2, two fields containing an estimated 1,000m. barrels of petroleum and 408,000m. cu m of natural gas, was initiated by Sakhalin Energy Investment, comprising Mitsui and Mitsubishi (of Japan), Marathon (of the USA) and RoyalDutch/Shell (Netherlands/United Kingdom). Sakhalin-3, backed by Mobil (now ExxonMobil) and Texaco (now ChevronTexaco—of the USA), was seeking to develop what was potentially the largest field on the Sakhalin shelf, containing an estimated 320m. tons of recoverable reserves. It was hoped that the proceeds from the ongoing projects would help to alleviate the high level of poverty in the region. In July 1998 the federal premier, Sergei Kiriyenko, signed a resolution extending a federal programme on social and economic development of the Oblast, to be financed by proceeds from Sakhalin-1 and Sakhalin-2, until 2005. In July 2002 it was announced that Rosneft was to undertake the development of a further project, Sakhalin-5, in association with British Petroleum (United Kingdom). In addition, food-processing (largely of fish products) was a significant industrial sector in the Oblast, accounting for 31.6% of such activity in 2001.

Sakhalin Oblast's economically active population totalled 323,000 in 2001, when 12.0% of the labour force were unemployed. The average monthly wage in the region amounted to some 6,735.7 roubles in mid-2002. The 2001 budget showed a deficit of 428m. roubles. In the same year exports from the Oblast were valued at US $331.1m. and imports to the Oblast were worth $168.8m.; total foreign investment in the region amounted to some $388.9m. At 31 December 2001 4,856 small businesses were registered in the Oblast.

Directory

Governor: IVAN MALAKHOV; 693011 Sakhalin obl., Yuzhno-Sakhalinsk, Kommunisticheskii pr. 39; tel. (4242) 72-19-02; fax (4242) 23-60-81; e-mail webmaster@ adm.sakhalin.ru; internet www.adm.sakhalin.ru.

Chairman of the Regional Duma: VLADIMIR I. YEFREMOV; 693000 Sakhalin obl., Yuzhno-Sakhalinsk, ul. Chekhova 37; tel. (4242) 42-14-89; fax (4242) 72-15-46; e-mail chairman@duma.sakhalin.ru; internet www.duma.sakhalin.ru.

Chief Representative of Sakhalin Oblast in the Russian Federation: VLADIMIR I. SHAPOVAL; 103025 Moscow, ul. Novyi Arbat 19/1132; tel. (095) 203-79-09; fax (095) 023-84-56; e-mail prsakh2001@mail.ru.

Head of Yuzhno-Sakhalinsk City Administration (Mayor): FEDOR I. SIDORENKO; 693023 Sakhalin obl., Yuzhno-Sakhalinsk, ul. Lenina 173; tel. (4242) 72-25-11; fax (4242) 23-00-06; internet yuzhno.sakh.ru.

KRASNOYARSK KRAI

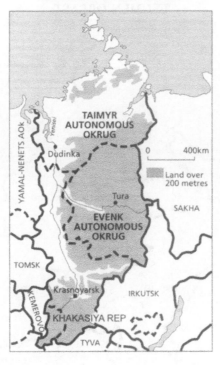

ARCHANGEL OBLAST

TYUMEN OBLAST

PART THREE
Select Bibliography

SELECT BIBLIOGRAPHY

Alekseev, M. A., (Ed.). *Centre–Periphery Conflict in Post-Soviet Russia: A Federation Imperilled.* Basingstoke, Macmillan, 1999.

Bahry, D. *Outside Moscow: Power, Politics and Budgetary Policy in the Soviet Republics.* New York, NY, Columbia University Press, 1987.

Bassin, M. *Imperial Visions: Nationalist Imagination and Geographical Expansion in the Russian Far East.* Cambridge, Cambridge University Press, 1999.

Baxendale, J., Dewar, S., and Gowan, D. *The EU and Kaliningrad: Kaliningrad and the Impact of EU Enlargement.* London, Kogan Page, 2000.

Blum, D., (Ed.). *Russia's Future: Consolidation of Disintegration.* Oxford, Westview, 1994.

Bradshaw, M. J. *Regional Patterns of Foreign Investment in Russia.* London, Royal Institute of International Affairs, 1995.

The Russian Far East. London, Royal Institute of International Affairs, 1999.

Bradshaw, M. J., (Ed.). *The Soviet Union: A New Regional Geography?* London, Belhaven Press, 1991.

The Russian Far East and Pacific Asia. London, RoutlegeCurzon, 2001.

Bukharayev, Ravil. *The Model of Tatarstan: Under Mintimer Shaimiyev.* London, RoutledgeCurzon, 2001.

Centre for Co-operation with Non-members. *A Regional Approach to Industrial Restructuring in the Tomsk Region.* Paris, Organisation for Economic Co-operation and Development, 1998.

Chenciner, R., (Ed.). *Daghestan: Tradition and Survival.* London, Caucasus World, 1997.

Colton, T. *Moscow: Governing the Socialist Metropolis.* Cambridge, MA, Harvard University Press, 1995.

Comité Tchetchenie. *Tchetchenie: Dix Clés pour Comprendre.* Paris, La Découverte, 2003.

Dellenbrant, J. A. *The Soviet Regional Dilemma: Planning, People and Natural Resources.* London, M. E. Sharpe, 1986.

Dolkinskaya, I. *Transition and Regional Inequality in Russia: Reorganization or Procrastination?* Washington, DC, IMF, 2002.

Dunlop, J. B. *Russia Confronts Chechnya: Roots of a Separatist Conflict.* Cambridge, Cambridge University Press, 1998.

Easter, G. M. *Reconstructing the State: Personal Networks and Elite Identity in Soviet Russia.* Cambridge, Cambridge University Press, 2000.

Evangelista, M. *The Chechen Wars: Will Russia Go the Way of the Soviet Union?* Washington, DC, Brookings Institution Press, 2002.

Fairlie, L. D., and Sergounin, A. *Are Borders Barriers? EU Enlargement and the Russian Region of Kaliningrad.* Helsinki, Finnish Institute of International Affairs, 2001.

Forsyth, J. *A History of the Peoples of Siberia.* Cambridge, Cambridge University Press, 1994.

Fowkes, B. *Russia and Chechnia: The Permanent Crisis*. Basingstoke, Macmillan, 1998.

Freinkman, L. *Subnational Budgeting in Russia*. Washington, DC, World Bank, 2000.

Friedgut, T. H., and Hahn, J. W., (Eds). *Local Power and Post-Soviet Politics*. Armonk, NY, M. E. Sharpe, 1995.

Gall, C., and de Waal, T. *Chechnya: Calamity in the Caucasus*. New York, NY, New York University Press, 1998.

Gel'man, V., Ryzhenkov, S., Brie, M., et al. *The Comparative Politics of Russia's Regions*. Lanham, MD, Rowan & Littlefield, 2003.

Gibson, J., and Hanson, P., (Eds). *Transformation from Below: Local Power and the Political Economy of Post-Communist Transitions*. Cheltenham, Edward Elgar, 1996.

Glatter, P. *Tyumen: The West Siberian Oil and Gas Province*. London, Royal Institute of International Affairs, 1997.

Gorenburg, D. P. *Minority Ethnic Mobilization in the Russian Federation*. Cambridge, Cambridge University Press, 2003.

Grant, B., and Pika, A., (Ed.). *Neotraditionalism in the Russian North*. Washington, DC, University of Washington Press, 1999.

Hahn, J., (Ed.). *Democratization in Russia: The Development of Legislative Institutions*. Armonk, NY, M. E. Sharpe, 1996.

   Regional Russia in Transformation. Washington, DC, Woodrow Wilson Center Press, 2001.

Hanson, P. *Regions, Local Power and Economic Change in Russia*. London, Royal Institute of International Affairs, 1994.

Hanson, P., and Bradshaw, M. J., (Eds). *Regional Economic Change in Russia*. Cheltenham, Edward Elgar, 2000.

Herd, G. P., and Aldis, A. *Russian Regions and Regionalism*. London, Routledge-Curzon, 2002.

Hill, F. *Russia's Tinderbox: Conflict in the North Caucasus and its Implications for the Future of the Russian Federation*. Cambridge, MA, Harvard University Press, 1995.

Hill, F., and Gaddy, C. G. *The Siberian Curse: How Central Planners Left Russia Out in the Cold*. Washington, DC, Brookings Institution Press, 2003.

Human Rights Watch. *Russia, the Ingush–Ossetian Conflict in the Prigordnyi Region*. New York, NY, Human Rights Watch, 1996.

Huskey, E. *Presidential Power in Russia*. Armonk, NY, M. E. Sharpe, 1999.

Hutcheson, D. *Political Parties in the Russian Regions*. London, RoutledgeCurzon, 2003.

Jacobs, E. M., (Ed.). *Soviet Local Politics and Government*. London, HarperCollins, 1983.

Jaimoukha, A. *The Circassians*. London, Caucasus World, 2001.

Joenniemi, P., and Prawitz, J. *Kaliningrad: The European Amber Region*. Aldershot, Ashgate, 1998.

Kirkow, P. *Russia's Provinces: Authoritarian Transformation versus Local Autonomy.* London, Macmillan, and New York, NY, St Martin's Press, 1998.

Kondrashev, S. *Nationalism and the Drive for Sovereignty in Tatarstan, 1988–92: Origins and Development (Studies in Diplomacy).* New York, NY, St Martin's Press, 1999.

Koropeckyi, I. S., and Schroeder, G. E., (Eds). *Economics of Soviet Regions.* New York, NY, Praeger, 1981.

Kotkin, S., and Wolff, D., (Eds). *Rediscovering Russia in Asia: Siberia and the Russian Far East.* New York, NY, M. E. Sharpe, 1995.

Krickus, R. J. *The Kaliningrad Question.* Lanham, MD, Rowman and Littlefield, 2002.

Lapidus, G. W., (Ed.). *The New Russia: Troubled Transformation.* Boulder, CO, Westview, 1995.

Lavrov, A. M., Makushkin, A. G., et al. *The Fiscal Structure of the Russian Federation: Financial Flows between the Centre and the Regions.* Armonk, NY, M. E. Sharpe, 2001.

Lieven, A. *Chechnya: Tombstone of Russian Power.* New Haven, CT, Yale University Press, 1998.

Lincoln, W. B. *The Conquest of a Continent: Siberia and the Russians.* New York, NY, Random House, 1994.

McAuley, M. *Russia's Politics of Uncertainty.* Cambridge, Cambridge University Press, 1997.

Mandelstam Balzer, M. *The Tenacity of Ethnicity.* Princeton, NJ, Princeton University Press, 1999.

Manezhev, S. A. *Russian Far East.* London, Royal Institute of International Affairs, 1993.

Melvin, N. *Regional Foreign Policies in the Russian Federation.* London, Royal Institute of International Affairs, 1995.

Minakir, P. A., and Freeze, G. L., (Eds). *The Russian Far East: An Economic Handbook.* Armonk, NY, M. E. Sharpe, 1994.

Moses, J. C. *Regional Party Leadership and Policy-Making in the USSR.* London, Praeger, 1974.

Mote, V. L. *Siberia.* Boulder, CO, Westview, 1998.

Murray, W. E., and Bradshaw, M. J. *Rising Tensions in the Natural Resource Market of Pacific Asia and the Role of the Russian Far East.* Birmingham, University of Birmingham, 1997.

Orttung, R. *From Leningrad to St Petersburg: Democratization in a Russian City.* New York, NY, St Martin's Press, 1995.

Orttung, R., (Ed.). *The Republics and Regions of the Russian Federation: A Guide to Politics, Policies and Leaders.* Armonk, NY, M. E. Sharpe, 2000.

Orttung, R., and Reddaway, P. *Dynamics of Russian Politics: Putin's Federal-Regional Reforms.* Lanham, MD, Rowan & Littlefield, 2003.

Pascal, E. *Defining Russian Federalism.* New York and London, Praeger, 2003.

Politkovskaya, A. *A Small Corner of Hell.* Chicago, IL, University of Chicago Press, 2003.

Reid, A. *The Shaman's Coat*. London, Weidenfeld and Nicolson, 2002.

Rigby, T. H. *Political Elites in the USSR: Central Leaders and Local Cadres from Lenin to Gorbachev*. Aldershot, Edward Elgar, 1990.

Rorlich, A.-A. *The Volga Tatars: A Profile in National Resilience*. Stanford, CA, Hoover Institution Press, 1986.

Ross, C. *Local Government in the Soviet Union: Problems of Implementation and Control*. London, Croom Helm, 1987.

Ruble, B. *Leningrad: Shaping a City*. Berkeley, CA, University of California Press, 1990.

Rutland, P. *The Politics of Economic Stagnation in the Soviet Union: The Role of Local Party Organs in Economic Management*. Cambridge, Cambridge University Press, 1993.

Scalapino, R. A., and Akaha, T., (Ed.). *Politics and Economics in the Russian Far East*. London, Routledge, 1997.

Schiffer, J. R. *Soviet Regional Economic Policy: The East–West Debate over Pacific Siberian Development*. London, Macmillan, 1989.

Seely, R. *The Russo—Chechen Conflict 1800–2000*. London, Frank Cass, 2001.

Segbers, K. *Explaining Post-Soviet Patchworks Vol. 3: The Political Economy of Regions, Regimes and Republics*. Aldershot, Ashgate, 2001.

Smith, G., (Ed.). *The Nationalities Question in the Soviet Union*, 2nd edn. London, Longman, 1996.

Smith, S. *Allah's Mountains: The Battle for Chechnya*. London, I. B. Tauris, 2000.

Ssorin-Chaikov, N. V. *A Social Life of the State in the Siberian Subarctic*. Stanford, CA, Stanford University Press, 2003.

Stephan, J. J. *The Russian Far East: A History*. Stanford, CA, Stanford University Press, 1996.

Stavrakis, P. J., de Bardeleben, J., and Black, L., (Eds). *Beyond the Monolith: The Emergence of Regionalism in Post-Soviet Russia*. Washington, DC, Woodrow Wilson Press Centre and John Hopkins Press, 1997.

Stoner-Weiss, K. *Local Heroes: The Political Economy of Russian Regional Governance*. Princeton, NJ, Princeton University Press, 1997.

Thornton, J., (Ed.) *Russia's Far East: A Region at Risk*. Seattle, WA, University of Washington Press, 2002.

Thubron, C. *In Siberia*. London, Penguin, 2000.

Tichotsky, J. *Russia's Diamond Colony*. Reading, Gordon & Breach, 2000.

Valencia, M. *The Russian Far East in Transition: Opportunities for Regional Economic Co-operation*. Boulder, CO, Westview, 1995.

Wallich, C. I., (Ed.). *Russia and the Challenge of Fiscal Federalism*. Washington, DC, World Bank, 1994.

Weinberg, R. *Stalin's Forgotten Zion: Birobidzhan and the Making of a Soviet Jewish Homeland*. Berkeley, CA, University of California Press, 1998.

Wood, A, and French, R. A., (Eds). *The Development of Siberia: People and Resources*. London, Macmillan, 1989.

Zelkina, A. *The Chechens*. London, Caucasus World, 2001.

PART FOUR
Indexes

Alphabetic List of Territories

(including a gazetteer of alternative names)

126	Adygeya.	*Republic*
	Aga-Buryat AOk.	*see Chita*
	Alaniya	*see North Osetiya*
242	Altai.	Krai
245	Altai.	Republic
289	Amur	Oblast
92	Archangel	Oblast
95	Nenets AOk	Autonomous Okrug
	ASSR Nemtsev Povolzhyya/ASSR der	
	Wolgadeutschen (Volga-German ASSR).	*see Saratov*
130	Astrakhan	Oblast
	Balkariya	*see Kabardino-Balkariya*
	Bashkiriya	*see Bashkortostan*
177	Bashkortostan	Republic
47	Belgorod.	Oblast
	Birobidzhan	*see Jewish AOb*
50	Bryansk.	Oblast
249	Buryatiya	Republic
133	Chechen—Nokchi Republic	Republic
	Checheno-Ingush ASSR	*see Chechen—Nokchi Republic or Ingushetiya*
	Chechen Republic of Ichkeriya	*see Chechen—Nokchi Republic*
	Chechnya	*see Chechen—Nokchi Republic*
225	Chelyabinsk	Oblast
	Cherkessiya	*see Stavropol (Karachayevo-Cherkessiya)*
252	Chita	Oblast
255	Aga-Buryat AOk	Autonomous Okrug
	Chkalov	*see Orenburg*
	Chukchi AOk	*see Chukot AOk*
292	Chukot AOk (Chukotka)	Autonomous Okrug
182	Chuvash Republic (Chuvashiya)	Republic
	Circassia (Cherkessiya)	*see Karachayevo-Cherkessiya*
140	Dagestan.	Republic
	Dolgano-Nenets AOk.	*see Krasnoyarsk (Taimyr AOk)*
	East Vogul (Ostyako-Vogulskii) National Okrug	*see Tyumen (Khanty-Mansii AOk—Yugra)*
	Evenk AOk	*see Krasnoyarsk*
	Far Eastern Republic.	*see Chita Oblast, etc.*
	Gorkii	*see Nizhnii Novgorod*
	Gorno-Altai AO	*see Altai (Republic)*
	Gorskaya People's Republic	*see Kabardino-Balkariya, etc.*
	Ichkeriya.	*see Chechnya*
	Ingodinskoye Zirnove.	*see Chita*
144	Ingushetiya	Republic
257	Irkutsk	Oblast
260	Ust-Orda Buryat AOk	Autonomous Okrug
53	Ivanovo	Oblast
295	Jewish AOb (Birobidzhan)	Autonomous Oblast
149	Kabardino-Balkariya	Republic
	Kabardiya	*see Kabardino-Balkariya*
	Kalinin	*see Tver*
98	Kaliningrad	Oblast
153	Kalmykiya	Republic
55	Kaluga	Oblast

331

Federal Okrugs

Economic Areas

For Product Safety Concerns and Information please contact
our EU representative GPSR@taylorandfrancis.com Taylor & Francis
Verlag GmbH, Kaufingerstraße 24, 80331 München, Germany

T - #0012 - 270225 - C0 - 234/156/19 [21] - CB - 9781857432480 - Gloss Lamination